HTML Stylesheet Sourcebook

Ian S. Graham

WILEY COMPUTER PUBLISHING

John Wiley & Sons, Inc.
New York • Chichester • Weinheim • Brisbane • Singapore • Toronto

Publisher: Robert Ipsen
Editor: Cary Sullivan
Assistant Editor: Pam Sobotka
Managing Editor: Mark Hayden
Text Design & Composition: Benchmark Productions

Designations used by companies to distinguish their products are often claimed as trademarks. In all instances where John Wiley & Sons, Inc., is aware of a claim, the product names appear in initial capital or ALL CAPITAL LETTERS. Readers, however, should contract the appropriate companies for more complete information regarding trademarks and registration.

This text is printed on acid-free paper. ∞

Library of Congress Cataloging-in-Publication Data:

Graham, Ian S., 1955–
    HTML stylesheet sourcebook / Ian S. Graham.
        p.   cm.
    Includes index.
    ISBN 0-471-19664-9 (pbk. : alk. paper)
    1. HTML (Document markup language) 2. World Wide Web (Information retrieval system: 3. Electronic publishing.   I. Title.
    QA76.76.H94G733   1997
    005.7'2--dc21   97-26970
                                                              CIP

Printed in the United States of America

10 9 8 7 6 5 4 3 2 1

Contents

Preface ix

Chapter 1 Introduction to HTML and Stylesheets 1

The Early Days of the Web 3
 The Splintering of HTML 3
 Reestablishing an HTML Standard 4
 HTML Is Not Enough 5
Introduction to Stylesheets 6
 Stylesheets and Word Processors 6
 Stylesheets and HTML 8
 Advantages of the Stylesheet Approach 9
 Approaches to Stylesheets 9
A Simple Stylesheet Example 12
 CSS Core and Advanced Features 16
 Property Inheritance 17
 Default Properties 18
 Browser Handling of Stylesheet Errors 20
Chapter Summary 21
Chapter Exercises 21
References 22

Chapter 2 HyperText Markup Language Review 25

Markup Language Review 26
 Defining HTML: The Document Type Definition 27
 Allowed Characters in HTML Documents 27
 Comments in HTML Documents 28
HTML Markup Model 28
 Empty Elements 29
 Element Nesting 29
 Element Attributes 29
 Case Sensitivity 31
 Browsers and HTML Errors 32
Structural Rules of Markup 33
 HEAD Content 33
 BODY Content 34

Contents

HTML and Stylesheets—New Markup 41
Element Specifications Key 41
META Specification of the Stylesheet Language 50
The Importance of Valid HTML 50
Readability without Stylesheets? 56
Chapter Summary 57
Chapter Exercises 58
References 59

Chapter 3 Stylesheets Tutorial, Part 1: Fonts and Typefaces **61**
Introduction to Typefaces and Fonts 62
Where Fonts Come From 63
Font Name and Name Variability 63
Font Naming on Computers 64
Digital Font Formats: Bitmapped and Scalable 65
Specifying Font Variants Using CSS 66
Font Names and Generic Font Families 67
Specifying Font Sizes 69
Display Resolution and Appropriate Fonts 70
Stylesheet Syntax: Rules, Selectors,
Declarations, and Properties 71
CSS Rule Selectors 73
Stylesheets and Font Specifications 77
Example 1: Simple CSS Selectors and Rules 78
Example 2: Some More CSS Selectors and Rules 83
Example 3: Font Family and Style Specification 87
Example 4: Specifying Font Weights 98
Example 5: Specifying Font Sizes 101
Chapter Summary 104
Chapter Exercises 105
References 107

Chapter 4 Tutorial, Part 2: Text Formatting Control **111**
Text Formatting Introduction 112
Horizontal Text Spacing 112
Text Variation: Color, Underlines, and Case Control 113
Vertical Alignment of Letters, Text, and Images 114
Formatting within Text Blocks 114
CSS Syntax: Complex Selectors and CSS Comments 117
Pseudo-Element-Based Selectors 118
Grouped Selectors 120
Comments in CSS Stylesheets 121
Contextual Selectors 122
Stylesheets and Text Formatting 125
Example 6: Text Formatting 128

Example 7: Vertical Alignment   131
Example 8: Line Height in Block Elements   139
Example 9: Text Indent, Alignment, and Whitespace   141
Chapter Summary   146
Chapter Exercises   148

Chapter 5 Tutorial, Part 3: Formatting and Positioning of Elements   **151**
Introduction to the CSS Formatting Model   152
Formatting Types: Block-Level, Inline, and Floating   154
Display of Formatting Elements   156
Formatting Details of the Formatting Box   159
Specifics of Element Formatting   166
Block-Level Formatting   166
Floating Elements   188
Special Issues for TABLE Formatting   204
TABLEs and Property Inheritance   204
TABLE Formatting Bugs   206
Chapter Summary   209
Chapter Exercises   211

Chapter 6 Tutorial, Part 4: Backgrounds, Miscellaneous Properties and the Stylesheet Cascade   **213**
Browser Canvas and Element Backgrounds   214
Background Colors   214
Background Images   215
Background Property Examples?   228
External Stylesheets, and the Stylesheet Cascade   228
Including Stylesheets in HTML Documents   229
Multiple Stylesheets and the CSS Cascade   235
Evaluating the Stylesheet Cascade   236
Stylesheet Design and Management   246
Chapter Summary   248
Chapter Exercises   249

Chapter 7 Example Stylesheet Designs   **251**
Appropriate HTML Markup Design   251
Design Example 1: Title Page   254
Designing the HTML Markup   255
Creating Associated Stylesheet Rules   255
Design Example 2: A Stylized Heading   258
Structuring the HTML Markup   258
Creating the Stylesheet Rules   260
Design Example 3: A Decorative Page   264
The Background   264
The Navigation Icons   264

Formatting the Text Column   265
HTML-Based Styling   267
Design Example 4: Chapter Cover Page   267
Page Markup Design   268
Stylesheet Rule Design   270
Design Example 5: Newspaper Web Page   275
Default Stylesheet Rules   278
Page Title or Banner   278
Major News Column   279
Navigation Bar   282
Main News Article Page   283
Assembling the Documents: External Stylesheets   285
Backward Compatibility   290
Stylesheet Reuse   290
References: Additional CSS Designs   293
Stylesheet Sourcebook Gallery   293
Microsoft CSS Gallery   293
Generationweb.com CSS Gallery   293

Chapter 8 CSS Language Reference   **297**
CSS Syntax   297
Comments in Stylesheets   298
Case Sensitivity   298
Property Inheritance   298
CSS Selectors   299
Including Stylesheets in HTML Documents   304
Importing Stylesheets: The @import Statement   305
Increasing Declaration Importance with !important   306
Processing CSS Rules: Error Handling   306
Processing CSS Rules: The Cascade   306
Length Units   307
Color Units   308
URLs as CSS Values   309
CSS Property Specifications   310
Status of CSS Support in Current Browsers   347

Chapter 9 Advanced Features/Future Developments   **351**
Positioning and Z-Ordering of Elements   352
Absolute Positioning   354
Relative Positioning   359
Absolute Positioning within Another Element   361
Visibility of Elements, and Element Transparency   365
Review of Positioning CSS Properties   368

Scripted Stylesheets and the Document Object Model   374
  Netscape's JavaScript Stylesheets   375
  The Microsoft Approach   377
Font Downloading and Dynamic Fonts   378
  Netscape Dynamic Fonts   379
  Microsoft Font Embedding   381
  Font Matching and PANOSE Numbers   381
  Fonts and Character Sets   382
Aural Cascading Stylesheets   383
Printing and Other Alternate Media   385
  Alternate Media Types   386
CSS-Aware Software   388
References   389

Appendix A Color, Color Codes, and Color Names   **391**
Color Specification In CSS   392
  CSS Named Colors   392
  Extended Named Colors   394
  Explicit RGB Color Codes   397
Limited Numbers of Colors: The Colormap   398
  Default System Colormaps   398
  Color Substitution and Dithering   398
Standardized Color—Standardized RGB   399

Appendix B CSS Length Units   **401**
  Problems with Percentage Length Values   402
Defining Length Units   404
Length Units and Printing Support   404

Glossary   **407**
Index   **413**

Preface

This book is about a new technology, called *stylesheets,* that will revolutionize the way Web pages are designed and delivered. Before stylesheets, Web page design was a crafty mix of images, HTML tables, and formatting-specific HTML markup, the product often being documents containing dozens of small images, complicated tabular structures, and precious little text. The pages often looked great, but were in practice less than successful, because of the long download times (since many image files were needed in the page), or because the page was unviewable by browsers with image loading turned off. As a result, the design process was a complicated (and expensive) compromise of design versus functionality. At the same time, the resulting pages were non-recyclable—each page was so cluttered with formatting-specific features, that switching to a new design meant rewriting all the documents, at considerable cost.

The *stylesheet* approach is designed to solve most of these problems. A stylesheet is a specification, written in a stylesheet language, for how an HTML document should be formatted and displayed. Thus, stylesheets are designed to work *with* HTML, where the HTML document contains the text (and links other content, such as embedded images) to be displayed, and where the stylesheet specifies how this content should be formatted and presented.

On the Web, stylesheets are written in a language called *Cascading Stylesheets,* or *CSS,* a language specifically designed for Web-based electronic documents. CSS provides for unprecedented control over page layout and presentation, and lets Web designers bypass the graphically intense formatting "tricks" of previous design approaches, to instead lay out the text content however they desire. At the same time, the separation of stylesheet from content enormously simplifies the task of document management. For example, to change the design of a page, an author need only pull out the old stylesheet and plug in a new one. Indeed, the same stylesheet can be shared by thousands of documents, so that updating a single stylesheet can instantly update the look and layout of thousands of pages. Indeed, stylesheets are the wave of the future, with all new browsers (and many HTML editors) claiming support for CSS in their most recent product offerings.

This book is designed for those interested in learning how to use the Cascading Stylesheet language, and how to apply this new approach to the design of Web pages. Thus, this book is designed for Web page designers. It was written on the assumption that the reader knows the basic HTML, although the HTML review in Chapter 2 provides most of the fundamentals needed to understand the rest of the book. The book does not assume that the reader understands the details of typography and layout, and includes, within the text, descriptions of the relevant issues and terminology.

The book is organized into nine chapters. Chapter 1 begins with a brief overview of the Web, and explains how we have arrived at the point where HTML stylesheets are both necessary and possible. The chapter then outlines the basic ideas behind the stylesheet approach, and describes the relationship between stylesheets and markup languages such as HTML.

Chapter 2 provides a brief review of the HyperText Markup Language, or HTML. Stylesheets are designed to work with HTML documents: HTML documents describe the content to be displayed, and stylesheets specify the layout and design. However, for this procedure to work, the HTML documents must use "correct" HTML markup, as the stylesheet rules are intimately tied to the correctness of this underlying structure. This chapter briefly reviews the ideas behind HTML, and describes features that have been added to HTML in support of stylesheets.

Chapters 3 through 6 are the tutorial chapters of this book. They provide a step-by-step exposition of the CSS language syntax, the different CSS properties, complete with examples. Chapter 3 covers font issues, and the basic aspects of the CSS language, while Chapter 4 looks at additional text-level formatting controls, such as text transformations (underlining, case control), word and letter spacing, line heights, line indents, horizontal text alignment, and vertical positioning of text. This chapter also delves into details of CSS selectors—the part of CSS that defines where particular formatting instructions should be applied.

Note   Incomplete Browser Support for CSS

All current browsers that claim support for CSS do so incompletely, and imperfectly. Indeed, most CSS-capable browsers have several bugs in their CSS implementations. These bugs can lead to enormous confusion when authoring stylesheet-enabled documents, since the associated formatting commands work incorrectly, and unpredictably.

This book attempts to note as many of these many limitations and problems as possible. However, this list will change, as new problems are discovered and as newer, updated software is released. An up-to-date description of browser capabilities will be found at the book's supporting Web site, described at the end of this Preface.

Chapter 5 is perhaps the most complicated tutorial chapter, and covers details of the CSS layout model—the model by which paragraphs, floated elements (such as floating images), and inline elements are formatted and positioned on the display. Many examples are provided to explain how this works, and to illustrate the more complicated aspects of this process.

Chapter 6 is the final tutorial chapter. It describes CSS properties that define how a background image or color should be painted *underneath* an element on the display (e.g., beneath a paragraph or a heading), using several examples to illustrate this procedure in practice. The chapter also completes the description of CSS language syntax, by describing mechanisms for including external stylesheets in a stylesheet or an HTML document, and by explaining the CSS *cascading mechanism* that specifies how conflicting stylesheet rules are resolved. The cascading mechanism determines how a large stylesheet is "distilled" to leave an unambiguous collection of CSS rules that describe how a document should be rendered.

Chapter 7 takes the knowledge gained in Chapters 3 through 6 and applies it to five CSS design examples. These examples employ all the features of CSS to develop sophisticated page layouts, and each provides a detailed description of the process that led to the given HTML markup and CSS designs. Issues covered include: designing appropriate HTML markup; creating pages that work well even in the absence of CSS; and the design of large stylesheet systems for use with large HTML document collections.

Chapter 8 is a CSS reference chapter, and contains a brief summary of the language syntax, plus descriptions of all the CSS properties, listed in alphabetical order. This chapter is a useful reference when designing stylesheets, allowing the reader to quickly discover the function of a particular CSS property, and the places it can be used. Each description is complete with a list and description of allowed values, and references to locations in Chapters 3 through 6 where the property is described in more detail.

Chapter 9, the last chapter of the book, describes new CSS features that are just now coming into use, as well as up-and-coming ideas that are likely to be implemented in the near future. Topics covered include: positioning of elements using CSS (currently implemented on Netscape Navigator 4 and Microsoft Internet Explorer 4); scripting interfaces to stylesheets (JavaScript Accessible Stylesheets on Navigator 4, the document object model on MSIE 4); downloadable fonts (implemented on Netscape Navigator 4); font descriptions and font embedding; and stylesheet extensions for printing and in support of aural presentations of documents. Finally, this chapter briefly lists some software that currently supports CSS, and provides a reference list for additional information on these newer issues.

A book can only teach the rules of the technology, and some of the tricks of the trade. After that, you are on your own—it is your own innovation and design skill that will take the CSS tools and produce attractive and useful Web resources. So—go out there, start styling, and have fun!

The Supporting Web Site

Instead of a CD-ROM, this book comes equipped with a supporting Web site. This site contains all of the example documents listed in this book, hypertext links to all the book (hypertext) references, regular updates and corrections, and links to sites. These updates include additional material assembled after this book went to press, such as new CSS example documents and new hypertext references to additional resources. The Web site is available at the URL

    http://www.wiley.com/compbooks/Graham

Much of the material at the site can be downloaded (as a ZIP or UNIX tar archive) to your own computer, and installed locally, giving you an up-to-date list of resources and examples. After all, who needs a CD-ROM, when you've got the Web?

Acknowledgments

I would first like to thank Håkon Wium Lie and Bert Bos of the World Wide Web Consortium (W3C) for writing the specifications for the CSS language, and for "evangelizing" stylesheet concepts to the point where the language is now implemented by all major browser vendors. The fact that we now have stylesheets is largely due to their efforts. We all owe them a debt of gratitude.

I would further like to thank Håkon and Chris Lilley (also of the W3C) for their correspondence over the past several months, in which I would generally pose a question about CSS syntax or formatting, and they would return detailed answers. This obscenely one-sided exchange (for which I owe them greatly) helped clarify some of the thornier formatting issues, resulting in a book that is both better and more accurate. In the same vein, I must thank all the participants of the *www-style* mailing list, whose letters, comments, and occasional "rants" have always been intellectually stimulating, and have often been useful in understanding the subtler issues of stylesheet languages and design. It is nice to know that alongside the growing, commercialized Web, there remains the intellectually vigorous community that began it all.

Once a manuscript is finished and sent to the publisher, it begins to mutate, and, via what to me is an unfathomable process, the text and graphic files are transformed from a messy typescript into an attractively designed book. This is accomplished through the efforts of the publisher, and I would very much like to thank the supporting cast at Wiley Computer Publishing who made this happen so successfully. In particular I would like to thank my editor Cary Sullivan (who, like all good editors, "conned" me into writing the book), my assistant editor, Pam Sobotka, the copy editor, Jodi Beder (who did the dirty job of reading the manuscript, and polishing up my "...maze of twisty sentences, all alike") and the managing editor, Mark Hayden (who actually took the jumbled text and figures and converted it all into a printed book). I am greatly indebted to them for the fine quality of the final product.

I would also like to thank all my friends and colleagues at the Information Commons at the University of Toronto, who patiently watched me come perilously close to losing my mind as I wrestled with the completion of this book. I must particularly thank my friends and colleagues at the Center for Academic Technology, most notably John Bradley (now at King's College, London), Allen Forsyth, and Rudy Ziegler, for their pleasant company and enthusiastic support for this book-writing effort. Finally, I must thank my director, Michael Edmunds, who, when all seemed beyond hope, granted me a leave of absence to finish the book, no doubt much against his better judgment!

Last, I wish to thank my wife, Ann Dean, who carefully edited the manuscript, and who performed a list of other important tasks too numerous (and too intimidating) to list. Suffice it to say that without her enormous and unswerving support, this book would not have been possible.

Chapter

1

Introduction to HTML
and Stylesheets

It is now hard to remember a time when people had never heard of HTML, URLs, or Netscape. But, if we were to set the clock back to 1993, this indeed would be the case. In 1993, the Web was still just an experiment in information distribution, based upon the ideas of Tim Berners-Lee, a computer scientist and researcher at CERN, the European Centre for Nuclear Research located in Geneva, Switzerland. At the time, Berners-Lee was interested in the problem of cooperative work at CERN, where experiments often involved several collaborating institutions and hundreds of researchers and technicians, located at laboratories around the world. Components of an experiment would be built at the home laboratories of the partner organizations—perhaps in Japan, Canada, or Germany—and then shipped to Geneva. However, these components were not independent, and the construction of an experiment required much cooperation and collaboration between groups. Tim believed that the Internet offered a way of improving this cooperation, if only the appropriate tools could be created.

One of the main issues was shared documentation—how, for example, could a group working in Japan make the technical notes for their particular component of a project available to collaborators in Switzerland or Canada? At the time, there was no simple answer, as the different parties used many different and often proprietary document preparation systems, running on many different computers (e.g., Windows 3.1,

I

UNIX, IBM mainframes, NeXT, DEC VAXes) and supporting input and display devices ranging from fancy graphical displays to simple text terminals. There was therefore no universal format suitable for document preparation, and no simple way of distributing the information to everyone.

Berners-Lee realized that a new information distribution system was needed—one that was both *platform independent* and *distributed*. Platform independence was important so that all users could access the system irrespective of the computers and display devices they were using. At the same time, the system needed to be *distributed* so that each user could prepare material on his or her own computer and relate it to the documents and resources prepared by others. Finally, there was a need for an easy way to publish the material via the Internet, and thereby make it accessible to all.

These criteria led Berners-Lee to develop the three technologies that are the cornerstones of the World Wide Web: the **H**yper**T**ext **M**arkup **L**anguage (*HTML*) for composing universally readable documents, **U**niform **R**esource **L**ocators (*URLs*) for referencing other documents or resources accessible via the Internet, and the **H**yper**T**ext **T**ransfer **P**rotocol (*HTTP*) for publishing and distributing the resources. From the point of view of someone preparing documents for publication on the Web, the most important components are HTML and URLs. The key features are:

1. The *platform-independent* way of describing a document's content. HTML uses a *semantic markup* model, and is designed to mark the document text according to the structure of the text (paragraphs, headings, addresses, etc.), and not according to the desired formatting. In principle, this means that documents can be displayed on almost any device (graphics or plain text displays, or even a Braille printer), with each display converting the marked-up text into a presentation format appropriate to the device's capabilities.

2. The support, by HTML, of *hypertext links* between documents. This makes it easy to write a document and connect it, via these links, to related material. The destinations of these hypertext links are indicated, in turn, by URLs embedded within the HTML markup.

3. The fact that URLs can point not only to other HTML documents, but to any type of Internet resource. In particular they can point to resources available from other Internet services such as Gopher, FTP, or e-mail. Thus, the model unifies the many Internet-based technologies under a single presentation framework.

I stress these three points because they focus on HTML documents as *simply structured, platform-independent* containers of information—where that content is both regular text (and inline images) and the hypertext relationships encoded within the text. Indeed, the focus of the initial Web developers was on developing tools for communicating this information content, with little effort put towards the presentation of that content.

Recently, of course, this focus has expanded, due to the growing commercial interest in the Web as a general-purpose, commercial medium. This new focus has driven much of the recent technological innovation of the Web, and particularly the move towards better stylistic formatting capabilities—mediocre formatting is simply no longer acceptable to the general public, nor to investors considering billion-dollar investments in new technology companies. There is thus a growing demand for professional styling and layout capabilities consistent with modern media expectations. On the Web, this goal is to be accomplished using *stylesheets*—a new language that expresses typographic and layout features to be applied to an HTML document. However, as we shall see, it took some time to come to the point where such a language was both possible and widely supported.

The Early Days of the Web

The core Web technologies, namely HTML, HTTP, and URLs, were designed to be easily expanded and upgraded—indeed, these early technologies were developed in public, using the public forums of appropriate Internet Engineering Task Forces (the working bodies that define the basic communication protocols of the Internet). In the early days of the Web, as it grew in popularity and developed a core following of innovative software developers, this open approach led to the development of new Web technologies, such as the CGI programming interface to Web servers, and the addition of **FORM** and **IMG** elements to the HTML language. These were important additions that turned the Web from an experimental information-distribution project into a nascent, general-purpose technology with important commercial uses. At the time, these changes were heavily debated in the various Internet forums. For example, when Marc Andressen (then at NCSA, now better known as the co-founder of Netscape) added **IMG** element support into his experimental Web browser, Mosaic, it was considered an audacious and controversial act!

This developmental approach proved to be both good and bad. It was good in that it meant that much effort was spent on developing an easy and coherent way of distributing and relating information. Because of this, the early evolution and growth of the Web distribution model happened quickly. Indeed, HTML and URLs were easy for nontechnical people to understand and master, which led to the rapid growth of Web publishing by a wide cross-section of Internet users (somewhat to the surprise of Tim Berners-Lee, who thought that people would never hand-edit documents, or URLs, without using the equivalent of an HTML "word processor").

It was bad in that the mechanisms in place for evolving the Web technologies could not keep pace with the demand, with the changing development environment—what was once the realm of a few dedicated experts soon became a commercial venture involving thousands of developers and millions of "customers," not all of whom wished to reveal their "secrets" by discussing proposed developments in a public forum. As the demand grew for new changes and improvements to HTML (after all, if you could include beautiful image files within your documents, why did the pages themselves have to look so ugly?) the standards-based development approach started to break down, and software companies started to strike out on their own.

The Splintering of HTML

As a result of customer and corporate demand, the new commercial browser companies (led by Netscape) began to add new HTML elements and new element attributes that supported presentational features such as document background images and background colors, control over text color, size, and font face, "floating" image alignment, and so on. These HTML "extensions" added significantly to the vocabulary of a document designer and provided primitive tools a designer could use to develop attractive, elegantly designed Web pages.

However, the "HTML extensions" approach brought with it a number of problems, not least of which was maintaining platform-independent access to Web resources, as envisioned by the Web's creators. The first versions of HTML were designed as a consensus amongst the language developers, such that all early Web browsers essentially supported the same "standard" version of HTML. However, as different companies (primarily Netscape and Microsoft) have started to introduce new HTML elements outside the standards process, the result has been a growing lack of *layout* portability, or *universality*. Since the proprietary markup additions are browser-specific and largely tied to special text formatting, they are not portable; they counted on the user having the appropriate computer hardware (to support the requested formatting style) and software (to support the new, nonstandard element). For example, **BLINK**, designed to produce blinking text, is not terribly useful to a blind reader and, moreover, does not work on non-Netscape browsers. Similarly, heavy emphasis on background images, **TABLE**-based layout, **FONT, MARQUEE,** or other format-specific markup can yield pages that are complicated to author and extremely browser-specific—documents specifically prepared for Microsoft's browser and using all the Microsoft HTML extensions can be essentially unviewable on other browsers, such as Netscape's. Thus it has become harder and harder to write universally viewable documents—which was one of the reasons for HTML in the first place!

A second major problem is document *design* and *maintenance*. Documents that use HTML elements to specify detailed formatting and layout become large and unwieldy, cluttered with a seemingly endless collection of formatting-specific markup tags. This, in turn, makes it difficult to maintain the documents, since each subsequent editor of the document (where "editor" can mean either the person modifying the document or some special editing software) must understand all the HTML "tricks" used to create the particular design, and must know if the pages were designed to look best on Netscape Navigator, Microsoft Internet Explorer, or some other browser. Indeed, some Web sites, in their efforts to surmount this problem, have gone so far as to design two or three versions of the same document, each one optimized for the particular features of Navigator, MSIE, or some other browser.

Finally, the lack of standardized formatting makes it difficult to *manage* the ever larger document collections hosted at many Web sites. Updating and managing any collection requires editing and modifying the content page-by-page. Ideally, administrators might automate this process as much as possible, by using small batch-processing programs (essentially automated HTML editors) to do regular updating and maintenance. However, without a standardized version of HTML, and given the haphazard rules by which documents are routinely created, it is difficult to create generic tools for maintaining and updating content—after all, what should an HTML editing script do with markup tags it does not understand, or tags that are just plain wrong? For individual users editing their own pages by hand, this is not a great problem. But for large-scale users, such as corporate sites or Web publishing businesses managing thousands of pages, this creates enormous and expensive management problems.

Reestablishing an HTML Standard
The various companies involved in Web development realized that this process of splintering could not continue, as the growing incompatibilities threatened to stifle both the growth of the Web and

market acceptance of their Web products and services. In the World Wide Web Consortium (W3C), the companies found a forum through which they could establish a "standard" version of HTML that would be supported by all major vendors. The current product of this standard is the de-facto standard known as HTML version 3.2. Note that this process has not stopped companies from introducing their own special markup, but it has ensured a common HTML denominator supported by all companies.

HTML 3.2 represents a consensus of how browsers currently implement HTML, and includes all the standard semantic markup elements (e.g., **Hn, DIV, BLOCKQUOTE,** and **P**) as well as some of the presentational markup elements that are now widely implemented (e.g., **B, I, FONT**). However, the HTML 3.2 standard stresses the importance of the semantic approach—namely that HTML is a tool for marking up a document's structure and not its stylistic features, and that the presentation details should be largely left up to the browser.

This point is still emphasized because the basic rationale behind this approach—to make the documents as platform independent as possible—is just as important today as it was at the beginning, when platform independence was the driving factor. In fact, today there is perhaps even more variability in the ways an HTML document might be displayed, or in the ways it might be used. For example, today's document designer needs to consider:

1. **Different size/resolution display devices.** Computer displays can range from 320 × 480 pixel (or smaller) PDA displays, capable of only black and white, or perhaps 16 shades of gray, to 1600 × 1280 pixel monitors capable of millions of colors.

2. **Alternative display media.** There are browsers based on screen readers that convert text to speech, and also browsers, under design, that convert the text into Braille. Some documents will also be printed to paper, which calls again for different formatting details (e.g., page breaks).

3. **Alternatives for elements that some browsers cannot handle.** For example, what should a browser do if it is unable to run the requested Java applet, or it does not have the plug-in required to view the requested data?

Appropriate markup can deal with the third of these points, as standards-based HTML has mechanisms that let an author provide alternative blocks of the document for use by browsers unable to process a document's more advanced features. At the same time, the first two considerations can be handled by using semantic HTML markup that can be appropriately processed by the different possible displays. The point is simply this: If a designer uses standard HTML and follows the platform-independent HTML markup approach, he or she can transparently design pages that *will work* regardless of the display type or other capabilities of the browser.

HTML Is Not Enough

However, for today's designers, this purely structural approach is not sufficient. Today's document authors also want control over the presentation and formatting of the displayed product. This is a complicated issue, given the wide variety of possible display devices—how, for example, should an

HTML document simultaneously specify the desired presentation of a heading for a text-to-speech synthesizer, a Braille reader, and a printer?

Although, in principle, such instructions could be embedded in a document as element attributes or as new elements, it is clearly impossible for each and every HTML document to contain the formatting instructions needed by all presentation options—particularly when the author may have no idea of how some of these devices work! This, plus the fact that HTML was simply not designed to specify formatting details, leads to the conclusion that there must be a better way— that is, a way of specifying detailed formatting and presentation information without turning HTML itself into an unwieldy and cumbersome language. This is the role of stylesheets.

Introduction to Stylesheets

So, what is the best way to add extensive formatting information? It has already been argued that it is a bad idea to use the text markup language to express both structural and formatting information—the documents simply become too difficult to maintain, while the language becomes too unwieldy to modify and update. A better choice is to specify the formatting instructions as an entity separate from the text markup, and to specify these instructions using a language designed for formatting details. Although this approach is more complicated, in the long run it allows for greater flexibility in developing the markup and formatting languages (since they can be developed independently), and greater flexibility in the design of documents.

This is called the *stylesheet* approach. This approach turns the act of designing documents into a two-part process. In the first part, an author marks up the document itself, for example using HTML, to denote the main structural components, and to distinguish these components (headers, body, footers, etc.) one from another. In the second part, the author designs a collection of formatting instructions that will specify the desired formatting for the different structural components. This collection of instructions is called the document *stylesheet*, as it contains the formatting or styling information.

The stylesheet approach also means that the *display* of a document becomes a two-stage process. In the first stage, the document is obtained and is passed to the formatting software. In the second stage, the formatting software obtains the formatting instructions, and uses these instructions to determine how the various component elements of the document should be formatted for display. As a way of reflecting this process, we often say that a stylesheet is *applied to* the document as it is being rendered.

Stylesheets and Word Processors

It is worth noting that this approach is not limited to HTML—any markup language can use this approach. In fact, this is the technique used by all documentation systems based on Standard Generalized Markup Language (*SGML*)—HTML is a particular instance of an SGML language. Of course, most people have never heard of SGML. Nevertheless, the concept of stylesheets should be familiar to you if you have used a modern word processor such as Word or WordPerfect, although you may not be aware of it—these word processors also use stylesheet mechanisms to allow authors to globally change formatting of headings, paragraphs, lists, and so on.

For example, consider preparing a document using Microsoft Word (an example used out of familiarity with the product, and not as an endorsement). One of the most important menus on the Word formatting toolbar is the *style menu*—this menu lets a Word user select *styles* to be applied to a selected block of text. The markup process is accomplished by first selecting a desired block of text, and then using the style menu to select the style appropriate to that text.

With Word as with other similar word processors, users can create their own custom styles, which can be saved to a stylesheet file or, as it is known under Word, a *document template*. With Word, the default template is a file named ***normal.dot***: This file contains a list of all the defined styles, along with the formatting instructions to apply to text marked by each style. Authors can also create their own named styles, and by saving these styles in custom document template files (e.g., ***mytemplate.dot***), create their own document stylesheet. Figure 1.1 illustrates the style modification menus provided with Word 7 that let a user create new styles or modify old ones.

Figure 1.1 Style modification and creation tools provided with Microsoft Word 7. Text can be marked with a particular style, while the document template or *stylesheet* contains the formatting instructions to associate with this style.

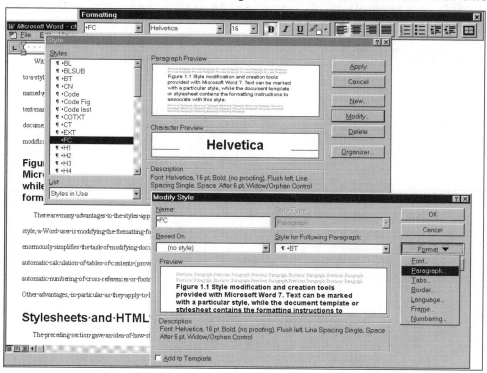

There are many advantages to the styles approach. For example, by modifying the formatting for a particular style, a Word user is modifying the formatting for *all* text sections marked by that style—this enormously simplifies the task of modifying a document's layout and styling. Other possible advantages include the automatic calculation of tables of contents (provided that headings are marked by an appropriate "heading" style), the automatic numbering of cross-references or footnotes, and the automatic tabulation of indexes and cross-references.

Stylesheets and HTML

The preceding section gave an idea of how stylesheets and style information work in theory and on everyday word processors. It is now time to look at some more concrete details, and see how the styles approach can work in practice with HTML documents. Figure 1.2 illustrates the stylesheet approach as applied to HTML documents.

The top portion of Figure 1.2 contains sample stylesheet instructions that define formatting properties for **P** elements—that is, for paragraphs. The letter **P** (placed in boldface in Figure 1.2 to make it stand out) initiates the group of instructions, and the actual formatting instructions are

Figure 1.2 An example of stylesheet instructions and the associated HTML document. Part A shows stylesheet instructions that specify formatting of HTML P (paragraph) elements. An example HTML document to which these instructions can be applied is illustrated in Part B.

A) Stylesheet instructions

```
P { left-margin: 5cm;
    font-family: garamond, "times new roman", times, serif;
    font-style:  italic;
    color:       black;
  }
... more style instructions ...
```

B) Example HTML document content

```
<H2>bleeble blabble blobble blub! <H2>
<P>The above phrase is strongly reminiscent of the
mating song of the long necked bandlesnnarf, a wily
bird long thought extinct, but now known to live in the
deepest haunts of lower Mongolia. But why, nobody knows.
</P>
<P>Of course, very few have actually seen the
long necked bandlesnnarf, least of all those of us who
have never left the joys of Toronto Ontario. But
even given this handicap, Prof. McGillicutty's slide
presentation tonight ...
</P>
```

enclosed within curly brackets—the stylesheet language rules define how the instructions are written and how they are related to the markup. The instructions in Figure 1.2, discussed in more detail later, are relatively straightforward—they simply specify the desired left margin for the text within the paragraph, as well as the font family, font style, and desired color for the text.

A browser that understands stylesheet instructions would apply these instructions to every **P** element in the document; thus in the HTML code example of Figure 1.2, the two paragraphs would be formatted using the indicated *formatting rules*. However, the rules would not affect the preceding **H2** heading, as headings require their own rules, independent of those for paragraphs.

Advantages of the Stylesheet Approach

There are several advantages to the stylesheets approach, and to separating stylesheets from the text and text markup. First, different stylesheets can be applied to the same document, allowing the same content to be presented in a number of different ways. This lets authors *restyle* the content, or redirect their content to a new audience, without modifying the original HTML document. Figure 1.3 illustrates how different stylesheets can in principle produce a wide variety of document renderings.

The second advantage to the stylesheet approach is in the area of document maintenance. If an entire collection of documents is formatted according to a single well-defined set of stylesheet rules, maintained in a single stylesheet file, then changes to this one stylesheet will modify the presentation of every one of these documents in a uniform way. This makes it is easy to modify and update the presentation of a few documents or of an enormous collection of documents, simply by modifying the stylesheet that applies to them. Thus, the global look of a Web site can be changed by modifying a single stylesheet page.

A third advantage is consistency. Because a stylesheet can be shared by any number of documents, an author can guarantee that all the documents will have the same design and layout, or the same look and feel. Uniformity of layout is an important aspect of Web site design, and stylesheets make it much easier to manage and update a collection consistently and efficiently.

The final advantage is simplicity of markup, and simplicity of style. Because the formatting information is not part of the HTML, document markup can be kept simple and concise, while the markup language can be kept simple and straightforward—which was one of the strengths of HTML in the first place. Similarly, the stylesheet language can also be simple, since it only describes styling and is not concerned with specific features of the markup language. Furthermore, a new presentation device—for example, a Braille touchpad, text-to-speech conversion, or perhaps a holographic projector—simply requires a new stylesheet language appropriate to that medium, but no changes to the marked-up document.

Approaches to Stylesheets

By now you should be entirely sold on the idea of stylesheets, and if not—well, you're going to use them anyway, so tough luck! In either event, it is time to describe the different types of stylesheet languages, and how the formatting instructions can be related to HTML documents. There are two very distinct approaches to stylesheet languages, and this section begins by reviewing these approaches. This is followed by a brief description of mechanisms for relating the instructions to HTML elements.

Figure 1.3 An illustration of the relationship between the stylesheet instructions and the marked-up document. The stylesheet instructions are applied to the document at the formatting stage, producing the displayed output. Different stylesheets can produce different displayed outcomes, without requiring any changes to the HTML document itself.

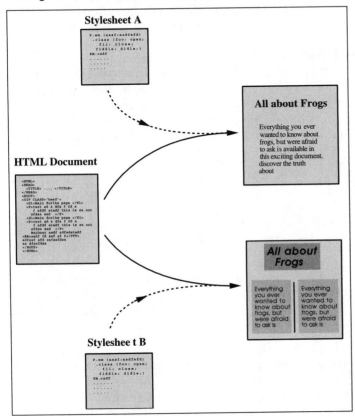

Rules-Based Formatting: Cascading Stylesheets

The two approaches to stylesheet languages can be described as *rules*-based and *procedure*-based. A rules-based language gives stylesheet instructions as a list of statements or *declarations* about how a particular element, or group of elements, should be presented. For example, the stylesheet snippet in Figure 1.2:

```
P {
    left-margin: 5cm;
    font-family: garamond, "times new roman", times, serif;
    font-style: italic;
    color:      black;
}
```

is an example of rules-based stylesheet instructions, as the declaration simply lists the formatting instructions that should be applied when formatting the indicated element, here a **P**.

Rules-based formatting has the advantage of simplicity—it is easy to construct a set of formatting rules that are both simple to express and simple for people to understand and appreciate. Most readers will be able to understand what the above instructions mean without even reading the rest of this book! At the same time, the rules can be significantly more complicated than those in this simple example, and can encompass most of the standard formatting needs of online document presentation.

The stylesheet language currently in use on the Web is rules-based. This language, known as Cascading Stylesheets, or *CSS*, is designed to be both simple to use and expressive of the most common styling features demanded by document authors. The stylesheet code shown in Figure 1.2 is an example CSS rule—here specifying the desired formatting for paragraphs. Note how simple and easy this is to understand. This simplicity was the key goal of the CSS approach, as the designers of CSS, led by Håkon Lie and Bert Bos of the World Wide Web Consortium, wished to create a language that would be both easy to use and easy to understand by graphics designers who knew a lot about typography and graphic design, but little about SGML or computer programming. Note, for example, the similarities between the instructions given in Figure 1.2 and the Microsoft Word style instructions illustrated at the bottom of Figure 1.1.

At present, CSS is the only stylesheet language in use on the Internet, and this book is focused on the CSS language and on how to create CSS stylesheets. There are, however, other stylesheet approaches. One in particular bears mentioning here, as it may in the long run provide a more powerful approach to styling on the Web.

Procedural Formatting: DSSSL Stylesheets

Simplicity comes at a price, and rules-based formatting such as CSS has important limitations: If you want to format something in a way that is not described by the formatting declarations supported by the language, then you're simply out of luck.

Such limitations can be avoided by using a *procedural* approach. With a procedural language, the formatting instructions are expressed as procedural functions that act much like small computer programs. In fact, that is rather what a procedural formatting stylesheet looks like: a small program that produces the formatting rules as its *output*, where the program input can consist of other formatting rules, plus information about the local display environment and the document being formatted.

There already exists a general-purpose procedural stylesheet language designed for SGML applications (as mentioned earlier, SGML is the language upon which HTML is based). This language is called the Document Style Semantics and Specification Language, or *DSSSL*. DSSSL is an extremely sophisticated stylesheet language designed explicitly for SGML-based languages and with abilities that far exceed those of CSS. A simple example of a DSSSL stylesheet is shown in Figure 1.4.

It does not take a rocket scientist to see that DSSSL is more complicated than CSS! While learning CSS is similar in difficulty to learning HTML, the task of learning DSSSL has been compared (perhaps unfairly) to learning a sophisticated programming language such as C++ or Java—tasks hardly for the timid.

Figure 1.4 An extract from a DSSSL stylesheet, taken from an introductory DSSSL tutorial prepared by Daniel M. Germán of the Department of Computer Science, University of Waterloo. The full tutorial is available at:

`http://csg.uwaterloo.ca/~dmg/dsssl/tutorial/tutorial.html`

```
;;;;;;;;;;;;;;;;;;;;;;;;;;;;;;;;;;;;;;;;;;;;;;;;;;;;;;;;;;
; Adding constants
(define *titleFontSize*        18pt)
(define *fmFontSize*           (/ *titleFontSize* 2))
(define *fmIndent*             3cm)
(define *fmSpaceBefore*        0.5cm)

(define *textFontSize*         10pt)
(define *textSpaceBefore*      (/ *textFontSize* 2))

(define *personaetitleFontSize* (+ *textFontSize*   3pt))
(define *personaIndent*          1.5cm)
(define *personaSpaceBefore*    (/ *textFontSize* 2))

(define *pgroupIndent*           (+ *personaIndent* 0.5cm))
;;;;;;;;;;;;;;;;;;;;;;;;;;;;;;;;;;;;;;;;;;;;;;;;;;;;;;;;;;;
; This version adds some page the title of the play
;;;;;;;;;;;;;;;;;;;;;;;;;;;;;;;;;;;;;;;;;;;;;;;;;;;;;;;;;;;
(root
  (make simple-page-sequence
; margins
        left-margin:             2cm
; default font
        font-size:               *textFontSize*
        line-spacing:            *textFontSize*
        right-margin:            2cm
        top-margin:              2cm
        bottom-margin:           2cm
        (process-children))
)
..... ; rest deleted to save space ..
```

This book does not provide details about DSSSL. If you are interested in finding out more about these advanced issues, you are encouraged to pursue the DSSSL references at the end of this chapter.

A Simple Stylesheet Example

The next chapters provide details of how CSS stylesheets rules are related to HTML elements. As an introduction, this section looks at a simple HTML document and a related stylesheet that illustrate the basic mechanisms. This is also a good opportunity to introduce the vocabulary of stylesheets. Earlier in this chapter we introduced the words *rules, declaration,* and *markup element* rather freely, since the general meaning was implied by the context. Here more concrete examples will be given that help define these terms.

Figure 1.5 shows an example stylesheet, containing a number of stylesheet *rules*, where a *rule* is simply a combination of stylesheet *declarations* (statements about what type of formatting properties should be applied) plus a *selector* that indicates the selection of markup elements to which the rule should be applied. For example, in Figure 1.5 the rule:

```
BODY {
    font-family:  "times new roman", times, serif;
    background:   white;
    color:        black ;
    margin-left:  10%;
    margin-right: 10%;
    text-align:   justify;
}
```

Figure 1.5 An example CSS stylesheet. This stylesheet contains stylesheet rules for the BODY, P, and DIV elements, and also for specific classes of DIV and P elements.

```
BODY {         font-family:   "times new roman", times, serif;
               background:    white;
               color:         black ;
               margin-left:   10%;
               margin-right: 10%;
               text-align:    justify;
          }
H1,H2,H3  { font-family:    gill, arial, helvetica, sans-serif; }
H2,H3     { margin-left:    2%; }
H1        { text-align:     center; text-transform: uppercase; }
DIV.abstract{ margin-left:  20%;
               margin-right:  20%;
               font-size:     smaller;
          }
P         { text-indent:    5em;}
A:link    { color: black;   text-decoration: underline }
A:visited { color: gray;    text-decoration: none }
.goofy    { color:          #FFFF00;
               font-family:   arial;
               background:    blue;
               text-decoration: blink;
          }
```

contains the selector BODY, to indicate that the rule should be applied to **BODY** elements. This selector is associated with six declarations. The declarations associated with a given selector are grouped together by curly brackets, while each declaration in the group is ended with a semicolon.

This particular rule specifies properties for the body of the document: that is, for everything that is to be displayed. The six declarations give the desired font (as a sequence of font names, in decreasing order of preference), the desired background color (white), the desired text color (black), the desired left and right margins (here as a percentage of the display window width), and the desired alignment of the text (justified).

One can see, however, that several properties, such as the font size, are not specified. Although these features could be specified, this stylesheet instead uses the default settings of the browser displaying the document. Thus the font size and style are determined by the settings of the browser.

There are several other types of rules in Figure 1.5, all of which will be discussed in detail in later chapters. Briefly,

```
H1,H2,H3   { font-family:  gill, arial, helvetica, sans-serif }
```

is an example of a grouped rule, where the declarations to the right (the font to use) are applied to any of the comma-separated elements listed to the left. On the other hand, the rule

```
DIV.abstract   { margin-left:    20%;
                 margin-right:   20%;
                 font-size:      smaller;  }
```

uses a *class-based selector,* such that this rule applies only to **DIV** elements that take the attribute value assignment **CLASS**="abstract". Thus, this rule will only apply to certain **DIV** elements, and not others. The rule

```
.goofy    { color:            #FFFF00;
            font-family:      arial;
            background:       blue;
            text-decoration:  blink;    }
```

also uses a class-based selector, but since no particular element name is specified, this rule applies to any element with the attribute value **CLASS**="goofy". Finally, the rule

```
A:visited    { color: gray; text-decoration: none }
```

employs a *pseudo-class* selector (which is CSS jargon for a property of an element that is "like" a **CLASS,** but that is based on information obtained from the browser itself and is not obtained from the HTML markup). Here, for example, the pseudo-class selector refers to **A** elements that are hypertext links that have previously been accessed or *visited.*

At this point it is easier to get a feel for what the stylesheet does by way of an example. Figure 1.6 is a simple HTML document to which the stylesheet in Figure 1.5 has been added. Note how the stylesheet content is placed inside a **STYLE** element. **STYLE** is a new addition to **HTML,** designed to contain stylesheet content. It can only appear inside the document **HEAD.**

Figure 1.6 An example HTML document to which the stylesheet in Figure 1.5 can be applied—here the stylesheet document is placed inside the HTML document, contained within a STYLE element. Note the use of CLASS attributes to *subclass* elements.

```
<HTML><HEAD><TITLE>Example Of CSS Stylesheets</TITLE>
<STYLE>
BODY {
        font-family:    "times new roman", times, serif;
        background:     white;
        color:          black ;
        margin-left:    10%;
        margin-right:   10%;
        text-align:     justify;
    }
H1,H2,H3        { font-family:  gill, arial, helvetica, sans-serif;   }
H2,H3           { margin-left:  2%;                                   }
H1              { text-align:   center; text-transform: uppercase;    }
DIV.abstract    { margin-left:  20%;
                margin-right:   20%;
                font-size:      smaller;
                }
P               { text-indent:  5em; }
A:link          { color: black; text-decoration: underline; }
A:visited       { color: gray;  text-decoration: none }
.goofy          { color:        #FFFF00;
                font-family:    arial;
                background:     blue;
                text-decoration:blink;
                }
</STYLE></HEAD>
<BODY>
<H1>An Example Illustration of CSS Stylesheets</H1>
<DIV CLASS="abstract">
<P>This document tests stylesheet support. A stylesheet
    can prescribe formatting rules for elements based on the
    element name, or on specific elements according to their
    CLASS. A stylesheet can also prescribe generic formatting
    instructions for all elements with the same CLASS.
</P>
<P>For example, if
    <A HREF="test.html">stylesheets are working</A>, this
    abstract should be in a slightly smaller font, with
    a slightly larger indent than paragraphs outside the abstract.
    Also, unexplored links, such as the one at the beginning of
    this paragraph, should be in black text and underlined,
```

Continued

Figure 1.6 *Continued*

```
      whereas already explored hypertext links, such as the text
      at the end of this sentence, should be in
      <A HREF="donetest.html">gray, and not underlined</A>.
</P>
</DIV>
<H2>Introduction to Stylesheets</H2>
<P>The CLASS attribute lets an author mark elements for special
      formatting, but also for special meanings. For example,
      by marking the above section with <B>CLASS="abstract"</B>
      we not only mark the meaning behind the section, but provide
      a way for CSS rules to specify special formatting for the
      entire abstract — CSS rules can be applied to particular classes.
</P>
<P>Note also how the CSS rules are <EM>inherited</EM> by child
      elements — that is, by elements within other elements. Thus
      the paragraphs inside the DIV with CLASS="abstract" inherit the
      extra indents and smaller font size of the surrounding DIV.
</P>
<H3>Generic Class Styling</H3>
<P>Styling can also be applied to generic CLASSes. For example,
      <EM CLASS="goofy"> this line of text </EM> and
      <STRONG CLASS="goofy"> this line of text </STRONG> are both
      of the same class: <B>CLASS="goofy"</B>. They can thus both
      take on properties of this generic class.
</P>
</BODY></HTML>
```

Figure 1.7 shows this document as displayed by a browser (here, Netscape Navigator 3) that does not understand CSS stylesheets. As you can see, the document is displayed clearly, but without any special formatting. It is still easy to read and understand (because the HTML markup reflected the structure of the document) even without the applied stylesheet.

Figure 1.8 shows the same document as displayed by Microsoft Internet Explorer 3 (MSIE 3). This browser does understand an early version of CSS, and applies the CSS rules when formatting the page. Note, however, that MSIE does not understand or cannot properly process all the declarations. For example, it does not properly process the `font-size: smaller` declaration associated with the `DIV.abstract selector`. This rule actually produces larger text: apparently, at this default font size, MSIE does not have a smaller font available, and so it erroneously chooses a larger one instead! Also, in Figure 1.8 one can see that MSIE does not remove the underlines from the visited hypertext anchors, or justify the text in the document as requested by the `text-align: justify` declaration associated with the **BODY** element.

CSS Core and Advanced Features

The font size problem identified in the analysis of Figure 1.8 is typical of early-stage technology—MSIE 3 was the very first browser to support stylesheets, and was released while the CSS specification was still being finalized. It is thus not surprising that a few things don't work quite right! On the other hand, the fact that the browser does not justify the text is not actually a failing of the browser's interpretation of the CSS rules. Because CSS was designed to express a wide range of desired formatting, it allows for capabilities (such as text justification) that may not possible with many browsers. Thus CSS declarations are divided into two categories:

- **CSS Core Features**—those declarations that every CSS-compliant browser must be able to process.

- **CSS Advanced Features**—those declarations that may, in fact, not be properly processed by a browser. In general, the CSS specifications specify what a browser should do if it is unable to handle a particular declaration.

As you probably guessed, `text align: justify` is an advanced CSS feature: The CSS specification lets a browser treat the justify value as either left or right alignment, depending on which is appropriate (e.g., left for English or Russian, right for Arabic or Hebrew).

Property Inheritance

Stylesheets are most useful when they let an author specify the minimum necessary information—after all, why must a rule specify the font size and family, if the only thing that needs to be added is some text color, or italics? CSS supports this type of minimal markup through several mechanisms, one of which is known as *property inheritance*. Inheritance means that the formatting properties of any element are inherited from the element that it lies directly inside. This idea is obvious from standard HTML. For example, if we have the markup

```
<P> This is a paragraph containing <EM>outrageous</EM> text
```

then the text inside the **EM** inherits the font size and family of the surrounding **P**,[1] and simply modifies the enclosed text as appropriate (usually by italicizing it). Thus, if the above text were subject to the stylesheet rule

```
P {font-family: arial; font-size: 24pt; color: blue}
```

then the **EM** element would inherit the font family, size, and color of the surrounding paragraph, but would override these properties using the specified rules, to produce the word "outrageous" in 24 point Arial font, with blue text, and in italics (which is very definitely emphasized!).

Inheritance also allows for two basic types of CSS property values. *Absolute* values are those that specify the desired property value in an absolute sense, for example `font-size: 24pt`. On the other hand, *relative* values specify the desired property relative to the inherited value, for example `font-size: smaller` for a font size smaller than that of the parent element.

Not all properties are inherited, as, in some cases, inheritance is not sensible. For example, an element does not inherit a background color or image, since it instead lies "on top" of the background; nor does it inherit margins. In most cases it is obvious when a property cannot be inherited. The detailed property specifications found in Chapter 8 explicitly state whether a property is inherited or not.

Figure 1.7 Rendering, by the Netscape Navigator 3 browser, of the document listed in Figure 1.5. Navigator 3 does not understand stylesheets, and ignores the style instructions.

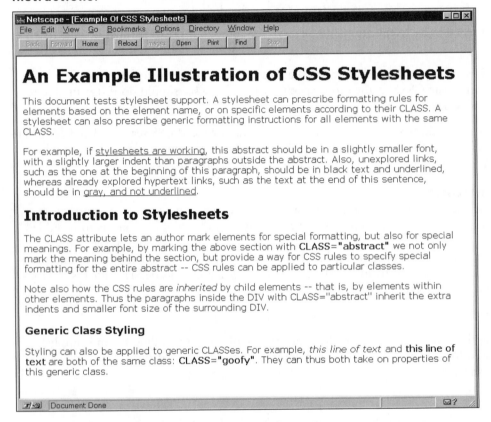

Default Properties

Default properties are those inherent in the browser—that is, the properties associated with each markup element, as defined by the browser itself. Sometimes this collection of properties is also called the *default stylesheet*. In the absence of any other property specifications, relative properties in a stylesheet will be evaluated relative to these natural defaults.

The default values can vary significantly from browser to browser, and may be modified by the user. For example, a user can modify the default background colors, the default text font, and, in some cases, the default fonts and alignment options specific to different levels of headings. In the future, browsers will let users specify their own default stylesheets, thereby defining a much more sophisticated set of default properties. Also, the user can (and usually does) constantly modify the size of the browser window, which in turn affects the default size of the drawing *canvas* (the region of the display into which the browser renders the document).

Figure 1.8 Rendering, by the Microsoft Internet Explorer 3 (MSIE 3) browser, of the document listed in Figure 1.5. The MSIE 3 browser understands CSS, and formats the document as per the stylesheet instructions—albeit with a few small problems, as discussed in the text.

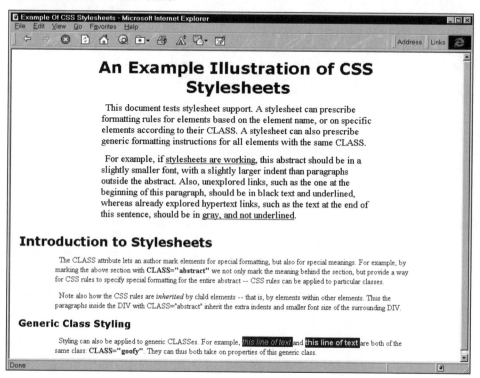

The instinct of many authors is to override default settings by using absolute declarations for all display properties (font sizes and faces, positions of paragraphs, etc.) to maximize the author's control over the rendering of the document. In general, this is not a good approach, for several reasons. First, the author might get the idea that he/she has absolute control over the canvas onto which the document will be displayed, despite the fact that this is simply not the case—don't forget about variability in the browser window size. Also, there are many cases where the user may need, for specific reasons, to impose particular style settings. Some simple and obvious examples are:

- a visually impaired user who wants particularly large font sizes so that the text is easy to read

- a teacher using a video projector to display the document, and who needs larger fonts, and perhaps a different font face, to make the text legible to the class

- a user who wants to shrink the font, so that the document can be printed on fewer pages of paper

CSS does provide mechanisms whereby a browser user can "insist" on using his or her own style settings, and override the settings recommended by the author—these mechanisms are discussed later in this book. Nevertheless, this problem is mitigated if the author instead uses absolute quantities only for those properties that absolutely must be absolute, and specifies everything else using relative quantities that work with inherited stylesheet properties.

Browser Handling of Stylesheet Errors

The final issue to discuss in this chapter is how a CSS-enabled browser handles "mistakes" or "non-understood" CSS instructions or markup. In general, the rule is that the CSS *parser* (the part of the browser that reads and interprets CSS rules) should simply ignore the parts that it does not understand. For example, the rule

```
P { text-align:  justify;
    font-style:  italic;
    blood-type:  ABnegative;
    font-size:   12em;
    background:  "blue";
  }
```

contains two illegal declaration's—as far as I know, paragraphs never have blood types, while color keywords, such as the name `"blue"`, cannot appear inside quotation marks. According to the CSS error-handling procedure, a CSS parser should ignore these two declarations, and format the paragraph according to the three properly written declarations.

If the selector portion of the rule is illegal, then the entire rule should be ignored. For example,

```
P.abstract.subset   { text-align:  justify;
                       font-style:  italic;
                       font-size:   12em;
                     }
```

is illegal due to the extra period in the subclassing portion—periods are not allowed in a class name—so that the CSS parser will skip this rule completely.

The Truth About Stylesheet Processing

Unfortunately, some browsers are not very good at parsing CSS rules, and often discard entire rules, or several declarations within a rule, even when only one of the declarations is invalid. Typical mistakes that cause this sort of problem are: errors in the property value, missing semicolons at the end of the declaration, or missing curly brackets before or after a collection of declarations.

Chapter Summary

Stylesheets specify formatting details specific to a set of HTML elements. A stylesheet is a collection of instructions that specify how particular elements of a document should be formatted. The instructions can also be related to different classes of an element, provided the markup elements take **CLASS** attributes.

Stylesheets are independent of HTML. Stylesheet instructions are written in a language that is independent of HTML, although the application of stylesheets to HTML documents is the topic of this book.

Cascading Stylesheets (CSS) is the currently deployed Web stylesheet language. CSS is a simple rules-based language for specifying formatting details, and permits instructions similar in form to those found in standard word processing programs such as Word or WordPerfect. The currently deployed version of CSS is known as CSS Level 1 or *CSS1*. The Document Style Semantics and Specification Language, or *DSSSL*, is an alternative and more powerful approach to stylesheets. There are currently no browsers that support this alternative.

The CSS specification has two parts: *core* and *advanced* features. Core features must be supported by a CSS-compliant browser, while advanced features may not be supported. In general, CSS1 indicates how a browser should handle unsupported features.

CSS stylesheets can be placed within an HTML document by placing the instructions within a **STYLE** element, which must appear in the document **HEAD**.

CSS stylesheets consist of *rules* to be applied to a given element or elements. A rule consists of *selectors* (to indicate the element or elements to which the rule should be applied) and one or more *declarations*. Each declaration consists of a *property* to be applied to the element, plus the *value* to be assigned to that property.

CSS properties are often *inherited* from parent elements. Thus, an **EM** element within a **P** inherits the font properties passed to it from the surrounding paragraph element. However, not all properties are inherited.

Default CSS properties are obtained from a browser's default settings. Default properties, such as the font size, margins, display area size and width, the background color, and so on, are defined by settings configured into the browser. These settings vary from browser to browser, and according to the preferences of the user. These settings are also called the *default stylesheet*.

CSS declarations containing errors are *ignored* by the CSS parser. If any part of a declaration is in error, then the entire declaration is ignored. If there is an error in the selector, then the entire *rule* is ignored.

Chapter Exercises

It's perhaps a bit early to ask you to construct your own stylesheets, but it is not too early to ask you to modify an existing one. It is a useful exercise to take the document listed in Figure 1.5

and modify the stylesheet instructions to get a feel for how things work. It is actually quite useful to create stylesheets with errors in the declarations or the rules—this will help you to see how the browser handles these conditions, and is useful for helping you to diagnose such problems when designing your own stylesheets. In general, a browser does not tell the user when it encounters an error in a CSS rule, so that an author is left largely to his or her own intuition to discover CSS mistakes.

As a second exercise, try varying the default browser properties (using the browser's "Preferences" menu) and observe how this affects the displayed document. Then, by playing with absolute and relative property declarations, you can get a feel for the control that an author has over the presentation of the document.

Like all the documents and code examples in this book, the documents listed in this chapter are available over the Web from the author's Web site. The home page for the Web site is:

`http://www.utoronto.ca/ian/books/style/`

from which all figures can easily be located.

References

Additional information about stylesheets is found at the URLs listed below. Note that all the URLs listed as references in this book are accessible through the book's Web site, and that the URLs at the Web site will be updated as new resources are added, or old ones are moved or deleted.

General Stylesheet Information
http://www.w3.org/pub/WWW/Style/ (W3C stylesheets overview)

news:comp.infosystems.www.authoring.html (HTML authoring newsgroup)

General CSS Information
http://www.w3.org/pub/WWW/TR/REC-CSS1 (CSS Specifications)

http://www.htmlhelp.com/reference/css/ (Web Design group CSS review)

Other Books on CSS
10 Minute Guide to HTML Style Sheets, by Craig Zacker, Que Corp., 1997.

Cascading Style Sheets: Designing for the Web, by Håkon Wium Lie and Bert Bos, Addison-Wesley, 1997.

DSSSL Information
http://csg.uwaterloo.ca/~dmg/dsssl/tutorial/tutorial.html (Introductory DSSSL tutorial)

http://itrc.uwaterloo.ca/~papresco/dsssl/tutorial.html (More detailed DSSSL tutorial) http://sunsite.unc.edu/pub/sun-info/standards/dsssl/ DSSSL Information, including DSSSL-Online and examples)

http://www.jclark.com/dsssl (DSSSL draft standard)

http://sunsite.unc.edu/pub/sun-info/standards/dsssl/draft/ (Draft DSSSL standard—DynaText format, with Windows 3.1/95 viewer)

news:comp.text.sgml (SGML newsgroup; also DSSSL)

Endnote

1. The **P** element is also called the *parent* of the **EM** element that lies inside it, while the **EM** is called the *child* of the **P**.

2

HyperText Markup
Language Review

As mentioned in Chapter 1, stylesheets are applied to documents that are already marked up with a markup language, for example HTML. In this approach, the markup organizes the document into distinct, logical parts (headings, paragraphs, lists, and so on), while the stylesheet defines formatting details that apply to these parts. Given a well-marked-up document or family of documents, this separation makes it easy to design an associated stylesheet that prescribes the desired layout and formatting, and that also can be changed when the author decides to update the look of the material.

However, this is possible only if the document is properly marked up: that is, if the author has marked up the document *accurately*, so that the rules of the markup language are properly observed, and *structurally*, so that the components of the document are well identified. The former is necessary because errors in the markup can badly confuse the browser as it tries to format the page (an example will be given later). The latter is important so that different styling can be specified for the different parts. For example, if an author wants different styling and layout for the page header, body, and footer, he or she will need to structure the document into these three parts, so that appropriate stylesheet instructions can be specified for the different pieces.

Thus, becoming a stylesheet designer means more than just learning a new stylesheet language—it also means having a well-grounded understanding of the *markup* language. The purpose of this chapter is thus to review the HyperText Markup Language (HTML) and discuss the relationship between HTML and stylesheets.

This chapter is not a substitute for a detailed reference on HTML, and you are encouraged to obtain a good HTML reference book, if you don't have one already (my own *The HTML Sourcebook*, now in its third edition, is, in all modesty, an excellent choice). Note that you need a book that explains the detailed rules of HTML, and not one that just discusses "cool Web page design" or "HTML design tricks." Such tricks often play fast and loose with the rules of HTML, and are thus not a good introduction to proper HTML design.

This chapter is divided into eight sections. The first two sections review the design of markup languages, with an emphasis on HTML, and describe the important structural rules associated with the authoring of an HTML document. This is followed by a review of the different markup elements of HTML, organized according to their general types: **HEAD**-level, **BODY**-level, and so on. The body-level elements are further divided into groupings that are relevant to a stylesheet's understanding of the markup; namely, *block* elements (those that define blocks of text, like paragraphs), *list-item* elements (those that have list item decorations, such as bullets or numbers), and *inline* elements (elements that affect formatting of text inline within a block). Other groupings, also relevant to formatting issues, are also described.

The fourth section looks in detail at the newer HTML elements and attributes introduced in support of stylesheets. The elements discussed include **STYLE, SPAN,** and **LINK,** with attribute **REL**="stylesheet", while the new attributes include **CLASS, ID,** and **STYLE.** Examples are provided to illustrate what these elements do and how they relate to stylesheet formatting.

The fifth section provides an overview of the HTML markup model, and a discussion of the importance of valid HTML markup. This is accomplished using simple examples that illustrate how markup errors can make stylesheet-based formatting quite unreliable, often to the point of being unusable. The purpose of this section is to reiterate the importance of correct markup design as a tool for easy document and stylesheet design. After all, a main point of stylesheet-based layout is to make a Web designer's job easier, not harder!

Finally, the last three sections provide a chapter overview, a short list of chapter-related exercises, and a brief reference list of related books and Internet resources. Recall also that all the example documents in this book, and the online examples, are available (and downloadable) from the book Web site; the URL is given in the Preface and at the end of Chapter 1.

Markup Language Review

As mentioned in Chapter 1, the HyperText Markup Language is designed to specify the logical organization of documents, with extensions that allow for inline images, fill-in forms, embedded objects and programs, and hypertext links to other Internet resources. This approach reflects the fact that in a distributed environment like the Web, individuals viewing a document can use browsers of very different capabilities. It is thus more sensible to specify the underlying structural features of the document (i.e., paragraphs, headings, lists, etc.) and leave the presentation details up to the browser or an associated stylesheet.

From an author's point of view, HTML consists of *markup tags* that are embedded within the document text. These tags are just strings of regular text, so that an HTML document can be prepared using a simple text editor. Structurally, the tags divide the document into blocks called elements; for example, the sequence

```
<EM> some emphasized text </EM>
```

is an **EM** *element* consisting of the *start tag* `<EM>`, the *stop tag* `</EM>`, and the text content `some emphasized text`. The HTML language specifications define the allowed elements (e.g., that **EM** is a valid element), and where the different elements can be placed within the document.

Defining HTML: The Document Type Definition

The rules for HTML are defined via the International Standards Organization's (ISO) Standard Generalized Markup Language, or SGML. SGML is a tool for defining markup languages like HTML (HTML is just one example). The details of SGML are fortunately not critical to Web page designers. One component that is useful is the definition of the HTML syntax, contained in a file called a document type definition, or DTD. This is a simple text file containing all the rules for HTML, and can be used, in combination with an SGML parsing program, to check the syntax of any HTML document. There are many commercial packages that do this, including HTML editors such as SoftQuad's HoTMetaL and InContext's Spider. There are also several resources on the Internet that provide "over the Web" checking or validation. Additional information about syntax checking is found in the references at the end of this chapter.

HTML is a rapidly evolving language. The current standard version of HTML is known as HTML version 3.2, or HTML 3.2. There are also many "enhancements" or "additions" to this language currently in use. Some of these enhancements (such as the additions to support stylesheets) arose from the HTML standardization process, and are widely supported, while others are specific to certain browser vendors (i.e., Netscape and/or Microsoft), are not in wide use, and are unlikely to be integrated into future standards. Because the proprietary elements are not likely to be integrated into standard HTML, an author should be wary of using them.

Allowed Characters in HTML Documents

As illustrated in Figure 1.6, an HTML document is just a simple text document. An HTML document can contain any of the valid **printable** characters from the 8-bit ISO Latin-1 character set,[1] which is the standard set used on most modern computers. The ISO Latin-1 character set supports 256 different characters ($2^8 = 256$), consisting of the 128 characters of the seven-bit ($2^7 = 128$) US-ASCII character set—the characters that appear on a standard U.S. English keyboard—plus 128 additional characters that use the eighth bit. These extra 128 positions contain many of the accented and other characters common in Western European languages.

Future versions of HTML will support a much larger set of characters by using the 16-bit Unicode character set. This set can represent up to 65,536 characters ($2^{16} = 65,536$) and contains the characters and symbols required by most of the world's languages. Fortunately, the first 256 characters of Unicode are the same as the characters in ISO Latin-1. Unfortunately, there is very little current software supporting this character set, although this situation will change in the near future.

Entity References

On many keyboards it is difficult to type non-ASCII characters. Partly for this reason, HTML has mechanisms for representing non-ASCII characters using ASCII character sequences. The most important of these is called an *entity reference*, which references characters using symbolic names written entirely in ASCII. For example, the entity reference for the character é is é.

The HTML specification defines a complete list of entity reference names corresponding to all the non-ASCII characters in the ISO Latin-1 character set. Lists of these are found in most books on HTML, and are also found at the URL:

```
http://www.utoronto.ca/webdocs/HTMLdocs/Book/Book-3ed/appa/en_test.html
```

Comments in HTML Documents

In HTML documents, comments are surrounded by the special character strings <!-- and -->. Here, the text between and including the two strings is a comment, and is not be displayed by a browser. Some examples are:

```
<!-- This is a comment --  >

<!-- This is also a comment
     This comment spans more than one line. Note that some very,
     very old browsers do not understand multiline comments.
  -- >
```

HTML Markup Model

Given this introduction, we will now briefly review the structure and organization of a simple HTML document. This discussion is based on the HTML document illustrated in Figure 2.1. The rendering of this document by the Netscape Navigator 3 browser is shown in Figure 2.2.

As mentioned previously, an HTML document is simply a text file in which certain strings of characters, called *tags*, mark regions of the document and assign special meanings to them. In the jargon of SGML, these regions and the enclosing tags are called *elements*.

This structure is clearly illustrated in Figure 2.1. The tags are the strings of characters surrounded by the less than (<) and greater than (>) characters. The first thing inside the tag is the element *name* (also called element *type*), which identifies the element and indicates what the element means. If the tag begins with the sequence <name (where *name* is the element name or type), then the tag marks the start of an element, and is called a *start tag*. On the other hand, if the tag begins with the sequence </name, then the tag marks the end of an element, and is called a *stop tag*. For example, the markup

```
<H1>A Simple Example HTML Document</H1>
```

illustrates the start tag, end tag, and content for an **H1** heading element.

Elements that mark selections of text are often called *containers*—the **H1** element just illustrated is one example. Most elements are containers, marking regions of the document into blocks of text which, in turn, may contain other elements marking other blocks of text, and so on. A document is then a *hierarchy* of HTML elements, with the complete hierarchy defining the entire document. This hierarchical character is an important aspect of HTML markup, and is illustrated in more detail a bit later.

In some cases, end tags are optional. This is so when the end of an element can be unambiguously determined from the surrounding elements. For example, in the markup

```
<P> here is a paragraph
<P> here is another paragraph </P>
```

the end tag after the first paragraph is optional, since the second `<P>` tag starts another paragraph, and by implication ends the preceding one. Note that in Figure 2.1, all end tags `</P>` are included. Some browsers have trouble applying stylesheets to HTML documents when end tags are absent, so it is best to put them in.

Empty Elements

Some elements (such as the **BR** [line break], **IMG** [insert an inline image], and **HR** elements) do not "contain" anything, and are called *empty* elements. In HTML, empty elements cannot have end tags.

Element Nesting

Elements are always *nested*, with this nesting reflecting the *hierarchical* structure of the document (for example, emphasized text inside a paragraph, inside a form, inside the **BODY**). However, elements can never overlap. Thus the following markup from Figure 2.1

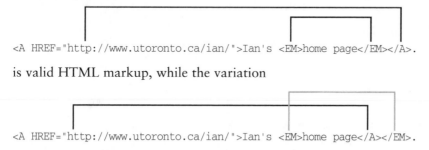

```
<A HREF="http://www.utoronto.ca/ian/">Ian's <EM>home page</EM></A>.
```

is valid HTML markup, while the variation

```
<A HREF="http://www.utoronto.ca/ian/">Ian's <EM>home page</A></EM>.
```

is not, as the two elements are not nested, but overlap.

In addition, elements are also restricted in terms of where they can appear—for example, **H2** elements cannot contain **P** elements, and vice versa. This point is discussed later in more detail.

Element Attributes

Many HTML elements can take *attributes*, which are quantities that specify properties relevant to that particular instance of the element. For example, the **A** (hypertext anchor) element takes the

Figure 2.1 A simple example HTML document.

```
<HTML>
<HEAD> <TITLE>HTML Example Document</TITLE>
  <!-- Note that there is no stylesheet -->
</HEAD>
<BODY BGCOLOR="#ffffff">
<DIV CLASS="part1">
  <H1>A Simple Example HTML Document</H1>
  <P>This is a simple, example HTML document. There is nothing
     fancy here — it is only to illustrate the basic features
     of HTML markup. Note how HTML elements can take attributes,
     as in the <B>CLASS</B> attribute of the <B>DIV</B> element.</P>
  <P>Another attribute example is the following link to
     <A HREF="http://www.utoronto.ca/ian/">Ian's <EM>home page</EM></A>.
     The <B>HREF</B> attribute takes, as its value, the URL of the
     resource to which the associated text should be linked. </P>
  <DIV CLASS="subpart">
    <H2>Famous Words, by Jack Handley</H2>
     <BLOCKQUOTE>
        <P>Is there anything more beautiful than a beautiful,
           beautiful flamingo, flying across in front of a
           beautiful sunset? And he's carrying a beautiful
           rose in his beak, and also he's carrying a very beautiful
           painting with his feet.</P>
        <P>And also, you're drunk.</P>
     </BLOCKQUOTE>
     <P>Paraphrased by Ian Graham <BR> 1 April 1997 </P>
  </DIV>
</DIV>
<DIV CLASS="footer">
  <HR SIZE=2">
  <TABLE WIDTH="100%">
    <TR>
      <TD ALIGN="left">  <EM>Ian Graham</EM>                 </TD>
      <TD ALIGN="right"> <EM>Tremendous Stories Pages</EM> </TD>
    </TR>
</TABLE>
</DIV>
</BODY></HTML>
```

HREF attribute, which specifies the target of a hypertext link. Most attributes are assigned values. For example, **HREF** is assigned the URL of the target document for a hypertext link, as in:

```
<A HREF="http://www.utoronto.ca/ian/">Ian's <EM>home page</EM></A>.
```

Attributes are always defined inside the start tag. Attributes are often optional.

Figure 2.2 Display, using the Netscape Navigator 3 browser, of the document listed in Figure 2.1.

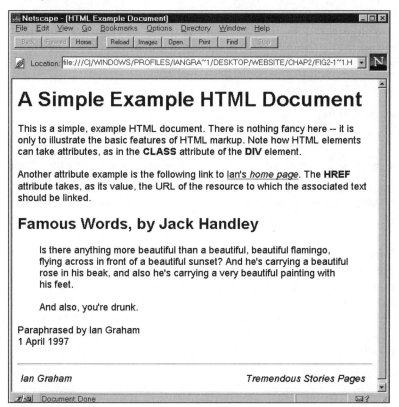

Case Sensitivity

Element and attribute names inside the markup tags are case-*insensitive*. Thus, the strings <H1> and <h1> are equivalent, as are the markup examples

```
<A HREF="http://www.utoronto.ca/ian/">Ian's <EM>home page</EM></A>
```

and

```
<a hReF="http://www.utoronto.ca/ian/">Ian's <em>home page</eM></A>
```

Element and attribute names are usually written in uppercase to make the tags easier for a developer to read.

While element and attribute names are case-insensitive, the *values* assigned to attributes are often case-sensitive. An obvious example is a URL assigned to an **HREF** attribute. Attributes that are case-sensitive must always be surrounded by double quotes.

Attribute Values as Literal Strings

Formally, HTML has two mechanisms for handling attributes values: *literal strings*, and *name tokens*. A literal string is just that—a string of characters to be accepted literally as typed by the author, including the preservation of case. Literal strings given as attribute values must be surrounded by double quotation marks. Literal strings can contain any sequence of printable characters, including HTML entity references—a browser will transform these references back into the desired characters before doing anything with the string. For example, if an anchor element is written as:

```
<a href="http://funky.com/dir/&lt;file-2&gt;">get this weird file</A>
```

then the URL that is actually accessed will be:

```
http://funky.com/<file-2>
```

as `&lt;` is the entity reference for the less-than symbol, and `&gt;` is the reference for greater-than.

Most attributes that can be assigned arbitrary, author-defined strings, such as **HREF** and **SRC** (uniform resource locators), **ALT** (**IMG** elements), and **NAME** (fragment identifiers for anchor elements), are handled as literal strings.

Attribute Values as Name Tokens

Name tokens are restricted character strings: They can only contain the letters a–z or A–Z, the numbers 0–9, periods (.), and hyphens (-), and must begin with a letter. Unlike literal strings, name tokens are *case-insensitive*, so that the token abba is equivalent to ABbA. Name token attribute values do not need to be surrounded by quotation marks, as in the string "text" in the assignment **TYPE**=text. However, as it is never an error to include quotation marks, it is safer to leave them in, since it is not always obvious that a value is a name token or a literal string.

Name tokens are used for values defined as part of HTML, such as the value "text" in the element `<INPUT TYPE="text"...>`. In these cases, the HTML DTD specifies the allowed name token values.

Browsers and HTML Errors

In general, a browser *ignores* elements or element attributes that it does not understand. For example, the **BLINK** element is Netscape-specific; on many other browsers, the `<BLINK>` ... `</BLINK>` tags are usually ignored, and the enclosed text is rendered as regular text. Similarly, in HTML 3.2, paragraphs can be centered using the **ALIGN** attribute, that is, `<P ALIGN="center">`. If a browser does not understand this attribute or the value assigned to it, it simply ignores the attribute and uses its own default paragraph alignment.

If there is an error in the HTML markup, a browser will try and present the document as best it can. In general, browsers contain internal software that attempts to "fix" the most common HTML coding errors. However, not all browsers do so in the same way, so authors should take care to eliminate all possible HTML errors in their documents. This is particularly important if stylesheets are involved, as discussed at the end of this chapter.

Structural Rules of Markup

It was mentioned earlier that there are rules stating where elements can appear; for example, **H1** elements cannot contain **P** elements, and vice versa. These content rules are an important part of the language, and reflect the use of HTML to define *logical* structure. Thus, **H1** cannot contain **P** because it is not sensible to have paragraphs inside headings. Once again, the HTML DTD defines these content rules. This section does not give details of these rules, but does outline the basic structure for a document. The references at the end of the chapter provide additional information on this subject.

Every HTML document is composed of two primary parts, and three main HTML elements. The two main parts are the document head and body, contained within the **HEAD** and **BODY** elements respectively, with the **HEAD** always appearing before the **BODY**. These elements are in turn contained within an **HTML** element that defines the bounds of the document. Thus, the basic markup for every HTML document should be:

```
<HTML>
     <HEAD>
     ... head content....
     </HEAD>
     <BODY>
     ... body content....
     </BODY>
</HTML>
```

where the omitted content is noted in italics. An example of this structure is shown in Figure 2.3—this is just the document listed in Figure 2.1, but with the range of the different elements within the document marked in the margin to the left of the document. The hierarchical nature of the nested elements is clearly evident.

HEAD Content

The **HEAD** of an HTML document contains document meta-information. This is information *about* the document. Consequently, the only elements allowed inside **HEAD** are those that express or contain meta-information. There are seven such elements, most of which can appear only in the **HEAD**, and not in the **BODY**. There are, however, two exceptions to this rule: **SCRIPT** and **ISIN-DEX** can also appear in the **BODY**.

Most **HEAD**-level elements are empty. The non-empty elements can contain only text, and cannot contain other HTML markup. Thus head-level elements cannot nest within other head-level elements. This should be contrasted with the document **BODY**, where nesting of the elements is required to define the structure of the document.

The seven **HEAD**-level elements are summarized in the following list. Of these, only two are relevant to stylesheet issues: the **LINK** element, which can reference an external stylesheet to be applied to the document when displayed, and the **STYLE** element, which can directly contain stylesheet instructions.

BASE (empty)	Base URL (origin) for the document.
ISINDEX (empty)	Invokes a simple search interface that passes a search query to a remote server.
LINK (empty)	References a URL and expresses the relationship between the document containing the **LINK** element and the referenced resource. For example, **LINK** can reference a file containing stylesheet instructions that should be applied to the document.
META (empty)	Contains arbitrary meta-information about the document.
SCRIPT (non-empty)	Contains a program script associated with the document.
STYLE (non-empty)	Contains stylesheet instructions associated with the document.
TITLE (non-empty)	Contains a text title associated with the document (most browsers put this string in the browser window titlebar).

BODY Content

BODY contains the content to be displayed. Formally, the **BODY** should not directly contain text; instead, it should contain elements that in turn contain the text, with these elements organizing the document content and assigning it structural meaning.

There are some 85–90 different elements that can appear inside the **BODY** (the number supported depends on the browser). The purpose of these different elements is to define the structure of a document in a meaningful way—and thus there are elements for paragraphs (**P**), headings (**H1** to **H6**), block quotations (**BLOCKQUOTE**), emphasized text (**EM**), and so on.

These elements form a body-centric hierarchy within the document. Note how Figure 2.3 illustrates the hierarchy arising from the HTML document listed in Figure 2.1. Also note how the structure inside the **BODY** of even this relatively simple document is much more complicated than that of the **HEAD**.

With this richness of structure comes important rules about where the elements can nest—for example, and as mentioned earlier, heading elements (**H1**–**H6**) cannot contain **P** elements, and vice versa. Again, you are referred to a detailed HTML reference book to obtain the rules appropriate to a given element.

Types of BODY Content Elements

In general, the **BODY** content elements can be divided into three main categories: *block elements* (such as **P**), which define separable blocks or boxes of text; *inline elements* (such as **EM**), which define text segments or other content that appears inline within a block; and *meta-information elements* (such as **SCRIPT**), which define information related to the content of the body but that is not explicitly displayed as part of the content.

NOTE About Element and Attribute Notation

As mentioned earlier in the chapter, certain HTML elements and attributes are defined as part of HTML 3.2 (the current standard), others as part of the evolving standardization process (e.g., enhancements and additions in support of stylesheets), and others as proprietary extensions created by browser vendors. In this chapter, these three types of elements and attributes are indicated by *typography*. HTML 3.2 elements and attributes are in a boldface font, while elements or attributes developed as part of the standardization process but not yet integrated into "standard" HTML are shown in boldface italics. Last, proprietary HTML extensions are shown in underlined boldface. The following table gives some examples:

Description	Example Element	Example Attribute
HTML 3.2 elements and attributes	**BLOCKQUOTE**	**ALIGN**
Standardized HTML extensions	***SPAN***	***STYLE***
Proprietary HTML extensions (e.g., Netscape or Microsoft)	**<u>BLINK</u>**	**<u>TARGET</u>** (attribute of A element)

As is apparent from the preceding description, these categories strongly relate to the structural role of the elements. For stylesheet formatting purposes, it is also useful to define two additional categories of HTML elements that define additional properties related to element formatting: *list elements* are similar to block elements but take additional special formatting, such as a bullet or number in front of the element content; and *floating elements* are elements that are allowed to float to the left or right margin on the display area, subject to certain constraints.

As a final category, certain HTML elements are known as *replaced elements*. Such elements are essentially "replaced" by some kind of external data; for example, an **IMG** element is replaced by the referenced image.

All HTML elements intrinsically belong in one of the categories just mentioned; however, CSS lets an author modify the properties of an element using the `display` and `float` properties. `Display` lets an author explicitly set the type of an element to one of: "block" (block element), "list-item" (list-item element), or "inline" (inline element). The `float` property, which can take the value "left" or "right," can turn an element into a floating element, and specify the margin towards which it should float.

The following sections describe the different element types in more detail, while examples illustrating the special characteristics of each type are found throughout this book.

Block Elements

Block elements define distinct blocks of text, where a block is a (possibly multi-line) section of text extending from the left to the right margin, and is typically preceded and followed by a line break.

Figure 2.3 A listing of the document shown in Figure 2.1, here illustrating the hierarchical nature of the elements structure of the document. Note how every element lies within another element, and that the document is divided into two main components, the HEAD and BODY.

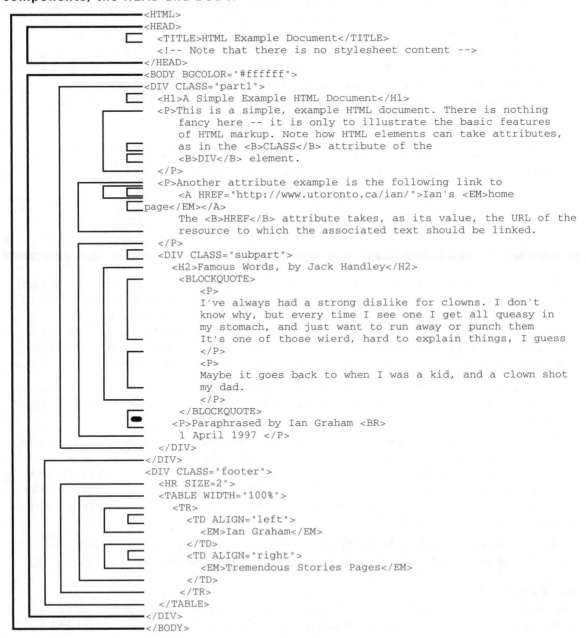

```
<HTML>
<HEAD>
  <TITLE>HTML Example Document</TITLE>
  <!-- Note that there is no stylesheet content -->
</HEAD>
<BODY BGCOLOR="#ffffff">
<DIV CLASS="part1">
  <H1>A Simple Example HTML Document</H1>
  <P>This is a simple, example HTML document. There is nothing
      fancy here -- it is only to illustrate the basic features
      of HTML markup. Note how HTML elements can take attributes,
      as in the <B>CLASS</B> attribute of the
      <B>DIV</B> element.
  </P>
  <P>Another attribute example is the following link to
      <A HREF="http://www.utoronto.ca/ian/">Ian's <EM>home
page</EM></A>
      The <B>HREF</B> attribute takes, as its value, the URL of the
      resource to which the associated text should be linked.
  </P>
  <DIV CLASS="subpart">
    <H2>Famous Words, by Jack Handley</H2>
    <BLOCKQUOTE>
        <P>
        I've always had a strong dislike for clowns. I don't
        know why, but every time I see one I get all queasy in
        my stomach, and just want to run away or punch them
        It's one of those wierd, hard to explain things, I guess
        </P>
        <P>
        Maybe it goes back to when I was a kid, and a clown shot
        my dad.
        </P>
    </BLOCKQUOTE>
    <P>Paraphrased by Ian Graham <BR>
    1 April 1997 </P>
  </DIV>
</DIV>
<DIV CLASS="footer">
  <HR SIZE=2>
  <TABLE WIDTH="100%">
    <TR>
      <TD ALIGN="left">
        <EM>Ian Graham</EM>
      </TD>
      <TD ALIGN="right">
        <EM>Tremendous Stories Pages</EM>
      </TD>
    </TR>
  </TABLE>
</DIV>
</BODY>
```

Paragraphs and headings are typical examples. HTML supports additional block elements that divide a document into logical components such as block quotations, addresses, lists, and so on. A complete list of block elements is given in Table 2.1.

The formatting difference between block and inline properties is displayed in Figures 2.4 and 2.5, which schematically illustrate the formatting for several different block and inline elements. Note how the block elements occupy large rectangular blocks on the page that span the full page width, while the inline elements occupy just the region needed to appear inline.

NOTE Avoid Using the CENTER Element

The block element **CENTER** is a purely formatting-based element, and is to be dropped (the official term is "deprecated") in future versions of HTML. It is also not accessible to CSS stylesheets, as defined by the official CSS specification. You are best advised to use the standards-based markup `<DIV ALIGN="center"> ... </DIV>` in place of `<CENTER> ... </CENTER>`.

The situation for HTML tables is somewhat more complicated. **TABLE** itself acts as a block element, and causes a line break both before and after the element. TD and TH are also block elements, but affect formatting differently, due to their nature as table cells—table cells define blocks, but these blocks are tiled on the display as per the layout specified by the table layout algorithm.

Table 2.1 Summary of HTML BODY Content Elements. In this table, the phrase *MSIE 3+ only* means that the element is supported only by Microsoft Internet Explorer 3 and later, while the phrase *Navigator 3+ only* means that the element is only supported by Netscape Navigator 3 and later. Note that all "Replaced" elements are also "Inline" elements.

HTML Block Elements

ADDRESS, BLOCKQUOTE, BR, CAPTION, CENTER, DD, DIR, DIV, DL, DT, FORM, H1, H2, H3, H4, H5, H6, HR, MENU, <u>MULTICOL</u> (Navigator 3+ only), OL, P, PRE, TABLE, TD, TH, UL, <u>WBR</u>

HTML List-Item Elements

LI

HTML Inline Elements

A, APPLET, B, *BDO*, BIG, <u>BLINK</u>, CITE, CODE, DFN, EM, <u>EMBED</u>, FONT, I, <u>IFRAME</u> (MSIE 3+ only), IMG, INPUT, KBD, <u>MARQUEE</u> (MSIE 3+ only), <u>NOEMBED</u>, <u>NOBR</u>, *OBJECT*, *Q*, S, SAMP, SELECT, SMALL, <u>SPACER</u> (Navigator 3+ only), *SPAN*, STRIKE, STRONG, SUB, SUP, TEXTAREA, TT, U, VAR

Continued

Table 2.1 *Continued*

HTML Meta-Information Elements

AREA, <u>BASEFONT</u>, <u>BGSOUND</u> (MSIE 3+ only), *COL, COLGROUP,* MAP, PARAM, <u>SERVER</u> (Navigator 3+ only), **SCRIPT**

HTML Replaced Elements

APPLET, <u>EMBED,</u> <u>IFRAME</u> (MSIE 3+ only), **IMG, INPUT,** *OBJECT,* **SELECT, TEXTAREA**

List-Item Elements

List-item elements are essentially the same as block elements, except that list elements take a list item decoration, such as a number or bullet. **LI** is currently the only such element in the HTML repertoire, as the other list-related elements, namely **DT** and **DD** (respectively, the terms and descriptions within a **DL** glossary list), are not formatted with any leading decoration, and are thus not list-item elements according to this definition.

List-item block formatting is illustrated in Figure 2.5. The details of CSS and list-item element formatting are discussed in Chapter 5.

Figure 2.4 Simple HTML document illustrating block and inline elements. The rendering of this document—with added graphics outlining the different formatted components—is shown in Figure 2.5.

```
<HTML>
<HEAD><TITLE>Amazing Example Element Document</TITLE></HEAD>
<BODY BGCOLOR="#ffffff" text="#afafaf">
<H1>Amazing Test Document</H1>
<P>This amazing test document illustrates some of the basic
   inline and block elements in HTML. Inline elements appear
   <EM>inline within a block, and may</EM> straddle line breaks.
   Block elements define text <STRONG>blocks</STRONG>, which
   are generally preceded and followed by a line break.
</P>
<UL>
   <LI>These are list items.
   <LI>List items are like block elements, except that they
       have leading decoration characters (bullets, etc.) and
       spacing around the decoration, in keeping with their list
       item character.
</UL>
</BODY></HTML>
```

Figure 2.5 Rendering, by NetManage WebSurfer browser, of the document listed in Figure 2.4. This figure has been annotated to outline the different block and inline elements. In this context, the drawing area or canvas can be thought of as the block defined by the BODY element itself.

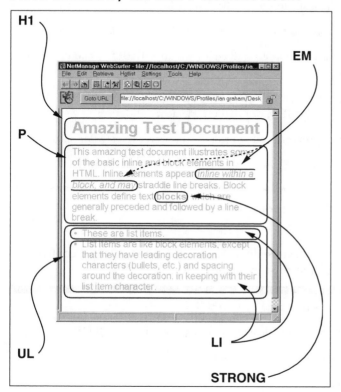

Inline Elements

Inline elements are elements that appear inline with the flow of text. Block element content often consists of text plus a variety of inline elements that define special properties of the text (e.g., text emphasis or highlighting), or that insert special objects into the element, such as form input elements and inline images. A complete list of inline elements is given in Table 2.1. Note that most HTML elements are inline elements, reflecting the many elements available for defining phrase-level markup (emphasis, superscripts, etc.), form input devices (text input lines, buttons, text input regions), inline images (**IMG**), and embedded applets or objects (**APPLET, EMBED,** and **OBJECT**).

Meta-Information Elements

Meta-information elements contain or refer to content that is not displayed by the document, but that is used by the browser in processing or creating the document, or in processing user input. The meta-information elements and their meanings are:

MAP, AREA	Specify regions and URL mappings for a client-side **IMG** element imagemap.
BASEFONT	Specifies the default font for the document. This element is likely to be dropped in future versions of HTML and should not be used. An author should instead use stylesheet mechanisms to specify the default font.
BGSOUND	Specifies a sound or audio file to play in the background (*MSIE 3+ only*).
COL, COLGROUP	Specify rules for drawing borders and edges within a **TABLE**. Valid only inside **TABLE** elements.
PARAM	Specifies a parameter for an **APPLET, EMBED**ded object, or **OBJECT**. Valid only inside **APPLET, EMBED,** or **OBJECT** elements.
SERVER	Contains JavaScript program code to run on the server (*Navigator 3+ only*).
SCRIPT	Contains script code (JavaScript or VBScript) to run on the browser.

Of these, only **BASEFONT** in any way affects the formatting of the document.

Replaced Elements

Replaced elements are those that are replaced by externally referenced content, either a control or an object of some sort. The replaced elements and their meanings are:

APPLET	Embedded applet (element to be superseded by **OBJECT**).
EMBED	Embedded special data type or program (element to be superseded by **OBJECT**).
IFRAME	Embedded external HTML document (*MSIE 3+ only*).
IMG	Embedded external image file.
INPUT	Embedded user input element, for use inside a **FORM**—the actual size and shape of the element depends on HTML attribute and CSS property values, and on the browser.
OBJECT	Embedded arbitrary data type or data handler (software). This is the successor to both **APPLET** and **EMBED. OBJECT** is only now becoming widely implemented (*Netscape/Microsoft Version 4*).
SELECT	Embedded selectable list element, for use inside a **FORM**. The actual size and shape of the element depends on HTML attribute and CSS property values, and on the browser.
TEXTAREA	Embedded text-input region, for use inside a **FORM**. The actual size and shape of the element depends on HTML attribute and CSS property values, and on the browser.

In general, replaced elements are treated as inline elements, and act rather like large words or letters embedded in the text. However, in HTML most of these elements (namely **APPLET,**

EMBED, IFRAME, IMG, and **OBJECT**) can be floated on the page, using the attribute assignment **ALIGN**="left" or **ALIGN**="right". Floating elements are discussed in the next section.

For CSS, the importance of replaced elements is that the actual size or content of the object is not known until it is loaded; for example, the size of an image is unknown until the image file arrives from the Web server. Although there are mechanisms in CSS (and to some extent HTML) that let the browser resize some types of objects to a desired region, this does not work for all embedded data—for example, images can be resized, while an interactive program control window cannot.

Floating Elements

Floating elements are elements that can float to either the left or right margin of the element within which they are contained, with the remaining content of the containing element flowing around the floated element. A simple illustration of this is shown in the HTML document in Figures 2.6, rendered for display by the Netscape Navigator browser in 2.7. This illustrates an **IMG** element as an inline element (the first displayed image), as a floated element floated to the left within a paragraph element (the second image), and finally as a floated element floated to the left within a **DIV** that subsequently also contains three paragraphs (the third image). Note how, in the latter two cases, the text flows around the floated element.

There are no default floating elements in HTML. However, as of HTML 3.2, the inline elements **APPLET, EMBED, IFRAME, IMG,** and **OBJECT** can take an attribute **ALIGN** with values "left" or "right" to float these elements to the left or right margin. Note that by floating an element, the element is transformed into a *block* element—the floated content defines a block around which all other content must flow.

CSS can be used to float any HTML element, via the property assignments `float: left` and `float: right`. These are the obvious generalizations of the HTML **ALIGN** attribute. Thus, in principle, a paragraph can be "floated" next to a group of other paragraphs, to give typographic features such as pull-quotes. Examples of this are found in Chapters 5 and 7.

HTML and Stylesheets—New Markup

Several HTML extensions were added to support stylesheets. These allow for inclusion of stylesheets *within* an HTML document, linking a document to an *external* stylesheet, and ways of relating CSS rules to specific *classes* of elements.

Only a few extensions to HTML were needed: three new elements, **STYLE, SPAN,** and **LINK** with attribute **REL**="stylesheet", plus three new attributes—**CLASS, ID,** and **STYLE**—for use by most body-content elements. Descriptions of these new elements and attributes, and of the roles served by them, are found in the following sections.

Element Specifications Key

Because HTML is an hierarchical language, it is important to know both what an element means and where it can be used. This information is given in the four lines at the beginning of each element's description in the following sections. The format is:

Figure 2.6 Simple HTML document illustrating floating elements. The rendering of this document—plus graphics outlining the different formatted components—is shown in Figure 2.7.

```
<HTML>
<HEAD><TITLE>Amazing Floating Examples!</TITLE></HEAD>
<BODY BGCOLOR="#ffffff" text="#afafaf">
<H1>Amazing Floating Text</H1>
<P>This amazing test document illustrates floating components,
   here a floating <B>IMG</B> This image <IMG SRC="happy.gif">
   does not float, and illustrates how replaced elements are
   treated as inline unless floated.
</P>
<HR NOSHADE>
<P><IMG SRC="happy.gif" ALIGN="left"> Here is a similar length
   paragraph, but this time containing the same image, but floated
   to the left using the <B>FLOAT</B>="left" attribute value.
   The image floats to the left, and all other text in the
   paragraph floats around the image.<BR CLEAR="all">
</P>
<HR NOSHADE>
<DIV>
<IMG SRC="happy.gif" ALIGN="left" HEIGHT="80" WIDTH="80">
   <P>This image is floated inside a <B>DIV</B>, and has
      <EM>paragraphs</EM> alongside it.
   </P>
   <P>This paragraph is quite long -- notice how the paragraph
      is still a rectangular box, but that the text flows
      around the floated image -- the floated image pushes
      the text out of a portion of the box
   </P>
   <P>Of course, this new paragraph can start below the image,
   so that the text can entirely fill the box
   </P>
</BODY></HTML>
```

Usage:	<NAME> ... </NAME>
Can Contain:	**element list**
Can Be Inside:	**element list**
Attributes:	**attribute list**

where **element list** is a list of allowed elements, and **attribute list** is a list of allowed attributes.

Usage:	Shows how the element is used. An end tag indicates that an element is a container (the *Can Contain* field lists the elements that are allowed inside the element). If the end tag is enclosed by parentheses, then it is optional. If no end tag is given, then the element is empty.
Can Contain:	Indicates what elements can go inside this element. The string "**characters**" indicates elements that can contain text. Elements that are proposed as part of the HTML standardization process are shown in boldface italics. Underlined elements are proprietary extensions by browser vendors.
Can Be Inside:	Indicates the elements inside which this element can be directly placed. Elements that are proposed as part of the HTML standardization process are shown in boldface italics. Underlined elements are proprietary extensions by browser vendors.
Attributes:	The names of the attributes that can be taken by the element. The word "none" means that the element takes no attributes. Attributes proposed as part of the HTML standardization process are shown in boldface italics. Underlined attributes are proprietary extensions by browser vendors.

Figure 2.7 Rendering, by NetManage WebSurfer browser, of the document listed in Figure 2.6. This figure has been annotated to outline the different block and inline elements—note how, in the last two sections, the IMG has been "floated" to the left, and in so doing, has been transformed into a "block" element.

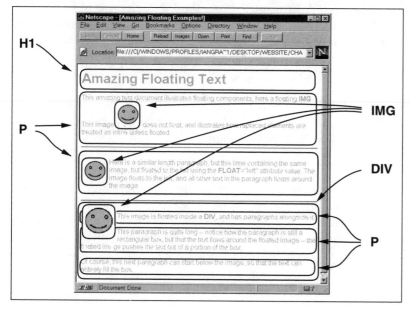

Shorthand for Character Highlighting Elements

To reduce the length of the descriptions, some *Can Contain* and *Can be Inside* fields refer to "character highlighting" elements. These are inline elements that mark text for special formatting or semantic meaning, such as **B** or **EM**, but excluding hypertext anchors. The complete list of elements in this category is:

Character highlighting:	B, *BDO*, BIG, <u>BLINK</u>, CITE, CODE, DFN, EM, FONT, I, KBD, <u>MARQUEE</u>, <u>NOBR</u>, Q, S, SAMP, SMALL, *SPAN*, STRIKE, STRONG, SUB, SUP, TT, U, VAR

LINK Element: Referencing External Stylesheets

Usage:	`<LINK>`
Can Contain:	empty
Can Be Inside:	**HEAD**
Attributes:	**HREF, ID, REL, REV, TITLE,** *TYPE*

   LINK is an empty, head-level element that describes a *relationship* between a document and another documents or resource: the mandatory **HREF** attribute contains the URL of the second resource, while the attribute **REL** (or **REV**, one must be present) defines the relationship between the two resources connected by the **LINK**. All the other attributes (**ID, TITLE,** and **TYPE**) are optional. **ID** can take a name token value and, in principle, allows the **LINK** element to be itself the target of a hypertext link, while **TITLE** can take a string that describes the target or purpose of the link. Finally, **TYPE** gives the MIME type of the target resources—for example, "text/html" for an HTML document.

Stylesheet MIME Types

The most important current use of **LINK** is for referencing external stylesheets to be applied to a document, and this is the purpose of interest to us—after all, this is a book about stylesheets! To reference a stylesheet, the appropriate form for the **LINK** element is

```
<LINK REL="stylesheet" TYPE="mime/type" HREF="url">
```

where the assignment **REL**="stylesheet" indicates that the target resource is a stylesheet, `url` is the URL pointing to the stylesheet document, and `mime/type` is the MIME type for the stylesheet—thus, **TYPE** allows for different possible stylesheet languages. For CSS stylesheets, the proper MIME type assignment is **TYPE**="text/css". For DSSSL stylesheets, the proper value is "application/dsssl", while for *JavaScript Accessible Stylesheets* (see Chapter 9), the value is "application/javascript".

   Note that a document can contain more than one **LINK** element referencing external stylesheets. For example, a document **HEAD** could contain the markup

```
<HEAD>
  <TITLE>HTML document Title</TITLE>
  <LINK REL="stylesheet" TYPE="text/css" HREF="./styles/default.css">
  <LINK REL="stylesheet" TYPE="text/css" HREF="./styles/sheet1.css">
  <LINK REL="stylesheet" TYPE="text/css" HREF="./styles/mods1.css">
</HEAD>
```

to indicate three different external stylesheets. The browser will simply load the three stylesheets one after the other, and will process them sequentially in the order in which they were loaded.

Some proposed extensions to the **LINK** element are described in Chapter 9.

STYLE Element

Usage:	`<STYLE> ... </STYLE>`
Can Contain:	characters
Can Be Inside:	**HEAD**
Attributes:	*TITLE, TYPE*

STYLE contains stylesheet instructions to be applied to the document. **STYLE** can take two optional attributes: **TITLE** and **TYPE**. The value for **TITLE** is a title to associate with the stylesheet. If more than one stylesheet is available to a document (for example, one from the **STYLE** element and others from **LINK** elements), the **TITLE** can be used as a label for the stylesheet, and the user may have the choice of selectively disabling the different stylesheets. There are currently no browsers that provide this functionality. Some proposed extensions to the **STYLE** and **LINK** element syntax in support of this functionality are discussed in Chapter 9.

TYPE gives the MIME type for the stylesheet content: for CSS stylesheets, the assignment should be **TYPE="text/css"**. Note that this also sets the type for any stylesheet instructions included in **STYLE** attributes associated with body content elements. **STYLE** attributes are discussed later in this chapter.

STYLE allows rendering information to be placed within the current document, rather than as a second file referenced through a **LINK** element. **STYLE** thus allows for browsers that support stylesheets but do not support **LINK** elements—the experimental browsers *Arena* and *Amaya* fall into this category. **STYLE** has two other important uses: (1) for development and testing of stylesheets (which, after development, may be moved to external stylesheet files), and (2) for customization of an external stylesheet. In this regard, you can use a linked stylesheet to specify the broad details of the layout, with the content in the **STYLE** element providing small-scale, local modifications.

Hiding Stylesheets from Older Browsers

A browser that understands **STYLE** will interpret the content as stylesheet instructions, and will not display the instructions to the reader. However, older browsers that do not understand **STYLE** can be confused by this element, and may think that the element content is actually text that should be displayed.

Fortunately, the CSS syntax lets a stylesheet author place the entire **STYLE** element content inside an HTML comment. This hides the stylesheet from older browsers that do not understand stylesheets, and makes the document smoothly compatible with older software such as lynx, or versions of Netscape Navigator or Internet Explorer prior to version 3, which would otherwise display **STYLE** content. The following example illustrates the use of HTML comments to "hide" the stylesheet content from older browsers; the HTML comment start and stop tags are shown in boldface:

```
<STYLE>
<!--
    BODY {margin-left: 4%; margin-right: 4%;
          color: black; background-color: white; }
    P    {margin-left: 5%; text-indent: 5em; }
-->
</STYLE>
```

SPAN Element: Select Text for Special Formatting

Usage:	<SPAN> ... </SPAN>
Can Contain:	characters, character highlighting, A, BR, IMG, <u>BASEFONT</u>, MAP, <u>NOSCRIPT</u>, SCRIPT, <u>SPACER</u>, WBR, APPLET, <u>EMBED</u>, <u>NOEMBED</u>, *OBJECT*, INPUT, SELECT, TEXTAREA
Can Be Inside:	ADDRESS, BLOCKQUOTE, BODY, CENTER, DIV, FORM, MULTICOL, PRE, Hn, DD, DT, LI, P, TD, TH, APPLET, <u>NOEMBED</u>, *OBJECT*, A, CAPTION, character highlighting
Attributes:	*CLASS, ID, STYLE*

SPAN marks text for special formatting as defined by an associated stylesheet rule; in the absence of stylesheet instructions, **SPAN** does not affect formatting. Document authors should think of **SPAN** as a general-purpose replacement for **FONT**.

SPAN can take three optional attributes—**CLASS, ID,** and **STYLE**—added in support of stylesheets. These attributes are supported by almost all body-content elements, and not just **SPAN**. Because of their important role in stylesheets, the attributes are discussed separately in the next section.

The following markup illustrates two uses of **SPAN** (the tags are in boldface, the element content in italics):

```
<P> Here is a simple paragraph of text, with <SPAN CLASS="special">
    specially formatted text </SPAN> within it. Note how the formatting
```

of this text must be specified by style instructions inside a
<B>STYLE</B> element or within an external stylesheet referenced
via a <B>LINK</B> element. On the other hand,
<SPAN STYLE="background-color: blue; color: red"> *this section
of text***</SPAN>** will be formatted with a blue background and red
text, as the styling instructions are explicitly given by the
<B>STYLE</B> attribute.
</P>

CLASS Attribute

Usage: CLASS="*name*" (optional)

Valid with: All block, list-item, and inline elements *except*: CENTER, <u>BLINK</u>, <u>EMBED</u>, FONT, <u>IFRAME</u>, <u>MARQUEE</u>, <u>MULTICOL</u>, <u>NOEMBED</u>, <u>NOBR</u>, <u>SPACER</u>, and <u>WBR</u>. Also does not apply to meta-information elements (See Table 2.1).

CLASS specifies a *class name* for an element; it makes possible element *subclassing*[2]—for example, <P CLASS="type2"> to subclass the paragraph as one of class "type2". Multiple elements can take the same CLASS attribute value, so that subclassing is very useful for defining the structural nature of a document. For example, in the following markup of a poem, <DIV CLASS="poem">, <DIV CLASS="poem-body">, and <P CLASS="verse"> mark the poem structure:

```
<DIV CLASS="poem">
    <H2 CLASS="poem-title">Revenge of the Faerie Queene</H2>
    <H2 CLASS="poem-author">Abercromb J. McGillibrance </H2>
    <DIV CLASS="poem-body">
        <P CLASS="verse">
            To be a happy wanderer<BR>
            Alone amongst the seas<BR>
            At last without my wallabee<BR>
            But with tasty herbal teas
        </P>
        <P CLASS="verse">
            ... second verse, same as the first ...
        </P>
        <P CLASS="verse">
            ... and yet more witty verse ...
        </P>
<P CLASS="verse">
            ... just like Jesse Berst... ...
        </P>
    </DIV>
</DIV>
```

Note that class values need not have such obvious structural meanings (and, unfortunately, that I am not a very good poet).

In HTML 3.2, the value for **CLASS** must be a *name token*, as described previously in this chapter.

CSS stylesheets can specify rules that apply to all elements with a specific class value, or to specific combinations of element type and class. Class values are indicated within CSS selectors by preceding the value by a period (recall that the selector is the part of a rule that indicates to which elements the rule applies). For example, the rule

```
.poem-author {color: blue}
```

applies to any element of **CLASS**="poem-author", whereas the rule

```
P.verse {color: blue}
```

applies only to paragraphs of **CLASS**="verse".

Note the use of the period to separate element name from class value. This special use can create problems if the **CLASS** value itself contains a period. CSS syntax rules use the backslash character to "escape" special characters such as the period. For example, given the class assignment

```
CLASS="marvin.gardens"
```

the CSS selector for this class would be

```
.marvin\.gardens
```

However, this escape mechanism is not widely supported, as described in the following paragraph.

Problems with CLASS Values

Internet Explorer 3 does not understand the backslash escape mechanism within CSS selectors, so that document and stylesheet authors should avoid **CLASS** values that contain periods. Also, early prerelease versions of Netscape Navigator 4 treat class attribute values as *case-sensitive,* treating the class values "Marvin" and "marvin" as distinct. Thus, for the present, a document and stylesheet author should:

- avoid periods in **CLASS** values

- assume that **CLASS** values are case-sensitive

ID Attribute

Usage: ID="*name*" (optional)

Valid with: All block, list item, and inline elements *except*: CENTER, <u>BLINK</u>, <u>EMBED</u>, FONT, <u>IFRAME</u>, <u>MARQUEE</u>, <u>MULTICOL</u>, <u>NOEMBED</u>, <u>NOBR</u>, <u>SPACER</u>, and <u>WBR</u>. Also does not apply to meta-information elements (See Table 2.1).

ID specifies a *unique* identifier for the element, meaning that within a given document, no two elements can have the same **ID** value. This is in distinct contrast to **CLASS**, where any number of elements can take the same **CLASS** value.

In HTML 3.2, the value for **CLASS** must be a *name token*, as described previously in this chapter.

CSS stylesheets can specify rules that apply to a specific **ID**, or to specific combinations of element type and **ID**. **ID** values in selectors are denoted by a leading hash character (#). For example, the rule

```
#xz23    {color: red}
```

applies to the element that has the attribute **ID**=“xz23”, whereas the rule

```
P#xz23 {color: blue}
```

applies to the element that has the attribute **ID**=“xz23”, but *only* if the element is a paragraph.

In principle, **ID**-labeled elements can be the targets of hypertext links: **ID** was initially designed to play the same role as the **NAME** attribute of the anchor element. However, this behavior is not supported by most current browsers.

As with **CLASS**, there are CSS problems when an **ID** attribute value contains periods, since the CSS parser will interpret this character as indicating the start of a class value string. Once again, CSS syntax rules solve this problem by allowing the backslash character to “escape” special characters such as the period. Note, however, that this escape mechanism is not supported in Internet Explorer 3, so it is safest to avoid periods in **ID** values.

STYLE Attribute

Usage:	STYLE=“*CSS-declarations*” (optional)
Valid with:	All block, list item, and inline elements *except*: CENTER, <u>BLINK</u>, <u>EMBED</u>, FONT, <u>IFRAME</u>, <u>MARQUEE</u>, <u>MULTICOL</u>, <u>NOEMBED</u>, <u>NOBR</u>, <u>SPACER</u>, and <u>WBR</u>. Also does not apply to meta-information elements (See Table 2.1).

A **STYLE** attribute contains stylesheet instructions to be applied to the content of the associated element. This avoids the need for a **STYLE** element in the document head, and is a way of burying location-specific styling instructions within the HTML markup. Note that this is not the recommended way of doing styling—it is better to put all stylesheet instructions inside a **STYLE** element, or in an external, linked stylesheet file.

The value assigned to **STYLE** must be a semicolon-separated collection of valid CSS declarations. Note that some declarations require quotation characters. Because of possible conflict with the double quotes used to surround the **STYLE** attribute value, authors must use single quotes for CSS properties placed as the value of a **STYLE** attribute.

The following are three simple **STYLE** attribute examples, in the context of a **SPAN**:

```
<SPAN STYLE="text-decoration: underline"> ... </SPAN>
<SPAN STYLE="background-color: blue; color: red"> ... </SPAN>
<SPAN STYLE="font-family: garamond, 'Times New Roman', serif"> ... </SPAN>
```

Note the single quotation marks around the "Times New Roman" font family specification.

META Specification of the Stylesheet Language

If a document lacks an external stylesheet or a **STYLE** element, the browser has no way of knowing the language used by **STYLE** attributes within the document. This situation can be resolved by using a **META** element to specify the default stylesheet language. The format is:

```
<META HTTP-EQUIV="Content-style-type" CONTENT="type/subtype">
```

where *type/subtype* is the MIME type of the stylesheet language. For CSS, this is just

```
<META HTTP-EQUIV="Content-style-type" CONTENT="text/css">
```

In the absence of this information, browsers should assume a default value, typically "text/css".

This use of **META** means that the default stylesheet type could also be indicated by an HTTP server response header field of the form:

```
Content-style-type: type/subtype
```

There are no current HTTP servers that return this field.

NOTE META Language Specification Not Currently Supported

At present, there are few browsers that understand this use of the **META** element, or this particular HTTP response header field. Authors should use **LINK** or **STYLE** elements to indicate the default stylesheet type.

The Importance of Valid HTML

HTML has rigorous rules stating where elements can and cannot go, with these rules largely flowing from the logic of document structure. For example, the rules state that **P** elements cannot contain headings (and vice versa), that **EM** (or other text-level markup) cannot contain block elements (e.g., **P** or **BLOCKQUOTE**), that **LI** elements cannot directly contain other **LI**'s but can contain other lists, and so on.

In principle, these rules seem rather simple, but in practice it is easy to make mistakes. This is because current browsers ignore HTML errors, or try to "guess" at how to fix the errors. Since most browser vendors try to design their products to mimic how their competitors handle such "mistakes," it is easy to build a badly written HTML document and never know that anything is wrong.

Unfortunately, this "graceful" error recovery mechanism breaks down when HTML is mixed with stylesheets. Since the CSS rules are intimately tied to the accuracy of the markup, even small markup errors can quite dramatically and unpredictably affect the formatting of a document. Consider, for example, the HTML document listed in Figure 2.8. There are two basic (and quite common) HTML errors in this document. The first error, marked by the first two comment strings, is obvious: The **DIV** element is opened and never closed. Instead, the author has "ended" the tag `<DIV CLASS="titles" ALIGN="center">` using `</CENTER>`. The second error is found later in the document, where the author has tried to strongly emphasize the first words ("And here we have") of the second paragraph—unfortunately the **STRONG** element overlaps the starting `<P>` tag, and is thus not properly nested inside the **P**.

Figure 2.8 Example HTML document illustrating two common HTML errors: The DIV element is not closed (here it was improperly closed by a `</CENTER>`), and the STRONG element associated with the second paragraph in the document is not properly nested inside the paragraph (note how this error is fixed in the final paragraph). Browser renderings of this document are found in Figures 2.9 and 2.10. Note that there are no stylesheet instructions. The HTML errors are noted in boldface, while the HTML comment strings describing the errors are in boldface italics.

```
<HTML><HEAD><TITLE>Test of CSS Handling of Erroneous Markup</TITLE>
</HEAD>
<BODY BGCOLOR="#ffffff">
<P><B>... REGULAR BLACK TEXT (for comparison purposes)</B></P>
<DIV CLASS="titles" ALIGN="center">          <!-- Error - DIV not properly
                                                  closed -->

<H1>The Main Title</H1>
<H2>A Gratuitous Subtitle</H2>
</CENTER>                                     <!-- Error- improper closing
                                                  of above DIV?-->

<P>Here is the first exciting example paragraph. This
   paragraph should be left-aligned, and have a ragged right
   edge. Of course, your mileage will vary, depending on how
   your browser interprets the HTML markup mistake surrounding
   the headings at the beginning of hte document: the
   centering of the headings is begun with a
   <B>&lt;DIV CLASS="titles" ALIGN="center"></B> element, while
   centering is turned of with a <B>&lt;/CENTER></B>.</P>
<STRONG><P>                      <!-- Error - STRONG overlaps <P> -->
   And here we have</STRONG> a paragraph that is improperly overlapped
   by a <B>STRONG</B> element. HTML rules state that this is not allowed,
   but most browsers simply emphasise the first words of the paragraph.
   Note, however, how badly this mistake can affect stylesheet-based
```

Continued

Figure 2.8 *Continued*

```
formatting.</P>
<P><STRONG>    <!-- same para. as above, but with properly nested STRONG -->
And here we have</STRONG> a paragraph that is improperly overlapped
by a <B>STRONG</B> element. HTML rules state that this is not allowed,
but most browsers simply emphasise the first words of the paragraph.
Note, however, how badly this mistake can affect stylesheet-based
formatting.</P>
</BODY></HTML>
```

Figure 2.9 shows the rendering of this document by Netscape Navigator 3. Note how Navigator 3 handles the first markup error: It "turns on" centering at the <DIV CLASS="titles" ALIGN="center"> tag, and then turns the centering off when it encounters the </CENTER>. The formatting associated with the **STRONG** element is handled similarly—the browser uses <STRONG>

Figure 2.9 Rendering of the document listed in Figure 2.8 by Netscape Navigator 3. Note how this browser resolves the HTML errors by (A) assuming that the </CEN-TER> tag was meant to end the centering initiated by the <DIV ALIGN="center"> tag; and (B) simply applying strong emphasis to the first few words of the second paragraph.

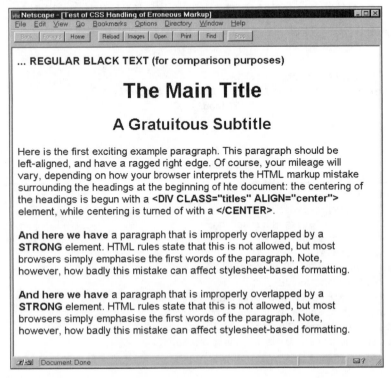

to "turn on" strong emphasis (boldface) and `</STRONG>` to turn off strong emphasis and return to the regular font.

Figure 2.10 shows the rendering of the document in Figure 2.8 by Internet Explorer 3. This browser handles the first error quite differently. One can clearly see that it does not use the `</CENTER>` tag to end the centering started by the `<DIV ALIGN="center">`. Internet Explorer 3 assumes that the `</CENTER>` tag is simply an error, and that the **DIV** element is not closed—it thus finds that the **DIV** is never closed, assumes that the **DIV** properties applies to the entire document, and centers everything in its path!

Neither Netscape Navigator nor Internet Explorer is "wrong" in its handling of these errors—given such mistakes, it is largely guesswork to determine what the author meant with the incorrect markup, and there is nothing to say that one browser's "guess" is better than another's. As mentioned earlier, most browser vendors try to make their browser "guess" in a manner similar to other browsers, so that some errors (such as the improperly nested **STRONG** element) go undetected. Unfortunately, such errors cause much greater problems when cascading stylesheets are used, as illustrated in the next example.

Figure 2.10 Rendering of the document listed in Figure 2.8 by Internet Explorer 3. Note how this browser ignores the `</CENTER>` tag, and assumes that the `<DIV ALIGN="center">` is never closed—and that centering applies through to the end of the document.

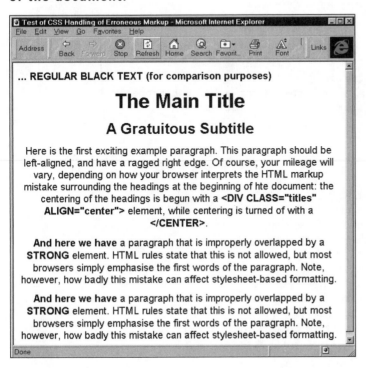

Figure 2.11 is a duplicate of the document in Figure 2.8, but now with stylesheet instructions in the head of the document. The stylesheet instructions imply the following formatting:

- Text inside **DIV** should be in a light green color (which will look like a light gray in the figures).

- Paragraphs should have left and right margins indented 10% from the window border (relative to the size of the window).

- Paragraphs inside a **DIV** should have 20% margins, and not 10% ones.

- Text inside **STRONG** elements should be underlined.

Figure 2.11 The example HTML document from Figure 2.8, but with added stylesheet rules. As in Figure 2.8, the boldface HTML comment strings show the locations of the markup errors. The rendering of this document—and the associated interpretation of the stylesheet rules—is found in Figures 2.12 and 2.13.

```
<HTML><HEAD> <TITLE>Test of CSS Handling of Erroneous Markup</TITLE>
<STYLE><!--
    DIV         {color: #55ff55;}
    DIV.titles  {text-align: center}
    P           {margin-left: 10%; margin-right: 10%}
    DIV P       {margin-left: 20%; margin-right: 20%}
    STRONG      {text-decoration: underline;}
-->
</STYLE></HEAD>
<BODY BGCOLOR="#ffffff">
<P><B>... REGULAR BLACK TEXT (for comparison purposes)</B></P>
<DIV CLASS="titles" ALIGN="center">        <!-- Error - DIV not properly
                                                    closed -->

<H1>The Main Title</H1>
<H2>A Gratuitous Subtitle</H2>
</CENTER>                                   <!-- Error- improper closing
                                                    of above DIV?-->
<P>Here is the first exciting example paragraph. This
   paragraph should be left-aligned, and have a ragged right
   edge. Of course, your mileage will vary, depending on how
   your browser interprets the HTML markup mistake surrounding
   the headings at the beginning of hte document: the
   centering of the headings is begun with a
   <B>&lt;DIV CLASS="titles" ALIGN="center"></B> element, while
   centering is turned of with a <B>&lt;/CENTER></B>.</P>
<STRONG><P>                      <!-- Error - STRONG overlaps <P> -->
   And here we have</STRONG> a paragraph that is improperly overlapped
   by a <B>STRONG</B> element. HTML rules state that this is not allowed,
   but most browsers simply emphasise the first words of the paragraph.
```

Figure 2.11 *Continued*

```
Note, however, how badly this mistake can affect stylesheet-based
formatting.</P>
<P><STRONG>   <!-- same para. as above, but with properly nested STRONG -->
And here we have</STRONG> a paragraph that is improperly overlapped
by a <B>STRONG</B> element. HTML rules state that this is not allowed,
but most browsers simply emphasise the first words of the paragraph.
Note, however, how badly this mistake can affect stylesheet-based
formatting.</P>
</BODY></HTML>
```

The renderings of this document by two stylesheet-aware browsers are shown in Figures 2.12 and 2.13: Figure 2.12 shows the rendering by MSIE 3, while Figure 2.13 shows the rendering by Netscape Navigator 4, prerelease 2. While both browsers only partially support CSS, they do support the properties used in this example.

Look at how the two documents interpret the **DIV** and **CENTER** tags. As before, the Netscape browser (Figure 2.13) assumes that the </CENTER> tag terminates the **DIV**, while Internet Explorer (Figure 2.12) does not. Note how strongly this affects the formatting—Internet Explorer applies the green text color, centering, and 20% paragraph margins to all the text in the document, while Netscape Navigator only applies the **DIV**-specified color modification and margins to the two headings, and does not apply these properties to the remaining paragraphs. In both cases, this is markedly different from the non-stylesheet rendered versions shown in Figures 2.9 and 2.10—indeed, in many ways, the non-stylesheet renderings look better than these stylesheets-aware examples!

Even more frustrating are the differences arising from the non-nested **STRONG** element. Internet Explorer 3 applies part of the specified formatting (the underline) to the entire element, but the boldface component just to the section bounded by the start and stop **STRONG** tags. Navigator 4, on the other hand, underlines the section bounded by the start and stop **STRONG** tags, implements a line break after the </STRONG> (perhaps assuming that the </STRONG> should close the paragraph), boldfaces the entire paragraph (since it just used </STRONG> to end the paragraph, so that the strong element is not yet closed), and resets the left and right margins to zero (since it was the paragraph that had the 10% margins, and the paragraph was implicitly closed by the </STRONG>).

The point to emphasize is that neither Netscape Navigator nor Internet Explorer is wrong in its presentation of the document. Given even simple HTML errors such as the ones illustrated here, browsers really have no clue as to what the author actually intended. Thus they are free (and obliged) to "guess" at the author's intentions, with often ridiculous results. And, with the huge number of formatting properties that can be controlled by an author through CSS, it is now less and less likely that two browsers will "guess" at the same rendering choice for a given markup mistake!

It is thus imperative that you, the stylesheet author, use accurate HTML markup. This is the only way that you can be sure that people will be able to read your work—and the only way to avoid enormous aggravation when authoring new stylesheets and new documents.

Figure 2.12 Rendering of the document listed in Figure 2.11 by Microsoft Internet Explorer 3. This browser properly understands the CSS rules used in this example. The differences between this rendering and that seen in Figure 2.13 are due to errors in the HTML markup.

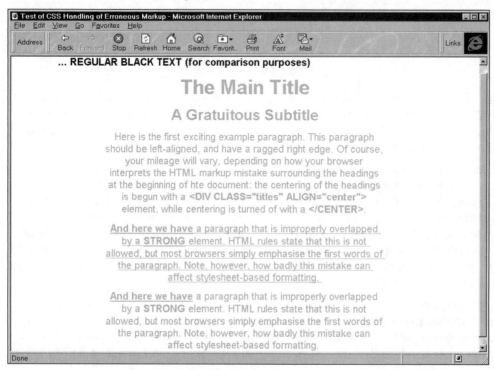

Readability without Stylesheets?

As a final point, recall how the document in Figure 2.11 looked when viewed by a browser that did not support stylesheets—such a rendering is shown in Figure 2.9. Although all the CSS-specified formatting details are missing, the document itself is easy to read and understand, since the elements preserve the document organization, and the browser's default display properties display the content clearly. This is an important point, since for the next year or so, many people will be using older browsers (Netscape 3 or earlier) that do not support stylesheets. Thus it is critical that the documents you prepare be understandable when viewed by browsers that do or do not support CSS.

If you start with well-defined markup, and then use stylesheets to define formatting on top of this structure, you will have no problems. However, if you use complex combinations of **TABLE**- and stylesheet-based layout to generate extremely complex layouts, it is quite likely that the document will be unreadable when stylesheets are not supported. If such compatibility is important to you, then be sure to check your documents with stylesheet removed, to make sure that all users can understand the content.

Figure 2.13 Rendering of the document listed in Figure 2.11 by Netscape Navigator 4 prerelease 2. This browser properly understands the CSS rules used in this example. The differences between this rendering and that seen in Figure 2.12 are due to errors in the HTML markup.

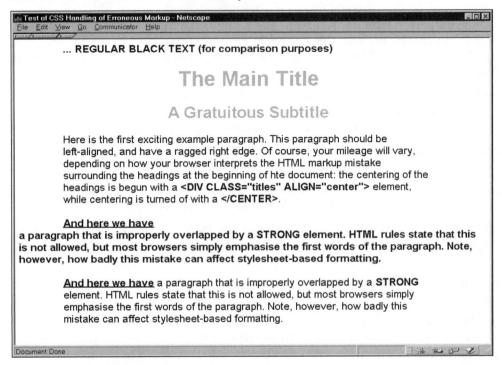

Chapter Summary

The HyperText Markup Language, or HTML, is a *text markup language.* HTML consists of markup *tags* that divide the document into blocks called *elements*. Elements are nested one within another, with a document's structure being defined by the nested structure of the elements.

HTML is defined using the Standard Generalized Markup Language, or *SGML*. SGML is a sophisticated meta-language for defining markup languages such as HTML. There are many other SGML-based markup languages, many of which are more complicated than HTML. The actual rules of the languages are specified by a special SGML file called a *document type definition*, or *DTD*.

HTML elements must *nest* one within another, and cannot *overlap*. Also, there are HTML rules, expressed in the DTD, that define where elements can and cannot nest. For example, an **H1** can contain **EM** elements, but cannot contain **P**.

Most HTML elements mark up document *structure*, and not *formatting*. Thus HTML has elements that define headings, paragraphs, lists, blockquotes, emphasized text, and so on. Formatting details were omitted (to a large extent) from HTML to make the language as platform-independent as possible.

HTML elements can take *attributes* that define special properties of the element. Attributes define the targets of hypertext links, the source for an inline image, the type of a form input element, and so on.

An HTML document has two main parts: a *HEAD* and a *BODY*. The document head is the first part of an HTML document, and contains document meta-information (e.g., the **TITLE,** **META, LINK,** or **STYLE** elements). The **BODY** contains the text to be displayed, and the markup elements related to the text.

BODY content elements fall into two main categories: *block* and *inline*. Block elements, such as **H1** or **P,** define rectangular blocks of text that can contain multiple lines. Inline elements, such as **EM, CODE,** or **IMG,** appear inline with the text that lies inside a block element.

LINK elements can reference *external stylesheets*. The stylesheet referenced by **LINK** will be loaded by a browser, and the instructions within the stylesheet will be used to format the document.

A STYLE element can contain *stylesheet instructions*. These instructions will be used to format the document, and will override any instructions specified in a **LINK**ed stylesheet.

SPAN elements define inline portions of text, and specify *special formatting* for them. SPAN is a stylesheet-aware generalization of HTML elements such as **FONT** or **BLINK**—these two elements should be avoided in stylesheet-aware documents.

The new CLASS attribute is used to *subclass* an element. Stylesheets can then specify formatting specific to a particular class, or even to a particular element type of a specified class.

The new ID attribute can give an element a *unique* ID label. Stylesheets can then provide formatting specific to a particular **ID,** or even to a particular element type that is of a given **ID.** Note that **ID** values must be unique in a document—no two elements in a document can have the same **ID.**

META can specify a *default stylesheet language* for a document. This functionality, however, is not yet widely supported.

Proper formatting is tied to the *accuracy* of the HTML markup. Because formatting is tied to elements and the content of the elements, an HTML document must be written to properly nest and close all elements. Any errors in element nesting or element closing can lead to enormous problems in document formatting.

Chapter Exercises

The first exercise should be to buy a good HTML reference text—one that outlines the proper rules for nesting and using the different HTML elements. Some books are listed in the reference section at the end of this chapter. Since accurate HTML is a key to designing reliable CSS-aware documents, it is always a good idea to have a good reference that will explain the proper use of the different language components.

As a second exercise, take the example document in Figure 2.11 and modify the content to intentionally add (and also remove) HTML markup errors. You will also want to see the results by previewing the page using one or more CSS-enabled browsers, in particular Navigator 4, Internet Explorer 3, or Internet Explorer 4, as these are the CSS-capable browsers that are most likely to be used by your readers. This will help familiarize you with the types of errors that arise when stylesheets are mixes with bad HTML.

As a final exercise, take CSS-enabled documents, comment out all the CSS rules, and preview the resulting "vanilla" HTML document. In many cases, your readers will be using older versions of Netscape or Internet Explorer (or other browsers) that do not support stylesheets, and this test will reassure you that the content is clear to the reader (if not as beautiful) in the absence of stylesheet formatting.

References

Web-based SGML Resources
http://etext.virginia.edu/bin/tei-tocs?div=DIV1&id=SG (Gentle SGML introduction)

http://www.lib.virginia.edu/etext/tagging-intro.html (Ibid.)

ftp://www.ucc.ie/pub/sgml/p2sg.ps (The above, but in PostScript)

http://www.sil.org/sgml/sgml.html (SGML reference collection)

http://www.w3.org/pub/WWW/MarkUp/SGML/Activity (W3C SGML activities summary)

ftp://ftp.ifi.uio.no/pub/SGML/ (Eric Naggum's SGML archive)

news:comp.text.sgml (SGML newsgroup)

Books on SGML
SGML on the Web: Small Steps Beyond HTML, by Yuri Rubinsky and Murray Maloney, Prentice Hall, 1997.

The SGML Handbook, by Charles F. Goldfarb, Oxford University Press, 1990 (the SGML "bible"—an advanced book, useful as a definitive reference).

HTML Specifications and Notes
http://ds.internic.net/rfc/rfc1866.txt (HTML 2.0 specifications)

http://www.w3.org/pub/WWW/MarkUp/Wilbur/ (HTML 3.2 information)

http://www.w3.org/pub/WWW/TR/WD-style (HTML 3 and stylesheets)

http://www.w3.org/pub/WWW/TR/WD-object.html (OBJECT element draft)

http://ds.internic.net.rfc/rfc2070.txt (HTML internationalization)

http://www.w3.org/pub/WWW/MarkUp/ (W3C HTML overview)

HTML Element Content Rules

http://www.utoronto.ca/webdocs/HTMLdocs/HTML_Spec/html.html (Author's HTML element content rules pages)

http://www.htmlhelp.com/reference/wilbur/overview.html (Web Design Group's HTML 3.2 overview)

HTML DTDs

http://www.w3.org/hypertext/WWW/MarkUp/MarkUp.html

http://www.utoronto.ca/webdocs/HTMLdocs/HTML_Spec/html.html (Author's collection of DTDs)

http://www.ucc.ie/html/dtds/htmlpro.html (HTML Pro DTD, by Peter Flynn)

http://www.cm.spyglass.com/doc/ (Spyglass archive of DTDs)

HTML Syntax Validation Tools/Sites

http://www.webtechs.com/html-val-svc/mirror_sites.html (Online validator)

http://ugweb.cs.ualberta.ca/~gerald/validate/ (Online validator)

http://www.spyglass.com/products/validator/ (Spyglass HTML validator—Windows 95)

Microsoft / Netscape HTML Extensions

http://home.netscape.com/assist/net_sites/html_extensions.html

http://home.netscape.com/assist/net_sites/html_extensions_3.html

http://home.netscape.com/eng/mozilla/3.0/relnotes/windows-3.0.html

http://www.microsoft.com/workshop/author/other/htmlfaq1.htm (Microsoft Internet Explorer 3.0 HTML FAQ)

http://www.microsoft.com/workshop/author/newhtml/ (Microsoft HTML references)

HTML Reference Books

The HTML Sourcebook, Third Edition, by Ian S. Graham, John Wiley and Sons, 1997.

HTML: The Definitive Guide, by Chuck Musciano and Bill Kennedy, O'Reilly and Associates, 1996.

Endnotes

1. A *character set* is simply a defined relationship between computer binary codes and a set of characters or symbols. *Printable* characters are just those that can be printed, as opposed to ones that cannot be printed, such as control characters (e.g., ESCAPE, ALT, CTRL).

2. Subclassing refers to the process of taking a specific *class* of element (e.g., **P**) and defining a specific *subtype* or *subclass* of the element (e.g., **CLASS**="verse").

Stylesheets Tutorial, Part 1: Fonts
and Typefaces

Chapter 1 gave a brief introduction to CSS stylesheets and their application to HTML documents, while Chapter 2 provided an overview of HTML, focusing on those aspects important in the design of documents that use stylesheets. Given this background, it is time to delve into the details of the CSS language, and to start introducing the formatting and layout concepts authors need to understand if they are to successfully use stylesheets.

Chapters 3 through 6 provide a step-by-step introduction to the usage and appropriate application of the different CSS Level 1 properties. They also provide important review information needed to understand the issues involved, and to appreciate the recommended design techniques.

This chapter covers topics related to font and typeface specification and selection. One of the goals of CSS has been to develop a way of unambiguously describing fonts and font characteristics, so that an author could specify a desired font, while at the same time allowing for graceful substitution of an appropriate alternative, should the desired font be unavailable to the computer displaying a document. This effort has largely been successful, with CSS providing a small and straightforward collection of properties for describing fonts and their characteristics.

However, to use these properties well, a CSS author must also understand the main issues related to fonts and typefaces. These issues include:

- How typefaces, fonts, and different font styles are named and described, both in general and in the specific context of CSS font properties.

- The styles and names of those fonts likely to be available on common computers.

- The different names that may be used for similar or equivalent fonts on a given computer, or on different computers running different operating systems.

- The different CSS properties that describe fonts and font characteristics, and how best to use them to create platform-independent documents.

This chapter is divided into three main sections. The first section is an introduction to fonts and typefaces. To Web designers coming from a typographic background, this section may seem incomplete, and a bit naive. This is intentional, and for two reasons. First, the section is intended as an overview for readers not terribly familiar with typographic issues, and for whom the full details would be overkill—the topic truly deserves its own book, and not just a small section of one chapter. Second, CSS supports far less control over typeface and font properties than is possible in advanced print publishing. Thus, the focus is on issues directly applicable to CSS and the Web, and largely avoids aspects not relevant to Web capabilities. In this regard, the section is useful even to those with a sound understanding of typefaces and fonts, as it will help them position their knowledge with respect to the capabilities and limitations of CSS.

The second section provides a brief introduction to the CSS language. This section explains how CSS *rules* (i.e., collections of stylesheet instructions) are written, and how they are applied to the elements of an HTML document. This brief introduction covers only some simple cases, which are, in turn, illustrated in the examples in the third section of the chapter. More complicated CSS rules are described and illustrated later in the book.

Finally, the third section uses example HTML documents containing CSS stylesheets to illustrate how CSS properties affect the typography of real Web pages. This section helps put into concrete form the font control properties described in the first section, and also illustrates how stylesheet rules are actually applied when a document is formatted. These examples also help illustrate the two basic characteristics of CSS: *inheritance*, whereby an element inherits the properties (e.g., font size or font face) of the parent element; and *cascading*, whereby formatting properties specified in one rule can be overridden by those specified in another.

Introduction to Typefaces and Fonts

A *font* or *typeface* is a collection of graphical symbols that share a common design or style and that usually correspond to the characters of a language. Most of the time we think of a font or typeface in terms of these characters, as in the symbol "A" that represents the indicated letter.[1]

In CSS, fonts are described using a variety of terms, most of which are hard to understand without some familiarity with the basics of fonts, font descriptions, and typeface design. The following discussion provides a brief introduction to help bring you up to speed on the main issues. If you are already familiar with fonts, you may prefer to skip ahead to the section titled "Specifying Font Variants Using CSS."

Where Fonts Come From

Fonts are designed by companies traditionally called *font foundries*. The name *foundry* comes from the original role of such companies, which was the design of the molds used to form the lead type used in printing. Until the 1970s, printing was a manually intensive craft, in which a typesetter (the person preparing the type) would combine a selection of molds to create a single line of type (for example, a single line from the page of a book), and would then pour molten lead into this line. When the lead hardened, it was removed, with the faces on this lead strip being the type used in the printing process to create the particular line of the book. A single page was composed of many such lines, painstakingly constructed one after the other and combined or set into a block for use on the printing press.[2] Printing is today a somewhat easier process—the lead-type printing process is now very rare, and has largely been supplanted by computerized typesetting technologies. At the same time, this has changed the business of font foundries, with today's firms selling digital representations for a font, rather than physical molds. This is done by designing computer algorithms that generate the fonts on computerized typesetting equipment or computer displays. In a sense, these algorithms are "digital molds," so that the name "foundry" is still quite appropriate. Some modern-day font foundries are Adobe, Bitstream, Monotype, and Microsoft (yes, they do that too!)—these names give a clear indication of the digital nature of modern typography.

Font Name and Name Variability

Upon developing a new font, a font foundry gives the font a name by which it will be known—some common examples are "Times Roman Bold," "Garamond Italic," or "Helvetica Narrow." These names are generally trademarked, and reserved for use by the company that registered the name. The base name of a font is often called the typeface *family name*, as there are generally many font variants (bold, italicized, etc.) that fall under the same name. For example, the Times Roman family consists of regular Times Roman, bold Times Roman, and many others.

The laws by which a typeface is protected vary significantly across the globe. The laws are particularly liberal in the United States, where anyone can create and distribute a font that reproduces the design of an already existing font, provided the imitation:

1. does not explicitly copy the digital format or formula used to create the characters, and

2. is distributed under a name *different from* that of the original font.

The Truth about *Font* and *Typeface*

The preceding discussion used the terms font and typeface more or less interchange-ably, as is common practice in today's world of desktop publishing; but, in fact, these two terms have somewhat different meanings. More precisely, a *typeface* (or face) con-sists of *all fonts* that share the same basic design, whereas a *font* is one particular instance of the typeface. All possible sizes or variants of the Times Roman style belong to the Times Roman typeface and are said to be in the same typeface *family*. Thus, when this book refers to the Times Roman font family, more correctly it should refer to the Times Roman *typeface* family.

A *font* is one particular instance of a typeface, with a specific weight, style, and size; for example, "Times Roman Bold Italic 12pt."

This distinction between typeface and font was important in the days of lead type, when fonts were made of real physical things (molds); it was then necessary to physi-cally separate the different fonts so that they didn't get mixed up, and it was very hard to tell two different fonts apart, since the molds all looked the same. This is no longer an issue, as software now enforces the separation of the fonts, so that the distinction between font and typeface is of less practical importance. Thus, today, the two terms are used more or less interchangeably.

The first condition is similar to software copyright law, whereby a company can sell software that mimics a competitor's product, provided it does not duplicate the actual computer code. The latter condition is required because, under United States law, *font names*, unlike the font's appear-ance, can be trademarked—for example, the name "Gill" is trademarked by the Monotype foundry, and cannot be used by anyone else unless they license the font from Monotype.

As a consequence of these rules, there are many foundries that now produce inexpensive copies of commonly used fonts, but under slightly different names. For example, the trademarked Times Roman font is available from vendors under such names as "English Times" or "London."

Font Naming on Computers

Font naming is an important issue on the Web, as different computer operating systems or applica-tions obtain their fonts from different foundries, such that the *same* font is often available across different systems (PC, Macintosh, UNIX) but under a different name. For example, the Times Roman font is available on all Microsoft operating systems under the name "Times New Roman," but is found on Macintoshes and most UNIX platforms under the name "Times."

When designing a CSS stylesheet, a CSS author must make allowances for these platform-depen-dent variations. In CSS, a stylesheet designer uses the `font-family` property to specify the desired font. To allow for variations in name, CSS lets an author specify multiple font names in the font-family specification; when displaying the document, the browser will look through the list, and use the first named font that it can find. Thus, this list should contain the font names found on different computers. For example, the specification for "Times Roman" might be given as:

```
font-family: "Times New Roman", "Times Roman", "Times"
```

to cover most possible platform-specific name variations.

Note that font copyright law is different in other countries. For example, font names as well as designs can be copyrighted in Germany, France, and many other countries, so that inexpensive imitations fonts are illegal in these jurisdictions.

Digital Font Formats: Bitmapped and Scalable

There are many different computer font formats, but they can be divided into two broad categories: *bitmapped* and *scalable*. Bitmapped formats store a font as the actual pattern of black dots that should be drawn to produce the symbols; consequently, bitmapped fonts are available only in fixed font sizes (e.g., 12pt, 14pt, 18pt) corresponding to the patterns stored in the font file. In principle, bitmapped fonts can be rescaled to other sizes, but the resized fonts are often of poor quality, since there is no easy of way of knowing how a particular pattern of dots should be shrunk or expanded to create the new pattern. For example, enlarged bitmaps tend to look "blocky," because of the inadequate "fill-in" of the spaces between the dots. A blowup of a bitmapped font is shown at the top of Figure 3.1, which illustrates both how the pixels are blocked in to create the desired symbols, and how poor a bitmapped font can look when rescaled to a larger size.

Scalable fonts, such as Adobe PostScript Type 1 and 3 or TrueType (a joint Microsoft/Apple format), use font-drawing algorithms to describe how the font should be drawn. Such fonts can be scaled to any desired size simply by changing the parameters used by the algorithm. When a particular sized font is requested, the algorithm calculates the best possible bitmap for the font, and draws it to the display (or to the typesetting device or printing engine).

Scalable fonts also use what are called *hinting* parameters—special parameters, designed into the font-drawing algorithm, that provide drawing "hints" appropriate to specific font sizes or size ranges. In general, scalable fonts look better on computer displays than equivalent bitmapped fonts, as the font-scaling algorithms adjust the font to look best at the chosen size.

All fonts, when rendered for display, can use *antialiasing* to improve font readability. Antialiasing means that, instead of displaying a character as an array of black or white dots, the character is drawn using black, white, and shades of gray. The text at the bottom of Figure 3.1 illustrates how antialiasing affects the font bitmap. Some scalable font formats have hinting parameters specifically related to font antialiasing.

Most computer fonts are scalable, but some computers offer both scalable and bitmapped versions of the same font, under slightly different names (this is usually done for backward compatibility with older software). For example, under Microsoft Windows, the Times Roman font is available as "Times," a bitmapped font, as well as "Times New Roman," a TrueType-format scalable font. For best results, stylesheet authors should use the scalable version.

Figure 3.1 A simple illustration of a font as displayed on a computer screen, magnified to illustrate the individual pixels. The upper figure shows standard bitmapped characters. The bottom half shows an antialiased font—antialiasing uses gray pixels to smooth the edges of the font, making the characters easier to read.

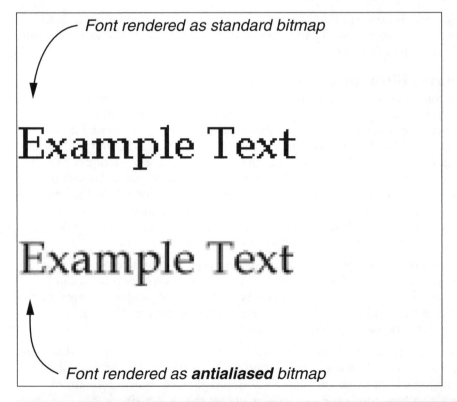

Font rendered as standard bitmap

Example Text

Example Text

*Font rendered as **antialiased** bitmap*

TIP Use Scalable Fonts

An author should, whenever possible, use font names corresponding to scalable fonts (e.g., TrueType or PostScript).

Specifying Font Variants Using CSS

A typeface or font family generally supports a number of variations upon the basic font, described by terms such as "regular," "bold," "italic," or "oblique." In general, these variations can be described using two main properties: the *weight* of the font (the darkness or width of the lines used to draw the symbols), and the *slant* or *style* of the font (the slant or italicized nature of the symbols). Traditionally, fonts are provided with names that specify these particular versions;

for example, the Times Roman font family provides a font under the name "Times Roman Bold Italics" to indicate this particular variant.

Unfortunately, the terms such as "bold," "regular," "italics," turn out to be very subjective—for example, one font family's "bold" may be equivalent, in apparent weight, to another family's "regular." Because these descriptive names are unreliable as an absolute specifier of a font's properties, they were avoided in CSS. Instead, CSS explicitly separates the terms that describe the family variants from the family name. Thus, a CSS author must specify font-family for the family of the desired font (e.g., "Helvetica" or "Times"), font-weight for the weight or degree of boldness of the font, and font-style for the slanted or italic nature of the font. These properties, in turn, take values that are well defined as part of the CSS specifications. The values are described in more detail in the third section of this chapter.

Some fonts are also available in other variants; an example is small caps, a variant wherein all the letters are in an uppercase typeface, with the lowercase letters being in a smaller font. CSS uses a font-variant property to indicate these options.

Of course, an author begins with a particular font's own idea of weight and style, and not with a CSS specification for the font. Thus, the author needs a way of converting information about the desired font into appropriate CSS weight and style specifications. Rules for doing so are presented later in this chapter.

Font Names and Generic Font Families

An author preparing a document for printing has access to literally thousands of different fonts. To a graphics designer, this richness of fonts is quite daunting. With thousands of fonts to choose from, with names ranging from Alleycat Bop to Zinjaro and styles ranging from the timid to the truly exotic, finding the ideal font for a particular purpose can be an exciting task. Fortunately, if the author has printed font samples and a collection of font diskettes or CD-ROMs, once the font is found, it can be loaded onto the system and used just as easily as the standard fonts. Design is thus limited only by time, patience, and budget—fonts are not, in general, free (a set of professional, multiple-font CD-ROMs can cost over $US 1500), and maintaining a professional font library can be an expensive task.

Unfortunately, all these wonderful fonts are not yet available on the Web. When a browser displays a Web document, it in general has access to only the fonts available on the local machine—this is often a small number of rather uninteresting fonts. For example, a PC equipped with Windows 3.1/95 and Netscape Navigator is likely to have only three font families—Arial, Times New Roman, and Courier New. Other fonts may be available, depending on what other software has been installed, but, in general, the selection is small compared with the expectations of a graphics designer. An author must be aware of these limitations, and must know what fonts are likely to be present on a given platform as well the alternative fonts to suggest should the desired font(s) not be available.

For Web applications, it is thus convenient to be able to group the font families into generic family groups. When an author specifies a desired font and a few possible alternatives, he or she can also specify the generic family to which the font belongs. Then, if none of the specific choices are available on the machine displaying the document, the browser can attempt to locate an available font that belongs to the same generic family.

CSS defines five generic font families, covering the most common character font groups. These families, along with some examples of fonts belonging in those categories, are listed in Table 3.1. *Serif* and *sans-serif* fonts are the standard proportionally spaced fonts used for text display; proportional spacing simply means that the spacing between letters varies to make the text easier to read (e.g., note, in this text, how the spacing around letters such as "t" or "i" is reduced). *Monospace* fonts are fonts with fixed spacing between the letters—such fonts are often used for computer code, as they reproduce the horizontal spacing in the program listing. Finally, *cursive* (handwriting-like) and *fantasy* (arbitrarily decorative) fonts are mostly used for decoration or headings, as they are not easy to read when used for bulk text, such as paragraphs. As discussed later, a CSS author should always list the generic font family as the last possible option of a font-family property value.

The most common groups for regular text are serif and sans-serif fonts. The word "serif" refers to the small strokes or lines added at the tips of strokes used to draw the character, as illustrated in Figure 3.2. It turns our that serifs make printed text easier to read, by providing a visual link between adjacent letters. Sans-serif fonts, such as Arial or Helvetica, do not have serifs, also as illustrated in Figure 3.2. In general, sans-serif fonts are somewhat less easy to read in print, although they are useful for highlighting text, or as a font for headings.

The situation is somewhat different on a computer display, where the lower resolution makes it hard to read small fonts containing serifs; thus it is often advantageous to use sans-serif fonts for regular text, particular at small font sizes.

Table 3.1 CSS Generic Font Families, with Examples

Generic CSS Family Name	Description	Examples (12 point)
cursive	Fonts drawn with a cursive or handwriting-like style.	*Ribbon 131 Bold BT, Shelley Volante BT*
fantasy	Nonstandard, decorative fonts	**Comic Sans MS**, 𝕭𝖑𝖆𝖈𝖐𝖑𝖊𝖙𝖙𝖊𝖗686 𝕭𝕿
monospace	Fonts where all symbols have the same width (sometimes called "typewriter" fonts)	`courier`
sans-serif	Fonts drawn with simple line segments, without serifs	**Arial**, Avant Garde
serif	Fonts drawn with simple line segments, with serifs	Times New Roman, Garamond

Figure 3.2 An illustration of serif and sans-serif fonts, using the "Times Roman," "Zapf Chancery," and "Helvetica" fonts as examples. Of these, only "Helvetica" is a sans-serif font.

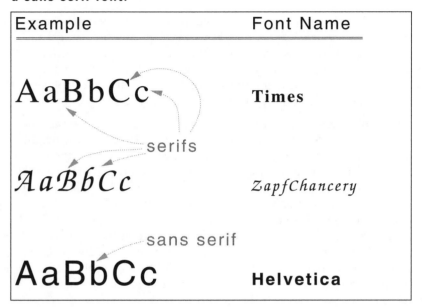

Specifying Font Sizes

Of course authors also must be able to specify the size of a font. However, in order to properly use font sizes and font size measurements, it helps to have a basic understanding of how fonts are described, and of how font sizes are measured. Figure 3.3 shows the basic structure of a font, showing the typical component dimensions. The *baseline* defines the line upon which the font is set, while the *ascender* defines the maximum height to which the font extends upwards, and the *descender* the maximum depth to which the font hangs down below the baseline. The *font size* is typically defined as the length from the bottom of the descender to the top of the ascender.

In principle, the absolute size of a font can be given in any desired units. However, the most common unit is the *point*. Points are particularly convenient for defining small lengths, such as the size of a font. A point, commonly abbreviated as *pt*, is a common typographic length unit, which in CSS is defined as 1/72 of an inch—that is, 72 points = 1 inch.[3] Thus specifying a 12pt font is the same as specifying a font that is 3/18" high.

There are also two important units that measure lengths *relative to* the size of a font. These units are useful because they scale with the font size; doubling the size of the font also doubles the size of these relative lengths. These units are thus useful for defining things such as the spacing between words, or paragraph indents. Then, if the size of the font is increased or decreased, the sizes of the spacing will remain appropriate to the newly adjusted size of the font.

Em and Ex Units

The first scalable unit is called an *em*. Traditionally, "1 em" was equivalent to the width occupied by the letter "m," so that the unit was convenient for defining horizontal spacing for paragraph indents (5 em being a typical indent length). However, in CSS, an em unit is defined as a length equal to the full size of the font. Thus, specifying the length "2 em" is equivalent to specifying a length equal to twice the height of the current font. Using this definition, an "em" unit depends only on the defined font size, and not on the font family or other font properties.

The second scalable unit is called an *ex*. An "ex" refers to the height of the "body" of the characters, and is called an "ex" (or the *x-height*) because this length is often equivalent to the height of the letter "x." For a given font size, ex lengths, unlike em lengths, vary depending on the font family. This is because different font families can have larger or smaller bodies relative to the full size of the font (corresponding to smaller or larger ascender/descender heights). This is illustrated in Figure 3.4, which shows, at the top of the figure, the fonts "Times Roman" and "Helvetica," both at the same font size. Note how the x-heights (and, not as obviously, the ascender and descender heights) are different for these two fonts, even though the fonts are of the same size. The bottom of the figure shows three short paragraphs, typeset using three different serif fonts, all of the same size. Once again, these different fonts have differing x-, ascender, and descender heights. As a result, the text in the paragraph formatted using the Times Roman font appears "smaller" than the text in the other two paragraphs, even through the fonts are of the same size.

Display Resolution and Appropriate Fonts

We have already mentioned how the palette of fonts available on a user's computer can be quite limited. At the same time, the limitations of computer displays impose important restrictions on font usability. The problem is the limited resolution of a computer display. A typographic designer generally prepares pages to be printed at a minimum resolution of 600 dots per inch (dpi), and usually much higher. A computer display, however, has a resolution of at best 100 dpi, and usually less. Thus, the highest resolution available on a computer is generally a factor of 10 or more poorer than that of a printed page.

The result is that many fonts that look wonderful in print look quite awful on a computer. Such problems typically arise with fonts that have fine-lined detail, such a script or decorative fonts, or fonts composed of multiple strokes, or with shading or shadows—in these cases, and particularly at small font sizes, the characters often turn into fuzzy smudges, since there is simply not enough resolution to display them properly (hinting on scalable fonts helps to mitigate this problem, to some degree). Fonts with these characteristics should thus be avoided in Web design, unless they are used at very large point sizes. The following pointers will help you select fonts appropriate for your documents.

1. Use simple sans-serif fonts for text that is particularly small (e.g., less than 10pt).

2. Use simple serif or sans-serif fonts for text that is to be read.

Figure 3.3 An illustration of font length measurements. The font size is defined as the length from the bottom of the descender to the top of the ascender, while one "ex" is equivalent to the height of the "body" of the characters. Note that not all characters of the same font size need to have the same ascender, descender, or body height (although the sum of these three quantities must be the same).

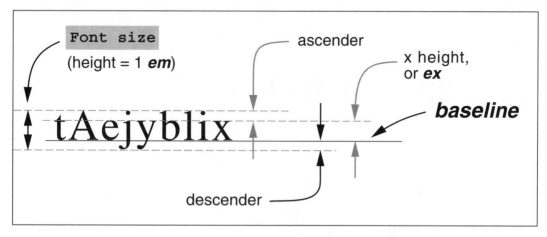

3. Use whatever fonts you want for decorations, headings, and so on, keeping in mind that uncommon fonts are probably not available to the reader viewing the document (and keeping in mind that a document that employ dozens of different fonts can look quite ridiculous!).

4. Be sure to offer font alternatives in your `font-family` property specification, particularly if you use exotic fonts that are likely to be unavailable to some readers.

5. Check your documents on a poor-quality display, and make sure that the text is clear and easy to read (provided you want it to be easy to read, of course!).

6. Avoid shadowed or decorative fonts, unless used at very large font sizes.

Stylesheet Syntax: Rules, Selectors, Declarations, and Properties

A CSS stylesheet consists of rules that specify how formatting should be applied to particular elements in a document. In general, a stylesheet contains many such rules. Each CSS rule begins with a *selector* that specifies the element or elements to which the rule applies, followed by one or more *declarations* that specify formatting *properties* for the element. Figure 3.5 provides two simple examples of CSS rules, and illustrates these basic component parts.

Figure 3.4 An illustration of different fonts of the same font size. Note that the heights of the fonts are the same, although the ascender, descender, and character body heights can vary between font families. As a result, text formatted using one font can appear "smaller" or "less dense" than the same text formatted in another, similar font of the same font size, as illustrated by the three example paragraphs.

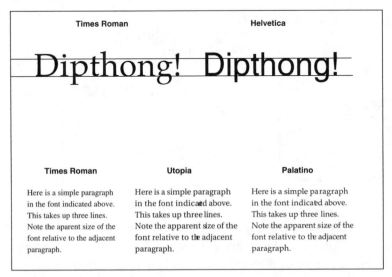

Each declaration has two parts: the *property*, which indicates the formatting property, and the *value* to be assigned to the property. Thus, the first rule in Figure 3.5 consists of the selector H1, the property `font-weight` (the weight, or degree of boldness, of the text), and the value `bold`. Note that the colon character (:) is the separator between a property and its associated value—the colon is a special character in declarations, and can appear only as a separator.

The collection of declarations associated with a selector is contained within curly brackets: The left curly bracket ({) marks the start of the collection, and the right curly bracket (}) the end. Each declaration is, itself, ended by a semicolon. However, the semicolon is optional if there is only one declaration, so that the first rule in Figure 3.5 could also be written as:

```
H1 {font-weight: bold }
```

Declarations do not need to be on separate lines, so that the second rule in Figure 3.5 could be written as:

```
H2{font-family: arial, helvetica, sans-serif; font-style: italics; font-weight: bold;}
```

However, it is easier for an author to read a stylesheet when each declaration stands alone.

Figure 3.5 Two example CSS rules, illustrating selectors and property declarations. A stylesheet will in general contain many such rules.

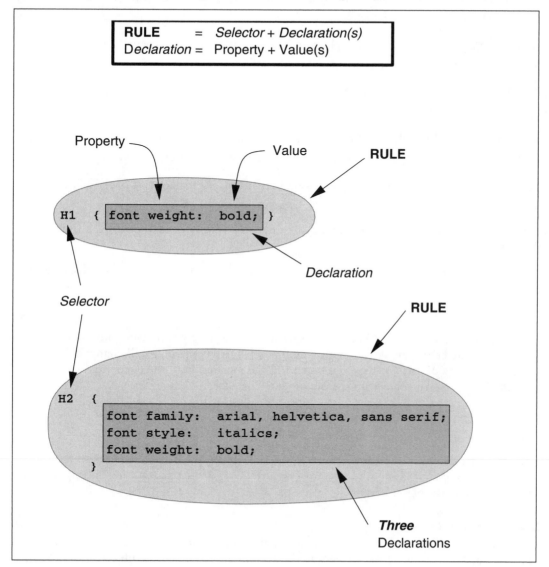

CSS Rule Selectors

Of course, rules are only useful given information specifying where the rules should be applied. This is the role of the *selector*. There are several types of CSS selectors that support rules specific to a generic element, to a specific class of an element, or even to elements contingent on their place within a document. More specifically, the types are:

1. **Simple selectors**—selectors based solely on element name.

2. **Class-based simple selectors**—selectors based on the **CLASS** attribute value of an element; may also be based on the element name.

3. **Pseudo-class-based simple selectors**—selectors based on the pseudo-class properties of an element; may also be based on the element name.

4. **ID-based simple selectors**—selectors based on the **ID** attribute value of an element; may also be based on the element name.

5. **Pseudo-element-based simple selectors**—selectors that apply to a particular subset of a given element, such as the leading line of a paragraph, or the leading letter of a line.

6. **Contextual selectors**—selectors based on a simple selector and the context of the selector; for example, a selector that applies only to **EM** elements inside an **H1**.

7. **Grouped selectors**—groupings of selectors, such that the same rule is applied to all selectors in the group.

In this chapter, we will consider selectors 1 through 4. The remaining types will be discussed in later chapters.

Simple Selectors

Simple selectors reference a single HTML element by name, and imply formatting instructions specific to the indicated element type. A rule with a simple selector is applied to all elements indicated by the selector, regardless of any **CLASS** or **ID** attributes associated with the element, and regardless of the location of the element within the document. For example, the rule

```
P {font-family: arial; font-size: 20pt}
```

is applied to all **P** elements, regardless of their place in the document.

Simple selectors are useful for defining overall properties applicable to *all* elements of a given type. Other selectors (such as class-based selectors, described next) can provide formatting instructions specific to a subset of these elements.

Class-Based Simple Selectors

Class-based selectors associate stylesheet rules with a particular subset or *class* of HTML elements. Elements are assigned a class using the **CLASS** attribute—a new attribute introduced into HTML to support class-based stylesheets. As an example, the HTML markup

```
<P CLASS="goofy">Here is some paragraph text </P>
```

assigns the paragraph element the indicated class value. Class values are useful for marking the specific function or purpose of a particular element. For example, the different sections of a research paper could be marked by **DIV** elements taking **CLASS** attribute values "abstract," "introduction," "section1," "references," and so on, to logically indicate the content of each section.

Stylesheet rules can be associated with specific classes of elements by appending the class name to the rule selector, separated from the selector by a period. For example, to associate special formatting with the paragraph element discussed previously, a stylesheet could have the rule

```
P.goofy { font-size: larger;  font-weight: bolder}
```

which indicates that all paragraphs of **CLASS**="goofy" should be displayed with a font that is larger and bolder than that of the default text. Note that there can be many paragraphs of **CLASS**= "goofy", and this rule will be applied to all of them.

A simple selector can also apply to all elements of a particular class, regardless of element type. This is accomplished by omitting the element name, and specifying just the name of the class— including the leading period to indicate that the selector is a class name. For example, the rule

```
.special2 { font-size: larger;  font-weight: bolder}
```

should be applied to any HTML element with **CLASS**="special2".

A single selector can be associated with at most one class; that is, a selector can specify, at most, one class in the rule. Thus, expressions such as `P.class1.class2` are not allowed.

CLASS is allowed with almost all body elements, the exceptions being those elements that are not displayed with the document (i.e., **AREA**, **MAP**, **PARAM**, and **SCRIPT**) and those that are formatting specific and destined to be entirely replaced by stylesheet rules (i.e., **CENTER** and **FONT**).

NOTE CLASS Allowed with Most BODY Elements

The **CLASS** attribute is supported by **BODY** and all **BODY** content elements except for **AREA**, **CENTER**, **FONT**, **MAP**, **PARAM**, and **SCRIPT**. **CLASS** is not supported by **HEAD**-level elements.

WARNING Multiple CLASS Values Not Supported

In HTML, a single **CLASS** attribute can take multiple values, provided they are separated by a space character, for example **CLASS**="value1 value2". However, current CSS implementations do not properly handle multiple CLASS attribute values. Authors should therefore use single-valued CLASS attributes whenever the value is designed for use with a stylesheet rule.

Pseudo-Class-Based Simple Selectors

Pseudo-class-based selectors are similar to class-based ones, except that the class-like information does not relate to HTML **CLASS** attribute values. Instead, pseudo-class information comes from the browser itself, and contains information about the status of the document or the status of particular elements within the document. CSS Level 1 defines just three pseudo-classes: `link`, to denote hypertext anchors that are unexplored by the user; `visited`, to denote hypertext anchors that were previously visited by the user; and `active`, to indicate active links—that is, links that are currently selected by the user.

CSS differentiates pseudo-classes from real classes by the separator character that precedes the class name or that links the class name to an element name—for pseudo-classes, the separator is a colon. Thus, the three pseudo-class selectors possible under CSS Level 1 are:

- `A:link`   Selects for unvisited links

- `A:visited`   Selects for visited links

- `A:active`   Selects for active links

since the three pseudo-classes are relevant only to **A** elements. Because these pseudo-classes apply only to anchor elements, the element name can be omitted (`A:link` becomes `:link`, and so on). Undoubtedly, future versions of CSS will permit pseudo-classes with other elements, so it is best to include the element name.

A selector cannot contain multiple pseudo-classes—thus selectors like `A:link:active` are forbidden.

NOTE Pseudo-Classes Not Well Supported

The pseudo-classes `:link`, `:visited`, and `:active` are not widely supported. MSIE 3 supports only the `:link` pseudo-class, while Navigator 4.0 partially supports `:link` and `:visited`. Here, partial support means that support of these pseudo-classes varies in an unpredictable way depending on the CSS rule context (that is, depending on location, in the document, of the anchor element to which the pseudo-class-based rule is being applied). This is a bug, and will be rectified in later releases of Netscape Navigator. The prerelease version of MSIE 4 supports all pseudo-class types.

Combining Class and Pseudo-Class Selectors A pseudo-class and a regular class selector can be combined, using the general form

`NAME.class:pseudoclass`

where *NAME* is the element name, *class* is the class name, and *pseudoclass* is the pseudo-class name. Note that the class name must appear first, followed by the pseudo-class name. For example, to create a rule that applies only to active anchor elements of **CLASS**="launcher", the selector would be:

```
A.launcher:active
```

ID-Based Simple Selectors

The CSS-inspired extensions to HTML also allow for **ID** attributes for most **BODY** content HTML elements. **ID** contains an element label, and was originally intended for labeling arbitrary elements as possible targets of hypertext anchors. As such, each **ID** label must be unique; that is, each **ID** value can appear only once in a given document. This is quite different from **CLASS**, as any number of HTML elements can take the same **CLASS** value.

As it did with **CLASS**, CSS provides a way for stylesheet rules to be bound to a particular **ID**-labeled element. The general form is to append the **ID** label to the selector element, separated by a hash character (#). For example, to specify formatting specific to **H1** elements with **ID**="#x23", the CSS rule could be:

```
H1#x23 { font-face: Arial; }
```

The element name can be omitted such that the rule applies to any element taking the given **ID** (much as with **CLASS**). Thus the above rule can also be expressed as:

```
#x23 { font-face: Arial; }
```

Note that according to the HTML specification for **ID** values, there can be at most one **ID**="x23" label in the same document. However, most browsers do not complain if there are multiple elements with the same **ID** value. In this case, current CSS-enabled browsers usually apply the stylesheet instructions to the first element in the document having the given **ID** value.

ID Allowed with Most BODY Elements

The **ID** attribute is supported by **BODY** and all **BODY** content elements except for **AREA, CENTER, FONT, MAP, PARAM,** and **SCRIPT**.

Stylesheets and Font Specifications

The first two sections of this chapter provided an overview of issues surrounding fonts, and also outlined the basic rules for defining stylesheet declarations and rules. In this third section, we will apply this knowledge in a practical way, using stylesheet rules to specify font properties for various components of a document. This will help to illustrate how the various font-related properties work, and will also help show how stylesheet rules are applied to the document.

CSS has five properties related to fonts. Briefly, these are:

Font-family	Specifies the family for the desired font, as a comma-separated list of possible font family names, in decreasing order of preference.
Font-style	Specifies the italicized or slanted nature of the font.
Font-variant	Specifies possible variants on the font; the only possible values in CSS Level 1 are "regular" for the regular font, and "small-caps" for small-capitalized lettering.
Font-weight	Specifies the line thickness or weight for the font.
Font-size	Specifies the size for the font.
Font	A shorthand property that can contain a mixture of the values set by the preceding five properties. This property is discussed in the next chapter.

The use of these properties in actual CSS stylesheets is illustrated in the remaining figures in this chapter. In all cases, the CSS stylesheet rules are contained within a **STYLE** element in the document head. Equivalently, the stylesheet can be placed in an external CSS document and then referenced from the HTML document using a **LINK** element of the form

```
<LINK REL="stylesheet" TYPE="text/css" HREF="url">
```

where `url` is the URL pointing to the CSS document.

Example 1: Simple CSS Selectors and Rules

The first example document is listed in Figure 3.6, and is shown rendered by the Internet Explorer 3.02 browser in Figure 3.7. This is a simple example that uses some simple font-related properties and that illustrates some simple CSS rules for applying those properties to the document.

There are four rules in the CSS stylesheet listed in Figure 3.6. The first rule,

```
.special   {font-family: "Swiss921 BT", "Arial Black", sans-serif}
```

uses a class-based selector, as indicated by the leading period in the selector string. As a result, this rule applies to *any* element taking the attribute **CLASS**="special". Looking to Figure 3.6, we see that this applies only to the **H2** heading at the beginning of the document. The instructions associated with this rule request that the heading be formatted using the "Swiss921 BT" font (the "BT" stands for *Bitstream*), and, failing that, using the "Arial Black" font. Finally, if Arial Black is not available, the browser should use the default sans-serif font. Figure 3.7 shows that, indeed, the computer displaying this document does support "Swiss921 BT," and this font is used to display the heading.

The second rule is also class-based, and applies to any element taking the attribute **CLASS**="special2". The second rule also requests a special font: in this case, the font "Comic Sans MS." If this font is not available on the computer displaying the document, then the browser should use the default font of the "fantasy" family. Fortunately the machine used in this example supports the Comic Sans MS font (this is one of the prerogatives of designing your own examples), so that this font is indeed used in Figure 3.7.

This second rule applies in two locations in Figure 3.7: to the **H1** heading at the beginning of the document, and to the **SPAN** element in the final paragraph. In both cases the selected text is displayed in this rather decorative font, as requested. The **SPAN**ed section within the final paragraph also shows how two fonts of the same font size can appear to the eye to be of quite different sizes. This phenomenon was described previously: Fonts having the same font size often have different "x-heights," which can lead to an apparent mismatch in the size of the font.

The third rule in Figure 3.7,

```
P.goofy    {font-style:  italic;
            font-family: Garamond, "Times New Roman", serif;}
```

is also a class-based selector, but here is specific to **P** elements of **CLASS**="goofy". In this document, this is true only for the second paragraph. Thus the two properties specified in this rule—use an italic font, and use the Garamond font if available (which indeed it is)—are applied to the formatting of this paragraph. Notice also how the text appears smaller than in the other paragraphs, which are formatted using the Times Roman font. Once again, although the fonts are of the same size, Garamond looks smaller, as it has a shorter character body.

The final rule in the stylesheet in Figure 3.7 is

```
EM         {font-weight: bold;
            font-family: arial, sans-serif}
```

which is a simple selector that applies to all **EM** elements. This rule requests that text inside **EM** elements be rendered in a bold Arial font. **EM** elements are found in the first and second paragraphs, and as can be seen in Figure 3.7, this text is indeed rendered in bold Arial. The **EM** text is also in italics because the *default* properties for **EM** elements call for italicization, and this property *cascades* through to the rendering of the element, since the value was not modified by any author-defined rules.

Default CSS Properties

The default properties notion is an important part of CSS. In CSS, *every* property associated with a particular element has a value, even if it is not specified in a stylesheet. The CSS specification defines default values for each property, listed in Chapter 8. These values can be overridden by explicit settings, as discussed in the following, or by property inheritance, as discussed in the next section.

At the same time, a browser generally applies a set of predefined formatting rules to the elements in a document. For example, a browser assumes that headings are of a particular font size and weight, that **EM** text should be in italics (and **STRONG** in bold), that lists have a certain indent and vertical spacing around the items, and so on. These browser-specified properties also specify the default font family and font size for the browser (in the case of Figure 3.7, the default font family is Times New Roman). Note that some of these default properties can be set by the user: For example, most browsers let the user select the default font family and size (usually using a dialog box or drop-down menus), and some even let the user set default heading alignment, or default margins for the page.

Figure 3.6 Example HTML document illustrating font-related stylesheet properties, and also illustrating simple CSS rules employing element- and class-based selectors. The rendering of this document by the MSIE 3.02 browser is shown in Figure 3.7. Stylesheet rules are in italics.

```
<HTML><HEAD>
<TITLE>Simple Test of Font Related Styles</TITLE>
<STYLE>
<!--
.special    {font-family:  "Swiss921 BT", "Arial Black", sans-serif}
.special2   {font-family:  "Comic Sans MS", fantasy}
P.goofy     {font-style:   italic;
             font-family:  Garamond, "Times New Roman", serif;}
EM          {font-weight:  bold;
             font-family:  arial, sans-serif}
-->
</STYLE>
</HEAD>
<BODY BGCOLOR="#ffffff">
<H1 ALIGN="center" CLASS="special2">Meeting Announcement</H1>
<H2 ALIGN="center" CLASS="special">Calling All Aardvarks!</H2>
<P>This note is to announce an upcoming meeting of
   <EM>Calling All Aardvarks</EM>, a new organization
   devoted to our furry forest friend, the aardvark. This
   largely uncelebrated animal is known for its friendly
   nature, unswerving <STRONG>devotion</STRONG> to community,
   and, of course, for eating ants. What animal could
   possibly make a better live-in companion?</P>
<P CLASS="goofy">Of course, not everyone is ready
   to have an aardvark as a pet. First, you must be
   <STRONG>willing</STRONG> to have lots of ants around the house
   -- after all, if you don't, then your new friend will have
   nothing to eat. <EM>And they</EM> must be live ants, as
   aardvarks don't like dead ones (or plastic ones,
   as discovered by Julian Bashir, our association
   president, some 8 years ago).</P>
<P>But what cost a <SPAN CLASS="special2">few ants</SPAN>,
   if in exchange for the kindest and gentlest of
   companions....</P>
<HR>
</BODY>
</HTML>
```

Figure 3.7 MSIE 3.02 rendering of the document listed in Figure 3.6.

Within CSS, an author should think of these default properties as being equivalent to a *default CSS stylesheet*: for example, if the browser's default font family and font size are "Times New Roman" and 12pt, then the corresponding default CSS rule for the font properties might be:

```
BODY    {font-size:      12pt;
         font-family:    "Times New Roman", "Times Roman", "Times", serif;
         font-style:     normal;
         font-weight:    normal;
         font-variant:   normal;
        }
```

The concept of a default stylesheet is important, as it lets the author construct simple stylesheets, similar in size to the one used in Figure 3.6, since it is necessary to specify only the formatting details *different* from those in the default stylesheet. Thus, to change the default font size in the document to 14pt, but not change any other properties, the stylesheet rule would be:

```
BODY {font-size:    14pt; }
```

CSS Property Inheritance

The rule given at the end of the previous section implies that the default font size for *every* element in the document will be 14pt, through what is known as *property inheritance*. In CSS, the principle of property inheritance states that, unless otherwise specified, an element inherits property values from the element within which it is contained (its *parent* element). For example, a **P** within a document **BODY** inherits the font specification defined for the **BODY**, while a **STRONG** element within a **P** inherits the font family associated with the **P**. Figures 3.6 and 3.7 illustrate this in practice: Here the default font is Times Roman, so that the first and third paragraphs inherit this font family, as does the **STRONG** element inside the first paragraph. Similarly, the **STRONG** element inside the second paragraph inherits the Garamond font from the parent element **P**, since the CSS rules for this **P** specifically request this font, overriding the Times Roman default.

The inheritance principle helps enormously in writing stylesheets, since properties that are inherited do not need to be stated over and over again. For example, specifying the rule

```
BODY {font-family: "Times New Roman", "Times Roman", "Times", serif }
```

means that the font family need not be specified in any other rules, unless the author wishes to override this font, for example to specify a different font for heading or emphasized text. A quick look at Figure 3.6 shows that this feature was used here—font family specifications are only present to override the value inherited from the parent element.

CSS Property Cascading

In complex stylesheets, it is common to find multiple stylesheet rules applying to the same element. For example, consider the simple document shown in Figure 3.8, and rendered for display in Figure 3.9. This document has three CSS rules that apply to paragraphs. The first rule applies only to paragraphs of **CLASS**="goofy", while the other two apply to any paragraphs at all. These rules also contain conflicting properties: For example, the first rule calls for normal (non-italicized) text, while the third rule calls for italics. How should these conflicts be resolved?

These rules are resolved according to the CSS cascading principle. In short: Given a collection of rules that apply to the same element, the properties that are applied are those that are *closest* to the element—thus, closer properties override ones that are further away. In CSS, a rule is closer to an element if the selector applies *more specifically* to the element. For example, a selector of the form P.goofy is more specific than the selector P, so that the properties associated with the selector P.goofy will override the properties specified by the other two selectors in our example.

Let us look at Figure 3.8 and see how this cascade plays out. Consider the first paragraph in Figure 3.8. This paragraph has no **CLASS** attribute, so only the second and third rules

```
P   { font-family: Arial, sans-serif;}
P   { font-family: Comic Sans MS;
      font-style: italic;              }
```

apply to this paragraph. The second rule has a font-family selector that requests the Arial font, while the third rule has two properties: one requesting the "Comic Sans MS" font and the other requesting that the font be in italics. This second declaration will certainly be used, so that the text will be italicized. In the case of the font family property, the browser will use the "last specified" value, namely the "Comic Sans MS" font. The result is the paragraph in the Comic Sans MS italic font, shown in Figure 3.9.

The second paragraph in Figure 3.8 has the attribute **CLASS**="goofy", so that all three rules,

```
P.goofy { font-style:  normal;            }
P        { font-family: Arial, sans-serif;}
P        { font-family: Comic Sans MS;
           font-style: italic;                }
```

apply here. However, the first rule, with selector `P.goofy`, is much more specific to this element than the other rules, so that all the properties specified by this rule will override those resulting from the other two rules. Thus, the font style is switched back to "normal," although the font family is left unchanged from the Comic Sans MS value set by the other two rules, since this more specific rule does not set the font family. The resulting paragraph is shown at the bottom of Figure 3.9, and is rendered in a regular Comic Sans MS font.

This simple example should give a feel for how cascading rules are applied to determine formatting properties for specific elements. The details are described in Chapter 6.

NOTE Default Stylesheets and Author Control of Presentation

If an author wants to control such features as default font size and face, page margins, and so on, he or she must set default properties for these characteristics in the document stylesheet. Only in this way can an author be sure to override any default font or size settings specified in the browser.

At the same time, next-generation browsers will give the reader the option of overriding the author-supplied stylesheet. This is required simply because users are the best judge of their own needs, and may need to override default settings to make the text usable: for example, to expand the font for readability by visually impaired users, or for reading when projected in a classroom. These issues are discussed in Chapter 9.

Example 2: Some More CSS Selectors and Rules

This example, shown in the document in Figure 3.10 and the browser renderings in Figures 3.11 and 3.12, looks at some additional, but slightly more complex, CSS rules—in particular, **ID**-based

Figure 3.8 Example HTML document that illustrates the cascading properties of CSS rules. The rendering of this document by a CSS-aware browser is shown in Figure 3.9. Stylesheet rules are in italics.

```
<HTML><HEAD><TITLE>Simple Cascade Demonstration</TITLE>
<STYLE><!--
P.goofy  { font-style:  normal;                }
P         { font-family: Arial, sans-serif;}
P         { font-family: Comic Sans MS;
             font-style: italic;               }
--></STYLE>
</HEAD>
<BODY BGCOLOR="#ffffff">
<H2 ALIGN="center">Amazing World of Cascade!</H2>
<P>
  No, this is not an advertisement for <EM>Cascade</EM>,
  the laundry detergent. This instead is a demonstration
  of stylesheet cascading, whereby properties are overridden
  by other properties specified by "closer" rules.</P>
<P CLASS="goofy">
  Why do you care? Simply because if you do
  not properly understand how cascading works, you will
  spend endless hours trying to figure out why
  your rules don't work properly!</P>

<HR>
</BODY></HTML>
```

selectors and at pseudo-class selectors. An **ID**-based selector relates a CSS rule to the **ID** attribute value of an element, and is very similar to the class-based selectors discussed in the previous examples. A pseudo-class selector, on the other hand, is based on class-like properties that are not determined from the HTML markup.

Let us first look at the rules that affect paragraph formatting. There are three such rules:

```
P        {font-family: verdana, sans-serif}
#foo     {font-family: arial;
           font-style:  italic;}]
.flub    {font-style:  normal;}
```

The first applies to any **P** element, while the second and third apply to any element with **ID**="foo" or **CLASS**="flub" respectively. Only the first rule applies to the first paragraph, which is thus rendered in the Verdana font, as shown in Figure 3.11. However, all three of these rules apply to the second paragraph, which means that cascading must be used to determine which properties will be applied.

CSS treats **ID**-based selectors as having a higher priority than **CLASS**-based ones. This makes sense, when you consider that any number of elements can have the same **CLASS** value, while only

**Figure 3.9 Rendering of the document shown in Figure 3.8 by the Netscape
Navigator 4 browser. The heading is rendered using the Times Roman font, while
the two paragraphs are rendered using Comic Sans MS.**

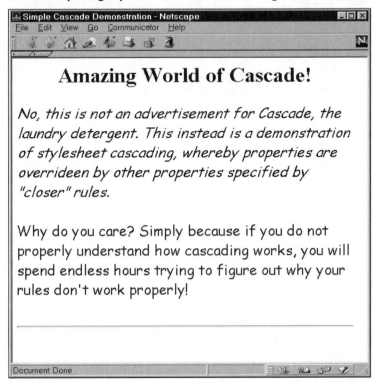

one element can have a given **ID**. As a result, the properties specified by **ID** override those set by
the other two rules, so that the second paragraph is presented in an Arial italic font.

Pseudo-class Selectors

Also of interest is the hypertext anchor in the second paragraph element in Figure 3.10, which in
Figure 3.11 is rendered in a Times Roman bold italic font. This is related to the `:link` pseudo-
class-based selector. In CSS, pseudo-class values select for class-like properties that are not coded
into the HTML document. In CSS1 there are only three such pseudo-classes, all related to hypertext links. These property names and their meanings are "link" (selects for unvisited hypertext
links); "visited" (selects for visited links); and "active" (selects for active links, where an active link
is defined as the state when the link is activated). A pseudo-class is indicated by preceding the
selector string by a colon, as in the `:link` selector at the top of Figure 3.10. This particular selector selects for all hypertext links, and requests a Times New Roman bold normal font. Note, however, that this browser does not properly set the font style property (this is a bug in MSIE 3.02).

Figure 3.10 A simple document illustrating ID, CLASS, and pseudo-class selectors. The rendering of this document by a CSS-aware browser is shown in Figures 3.11 and 3.12. Stylesheet rules are in italics.

```
<HTML><HEAD>
<TITLE>Simple Test of ID and Pseudoclass Selectors</TITLE>
<STYLE>
<!--
BODY      {font-family:  Garamond; }               /* Default font is Garamond */
P         {font-family:  verdana, sans-serif;} /* P's in Verdana          */
#foo      {font-family:  arial;
           font-style:   italic;}                 /* #foo in Arial italic    */
.flub     {font-style:   normal;}                 /* .flub is normal         */
:link     {font-style:   normal;
           font-family:  "Times New Roman";      /* Links are bold times    */
           font-weight:  bold;           }  /* New roman....           */
:visited {font-family:  "Arial Black";
           font-weight:  bold;           }
-->
</STYLE>
</HEAD>
<BODY BGCOLOR="#ffffff">
<H2> ID and Pseudoclass Selectors </H2>

<P>Here is a paragraph in the Verdana font, as specified
   by the rule associated with the selector <CODE>P</CODE>.
   Not terribly interesting, but I am sure you get the idea. </P>
<P CLASS="flub" ID="foo">Here is a paragraph of
   <B>CLASS</B>="flub" and <B>ID</B>="foo." This is
   affected by three rules: note how the rule with the
   ID-based selector is considered more specific to the
   <B>P</B> element than the rule with the CLASS-based
   selector, so that the font is set to Arial italic. This
   should be be compared with <A HREF="fig3-8.html">the
   previous examples</A> of purely class-based selectors.</P>

<HR>
</BODY></HTML>
```

Finally, Figure 3.12 displays the document after exploring the hypertext link. In this case, the rule with the :visited selector is applied to the anchor element content, so that it is now formatted using Arial Black, according to this rule. Unfortunately, Internet Explorer 3.02 does not properly format this situation, and does not allocate enough space for the text. Such problems are remedied in version 4 of the browser.

Figure 3.11 Display, by the MSIE 3.02 browser, of the document listed in Figure 3.10. Note in particular the formatting of the hypertext link using a bold Times Roman italic font.

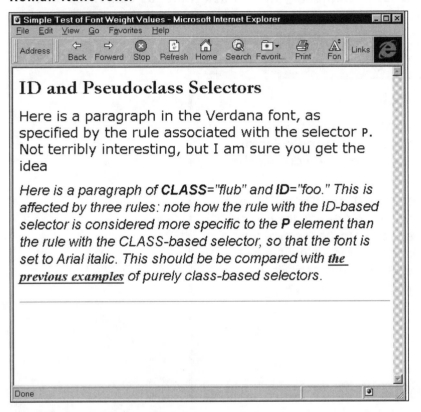

Example 3: Font Family and Style Specification
In this example, we will look at the different font-related properties, and discuss how they are used to select desired fonts.

Font Style
Font-style specifies the desired italicized or slanted nature for the font. In general, fonts can come in three slanted variations: a *normal* or roman style, corresponding to the default vertical font; an *oblique* style, which is essentially the same as the normal font but tilted at an angle; or an *italic* style, which is a variant that is slanted and more cursive than the standard font, and which often contains characters that are different in shape from the regular or *italic* versions. Figure 3.14 shows a comparison of the regular and italic variants, here for the Garamond font: Note how the italic version is slanted and cursive, and that the letter "a" is in fact drawn quite differently in the italic face.

Figure 3.12 Display, by the MSIE 3.02 browser, of the document listed in Figure 3.10, but *after* following (and returning from) the hypertext link. Note that the text within the link is now formatted using Arial Black italic, as compared with the bold Times Roman italic font used in Figure 3.11.

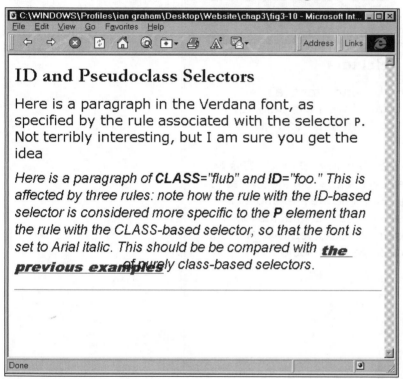

CSS defines three `font-style` property values that correspond to these three variations: `normal` for the normal or upright font; `oblique` for fonts that are slanted but do not have any added cursive features; and `italic` for fonts that are slanted and have extra cursive features. Note that you can only specify one style in a font style rule; the CSS specifications define the result should the desired style not be available.

Fonts themselves are described using a number of terms in addition to oblique and italic, although these alternative terms are usually equivalent to one of the three CSS values. Table 3.2 lists these common names alongside their CSS equivalents. This table will help you determine the correct CSS value appropriate to the font style you wish to use for your chosen font family.

Of course, the requested style may not be available, either because it just isn't—many computers have either an italic or an oblique variant of a font, but not both—or because the requested font family was not available, and the alternative being used does not support the desired style. CSS specifies the following rules for selecting an alternative style, given the indicated preferred value:

Table 3.2 CSS Font-Style Values and Their Relationship to Terms Commonly Used to Describe Fonts.

CSS Value	Common Terms Used in Traditional Font Descriptions
normal	roman, upright
oblique	oblique, slanted, incline
italic	italic, cursive, kursiv

`font-style: normal`	Choose the normal, unstylized version of the font (this is always available). This is the default value.
`font-style: oblique`	Choose the oblique version. If oblique is not available, look for an oblique font in the next font listed in the `font-family` declaration. If no oblique form is found, use the `normal` form of the font.
`font-style: italic`	Choose the italic version. If italic is not available, choose oblique; if oblique is not available, choose normal.

Some examples of font-style usage in CSS stylesheets are shown in Figures 3.13 and 3.14. Note that many commonly used computer fonts (e.g., Times New Roman or Garamond under Windows 95) do not have oblique versions.

WARNING Incomplete MSIE 3.0 Support

MSIE 3.0 does not support `font-style: oblique`. If you expect your documents to be viewed on MSIE 3.0, you should use `font-style: italic`.

Font Variant

Font variant selectors cover standard variations of a font that are not related to the family, style, or weight, but that are related to how the font is presented. CSS supports only two values for font variant. These are:

`font-variant: normal`—Choose the normal version of the font (this is always available). This is the default value.

`font-variant: small-caps`—Present the text using small-caps lettering; for example, the phrase "Angels in America" as "ANGELS IN AMERICA." If this variant is not available, the text will be presented without any modification in capitalization.

Figure 3.13 Simple document illustrating the `font-style` **and** `font-variant` **properties applied to the Garamond and Arial font families. Stylesheet content is in italics. The rendering of this document by an early beta version of Netscape Navigator 4.0 is shown in Figure 3.14. Note that this early version does not support the small-caps font variant.**

```
<HTML><HEAD>
<TITLE>Simple Test of Font Style and Variant</TITLE>
<STYLE>
<!--
DIV.gar     {font-family:  garamond;   }
DIV.ari     {font-family:  Arial;      }
P.normal    {font-style:   normal;     }
P.oblique   {font-style:   oblique;    }
P.italic    {font-style:   italic;     }
P.smallcap  {font-variant: small-caps:}
-->
</STYLE></HEAD>
<BODY>
<H1>Font-Style and Variant </H1>

<TABLE WIDTH="100%" CELLPADDING=5>
<TR BGCOLOR="#dddddd">
   <TD><B><I>STYLE</I></B>                               </TD>
   <TD><DIV CLASS="gar"><B>Garamond</B></DIV>            </TD>
   <TD><DIV CLASS="ari"><B>Arial</B>    </DIV>           </TD>
</TR><TR>
   <TD BGCOLOR="#eeeeee"><B>Normal </B>                  </TD>
   <TD><DIV CLASS="gar"><P CLASS="normal"> AaBbGgQqYyZz </P></DIV></TD>
   <TD><DIV CLASS="ari"><P CLASS="normal"> AaBbGgQqYyZz </P></DIV></TD>
</TR><TR BGCOLOR="#dddddd">
   <TD BGCOLOR="#eeeeee"><B>Oblique </B>                 </TD>
   <TD><DIV CLASS="gar"><P CLASS="oblique">AaBbGgQqYyZz </P></DIV></TD>
   <TD><DIV CLASS="ari"><P CLASS="oblique">AaBbGgQqYyZz </P></DIV></TD>
</TR><TR>
   <TD BGCOLOR="#eeeeee"><B>Italic </B>                  </TD>
   <TD><DIV CLASS="gar"><P CLASS="italic"> AaBbGgQqYyZz </P></DIV></TD>
   <TD><DIV CLASS="ari"><P CLASS="italic"> AaBbGgQqYyZz </P></DIV></TD>
</TR><TR BGCOLOR="#dddddd">
   <TD BGCOLOR="#eeeeee"><B>Small Caps</B>               </TD>
   <TD><DIV CLASS="gar"><P CLASS="smallcap">AaBbGgQqYyZz</P></DIV></TD>
   <TD><DIV CLASS="ari"><P CLASS="smallcap">AaBbGgQqYyZz</P></DIV></TD>
</TR></TABLE>
<HR>
</BODY></HTML>
```

Figure 3.14 Rendering of the document listed in Figure 3.13 by an early beta version of Netscape Navigator 4.0. Note how this browser does not understand the small-caps variant.

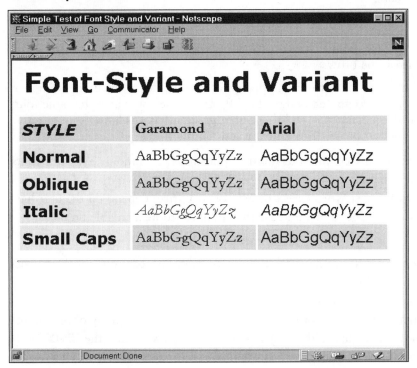

The example document in Figures 3.13 attempts to use `font-variant`. Note, in Figure 3.14, how this early beta version of Netscape Navigator 4 does not support this property.

There are many other possible font variants, such as outline or shadowed fonts, or fonts with small-cap numerals. There is currently no way in CSS to reference these variants.

NOTE `Font-Variant` Not Supported by Netscape Navigator 4, MSIE 3

The `font-variant` property is not supported by Netscape Navigator 4.0 or by MSIE 3. This property is also not supported by MSIE 4 beta 1.

Font Family

`Font-family` specifies the desired family for the font. If a family is not specified, then it is inherited from the parent element, as illustrated in the previous examples. The value for this property is given as a comma-separated list of fonts, in decreasing order of preference. Font names that consist of more than one word must be placed inside quotation marks. When formatting the document, the browser will look through the list of fonts from left to right, and will use the first one that is available. For example, the property

```
font-family: "Swiss921 BT", "Arial Black", sans-serif
```

requests first the "Swiss921 BT" font; failing that, the "Arial Black" font; and failing that, the default sans-serif font available on the browser.

As mentioned many times, it can be hard to select appropriate fonts, due to the limited number of fonts likely to be available on the computer, and to the different names by which the same font may be known. To ensure portable documents, and to ensure "graceful" degradation should the desired font(s) be unavailable, an author needs to follow a few simple rules:

1. **Where possible, use fonts that are common to multiple platforms.** Commonly available fonts and their system-dependent names are listed in Tables 3.3 through 3.7. Many of these fonts (such as those installed with Corel WordPerfect or Microsoft Office) depend on the user having installed a word processor/office suite, and are thus unlikely to be available on many browsers.

2. **Include the different operating-system names for the chosen font.** For example, for the "Times Roman" font, the selector should be:
   ```
   font-family: "Times new Roman", times
   ```
   since "Times New Roman" is the name for this font under the Microsoft family of operating systems, and "Times" is the name under the Macintosh operating system and the UNIX X-Windows windowing system. Note that font names that contain spaces must be placed inside single or double quotation marks.

3. **Provide alternative font names that would be appropriate replacements,** particularly if it is likely that the desired font is unavailable on some platforms. For example, suppose the desired font is "Footlight MT Light." This font comes as part of Microsoft Office, and is thus probably not available on all systems, so that alternatives should be offered. From Tables 3.6 and 3.7, we see that some possible alternatives are "Garamond" and "BernhardModBT." Thus the declaration might be:
   ```
   font-family: "Footlight MT Light", Garamond, "BernhardModBT"
   ```

4. **Give the CSS family name of the desired font as the final family option.** Then, if none of the specified fonts are available, the browser will (hopefully) select an appropriate, available font from this generic family. Following upon the preceding example, the full rule would be:
   ```
   font-family: "Footlight MT Light", Garamond, "BernhardModBT", serif
   ```
   where the final specification requests any available serif font should neither Garamond nor

BernhardModBT be available, and leaves the choice of font up to the browser.

At present, most systems do not have appropriate default fonts for the generic "cursive" or "fantasy" font family categories. Most next-generation browsers, however, will come with appropriate default fonts.

There is, of course, no guarantee that these rules will work under all circumstances! However, following these rules will make documents as universal as possible, given the current limitations on font availability.

NOTE Some Generic Font Families Not Supported by Navigator 4.0

Netscape Navigator 4.0 is not equipped with fonts appropriate to the generic "fantasy" or "cursive" font families. If these families are requested in a CSS rule, Navigator 4.0 will substitute the default sans-serif (for fantasy) or serif (for cursive) fonts. This is true even if there are cursive or fantasy fonts installed on the system, since the browser has no way of determining the true nature of these fonts (i.e., which are of type "fantasy", or which are of type "cursive"). MSIE 3, on the other hand, can make more reasonable substitutions for the "cursive" and "fantasy" types, as can MSIE 4.

Table 3.3 Standard Fonts on Default Windows 3.1/95/NT Systems, with Examples

Font Names	Example Text (12 Point Font)
A) Cursive Fonts	*(none)*
B) Fantasy Fonts	*(none)*
C) Sans-Serif Fonts	
Arial	Example Text (#$%{&}).
D) Serif Fonts	
Times New Roman	Example Text (#$%{&}).
E) Monospace Fonts	
Courier New	Example Text (#$%{&}).

Table 3.4 Standard Fonts on Default Macintosh Systems, with Examples

Font Names	Example Text (12 Point Font)	
A) Cursive Fonts	*(none)*	Continued
B) Fantasy Fonts	*(none)*	

Table 3.4 *Continued*

Font Names	Example Text (12 Point Font)
C) Sans-Serif Fonts	
Chicago	**Example Text (#$%{&}).**
Geneva	Example Text (#$%{&}).
Helvetica	Example Text (#$%{&}).
D) Serif Fonts	
New York	Example Text (#$%{&}).
Palatino	Example Text (#$%{&}).
Times	Example Text (#$%{&}).
E) Monospace Fonts	
Courier	`Example Text (#$%{&}).`
Monaco	`Example Text (#$%{&}).`

Table 3.5 Standard Fonts on UNIX X-Windows Systems, with Examples

Font Names	Example Text (12 Point Font)
A) Cursive Fonts	
Zapf Chancery	*Example Text (#$%{&}).*
B) Fantasy Fonts	*(none)*
C) Sans-Serif Fonts	
Helvetica	Example Text (#$%{&}).
Lucida (*on some systems:* "Lucida Sans")	Example Text (#$%{&}).
D) Serif Fonts	
TC Bookman	**Example Text (#$%{&}).**
New Century Schoolbook	Example Text (#$%{&}).
Palatino	Example Text (#$%{&}).
Times	Example Text (#$%{&}).
E) Monospace Fonts	
Courier	`Example Text (#$%{&}).`

Table 3.6 Fonts Provided with Microsoft Word/Office; Microsoft Internet Explorer 3 and Greater; or the Microsoft Set of Freely Distributable TrueType Fonts. These fonts are available on both Windows and Macintosh platforms.

Font Names	Availability			Example Text (12 Point Font)
A) Cursive Fonts				
Brush Script MT			O	*Example Text ($%{&}).*
B) Fantasy Fonts				
Arial Black	E	F	O	**Example Text (#$%{& {(**
Algerian			O	EXAMPLE TEXT (#$%{&}).
Bragadoccio			O	**Example Text (#$%{&}).**
Britannic Bold			O	**Example Text (#$%{&}).**
Comic Sans MS	E	F	O	Example Text (#$%{&}).
Desdemona			O	EXAMPLE TEXT (#$%{&}).
Impact	E	F	O	**Example Text (#$%{&}).**
Kino MT			O	Example Text (#$%{&}).
Playbill			O	Example Text (#$%{&}).
Matura MT Script Capitals			O	*Example Text (#$%{&}).*
Wide Latin			O	**Example Text (#$%{&})**
C) Sans-Serif Fonts				
Arial		F		Example Text (#$%{&}).
Arial Narrow			O	Example Text (#$%{&}).
Arial Rounded MT Bold			O	**Example Text (#$%{&}).**
Haettenschweiler			O	Example Text (#$%{&}).
Trebuchet MS		F		Example Text (#$%{&}).
Verdana	E	F	P	Example Text (#$%{&}).
D) Serif Fonts				
Book Antiqua			O	Example Text (#$%{&}).
Bookman Old Style			O	Example Text (#$%{&}).

Continued

Table 3.6 *Continued*

Font Names	Availability	Example Text (12 Point Font)
Century Schoolbook	O	Example Text (#$%{&}).
Colonna MT	O	Example Text (#$%{&}).
Footlight MT Light	O	Example Text (#$%{&}).
Garamond	O	Example Text (#$%{&}).
Times New Roman	F	Example Text (#$%{&}).
Georgia	F	Example Text (#$%{&}).
E) Monospace Fonts		
Courier New	F	Example Text (#$%{ &}).

Key to Availability

E	Comes with Microsoft Internet Explorer 3.02 and later
F	Comes as a free TrueType font from Microsoft; available from: http://www.microsoft.com/truetype/
O	Comes with Microsoft Word 6.0 / Microsoft Office 95 and 97
P	Comes with Microsoft Office 97 only

Table 3.7 Some of the Fonts Provided with Corel WordPerfect 6 and Later. Note that Corel WordPerfect 7 Suite contains over 150 fonts.

Font Names	Example Text (12 Point Font)
A) Cursive Fonts	
Brush Script MT	Example Text ($%{&}).
Ribbon 131Bd BT	Example Text (#$% {&}).
ShelleyVolante BT	Example Text (#$%{ &}).
B) Fantasy Fonts	
Swis721 BlkEx BT	Example Text (#$%{&}).
Swis721 BdOul BT	Example Text (#$%{&}).
Humanist 521 Cn BT	Example Text (#$%{&}).
Blackletter686 BT	Example Text (#$%{&}).
Brush738 BT	Example Text (#$%{&}).
Caslon Openface BT	Example Text (#$%{&}).

Continued

Table 3.7 *Continued*

Font Names	Example Text (12 Point Font)
Engravers Gothic BT	EXAMPLE TEXT (#$%{&}).
Onyx BT	Example Text (#$%{&}).
OzHandicraft BT	Example Text (#$%{&}).
C) Sans-Serif Fonts	
Humanist 521 BT	Example Text (#$%{&}).
Humanist 521 Lt BT	Example Text (#$%{&}).
D) Serif Fonts	
Arrus BT	Example Text (#$%{&}).
BernhardMod BT	Example Text (#$%{&}).
GeoSlab 703 Lt BT	Example Text (#$%{&}).
E) Monospace Fonts	(*none*)

Font Matching and Font Downloading

Of course the preceding procedure for defining appropriate `font-family` property values is both time-consuming and inefficient—after all, the author has no way of knowing if the user actually has a specific font. Thus, it would be nice if in addition to specifying an exact font, an author could also specify some generic font characteristics, which the browser could use to locate the local font that best matches those criteria.

This soon may be possible. In the near future, CSS may let the author specify the *PANOSE* number for the desired font. A PANOSE number is a numeric code that parameterizes several properties that describe a font. Font matching systems, common on many desktop publishing systems, can use PANOSE numbers to locate substitute fonts to replace those that are requested by a document, but unavailable. This idea, and its possible relationship to the next generation of CSS, will be discussed in more detail in Chapter 9.

A second alternative would be for the document to reference font files from a remote server, such that the browser could retrieve any desired fonts and use them at will. This approach has the advantage of providing near-ideal typographic control. But there are several problems, including copyright and payment—how will the users pay for fonts they have downloaded for use—and speed—font files are large, and would be slow to download.

Netscape believes they have found a way around these problems, via a compact font format known as *TrueDoc*. Developed by Bitstream, TrueDoc stores a scalable font-drawing algorithm in a tightly compressed format, which can be downloaded with an HTML document or stylesheet, and then used to generate the fonts in a document. Netscape has integrated support for TrueDoc into their Navigator 4 browser and also into their HTML editing tool—the tool can automatically create TrueDoc files when an author is preparing a document, and will save these alongside the document. Then, when the Netscape browser retrieves the document it also retrieves the font files, and can reproduce the desired fonts. Copyright is preserved by binding the fonts directly to the document that created them—thus the fonts cannot be reused by other applications.

The TrueDoc approach is exciting, but is also only available on Netscape Navigator 4. This technology is discussed in more detail in Chapter 9.

Example 4: Specifying Font Weights

Font weight defines the thickness or weight of the lines with which the font is drawn. Typically, words such as "light," "regular," "bold," and "black" are used to specify the weight of a particular font variant, but the actual words used—and the meanings of those words—varies greatly from font to font. For example, one family's "regular" font may actually have the same weight as another family's "bold." At the same time, not all font families come with the same number of weight variations—some fonts support only four or five weights, while others support nine.

This variability presents a great problem for stylesheets, where there is a need to specify relative (i.e., bolder or lighter weight) as well as absolute weights, in a largely font-independent way. This, of course, is because the author can never be sure what font will actually be available, and thus needs to be able to specify weight in a way that will work properly regardless of the actual font used.

Absolute Font Weights

The CSS specifications define nine different absolute weights, as integers ranging from 100 (lightest) to 900 (darkest) in steps of 100. The actual weight associated with these numbers will vary depending on the font—the scale, however, guarantees that each value has a weight that is at least as heavy as, and probably heavier than, the value below it. Thus 500 will be heavier than or equal to 400, and so on.

Named Font Weights

In addition to these numerical weights, CSS supports two named weights: `normal` and `bold`. These correspond, on the numerical scale, to the values 400 and 700 respectively. Most of the time, these are the only weights used, and correspond to the "regular" weight plus a "bold" weight used for emphasis. For much typography, an author can simply use these named weights, and not bother about the more complex numerical scale.

In some cases, of course, this two-weight limit is too restricting. For finer layout control, an author needs a way of properly mapping the known weight descriptions for a given font onto the proper CSS numerical values. This is complicated by the fact that not all fonts support nine different weights, and that different fonts use different font weight naming schemes. The procedures described below should let you turn any font weight into the correct CSS numerical value.

Fonts Supporting Nine Weights

Some fonts actually come with nine distinct weights. In these cases, the nine weights directly correspond to the CSS weight numbers, with 100 corresponding to the lightest weight, and 900 to the heaviest. Thus if you want to use the sixth weight value of a font that supports nine weights, you would use:

```
font-weight: 600
```

OpenType (a planned merging of the TrueType and PostScript Type 3 scalable font formats) fonts support nine weight values. Unfortunately, OpenType is still just a proposed font format, and is not in use.

Fonts Supporting Fewer Than Nine Weights

Most fonts support fewer than nine weights—and support these weights via a bewildering collection of names. The trick for a stylesheet author is to find out how these weight names relate to appropriate CSS numerical values. Then, the author can use the proper numeric code, knowing that the browser will convert this number into the appropriate weight—or into an appropriate weight for a substituted font, should the desired font not be available. This conversion process follows a complicated algorithm developed as part of the CSS specification. Fortunately, stylesheet authors do not need to know this algorithm. Unfortunately, they do need to know the appropriate procedure for determining the correct numeric weights, which is almost as complicated! This seven-stage procedure is as follows:

1. If there is a font family member labeled "book," "regular," "roman," or "normal," assign this font a weight of 400. The value 400 corresponds to the standard weight of any font.

2. If there is a font labeled "medium," and if step 1 already assigned a font to the weight value 400, then the "medium" font should be assigned a weight of 500. If step 1 did not assign a font to the value 400, the "medium" font should be assigned the weight of 400.

3. If there is a font labeled "bold," this font should be assigned a weight of 700. If there is no font specifically labeled "bold," but there are one or more fonts heavier than those assigned to 400 and/or 500, then the author must determine which font weight would correspond to a generic "bold" font, and assign this font weight the value 700.

4. If there are remaining font weights heavier than "bold," these should, in order of increasing weight, be assigned the weight values 800 and 900. If there are still unassigned and heavier weights, these should be assigned the weight of 900. For example, if there were fonts with weights "bold," "very bold," "super bold," and "super-duper bold," in increasing order of weight, then these would be assigned CSS numerical weights of 700, 800, 900, and 900 respectively (the last two are assigned the same numerical weight).

5. If there are remaining fonts with weights less than "bold" but greater than "medium" or, if there is no "medium," greater than the font assigned to 400, these should all be assigned to the unassigned value 600, and also possibly the value 500, provided 500 was not assigned at step 2.

6. If there are fonts with weights less than "normal," these should be assigned the values 300, 200, and 100 in order of decreasing weight.

7. If there remain any lighter font family members, these should all be assigned a weight of 100.

If you are feeling a bit woozy after this, don't worry—the preceding seven-step algorithm is possibly the most complicated aspect of CSS stylesheets. It's mostly downhill from here.

As an example, the ITC "Century Condensed" font comes in the four weights "light," "book," "bold," and "ultra." Following the above rules, these should be assigned the CSS weight values:

Weight Name	CSS Weight Value
light	300
book	400
bold	700
ultra	800

Figure 3.15 lists many of the common terms used in describing font weights, along with their "usual" relative position on the weight scale, from lightest to heaviest. Although this list corresponds, in many cases, to the actual CSS ordering, it is not always so—for complex font weighting schemes you must check your assignments using the above algorithm.

Of course a little theory is a nice thing, but a few examples help to bring issues into focus. Figure 3.16 is a simple HTML document that uses all the possible absolute font weight measures; the browser rendering of this document is shown in Figures 3.17 and 3.18. The font used is "Bookman Old Style." The only difference between Figures 3.17 and 3.18 is the font size: The font in 3.18 is larger than in 3.17.

It is clear from Figures 3.17 and 3.18 that the browser has attempted to create a scale of font weights from 100 to 900, in this case with three weight variants. Figure 3.18, however, looks a bit odd: The font at weight 500 is wider than the font at weight 600. Note that this problem is not restricted to Netscape Navigator, but occurs also with Internet Explorer, and is apparently an artifact of the rendering engine used to draw the fonts.

Relative Font Weights

The above absolute weight procedure is complex, and in many cases easily avoided. Usually, what the author actually wants to specify is a heavier or lighter weight relative to that of the surrounding text, for example to highlight emphasized text or to otherwise mark text as distinct from the surroundings. The safest way to do so is using the relative font weight assignments:

```
font-weight: lighter--a lighter-weight font
font-weight: bolder--a heavier-weight font
```

Figure 3.15 Typical words used to describe font weights and typical weight value assignments. Actual values depend on the particular font.

Lightest ◄——————————————————————————————► *Heaviest*								
Ultra light	Extra Light	Light Thin	Book Regular Roman Normal	Medium	Semi Semi-bold Demi Demi-bold	Bold	Heavy Black	Extra Black Super Ultra
100	200	300	400	500	600	700	800	900

By specifying a relative weight, an author in principle guarantees that the browser will choose a visibly lighter or heavier font, provided one is available. On the other hand, if the font used is of weight 400 and the author specifies a font of weight 500, then there is no guarantee that the browser will display a bolder font even if one is available, since the weight of 500 may in fact map onto the same weight as the surrounding text.

However, in practice these values are less useful than they seem, since there often is no "lighter" or "bolder" version available. This is illustrated in Figures 3.19 and 3.20. In this example, these properties are applied to **SPAN** elements—note that **SPAN** element content is also underlined to make the content stand out from the regular text. As can be seen in Figure 3.20, the values `lighter` and `bolder` do not always lead to a change in weight here because the font comes in only four weights, such that there are no fonts "lighter" than normal.

Note also that these `font-weight` property values do not work at all under MSIE 3.

Example 5: Specifying Font Sizes

The final font property is `font-size`, which specifies the size of the font, and does so using a variety of length units. Length units are used in various places in CSS, and are discussed in detail in Appendix B. There are essentially two ways to specify length: as an absolute length (e.g., inches or centimeters), or as a relative length. Absolute lengths can be given in inches (in), centimeters (cm), millimeters (mm), picas (pc), or points (pt). Absolute length is specified as a real number followed by the two-letter code corresponding to the units.

Absolute lengths are particularly useful for absolute typesetting, but not as useful on the Web, where an author never knows exactly how large the display really is, or the relationship between a given absolute length and a display pixel. For the Web, it is therefore better to be able to measure lengths in relative units. There are three relative length measures in CSS: em units (em), ex units (ex), and percentages (%).

When relative units are employed, `font-size` specifications determine the size relative to the font size in the *parent element*. For example, if the declaration

```
font-size: 1.5em
```

Figure 3.16 Simple HTML document demonstrating all the absolute font-weight property values. Renderings of this document by a CSS-aware browser are found in Figures 3.17 and 3.18. Stylesheet content is in italics.

```
<HTML><HEAD><TITLE>Simple Test of Absolute Font Weight Values</TITLE>
<STYLE><!--
.a100     {font-weight: 100}
.a200     {font-weight: 200}
.a300     {font-weight: 300}
.a400     {font-weight: 400}
.a500     {font-weight: 500}
.a600     {font-weight: 600}
.a700     {font-weight: 700}
.a800     {font-weight: 800}
.a900     {font-weight: 900}
.bold     {font-weight: bold}
.normal   {font-weight: normal}
-->
</STYLE> </HEAD>
<BODY>
<H1 ALIGN="center">Test of Absolute Font Weights</H1>
    <P CLASS="a100">Example Weight - 100     </P>
    <P CLASS="a200">Example Weight - 200     </P>
    <P CLASS="a300">Example Weight - 300     </P>
    <P CLASS="a400">Example Weight - 400     </P>
    <P CLASS="a500">Example Weight - 500     </P>
    <P CLASS="a600">Example Weight - 600     </P>
    <P CLASS="a700">Example Weight - 700     </P>
    <P CLASS="a800">Example Weight - 800     </P>
    <P CLASS="a900">Example Weight - 900     </P>
    <P CLASS="bold">Bold Text containing
       <SPAN CLASS="normal">normal</SPAN> text</P>
<HR>
</BODY></HTML>
```

is associated with a **P** inside the **BODY** of a document, and the font size within the **BODY** is 12pt, then the font size inside the **P** will be 18pt.

Pixel units (px) correspond to lengths measured as a number of pixels on the display. This is a very useful unit for absolutely fixing size on a computer display, but is not generalizable to other contexts: For example, a pixel has little meaning when printing to paper. Thus, pixels units are best avoided unless absolute positioning on the display is absolutely required, and provided high-quality print-format output is not important.

The document in Figure 3.21 demonstrates how these units work, using the two properties `font-size` and `text-indent`. This latter property, discussed in detail in the next chapter,

Figure 3.17 Display, by the Netscape Navigator 4 beta 3 browser, of the document listed in Figure 3.16. The font used is "Bookman Old Style."

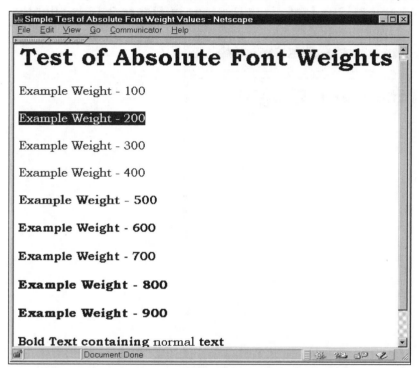

defines an indent for the first line of a paragraph or other block element. Note here that all the absolute length measurements have been adjusted to be the same absolute length.

Relative font units are a bit more complicated. In the case of the font-size property, all the relative units calculate a length relative to the font size of the *parent element:* in this case the **BODY.** For example, the declaration font-size: 200% calls for font size twice as big as that in the parent element. This is not the case with the text-indent property. For indents specified using em or ex units, the text indent is calculated relative to the *font size within* the element (in Figure 3.21, the **DIV** containing the content). However, with percentage units, the text indent is calculated relative to the width of the *entire* **DIV** element, which is unrelated to the size of the font.

Unfortunately, relative font size units did not work properly on Internet Explorer 3, and were somewhat problematic with early beta versions of Navigator 4 and Internet Explorer 4. For example, in Figure 3.22, the font of size "1ex" should actually be smaller than the font of size "1em," but is instead rendered with the same size. The document in Figure 3.21 thus serves as a good test of a browser's support for CSS length units.

Figure 3.18 Display, by the Netscape Navigator 4 beta 3 browser, of the document listed in Figure 3.16. The font being used is "Bookman Old Style." The only difference between Figures 3.18 and 3.17 is font size: The font in Figure 3.18 is slightly smaller.

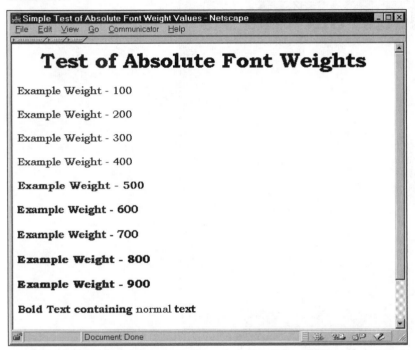

Font Property: Shorthand for Font Properties

Finally, we note that all the font characteristics—style, weight, family, variant, and size—can be grouped together and written down using a single `font` property declaration. This property also can include `line-height` property values (a property that defines the interline spacing within the text). A full discussion of this property is presented in the next chapter.

Chapter Summary

Computer font formats can be divided into two broad categories: *bitmapped* and *scalable.* Whenever possible, a CSS designer should use font names corresponding to scalable fonts.

The *baseline* defines the line upon which the font is set, *ascender* defines the maximum height, and *descender*, the maximum depth. The font size is generally measured from the bottom of the descender to the top of the ascender. Font sizes are usually specified in points. In CSS, 72 points equals 1 inch. Em units measure lengths relative to the font size, where 1 em is equal to the size of the font. Font sizes are specified in CSS via the `font-size` property.

The name for a font is also called the *typeface* family name. Knowledge of names is important because the `font-family` property references fonts through their names.

CSS supports five generic font family names: serif, sans-serif, monospace, cursive, and fantasy. Text is usually displayed in serif and sans-serif, with monospace reserved for applications such as computer code, and cursive and fantasy for decorations and headings.

The author should always offer font alternatives in the `font-family` specifications. The font-family declaration should list a selection of comma-separated fonts, with the generic family as the last specified option. Be sure to offer a selection of font names appropriate to different operating systems, and also appropriate to alternative fonts that may make a good substitute, should the desired font not be present.

The `font-style` property defines three possible styles of the font. Of the allowed styles, "normal" is always available, in contrast with "oblique" and "italic." Note that most current computer fonts do not support an oblique style. Internet Explorer 3 does not support the `font-style` property.

`Font-variant` yields variants not related to family, style, or weight. The only supported variant is "small-caps," for small-cap lettering. This variant is not supported by Navigator 4 or MSIE 3.

Font-weight is specified using the `font-weight` property. CSS supports nine numerical gradations of weight. Most fonts, however, support fewer than nine weights. By specifying keyword (e.g., "normal," "bold") or relative (i.e., "lighter," "bolder") values, an author can avoid absolute weights.

Font matching and font downloading will simplify font definition problems. In the future, CSS may let the author specify the PANOSE number for the desired font.

Every CSS rule begins with a *selector*, followed by one or more *declarations*. Each declaration has in turn two parts: a *property* and a *value*. The colon character (:) separates a property name from the associated value, while the entire selector ends with a semicolon (;). The set of declarations associated with a given selector is contained within curly brackets.

Selectors can be specific to a generic element, can depend on CLASS or ID values of an element, or can depend on an element's context. The selector types discussed in this chapter include simple selectors, class-based selectors, pseudo-class-based simple selectors, and ID-based simple selectors. Some selectors have a higher priority than other selectors. Details of priority evaluation are found in Chapter 6.

Property declarations must be included in the stylesheet if the author wants to ensure that the browser default values are overridden. Next-generation browsers will give the reader the option of overriding document-specified styling.

Chapter Exercises

For the first exercise, review Figures 3.6 and 3.7. Prepare your own event announcement, using the four stylesheet rules listed in Figure 3.6. Also try out the document using just the default family

Figure 3.19 Simple document illustrating the use of relative font weight values. The rendering of this document by a CSS-aware browser is shown in Figure 3.20. Stylesheet content is in italics.

```
<HTML><HEAD><TITLE>Test of Relative Font Weight</TITLE>
<STYLE>
<!--
BODY    {font-family: "Century Schoolbook"; }
SPAN    {text-decoration: underline; }   /* Underline SPANS for visibility */
P            {font-weight: 500;         }
SPAN.more   {font-weight: bolder;    }      /* "more" == "bolder"  */
SPAN.less   {font-weight: lighter;   }      /* "less" == "lighter" */
DIV         {font-style: italic;     }
-->
</STYLE></HEAD>
<BODY>
<H2 ALIGN="center">Relative Font Weight Values
     <BR>(Century Schoolbook Font)</H2>
<P>Here is a paragraph of text set with a default weight of 500.
   But now, here is some <SPAN CLASS="more">heavier weight</SPAN>
   text, produced using the value "bolder."  Alternatively,
   we can use the "lighter" value to produce <SPAN CLASS="less">light,
   and then <SPAN CLASS=less>even lighter</SPAN></SPAN> text.
</P>
<DIV ALIGN="center">
  <HR SIZE="2" NOSHADE WIDTH="60%">
  Note that the values "lighter" and<BR>
  "bolder" do not work at all in MSIE 3.
  <HR SIZE="2" NOSHADE  WIDTH="60%">
</DIV>
</BODY></HTML>
```

names "monospace," "cursive," "fantasy," "serif," and "sans-serif"—this will help illustrate the behavior should a browser not have any of the requested fonts—and will test your browser's support for these generic family names.

Commonly available fonts and their system-dependent names are listed in Tables 3.3 through 3.7. As a second exercise, review these tables, along with the font selection principles described in the "Font Family" section located earlier in this chapter. Using the announcement you prepared in the first exercise, try out the font selection rules by varying the fonts in the announcement. Experiment with the fonts as much as you like. Note how effective some fonts are—and how ineffective others are—due to the resolution limitations of a computer display.

Figure 3.20 Display, by the Netscape Navigator 4 beta 4 browser, of the document listed in Figure 3.19. Note how the relative font-weight values `bolder` **and** `lighter` **do not always produce the expected result!**

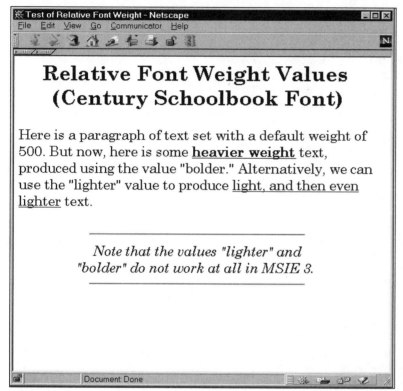

The third exercise examines font weights and font sizes. Begin by reviewing the seven-stage procedure provided in the "Fonts Supporting Fewer Than Nine Weights" section of the chapter. Duplicate Figure 3.16 using your own text (or by obtaining the file from the supporting Web site—see the Preface) and add some sample headings. Once you have completed the figure, try experimenting with variations in font size, family, and default weight, and observe the results—are the displayed weights for each numerical value consistent with those predicted by the seven-step process? Also try using the relative font weight rules, and observe how they are affected by varying default font sizes and weights.

References

Additional references for more advanced font issues are found at the end of Chapter 9.

Figure 3.21 Example document that exercises the different CSS length units to specify both font size and a text indent. The rendering of this document by a CSS-aware browser is shown in Figure 3.22. Stylesheet content is in italics.

```
<HTML><HEAD><TITLE>Simple Test of Font Sizes and Length Units</TITLE>
<STYLE><!--
BODY        {font-size:   12pt;} /* Specify the default font size */
DIV.inch    {text-indent: 0.166667in;   font-size: 0.166667in;      }
DIV.cmtr    {text-indent: 0.423333cm;   font-size: 0.423333cm;      }
DIV.mmtr    {text-indent: 4.233333mm;   font-size: 4.233333mm;      }
DIV.pica    {text-indent: 1pc;          font-size: 1pc;             }
DIV.point   {text-indent: 12pt;         font-size: 12pt;            }
DIV.pixel   {text-indent: 30px;         font-size: 30px;            }
DIV.emmm    {text-indent: 1em;          font-size: 1em;             }
DIV.pct     {text-indent: 10%;          font-size: 100%;            }
DIV.exxx    {text-indent: 1ex;          font-size: 1ex;             }
DIV.arb     {text-indent: 30;           font-size: 30;              }
-->
</STYLE></HEAD>
<BODY>
   <H1 ALIGN="center">Font Sizes and Length Units</H1>
   <DIV CLASS="inch"> Font size in inches. (0.166667in)           </DIV>
   <DIV CLASS="cmtr"> Font size in centimeters. (0.423333cm)      </DIV>
   <DIV CLASS="mmtr"> Font size in millimeters. (4.233333mm)      </DIV>
   <DIV CLASS="pica"> Font size in picas. (1pc)                   </DIV>
   <DIV CLASS="point">Font size in points. (12pt)                 </DIV>
<HR NOSHADE>
   <DIV CLASS="emmm"> Font size in em units. (1em)                </DIV>
   <DIV CLASS="exxx"> Font size in ex units.  (1ex)               </DIV>
   <DIV CLASS="pct">  Font size as a percentage. (100%; 10% indent)  </DIV>
<HR NOSHADE>
   <DIV CLASS="pixel">Font size in pixels.   (30px)               </DIV>
   <DIV CLASS="arb">  Font size; no specified units. (30)         </DIV>
</BODY></HTML>
```

General Font Issues

http://www.ora.com/homepages/comp.fonts/ (Font FAQ)

http://www.ora.com/homepages/comp.fonts/foundry.htm   (Names of font foundries)

http://fonts.verso.com/ (General topics associated with fonts and fonts on the Web)

news:comp.fonts (Newsgroup devoted to font issues)

http://www.fonts.com/fontlinks.htm (Font-related links)

Figure 3.22 Rendering of the document listed in Figure 3.21 by an early beta version of the MSIE 4.0 browser. Note that some of the property values are improperly calculated by the browser, as discussed in the text.

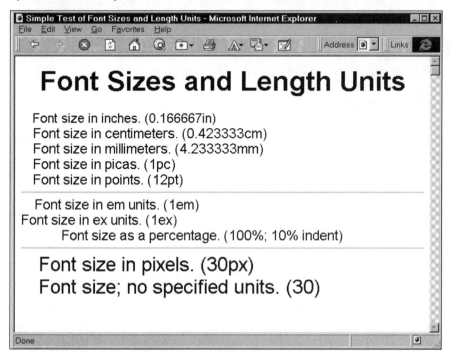

Microsoft Font Recommendations

http://www.microsoft.com/truetype/ (Microsoft font information)

Font Matching and Font Substitution

http://www.w3.org/pub/WWW/Fonts/Panose/pan2.html (PANOSE 2.0 white paper)

http://www.truetype.demon.co.uk/ttparam.htm (Parametric TrueType)

http://www.w3.org/pub/WWW/Printing/stevahn.html (W3C note on PANOSE and the Web)

Endnotes

1. There are also non-character-based fonts, such as Zapf Dingbats or Wingdings, that consist of graphical symbols or dingbats for use as decorations, highlighting or other purposes. In this section we focus on character-based fonts.

2. I once worked in a science museum, where I demonstrated the operation of a traditional molten-lead *Linotype* machine, dating from the 1960s. The demonstration involved assembling rows of molds to form a line of type, pouring molten lead into the row, and then assembling multiple rows together to form a printing block. It is amazing to see how quickly the technology has changed in only 30 years.

3. This is the same definition used in the PostScript language—a printing language employed by most high-quality computer printing systems. There are, however, several other common definitions of the "point." Length units are discussed in more detail in Appendix B.

4

Tutorial, Part 2: Text
Formatting Control

The previous chapter discussed text typefaces and fonts, and introduced the five related CSS properties `font-family`, `font-style`, `font-weight`, `font-variant`, and `font-size`. It also provided a brief introduction to the CSS language, using these properties to illustrate simple CSS declarations and rules.

Of course, there is more to text layout than just fonts, and more to the CSS language than the points discussed in Chapter 3. For example, an author needs to know how to:

- adjust word and letter spacing within selections of text

- add underlining or other "decorations" to text

- vertically align super- and subscripts, and align inline graphics with associated text

- modify the text color

- change the line spacing within a block of text, and add leading indents to a paragraph

These are the main topics of this chapter. The chapter begins with an introduction to these newer text-related layout concepts, introducing the standard terminology used in typographic layout, and relating these terms and concepts to the appropriate CSS properties. This section also mentions the cases where a particular type of formatting control is not possible within CSS.

Following the pattern set in Chapter 3, the second section introduces some additional characteristics of the CSS language: the concepts of pseudo-elements, the construction of contextual, grouped, and pseudo-element-based selectors, and the inclusion of "comments" within a given stylesheet.

The final section uses some example HTML documents to illustrate the formatting control allowed by the new text-related properties introduced in this chapter, giving some examples of typical applications of these elements.

Text Formatting Introduction

In print typesetting, a compositor[1] has enormous control over how the text should be presented. Beyond selecting the font or fonts to be used, the designer[2] also controls how densely the text should be set, the spacing between lines, text color, special decoration of the text (e.g., underlined or struck-through text), case selections (e.g., forced uppercase or lowercase text), leading line text indent (i.e., paragraph indents), and also text alignment (left-aligned, right-aligned, or fully justified text).

As you have no doubt guessed, CSS has properties for controlling all these aspects of text layout. To best understand how these properties work, it helps to have an understanding of the typesetting terminology surrounding these issues, which is the goal of this short section.

Horizontal Text Spacing

The term *tracking* describes the spacing between characters in a word. In traditional typesetting, tracking is described in vague terms such as "loose" or "very loose," which corresponds to wide gaps between letters, and "tight" and "very tight," corresponding to tightly spaced letters. "No tracking" implies that no letter-spacing adjustments have been applied, and that the spacing between letters is simply that defined by the font design. CSS defines a `letter-spacing` property for tracking control, although this is not a core CSS property, and is not widely supported. Tracking is illustrated in Figure 4.1.

Kerning, or *pair kerning*, refers to character spacing control that applies only between specific pairs of characters appearing in a specific order. Kerning is always used with proportional fonts to bring certain pairs of letters closer together, and is done to make the text density appear uniform. This is illustrated in Figure 4.1 using the letters A and W in the abbreviation "AW." Note how the kerning has reduced the space between the two letters, such that the "A" actually lies under the stem of the "W."

CSS Level 1 does not provide for control over kerning, and leaves all kerning control up to the browser and font defaults.

Space band has nothing to do with either telecommunication or electro-pop music—instead, it is the preferred space between words separated by whitespace. Like kerning, it is defined as part of a font's specification. For left or right-aligned text, the space band is a fixed distance. However, for justified text (aligned with both left and right margins), the space band between words is adjusted to make the text align with both margins.

Figure 4.1 An illustration of text tracking, kerning, and space band. *Tracking* adjusts the spacing between all characters in a selection of text, while *kerning* adjusts the spacing only between specific pairs of characters appearing in a specific order. The *space band* is the preferred (font-specific) space to leave between words separated by space characters.

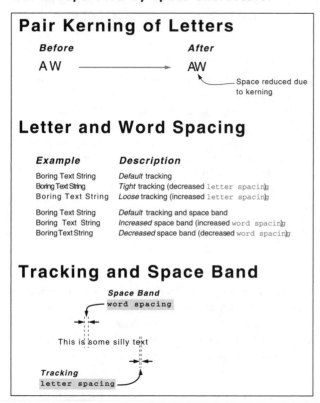

In CSS, the space band can be adjusted using the word-spacing property.

Text Variation: Color, Underlines, and Case Control

There are several other variations on text that are common in typesetting. For example, the color of the text is often modified, or the text may be underlined, or struck through with a line. There are no fancy typographic terms for these variants on a typeface. In CSS, these variants are handled by two properties: color, which affects the color of the typeface, and text-decoration, which controls the special decoration (underlining, etc.) applied to the text.

Text color adjustment is particularly common, but is largely useless in the absence of control over the background color—after all, choosing white text is not terribly useful unless the background can be switched to black. CSS provides several background control properties, among which is `background-color`. We will use this property in some of the examples later in this chapter, but defer a detailed discussion of background properties to Chapter 6.

Finally, there are text-transformation options—that is, converting text to uppercase or lower-case, or such that the leading letter of each word is in uppercase (useful for headings). In typesetting, these options are usually handled on an individual basis, so that there is no specific terminology for this process. However, for Web-based formatting, where the authored document cannot indicate such issues directly, it is convenient to have a stylesheet property to implement such conversions. In CSS, the relevant property is `text-transform`.

Vertical Alignment of Letters, Text, and Images

An important aspect of typography is the vertical offset and alignment of text. With text, common examples of such vertical offset are super- and subscripts, common in abbreviations, such as $13:00^h$ to indicate a time, or in simple mathematical expressions such as $x_{ij} = y^2$. Vertical offset/alignment is also important when non-text objects such as images are added to the flow of text. In this case, an author often needs to specify how the object should be vertically aligned so that, for example, the baseline of the image aligns with the baseline of the surrounding text. This is a role formerly taken on by the **ALIGN** attribute of **IMG** (or **APPLET** or **EMBED** elements) in HTML. Since this is a formatting issue, it is better to specify this information in a stylesheet.

CSS supports a `vertical-align` property for controlling the vertical alignment of elements inline with the flow of text. Note that this property applies to either inline text elements (such as that within a **SPAN**) or inline images.

Formatting within Text Blocks

The formatting concepts discussed so far apply to words or simple collections of words (or images) within a line. However, many text-formatting properties do not apply to simple *inline* text, but rather apply to blocks of text, such as paragraphs, floating boxes of text (such as Tip or Note boxes), and so on. Some simple examples are paragraph indents or text line spacing—obviously these concepts only apply if you have a block of text that needs a first-line indent, or that can have multiple lines with a well-defined line spacing.

As discussed in Chapters 1 and 2, CSS has a well-defined notion of the "type" of a markup element. For example, *inline* elements are those like **EM** or **SPAN** that appear inline within the flow of the text. On the other hand, block elements such as **P** or **BLOCKQUOTE** define blocks of text, with breaks before and after. When formatted for display, block elements define a "box" on the display, within which the content (for example the text of a paragraph) is contained. Concepts such as line spacing and text indents obviously apply to such blocks of text, whereas they are irrelevant to the formatting of inline elements like **EM**.

This chapter does not discuss block element formatting in much detail, and defers discussion of the many issues surrounding block elements to Chapter 5.

Controlling Line Spacing

The term *leading* (pronounced "ledding") refers to the vertical space occupied by a line of text, as illustrated in Figure 4.2. In most cases, leading is equivalent to line or inter-line spacing (generally

Figure 4.2 An illustration of text *leading*, or line height. *Leading* (pronounced "led-ding") is just the vertical space occupied by a line of text, and is generally equivalent to the vertical space between lines. In CSS, leading is controlled by the `line-height` property.

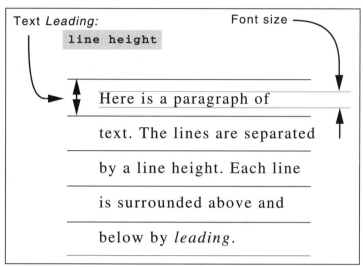

the distance from one text baseline to the next), although this equivalence is not always true—for example, if the two lines use different fonts with different font dimensions.

In CSS, leading is specified with the `line-height` property. The resulting space is split evenly above and below a line of text; that is, half the extra line height is added above the line, and half below. This is not important with respect to the spacing between lines, but is important for determining where the block of text starts (at the *top* of the leading above the first line of the paragraph), and ends (at the *bottom* of the leading below the last line of a paragraph). This is illustrated in Figure 4.3, which shows the default boundaries of a block of text (e.g., a paragraph): Note how the boundaries hug the text, but allow for the extra line height above the first line and below the last.

There are all sorts of other formatting issues associated with blocks of text, and these are discussed later in this chapter, and also in Chapter 5.

Aligning and Indenting Text

There are several common typesetting properties that can be applied to text within a block. The most common property is text alignment. Text within a block can be left-aligned with a ragged right margin, right-aligned with a ragged left margin, or justified with both margins vertically aligned. Also common is first-line (also called leading-line) text indent, the most obvious example being an indent for the first line of a paragraph. These formatting features of blocks of text are illustrated in Figure 4.4.

Figure 4.3 An illustration of the boundary around a block of text, such as a paragraph, and around an inline element. Note how the block hugs tightly to the text, but allows for the line height above the first line and below the last line in the block.

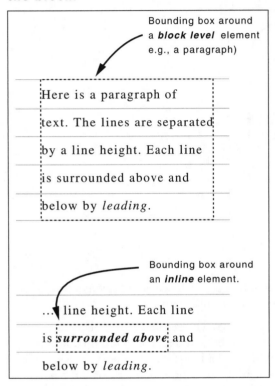

CSS provides two properties to control these aspects of block element formatting: `text-align`, to control alignment of text within the element, and `text-indent`, to set the indent for the first displayed line within the element.

First-Letter or First-Line Formatting

Another common feature in typography is special formatting for the first line or first letter of a block. Examples are capitalization of the text in the first line of text in the first paragraph of a section, or transforming the first letter in a paragraph into a *drop cap*—a significantly enlarged letter "floated" to lie in front of the associated block of text. Figure 4.5 illustrates these two formatting features.

CSS Level 1 has no properties specific for drop-cap lettering or first-line emphasis. However, CSS does support *pseudo-elements* that reference the first displayed letter, or the first displayed line of a block element. It is then left to the author to associate properties with the selector that provide the desired first-letter or first-line formatting. These special selectors are described in the next section. Note, however, that these selectors are not core features of CSS, and are not yet widely supported.

Figure 4.4 Formatting characteristics of blocks of text, illustrating right-aligned, left-aligned, and justified text, and a first- or leading-line indent (last two blocks). The dashed gray lines mark the edges of the element. Note that indents can be either positive or negative.

```
Left aligned                          Right  Aligned

Did you know that the                      Did you know that the
long tailed snow y flober bird        long tailed snow y flober bird
is the only bird known to dine        is the only bird known to dine
exclusively on weiners and                exclusively on weiners and
packaged foods?  Many have            packaged foods?  Many have
wondered how this                             wondered how this
three headed, fi ve footed             three headed, fi ve footed
wonder of the wild survived            wonder of the wild survived
before ...                                             before ...


Center Aligned                        Justified

    Did you know that the             Did   you   know   that   the
long tailed snow y flober bird        long tailed  snowy  flober bird
is the only bird known to dine        is the only bird known to dine
    exclusively on weiners and        exclusively   on   weiners and
    packaged foods?  Many have        packaged foods?   Many have
    wondered how this                 wondered      how      this
    three headed, fi ve footed        three headed,        five footed
    wonder of the wild survived       wonder  of  the  wild  survive
            before ...                before ...


Positive Indent                       Hanging Indent

        Did you know that the         Did you know that the long tailed
long t ailed snowy flober bird        snowy flober bird is the only
is the only bird known to dine        bird known to dine
exclusively on weiners and            exclusively on weiners and
packaged foods?  Many have            packaged foods?  Many have
wondered how ...                      wondered how ...
```

CSS Syntax: Complex Selectors and CSS Comments

Chapter 3 described the basic structure of CSS stylesheets, and introduced the concepts of stylesheet properties, declarations, selectors, and rules. It also introduced four basic types of selectors: those based on element name (e.g., EM); on an element's **CLASS** (`.intro` or `EM.blue`); on the **ID** attribute value (`#id23` or `DIV#fix3`); and also on an element's pseudo-class (`:link` or `A:visited`).

CSS supports three additional forms of selectors: pseudo-element-based selectors, grouped selectors, and contextual selectors. Pseudo-element-based selectors define "markup element–like" sections of an element, where the bounds of the section depend on page layout or formatting. Grouped selectors simply provide a way of assigning the same group of properties to more than one element—they are a convenient shorthand tool. Contextual selectors allow for context-based rules—for example, to specify properties that should only apply to **EM** elements located inside a particular **CLASS** of **DIV**.

Figure 4.5 An illustration of first-line text emphasis and drop-cap leading lettering. Note how the baseline of the drop-cap letter is aligned with the baseline of the adjacent line of text.

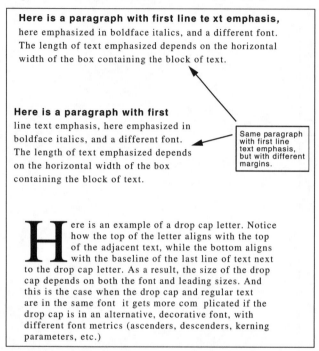

Pseudo-Element-Based Selectors

Pseudo-element-based selectors specify formatting for "element-like" blocks of text—"element-like" because they correspond to blocks of the document that cannot be formally marked up using HTML. This is a rather awkward definition, but the principle is simply demonstrated using an example.

Consider a "first-line" pseudo-element (which is, in fact, one of the pseudo-elements available in CSS). This element specifies the first displayed line in a block element. Obviously, the amount of text in the first line depends on the font size, browser window width, margins, and so on, so that the content cannot be selected by a real markup element. This is the intent of pseudo-elements: to denote sections of text that vary according to the vagaries of the display.

CSS supports just two pseudo-elements: for the first line and the first letter of a block of text. Like pseudo-classes, pseudo-element selectors are denoted by a leading colon, for example `:first-line` for the first-line pseudo-class. The `:first-line` pseudo-element, just described, selects for the first line of displayed text in a block element. The `:first-letter` pseudo-element, on the other hand, selects for the first letter in a block of text, and is designed to support formatting features such as drop-cap lettering.

Figure 4.6 shows an example document that uses these pseudo-elements. Unfortunately, at press time, there were no browsers that properly implemented these pseudo-elements, and thus this book does not include an example rendering of this document.

NOTE Pseudo-Elements Not Widely Supported

The `:first-line` and `:first-letter` pseudo-elements are *not* supported by Netscape Navigator 4.0 or earlier, or by MSIE 3. The `:first-letter` pseudo element, however, can be mimicked using a **SPAN** element that contains the first letter in a block element.

Figure 4.6 Example document illustrating first-letter and first-line pseudo-elements. The stylesheet content is shown in italics. Note the use of grouped selectors (the second rule in the stylesheet) and CSS comment strings. The attempt at providing drop-cap lettering, as expressed in the last CSS rule, will not currently work properly, for reasons discussed in the text.

```
<HTML><HEAD><TITLE>Test of Pseudo-Elements</TITLE>
<STYLE>
<!--
P                       {text-indent: 5em;}  /* Default Paragraph indent */
P.first, P.afirst       {text-indent: 0em;}  /* 'First' paragraph indent */
P.first:first-line      {text-transform: uppercase;
                         color: blue; }
/*
    The following is an attempt at drop-cap lettering. Note that
    this does not work properly, as CSS cannot properly specify
    the font sizes needed to properly align the drop cap.
*/
P.afirst:first-letter {font-family: "Blackletter686 BT";
                       font-size: 300%;
                       float: left; }
-->
</STYLE>
</HEAD>
<BODY BGCOLOR="#ffffff">
<H2>Test of Pseudo Elements</H2>

<P CLASS="first">Here is the first paragraph -- this one
    has a first line transform to uppercase, and will therefore
    have the first line in capital letters.</P>
<P>Here, in all its glory, is the second paragraph. This is a
    regular paragraph, but with a first-line indent of 5em
    (about 5 characters).</P>
```

Continued

Figure 4.6 *Continued*

```
<HR SIZE=2 NOSHADE WIDTH="80%">
<P CLASS="afirst"><SPAN CLASS="foo">H</SPAN>ere is the second example "starting" paragraph.
   This one has an first-letter selector rule that calls for drop cap
   leading lettering. Note that, for many browsers, drop-cap formatting
   does not work well, as the CSS mechanisms are too primitive to
   get the proper vertical alignment. </P>
<HR>
</BODY></HTML>
```

Problems with CSS Drop-Cap Lettering

In the current version of CSS, the `first-letter` pseudo-class is insufficient for proper drop-cap lettering. Recall that a drop cap must be sized such that the baseline of the drop cap aligns with the baseline of the bottom line of adjacent text, and the top of the drop cap aligns with the top of the ascender in the first line of displayed text (see Figure 4.5). For a drop-cap letter that spans n lines of text, this means that the drop-cap letter size (the x-height *plus* the ascender height for the drop-cap font) must be equal to $(n - 1)$ times the regular line spacing, *plus* the x-height and ascender height of the regular font (the height above the baseline in the first line of regular text). There is no mechanism in CSS for expressing this complicated relationship, and thus no way of properly specifying the desired size for a drop-cap font. It is likely that a future version of CSS will support a `drop-cap` property for specifying leading letters.

Note also that drop-cap lettering depends on language and context. For example, quotation marks preceding the first letter in a sentence should be included in the drop cap, while in some languages certain letter pairs are kept together in a drop cap.

Note that both currently defined pseudo-class selectors can only be associated with a block element; thus, expressions such as EM:`first-line` or STRONG:`first-letter` are invalid.

Grouped Selectors

There are often cases where the same rule is applied over and over again to different elements. For example, if an author wants to specify a particular font for all heading types, then this would require six stylesheet rules, one for each heading level.

This repetition can be avoided via grouped selectors, which simply apply the same collection of declarations to multiple selectors. Grouped selectors are created by including, to the left of the rule, a comma-separated list of the selectors to which the declarations should be applied. Then, any associated declarations are treated as applying to all the selectors in the group. For example, the selectors

```
H1  {font-family: arial, helvetica, serif}
H2  {font-family: arial, helvetica, serif}
```

```
H3  {font-family: arial, helvetica, serif}
H4  {font-family: arial, helvetica, serif}
H5  {font-family: arial, helvetica, serif}
H6  {font-family: arial, helvetica, serif}
P.abstract  {font-family: arial, helvetica, serif}
```

can be rewritten, using a grouped selector, as

```
H1, H2, H3, H4, H5, H6, P.abstract { font-family: arial, helvetica, serif}
```

which indicates that the desired font selection property should be applied to all headings and to all paragraphs of the indicated class. Another example of a grouped selector is found in the second CSS rule in Figure 4.6, namely:

```
P.first, P.afirst  {text-indent: 0em;}  /* 'First' paragraph indent */
```

which specifies a text indent for these two different classes of paragraph.

Grouped selectors are convenient for reducing the size of the stylesheet. They are also useful structurally, to group obviously related elements and properties together, as in the previous two examples. Then, should the author wish to modify the document style, it is easy to update the value at a single place in the stylesheet.

Comments in CSS Stylesheets

Figure 4.6 also illustrates CSS comments. It is often useful to include comment statements within a stylesheet, both as a reminder to yourself about the intent of a particular set of rules, and as a note, for future users of the stylesheet, explaining how the rules are designed to be used. In CSS, comments are included between the markers /* and */ (these are the same markers used to denote comments in the C programming language). The string /* indicates the start of a comment, while */ marks the end. Everything between these markers is treated as a comment, and is ignored by the stylesheet processor.

As illustrated in Figure 4.6, comments can be on one line, or they can span multiple lines. However, comments cannot nest, since the parser will treat the first */ string it encounters as the end of the comment. For example, consider the following "nested" comments:

```
/* here is the first comment with lots of silly words..
   /* and a second comment, supposedly nested within the first */
and here is the end of the first comment */
```

The CSS software interpreting this text will take the first /* (boldface in the example) as the start of the comment, and the first encountered */ (also in boldface) as the end. Consequently, the remaining "comment" text (in italics) is treated as CSS instructions, and produces a CSS error.

It is always a good idea to add comments to stylesheets, as it is easy to forget the reasoning behind a design, particularly a complex one. Figure 4.7 gives an example of how comments can be used to track the evolution and maintenance of a stylesheet.

Figure 4.7 An example CSS stylesheet, illustrating common uses for CSS comments. The text inside the comments is shown in italics.

```
/*
    Stylesheet for Advertising Web Site Project Number 21-312B
    Web Adjunct to "Buttered BonBon Campaign"
    See Rolf Born Zordle <r.bozo@BlorkleAdWeb.com> for
    campaign details.


    ----------------------------------------------------------------
    Stylesheet Author    Ian Graham  <ian@BlorkleAdWeb.com>
    Version              1.0
    Created              23 May 1997
    Last-Modified        24 May 1997
    Stylesheet URL       http://www.blorkle.com/priv/style/21312b.css
    ----------------------------------------------------------------


    The Design uses bold Verdana fonts for all headings, plus special
    alignment options to follow the print advertising model of the
    client, McGillicutty and Associates, the world's largest producer
    of buttered bonbons. Note that special margins selections were
    added to allow for the fact that many browsers do not have Verdana
    and use Arial (PCs) or Helvetica (UNIX) in its place -- this
    substitution led to spacing problems, which were resolved by
    adding extra borders on elements of CLASS="callout".

*/
BODY {
      font-family: verdana, arial, helvetica, sans-serif
      font-size: 16pt       /* need to fix size so copy fits in boxes   */
      font-weight: normal   /* need to fix weight for same reason       */
      background: black;
      color: white;
      margin-left:  2%;     /* use percents, but watch out for overflow!*/
      margin-right: 2%
      }
.....
```

Contextual Selectors

Stylesheet rules based on **CLASS** values, **ID** values, or element names are very useful, but often an author needs to specify styling dependent on an element's *context*. For example, an author may want **EM** text to be red except when inside a heading, in which case the color should be black. In principle, an author can force this behavior by giving all **EM** elements within headings a special class, and using this class to specify a different style. In practice, however, this is cumbersome—it is far easier if the stylesheet can specify rules that apply depending on element context. This eliminates the need for extra **CLASS** attributes in the HTML document, and also makes stylesheet rule construction easier and more obvious.

CSS supports this type of rule specification through *contextual selectors*. A contextual selector selects for elements contingent on their context *within* other elements. With contextual selectors, the content order for a selector is given as a space-separated list of simple selector names, read from right to left. For example, the rule

```
H1 EM {color: black}
```

states that text within **EM** elements that lie within an **H1** element should be rendered in black, while the rule

```
DIV.intro H1.main EM {font-style: oblique}
```

states that text within **EM** elements lying within **H1** elements of **CLASS**="main" that, in turn, lie within **DIV** elements of **CLASS**="intro", should be formatted in an oblique style.

Like simple selectors, contextual selectors can be grouped, allowing the same properties to be associated with more than one such selector. For example, the rule

```
H1 EM, H2 EM, H3 EM, H4 EM, H5 EM, H6 EM {color: black}
```

states that **EM** elements lying within *any* level of heading should be displayed in black.

Contextual selectors can specify multiple levels of context. For example, the rule

```
LI UL LI      {color: #666666; font-size: smaller}
```

applies to **LI** elements in **UL** lists that are in turn within an **LI** element, while the rule

```
LI UL LI UL LI {color: #dddddd; font-size: smaller}
```

applies to **LI** elements in **UL** lists that are in turn inside an **LI** element within a **UL** list that is in turn within an **LI**. Table 4.1 gives some other examples of contextual selectors.

Table 4.1 Some Example Contextual Selectors, with Explanations

CSS Rule	Explanation
UL LI	Selects for **LI** elements that are within **UL** elements.
H1 STRONG	Selects for **STRONG** elements inside **H1** headings.
DIV.sidebar H1	Selects for **H1** elements that lie inside **DIV** elements of **CLASS**="sidebar".
DIV.int P EM	Selects for **EM** elements lying inside **P** elements that, in turn, are inside **DIV** elements of **CLASS**="int".
DIV.sidebar P:first-line	Selects for the first-line pseudo-element of **P** elements that lie inside **DIV** elements of **CLASS**="sidebar".

Contextual, Not Parent-Child

It is important to realize that a contextual relationship is *not* the same as a parent child relationship.[3] For example, the rule

```
OL LI EM {font-weight: bold; }
```

applies to any **EM** element that is in some way contained within an **LI** that lies beneath an **OL**—the **LI** and **OL** do not need to be the direct parents of the **EM**. This rule applies to the **EM** element in the following markup:

```
<OL>
    <LI>First ordered list item
        <UL>
            <LI>Here is an <EM>emphasized</EM> unordered item
        </UL>
</OL>
```

even though the **EM** not directly inside an **LI** lying directly inside an **OL** list.

Figure 4.8 illustrates contextual selectors. The rendering of this document by the Internet Explorer 4 browser is shown in Figure 4.9.

There are several rules present in Figure 4.8. The first two rules apply to **EM** elements: The first rule sets the color "#00bbbb" (a shade of aqua) for all **EM** elements, while the second rule with grouped contextual selectors calls for black text for all **EM** elements lying inside heading elements. Looking to Figure 4.9, we can see that this is exactly what occurs (in a black-and-white figure, #00bbbb is a light shade of gray). Here the emphasized text within the **H2** heading is black, while elsewhere it is in gray.

The next three contextual rules apply to **LI** elements. The first of these sets the default color for **LI** elements within **UL** lists as "#666600" (a yellow-brown, rendered in the black-and-white figure as a dark gray), while the next two rules set the default color for doubly and triply nested unordered list **LI** elements as light gray (#666666) and black respectively. The second rule applying to **LI** elements also calls for a "smaller" font size—recall that the value "smaller" simply calls for a font smaller relative to that of the parent element.

The resulting rendering in Figure 4.9 follows this procedure. The second-level nested **LI** element within the **UL** list is in a dark gray and a smaller font—the rule with the selector LI UL LI applies here, and sets both the color and the font size. However, the triply nested LI element that follows is also subject to the rule with selector LI UL LI UL LI—thus the text here is black. The text is also reduced in size, since the font size property from the rule with selector LI UL LI is applied, which calls for a font size smaller than that in the parent element. Of course, the parent element is the previous **LI**, which already has a reduced font size. Thus, the size within this second-level **LI** element is reduced once again.

We last look at the **LI** elements nested within the **OL**. These are of course also "under" the **UL** list that encompasses all lists in this example. Therefore, these items are also subject to formatting specified by the UL LI contextual selector, so that the text is once again in a yellow-brown color (light gray in Figure 4.9).

NOTE Special Handling by Netscape Navigator 4 of Contextual Selectors Containing LI Elements

Netscape Navigator 4 treats CSS selectors that apply to **LI** elements (e.g., UL LI) as applying to the number or bullet associated with an **LI** element, and *not* to the content of the **LI**. As a result, on Netscape Navigator 4, the stylesheet associated listed in Figure 4.8 simply modifies the colors (and sizes) for the list item numbers or bullets, and does not affect the color or size of the text. With Netscape (and with other browsers) the properties of all list content can be modified by using selectors that contain only **UL** or **OL** elements. For example, the stylesheet rules in Figure 4.8 that apply to lists could be rewritten as:

```
UL          {color: #666600;}

UL UL       {color: #666666; font-size: smaller;}

UL UL UL    {color: black; }.
```

which yield identical formatting without the need for **LI** elements in the selectors. Thus, for best compatibility with all browsers, it is best to omit **LI** elements from the selectors.

Stylesheets and Text Formatting

The first two sections of this chapter gave an overview of the issues surrounding text formatting beyond the font-specific issues discussed in Chapter 3. In this third section, we will use example stylesheets to demonstrate the CSS properties that control these aspects of typography and layout. To summarize, these properties are:

Figure 4.8 Example document illustrating the use of contextual selectors. Stylesheet rules are shown in italics. Browser rendering of this document is shown in Figure 4.9.

```
<HTML><HEAD><TITLE>Test of Contextual Selectors</TITLE>
<STYLE>
<!--
EM {color: #00bbbb;}        /* grayish-aqua -- light gray on B/W display */
H1 EM, H2 EM, H3 EM, H4 EM, H5 EM, H6 EM {color: black;}
UL LI          {color: #666600;}    /*Yellow-brown gray on B/W display */
LI UL LI       {color: #666666; font-size: smaller;} /* light gray      */
LI UL LI UL LI {color: black; }
-->
</STYLE></HEAD>
<BODY>
<H2>Test of <EM>Contextual</EM> Selectors</H2>

<P>This example document tests formatting associated with
    <EM>contextual selectors</EM>. Contextual selectors specify
    formatting that depends on the context of an element.</P>
<UL>
   <LI>Here is an item in an unordered list. According to the
       stylesheet, this should be in a yellow-brown, and in the
       default font size.
       <UL>
          <LI>Here is an LI within a UL within an LI. According to
              the stylesheet, this text should be gray, and in a font
              slightly smaller than that in the parent element.
              <UL>
                 <LI>Here is an LI within a UL within an LI within
                     a UL. </LI>
                 <LI>Ditto. According to the stylesheet, this text
                     should be in a black, and in an
                     <EM>even smaller</EM> font size.</LI>
              </UL>
          </LI>
       </UL>
       <OL>
          <LI>Here is an LI within an OL within an LI within a UL.</LI>
          <LI>Ditto. Thus the UL LI selector applies, and the
              text is a yellow-brown.</LI>
       </OL>
   </LI>
</UL>
<HR SIZE=2 NOSHADE>
</BODY></HTML>
```

Figure 4.9 Rendering by the Internet Explorer 4 browser of the document listed in Figure 4.8. Note the application of the contextual rules to determine the list-item formatting.

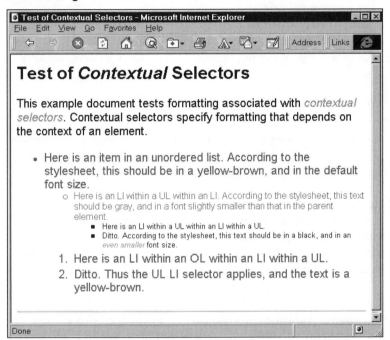

Color	Specifies the color for the displayed text
Background-color	Specifies the *background* color for the displayed text
* * Word-spacing	Adjusts the default spacing between adjacent words (Not supported by Navigator 4.0, MSIE 3)
* * Letter-spacing	Adjusts the default spacing between adjacent letters (Not supported by Navigator 4.0, MSIE 3)
Text-decoration	Sets optional decoration (underlining, etc.) for the text (Partially supported by Navigator 4.0, MSIE 3)
Text-transform	Sets text transformation properties (to uppercase, lowercase, etc.) for displayed text (Not supported by MSIE 3)
Vertical-align	Specifies desired alignment relative to surrounding text (Not supported by MSIE 3, partial support by Navigator 4.0)

Line-height	Specifies height of lines of text within a block element (Partially supported by Navigator 4.0, MSIE 3)
Font	Shorthand property for expressing font-related and line-spacing properties, all within one font property specification
Text-indent	Specifies text indent for the first displayed line in a block element
Text-align	Specifies alignment of text (left, right, or justified) within a block element (Partially supported by MSIE 3)
White-space	Specifies handling for whitespace characters (Not supported by MSIE 3; partial support by Navigator 4.0)

Note that the line-height, text-indent, and text-align properties apply only to *block elements*, and cannot be applied to inline elements such as **EM** or **SPAN**.

Example 6: Text Formatting

There are many ways that displayed text can be modified other than by varying font characteristics. In CSS, such variations are possible using the properties color, word-spacing, letter-spacing, text-decoration, and text-transform. The meanings and uses of these properties are relatively straightforward, and are outlined in the following.

Text and Background Colors

The color of the displayed text can be modified via the color property. This property can take as its value: a named color (e.g., red); a hexadecimal RGB code, as was common within HTML color attribute values (e.g., #F53B00); a "decimal" RGB code, with decimal values from 0 to 255 for each color channel (e.g., rgb(211,0,255)); or a "percentage" RGB code, with decimal percentages instead of decimal values (e.g., rgb(45%, 23.4%, 95%)). A list of named colors and a description of the CSS color model are found in Appendix A.

Of course, a change in text color may require a change in the background color to make the text readable. This can be accomplished using the background-color property, which takes the same values as color. In principle, the background can also be an image file, but we shall defer discussion of this option to Chapter 6, as there are several other properties related to background images and their placement and tiling on the display.

Color properties were used previously in this chapter in Figures 4.8 and 4.9. Figures 4.10 and 4.11 illustrate the use of color together with background-color to create a decorative heading style.

Spacing between Words and Letters

As discussed in the first section of this chapter, every font has its own default word and letter spacing. CSS lets an author modify these default values using the word-spacing and letter-spacing properties. These properties take as their values a length (absolute, relative, or percentage) value that changes the spacings relative to the default setting. Both positive and negative values are possible, with positive ones increasing the spacing, and negative ones decreasing it. The properties can also take the value normal, which returns the spacing to the font's default value. Relative or percentage values are always calculated relative to the font size.

These spacing controls are demonstrated in Figures 4.10 and 4.11. The second and third paragraphs illustrate the effect of modifying the letter spacing (the quantity in brackets indicates the value assigned to the letter spacing property). Note how reducing or increasing the letter spacing can make the text quite hard to read. The default letter spacing for a given font is carefully selected for maximum font readability. Thus, an author should be cautious about making large changes to this value. Some systems have restrictions on the allowed amount of "negative" letter-spacing offset, and will refuse to reduce the letter spacing below a preset minimum value.

Note that the word-spacing property varied in the first paragraph in Figure 4.11 has no affect on the actual word spacing. In general, word spacing is treated as a "rubber" quantity—that is, as a quantity that can be adjusted by the browser. For example, most browsers will ignore this property if the text is either left- or right-aligned.

Text Alignment and Word/Letter Spacing It will be seen later that the type of text justification strongly affects a browser's treatment of word and letter spacing. If text justification is requested, a text formatter justifies the text by adjusting the word and letter spacing to make the text fit. Consequently, the word and letter spacing properties can help control how the browser adjusts these quantities to justify the text.

NOTE Word-Spacing **and** Letter-Spacing **Not Widely Supported**

The word-spacing and letter-spacing properties are not supported by Netscape Navigator 4.0 or by MSIE 3.

Decorating Text with Underlines and Strikethrough

The text-decoration property can assign special formatting to the associated text. In CSS, the allowed values are underline for underlined text, overline for text with a line drawn on top, line-through for text with a line drawn through it, and blink for blinking text. Last, the value none removes any inherited decoration to yield undecorated text. These different values are used in Figure 4.12, and their effects (with the exception of blink, of course) are displayed in the list items at the top of Figure 4.13. Note that not all browsers support all these values—Internet Explorer, for example, does not support blinking text.

Transforming Text Case

Text case transformations are supported via the text-transform property. This property lets an author globally control the case for text within an element, converting all text to uppercase (via the value uppercase), or to lowercase (via the value lowercase), or capitalizing only the leading letters

**Figure 4.10 Example document illustrating color, word, and letter spacing proper-
ties. The rendering of this document by a CSS-aware browser is shown in Figure
4.11. Stylesheet rules are shown in italics.**

```
<HTML><HEAD>
<TITLE>Test of Text Formatting Properties</TITLE>
<STYLE>
<!--
/*  Set default font for entire document                         */
BODY          {font-family: verdana, arial, sans-serif;        }

/* Set fonts, colors and backgrounds for headings:
   rong -- red on light gray;
   wonb -- white on black                                       */
.rong         {color: red;   background: #bbbbbb;
               font-family: "Comic Sans MS", Arial, sans-serif; }
.wonb         {color: white; background: black;
               font-family: Garamond, serif;                    }

/* Now set classes for adjusted word and letter spacings        */
SPAN.wordp    {word-spacing:    1.0em;}    /* Add 1em to word space  */
SPAN.wordm    {word-spacing:   -0.2em;}    /* reduce word space 0.2em */
.times        {font-family: "Times New Roman"}
SPAN.lettp    {font-family: verdana;           letter-spacing:  0.2em}
SPAN.lettp3   {font-family: "times new roman"; letter-spacing:  0.2em}
SPAN.lettm    {font-family: verdana;           letter-spacing: -0.1em}
SPAN.lettm3   {font-family: "times new roman"; letter-spacing: -0.1em}
-->
</STYLE></HEAD>
<BODY BGCOLOR="#ffffff">
<H1><SPAN CLASS="rong">Test of Text
    <SPAN CLASS="wonb">Formatting</SPAN> Properties</SPAN></H1>
<P>
  <SPAN>               Test of varied word spacing (default)</SPAN><BR>
  <SPAN CLASS="wordp">Test of varied word spacing (1.0em)</SPAN><BR>
  <SPAN CLASS="wordm">Test of varied word spacing (-0.2em)</SPAN>
</P><P>
  <SPAN>Test of varied letter spacing (Verdana, default)</SPAN><BR>
  <SPAN CLASS="lettp">Test of varied letter spacing (+0.2em)</SPAN><BR>
  <SPAN CLASS="lettm">Test of varied letter spacing (-0.1em)</SPAN>
</P><P>
  <SPAN CLASS="times">Test of varied letter spacing
                      (Times, default)</SPAN><BR>
  <SPAN CLASS="lettp3">Test of varied letter spacing (+0.2em)</SPAN><BR>
  <SPAN CLASS="lettm3">Test of varied letter spacing (-0.1em)</SPAN>
</P><HR>
</BODY></HTML>
```

Figure 4.11 Display, by the Internet Explorer 4 browser, of the document listed in Figure 4.10. In this black-and-white figure, the color "red" is displayed as a dark shade of gray. Note how the word-spacing properties do not affect the spacing in this context, as discussed in the text.

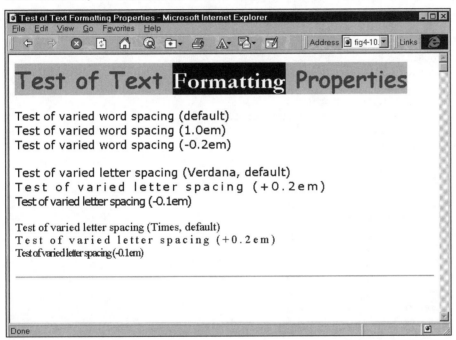

in the words (via the value `capitalize`). Typical results of the different transformations are shown in Figure 4.13—note how this version of Internet Explorer has a small bug in text capitalization, and "forgets" to capitalize the first letter of the first word.

The `text-transform` property, when combined with the `font-variant` property, can be used to produce small-caps versions of capitalized strings. This can be useful for abbreviations and acronyms such as NASA and NATO. In these cases, full-sized capital letters may appear overly heavy, although capitalization is still needed to mark the word as an abbreviation. A small-caps version of the string can be produced by using `text-transform: lowercase` to convert the text to lowercase, and `font-variant: small-caps` to convert this lowercase string to one composed of small capital letters. This application is illustrated at the bottom of Figures 4.13 and 4.14. Note that this does not look terribly nice on a computer display, although it does look good in print. In general, this transformation is best used in large blocks of text (as in pages of a book), and is less useful on a computer display.

Example 7: Vertical Alignment

Within lines of text, there is often a need to vertically align text with text, or inline objects (e.g., images) with text. In the former instance this could be alignment of super- or subscripts, while in

Figure 4.12 Example document illustrating the `color, text-decoration,` **and** `text-transform` **properties. Stylesheet rules are in italics. The rendering of this document is shown in Figure 4.13.**

```
<HTML><HEAD><TITLE>More Text Formatting Properties</TITLE>
<STYLE>
<!--
/* Set default font for document, and special heading formatting    */
/* heading formatting properties                                     */
BODY      {font-family: Verdana, arial, sans-serif}
CODE      {font-family: monospace;                     }
.bonw     {color: red;     background: #bbbbbb;
           font-family: "Comic Sans MS", Arial, sans-serif;    }
.wonb     {color: white;   background: black;
           font-family: Garamond, serif;                       }
/*  Now set properties for displaying                               */
/*  text-decoration properties.                                     */
SPAN      {color: red; }
.under    {color: black; text-decoration: underline;}
.blink    {color: black; text-decoration: blink;       }
.over     {text-decoration: overline;                  }
.strike   {text-decoration: line-through;              }
.upper    {text-transform: uppercase;                  }
.lower    {text-transform: lowercase;                  }
.caps     {text-transform: capitalize;                 }
.abbrev   {text-transform: uppercase;
           font-variant:   small-caps;                 }
-->
</STYLE>
</HEAD><BODY BGCOLOR="#ffffff">
<H1 ALIGN="center"><SPAN CLASS="bonw">More
    <SPAN CLASS="wonb">Text Formatting</SPAN> Properties</SPAN></H1>

<P>The <CODE>text-decoration</CODE> property lets an author specify:</P>
<UL>
  <LI><SPAN CLASS="over">lines on top of text</SPAN>;
      <SPAN CLASS="under">underlining of text</SPAN></LI>
  <LI><SPAN CLASS="strike">struck-through text</SPAN>;
      <SPAN CLASS="blink">blinking text</SPAN> (hard
      to see in print!)</LI>
</UL>
<P>Here are some <CODE>text-transform</CODE> examples:</P>
<DL>
  <DT><CODE>Capitalize</CODE> transform of "This is YOUR life!" gives:
  <DD><SPAN CLASS="caps">This is YOUR life!</SPAN>
  <DT><CODE>Uppercase</CODE> transform of "This is YOUR life!" gives:
```

Continued

Figure 4.12 *Continued*

```
  <DD><SPAN CLASS="upper">This is YOUR life!</SPAN>
  <DT><CODE>Lowercase</CODE> transform of "This is YOUR life!" gives:
  <DD><SPAN CLASS="lower">This is YOUR life!</SPAN>
  <DT><CODE>text-transform: lowercase</CODE> plus
      <CODE>font-variant: small-caps</CODE> applied to
    "NASA" in the phrase "Officials at NASA stated ..." gives:
  <DD><SPAN>Officials at <SPAN CLASS="abbrev">NASA</SPAN>
      stated ...</SPAN>
</DL>
<HR> </BODY></HTML>
```

the latter instance this could be alignment of a decorative graphic or logo (for example, an image as a "bullet"), or perhaps the alignment of a graphic containing text, where the author wants the image placed such that the baseline of the graphic's text aligns with the baseline of the real text.

Such alignment is possible in CSS via the `vertical-align` property. This property can take a number of keyword values that align the element with respect to the parent element, or with respect to the line containing the element. Finally, percentage values can be used to vertically translate the

Figure 4.13 Display, by the Internet Explorer 4 browser, of the document listed in Figure 4.12. In this black-and-white figure, the color "red" appears as a dark gray.

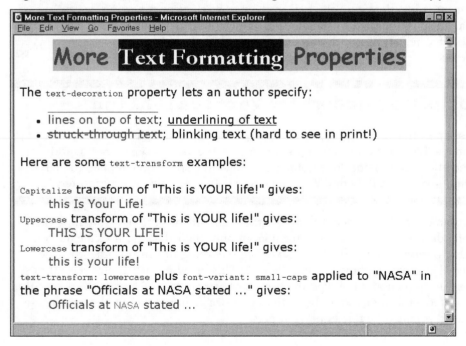

element as a percentage of the line height. The `line-height` property is discussed in the next example, so we defer discussion of this aspect of vertical alignment until then.

The following values define vertical alignments with respect to the parent element:

`baseline`	Align the text baseline of the element with the text baseline of the parent element. If the element does not have a baseline (for example, an **IMG**), align the bottom of the element with the baseline of the parent element. This is the default alignment.
`middle`	Align the vertical midpoint of the element with middle of the parent element. For text, the "middle" is defined as the position of the baseline plus half the x-height.
`sub`	Display the element as a subscript of the parent element.
`super`	Display the element as a superscript of the parent element.
`text-top`	Align the top of the element with the top of the parent element's text content. For text, the "top" is defined as the top of the longest ascender in the font.
`text-bottom`	Align the bottom of the element with the bottom of the parent element's text content. For text, the bottom is defined as the bottom of the longest descender in the font.

A diagram illustrating how these alignment options should work is found in Figure 4.14. With text alignment, the values `baseline`, `middle`, `text-top`, and `text-bottom` have no effect if the font inside the element is identical with the font in the parent element, since in this case the text bottom, middle, and top are aligned by default. However, if the font is changed, either in size or *metric* (relative sizes of x-height, ascender, and descender), then these `text-align` property values can re-align the text.

NOTE Incomplete Support for `Vertical-Align`

MSIE 3 does not support the `vertical-align` property. Netscape Navigator 4 supports this property for inline **IMG** elements, although in this case the values `superscript` and `subscript` have no effect. Navigator does not support this property when applied to inline elements containing text (e.g., **SPAN** or **EM**). Percentage values are also not supported.

Figure 4.15 contains an example document that tests these alignment options. Note how the text to be aligned is of a different color and typeface (Garamond) than the parent element, to ensure that all alignment options should affect the text. The rendering of this document by the Internet Explorer 4 beta 1 browser is shown in Figure 4.16. This browser mishandles several of these alignment options. In particular, note how the browser has *reduced* the size of the text that is subscripted or superscripted—this text should be of the same size as in the parent element. These errors should be corrected by the time this book is in press.

Figure 4.14 Diagram illustrating the correct alignment of text with text, and images with text. The thin gray line denotes the baseline of the surrounding text. These alignment options are tested by the document listed in Figure 4.15.

Value	*Example*
sub	sub _{script}
super	super ^{script}
baseline	goofy [image] text
middle	goofy [image] text
super	goofy [image] text
sub	goofy [image] text
text top	goofy [image] text
text bottom	goofy [image] text

Two other values, top and bottom, define alignment with respect to the line within which the element lies. The defined meanings are:

top	the top of the element with the top of the tallest element in the line, where the "top" is the top of an image or the top of the ascender of the associated text.
bottom	Align the bottom of the element with the bottom of the lowest element in the line, where the "bottom" is the bottom of an image or the bottom of the descender of the associated text.

These values are important in that they let an author align inline elements with other non-text objects in the line, such as other images. Note that the values mentioned earlier support only alignment with text, and not with non-text inline objects. Figures 4.17 and 4.18 show examples of the use of "top" and "bottom" values—here they are used to align two different images to each other, as well as to the text.

Figure 4.15 Example HTML document illustrating various text and image alignment values. The rendering of this document is shown in Figure 4.16. The stylesheet content is in italics.

```
<HTML><HEAD><TITLE>Vertical Alignment Test</TITLE>
<STYLE>
<!--
BODY      {font-family: Verdana, arial, sans-serif; }
SPAN      {color: #00dddd;
              font-family: garamond, serif;            }
/* SPANned text is a different color so it is easy to see,
   and a different font so that the font has, in principle,
   a different text bottom.                                   */
.base     {vertical-align: baseline;      }
.middle   {vertical-align: middle;        }
.subs     {vertical-align: sub;           }
.sups     {vertical-align: super;         }
.texttop  {vertical-align: text-top;      }
.textbot  {vertical-align: text-bottom;   }
-->
</STYLE>
</HEAD><BODY BGCOLOR="#ffffff">
<H2>Vertical Alignment Test</H2>
<P>A paragraph containing
   <SPAN CLASS="base">baseline-aligned</SPAN> text, and also<BR>
   text that is <SPAN CLASS="middle">middle-aligned</SPAN>, and <BR>
   text that is <SPAN CLASS="subs">subscripted</SPAN>, and
   text that is <SPAN CLASS="sups">superscripted</SPAN>, and <BR>
   text that is <SPAN CLASS="texttop">text-top aligned</SPAN>, and finally
   text that is <SPAN CLASS="textbot">text-bottom aligned</SPAN>.
   That's all, folks!</P>
<P>A paragraph containing:<BR>
   a<IMG SRC="icon.gif" CLASS="base">baseline-aligned image,
   a<IMG SRC="icon.gif" CLASS="middle">middle-aligned image,
   and also a<IMG SRC="icon.gif" CLASS="subs">subscript image,
   and a<IMG SRC="icon.gif" CLASS="sups">superscript image,
   followed by a<IMG SRC="icon.gif" CLASS="texttop">text-top
   aligned image,and finally
   a<IMG SRC="icon.gif" CLASS="textbot">text-bottom aligned image.
   That's all, folks!</P>
</BODY></HTML>
```

Problems with Top and Bottom Alignment

Top and bottom can lead to problems if there are two (or more) aligned items in a line, one top-aligned, the other bottom-aligned. Consider for example the line labeled "D)" in Figure 4.18; looking to Figure 4.17, we see that the shorter image should be "top" aligned, while the taller image should be "bottom" aligned. Unfortunately, these two conditions are mutually exclusive;

Figure 4.16 Rendering, by the Internet Explorer 4 beta 1 browser, of the document listed in Figure 4.15. Note how almost all the alignment options are improperly rendered, as discussed in the text.

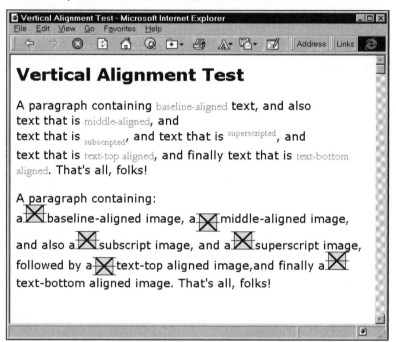

aligning the top of the short image with the top of the tall image means that the bottom of the tall image can never be aligned with the bottom of the short one, and vice versa. So, what does a browser do? As shown in Figure 4.18, Internet Explorer satisfies the first detected alignment, and ignores any "required" alignments that are subsequently impossible. However, there is no requirement for a browser to handle the conflict in this way, so that the rendering of such alignments is unpredictable.

Conflicts such as these can be resolved by creating another axis to which items should be aligned. This can be accomplished by placing text alongside the images, as is done in the line labeled "E)" in Figure 4.18. This line uses the same **IMG** alignment specifications used in "D)," but can now satisfy the alignment settings by aligning the bottom of the tall image with the bottom of the text.

There is one other strange situation that can occur, namely when two images, both of the same height and taller than the height of the text, are both "top" and "bottom" aligned. In this case, the images can be properly aligned to each other, but their position relative to the adjacent text is undefined, since neither the "top" nor the "bottom" is tied to the baseline of the associated text. This situation is illustrated in the inset labeled "F)" in Figure 4.18. Most browsers appear to handle this conflict by aligning the bottom of the images with the bottom of the text, but there is nothing in CSS to say that this is the appropriate behavior.

Figure 4.17 Example HTML document illustrating "top" and "bottom" alignment values. Browser rendering of this document is shown in Figure 4.18. The stylesheet content is in italics.

```
<HTML><HEAD><TITLE>Top and Bottom Alignment Test</TITLE>
<STYLE>
<!--
BODY      {font-family: Verdana, arial, sans-serif} /* Default font    */
TABLE     {background-color: #dddddd;}
.atop     {vertical-align: top;      }  /* Class for top-alignment     */
.abot     {vertical-align: bottom;   }  /* Class for bottom-alignment  */
-->
</STYLE>
</HEAD><BODY BGCOLOR="#ffffff">
<H2>Top and Bottom Alignment</H2>
<TABLE BORDER CELLPADDING=4 ALIGN="right"><TR><TD>
   <P><B>F)</B> <IMG CLASS="abot" SRC="icon3.gif">
   <IMG CLASS="atop" SRC="icon3.gif"> same <BR>size,
   "top" and "bottom"<BR>aligned.</P>
</TD></TR></TABLE>
<P><B>A)</B> <IMG SRC="icon2.gif"> and
   <IMG SRC="icon3.gif">, on the same line</P>
<P><B>B)</B> <IMG CLASS="atop" SRC="icon2.gif"> and
   <IMG CLASS="atop" SRC="icon3.gif">, both "top"
   aligned.</P>
<P><B>C)</B> <IMG CLASS="abot" SRC="icon2.gif"> and
   <IMG CLASS="abot" SRC="icon3.gif">, both "bottom"
   aligned.</P>
<P><B>D)</B> Two images alone -- first "top" and second "bottom" aligned:<BR>
   <IMG CLASS="atop" SRC="icon2.gif">
   <IMG CLASS="abot" SRC="icon3.gif"></P>
<P><B>E)</B> <IMG CLASS="atop" SRC="icon2.gif"> and
   <IMG CLASS="abot" SRC="icon3.gif"> on the same line, first
   "top" and second "bottom" aligned. The text resolves the alignment
   conflict.</P>
</BODY></HTML>
```

Finally, the alignment can be expressed as a percentage value, calculated with respect to the line-height property of the element. The specification is:

xxx%   Raise the baseline of the element the specified amount above the baseline of the parent, where *xxx*% is the percentage of the line-height property of the current element. Negative percentages will lower the element.

This form is discussed in the next example, after introducing the line-height property.

Figure 4.18 Rendering by the Internet Explorer 4 browser of the document listed in Figure 4.17.

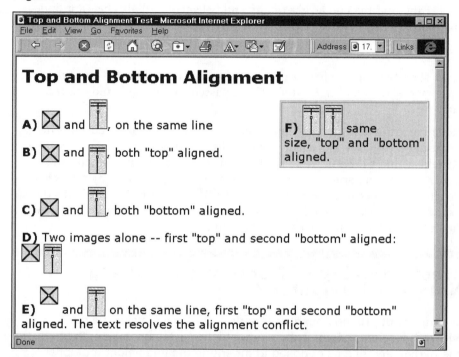

Example 8: Line Height in Block Elements

The `line-height` property defines the height of a line of text within a block element, and is defined as shown in Figure 4.2. As with all text-related properties, `line-height` is inherited from a parent element, although the inheritance rules are somewhat different than with other elements, as discussed a bit later.

The line height value can be specified as a length, in any of the fixed or relative units, or it can be given as a percentage. In the case of percentage values, the value is calculated as a percentage of the font size. Note that relative or percentage units are usually the best choice. In addition, the special keyword value "normal" specifies a default line height, the value of which depends on the font, and also possibly on the browser.

Finally, the line height can be specified as a simple numeric value, or ratio—for example, line-height: 1.5. A numerical value calls for a line height equal to the number *multiplied by* the size of the font.

This differs from percentage values in the way in which a child element inherits the line height from a parent: With percentages, the child inherits the actual line height, while with a numeric ratio, the child inherits the ratio, and not the specific height. For example, if the font size is 12pt and the line height is specified by either of

```
line-height: 150%;
line-height: 1.5em
```

then the line height will be 18pt, and the line height of any child element will also be 18pt, independent of the size of the font in these children. However, if the specification is

```
line-height: 1.5
```

then the line height will be 18pt, but the line height in any child element will be *1.5 times the font size* in that child element—that is, the *line height multiplier* is passed to the child, and not the absolute line height value.

These different characteristics of line height are illustrated in Figures 4.19 and 4.20. This document contains, in tabular format, two **DIV** elements: The one displayed on the left uses percentage values to specify a line height within the **DIV**, while the **DIV** on the right uses numerical ratios. These **DIV** elements, in turn, contain a paragraph at the default font size, followed by a **BLOCKQUOTE** taking a smaller font size. As can be seen, the **BLOCKQUOTE** on the right-hand side has a reduced line spacing, since in this case the line-height *ratio* was inherited from the parent **DIV**, and this ratio was applied to the reduced size font in this element.

NOTE Incorrect Handling of Numeric `Line-Height` Values by Netscape Navigator 4

Netscape Navigator 4 does not properly handle numeric `line-height` values (e.g., `line-height: 1.5`)—with Navigator 4, the child element inherits the actual length of the line height in the parent element, as opposed to inheriting the line height multiplier.

Vertical-align **and** *Line-height* As mentioned in Example 7, the vertical-align property can also define the vertical displacement of an inline element using percentage values. In this case, the displaced distance is calculated as a percentage of the line height, and is used to *vertically translate* the baseline of the element (or the bottom of the element, should it not have a baseline—e.g., an image) relative to the baseline of the parent element—usually the surrounding line of text. Positive values move the element upwards, while negative values move it downwards. Thus, a value of 100% would move an element up such that it is aligned with the line of text that preceded the line containing the translated element.

At present there are no browsers that support percentage vertical-alignment properties.

The Shorthand `Font` Property

The default line spacing is generally a characteristic of a given font. Thus, it is common to express together font and line spacing properties. CSS supports a shorthand font property that can, in a single declaration, specify the line spacing along with the five different font description properties. The general form is:

```
font: font-style font-variant font-weight font-size/line-height font-family
```

where the italicized strings refer to the values supported by the associated property. Note the use of a slash to separate the font size and line height values. As with the `font-family` property, alternative font family selections must be separated by commas. Note that `font-style`, `font-variant`, `font-weight`, `font-family`, and `font-size/line-height` property values can appear in any order. Here are some simple examples:

```
font: large
font: large/1.4 Garamond, "Times New Roman", serif
font: italic small-caps larger/120%
font: bold italic small-caps
```

Example 9: Text Indent, Alignment, and Whitespace

In the last example in this chapter, we look at the properties `text-indent`, `text-align`, and `white space`. The first two properties define a first-line indent and text alignment for block elements such as **DIV** or **P**. Both of these properties are inherited, so that specifying justified text plus an indent for a **DIV** implies the same justification and indent for any paragraphs inside the **DIV**.

The property `white-space` defines how a block element should handle whitespace characters—the characters such as spaces, tabs, or carriage returns that generally separate words. In most cases, a browser collapses multiple whitespace characters (spaces, tabs, carriage-returns, or line feeds) into a single word space. `White-space` lets an author disable this feature, such that the actual spaces, tabs, and carriage returns are displayed (as they are inside an HTML **PRE** element).

Text Indent

`Text-indent` defines the size of the first line text indent of a block element. The value can be expressed as an absolute or relative length, or as a percentage. Relative lengths are calculated relative to the font size in the element, while percentage values are calculated relative to the width of the *parent* element. Text indents can be positive or negative, with negative values pulling the leading line text out ahead of the margin, as illustrated in Figures 4.21 and 4.22.

The margin against which a `text-indent` is applied depends on the directionality of the text; thus for English and French, which read from left to right, the indent should be applied against the left margin, while for Arabic and Hebrew, the indent should be applied against the right margin. Current browsers do not have any understanding of text directionality, and always apply the indent at the left. This is what we see in the text indent examples given in Figure 4.21, and rendered in Figure 4.22. Of course, indents are not very sensible when applied to centered text!

Text Alignment

`Text-align` specifies how the text should be aligned within a block element. This property can take four values: `left` defines left-aligned text (the right text margin is ragged), `right` defines right-aligned text (the left text margin is ragged), `justify` specifies fully justified text (the text is flush smoothly with both left and right text margins), and `center` (the text is centered between

Figure 4.19 Example document illustrating the line-height property, and the two modes of property inheritance. Stylesheet rules are shown in italics. Browser display of this document is found in Figure 4.20.

```
<HTML><HEAD><TITLE>Test of Line-Height Property</TITLE>
<STYLE>
<!--
BODY          {font-family:      Verdana, arial, sans-serif}
DIV.fix       {line-height:      170%; }
DIV.ratio     {line-height:      1.7;  }
.small        {font-size:        smaller;}
P             {background-color: #dddddd}  /* shade for visibility */
-->
</STYLE>
</HEAD><BODY BGCOLOR="#ffffff">
<H2>Line Height Property</H2>
<DIV><P>Here is the first block of text, using the default
     line height. Note the resulting spacing for future
     reference!</P></DIV>
<TABLE BORDER CELLPADDING=4 WIDTH="100%"><TR><TD WIDTH="50%" VALIGN="top">
  <DIV CLASS="fix">
    <P>Here is a paragraph inside a <B>DIV</B> Of
       <B>CLASS</B>="fix". The line spacing is 170%
       of the parent element font size. Big, eh?</P>
    <BLOCKQUOTE CLASS="small">
       This blockquote is inside the same <B>DIV</B>,
       but is of <B>CLASS</B>="small." This reduces the font
       size — note that the line height is the
       same as in the preceding paragraph.</BLOCKQUOTE>
  </DIV>
</TD><TD WIDTH="50%" VALIGN="top">
  <DIV CLASS="ratio">
    <P>Here is a paragraph inside a <B>DIV</B> Of
       <B>CLASS</B>="ratio". The line spacing is 1.7
       times the current font size. Big, eh?</P>
    <BLOCKQUOTE CLASS="small">
       This blockquote is inside the same <B>DIV</B>,
       but is of <B>CLASS</B>="small." This reduces the font
       size — note how the line height is reduced to
       1.7 times the size of the current font!</BLOCKQUOTE>
  </DIV>
</TD></TR></TABLE>
</BODY></HTML>
```

the margins, and the left and right text margins are both ragged). Note that not all browsers support fully justified text. These browsers instead use left or right alignment, depending on the language of the document.

Figure 4.20 Display, by the Internet Explorer 4 browser, of the document listed in Figure 4.19.

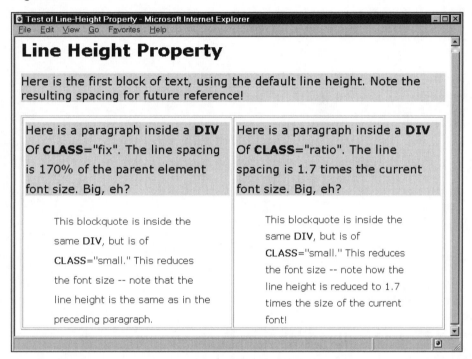

Figure 4.21 tests these four alignments on four paragraph elements, while Figure 4.22 shows the display of the document by Netscape Navigator 4 prerelease 3. Note that the first four paragraphs have a text indent of 10%, which indeed is interpreted as 10% of the parent (**DIV**) element width (essentially the width of the browser window). The last paragraph has an indent of –10%, which causes the text to actually disappear outside the browser window!

Note that MSIE 3 supports `text-align` but not the value `justify`, which it instead treats as left-aligned text.

White-space

In most cases, the browser ignores extra spaces, tabs, or carriage returns, or line feeds typed into the text, and collapses these into a single word space. This space is the formatted using as a *space band*, as defined in Chapter 3. The result is that the text is smoothly flowed across the display, and the author does not have to worry about the exact positioning of the text.

In some cases, however, an author may wish to preserve these whitespace characters. A typical example is the content of a **PRE** element, wherein the text is rendered in a monospace font, and preserved whitespace can be used to vertically align text, or to otherwise structure the text—indeed, this is what is done with all the CSS example listings in this book.

Figure 4.21 Example document illustrating the `text-indent` and `text-align` properties. Stylesheet rules are shown in italics. Browser display of this document is found in Figure 4.22.

```
<HTML><HEAD><TITLE>Text Indents and Alignment</TITLE>
<STYLE>
<!--
BODY     {margin-left: 4%; margin-right: 4%}
P        {text-indent: 10% }   /* indent 10% of element width */
.jleft   {text-align:  left;      }
.jright  {text-align:  right;     }
.justfy  {text-align:  justify;   }
.cent    {text-align:  center;    }
.lefty   {text-indent: -10%;      }
-->
</STYLE>
</HEAD><BODY BGCOLOR="#ffffff">
<H2>Text Indent and Alignment </H2>
<DIV CLASS="indent">
<P CLASS="jleft">This is a standard <EM>left-aligned</EM> paragraph.
    With left-to-right languages, this is the default alignment.</P>
<P CLASS="jright">This is a <EM>right-aligned</EM> paragraph.
    This is the default for right-to-left languages, such
    as Arabic or Hebrew. </P>
<P CLASS="justfy">Here is <EM>justify</EM>-ied text—the text
    should be smoothly flowed between the left and right margins.
    Many browsers do not support full justification between both
    margins, and default to left justified. </P>
<P CLASS="cent">This is <EM>center</EM>ed text—it should
    be centered within the element, with ragged left and
    right margins. Note that the first line does not appear
    centered, due to the text-indent on that line.</P>
<P CLASS="lefty">This paragraph has no special alignment, but
    has a <EM>negative</EM> text-indent of -10%. As a result,
    the text is indented outside the browser border.</P>
</DIV><HR></BODY></HTML>
```

The CSS `white-space` property lets an author control the browser's interpretation of the whitespace characters. There are three possible values. `Normal` tells the browser to process the characters in the normal way—that is, to collapse whitespace characters into a single space band, and to break the text to a new line only when necessary. On the other hand, the value `pre` tells the browser to preserve all these whitespace characters, and to include all the space, tab, and carriage return characters when displaying the content. Finally, the value `nowrap` tells the browser to collapse the text, but not to insert any line breaks unless explicitly indicated by a BR element.

Figure 4.22 Rendering by the Netscape Navigator 4 prelease 4 browser of the document listed in Figure 4.21. Note how the negative text indent associated with the final paragraph pushes the text outside the browser window!

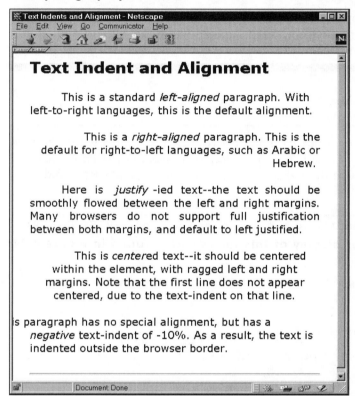

The effect of this property is illustrated in Figures 4.23 and 4.24. The first paragraph is formatted as per the "normal" method—the text is collapsed, and line breaks are introduced where needed. The second paragraph has the associated property white-space: pre. As a result, the tabs, carriage returns, and extra spaces are preserved. Note, however, that the text laid out in columns in Figure 4.23 is not so arranged in Figure 4.24. The text is not aligned because the font is not a monospace font; consequently, the letters are of variable width. A combination of the properties

```
whitespace: pre;
font-family: monospace;
```

reproduces the text layout behavior of the HTML **PRE** element.

NOTE Incorrect Handling of `White-space: nowrap` by Netscape Navigator 4

Netscape Navigator 4 does not properly handle the declaration `white-space: nowrap,` and mistakenly inserts line breaks to keep the text within the left and right margins (i.e., it treats `nowrap` as equivalent to `normal`).

Chapter Summary

Horizontal text spacing in text depends on: *tracking* (space between characters in a word), *kerning* (spacing control between specified pairs of characters), and *space band* (space between words). CSS provides control over tracking through the `letter-spacing` property, and space band through `word-spacing`.

Figure 4.23 Example document illustrating the `white-space` property. Stylesheet rules are shown in italics. Browser display of this document is found in Figure 4.24.

```
<HTML><HEAD><TITLE>Whitespace Property</TITLE>
<STYLE>
<!--
P          {margin-left: 5%; margin-right: 5%;}
H2         {text-align:  center;  }
.preform   {white-space:  pre;     }  /* Preserve spaces, tabs and CRs */
.norap     {white-space:  nowrap;  }  /* disable line wrapping */
-->
</STYLE>
</HEAD><BODY BGCOLOR="#ffffff">
<H2>Text Indent and Alignment </H2>
<H3>White-space: normal</H3>
<P>Here is a regular, everyday       paragraph,
    with a few carriage returns, some extra  spaces and        some     tabs.
    here  is    column    aligned    text
    this  does  not     align,       however.</P>
<H3>White-space: pre</H3>
<P CLASS="preform">Here is a regular, everyday       paragraph,
    with a few carriage returns, some extra  spaces and        some     tabs.
    here  is    column    aligned    text
    this  does  not     align,       however.</P>
<H3>White-space: nowrap </H3>
<P CLASS="norap">Here is a regular, everyday       paragraph,
    with a few carriage returns, some extra  spaces and        some     tabs. here  is    col-
umn   aligned    text this  does  not       align,       however.</P>
<HR></BODY></HTML>
```

Figure 4.24 Rendering by the Netscape Navigator 4 prelease 4 browser of the document listed in Figure 4.23. Note how the second paragraph, with property white-space: pre, **displays the hard-coded space, tab, and carriage return characters present in the original document.**

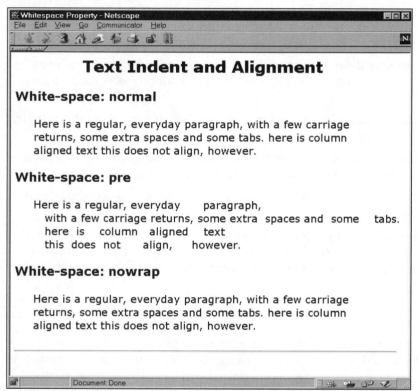

Vertical spacing around lines of text is known as *leading*. In CSS, this is specified by the line-height property.

Pseudo-element selectors specify formatting for *element-like* blocks of text. However, the first-letter pseudo-class is insufficient for proper drop capitals. Both currently defined pseudo-elements (first-line and first-letter) can only be associated with block elements.

Grouped selectors reduce the need to duplicate rules that are to be applied repetitiously to varying elements. Using grouped selectors reduces the size of the stylesheet and encourages the author to be consistent in the use of fonts and layout.

Adding *comments* to the stylesheet helps authors remember and track rules.

Contextual selectors cull for elements contingent on their context within other elements. Contextual selectors can be grouped, and can specify multiple levels of element nesting.

`Color` can modify the text color. Color changes can also be made to background—and often must be, to retain sufficient contrast between the text and the background.

`Text-align` and `text-indent` provide for text alignment and text indents within block elements. Negative text indent values will produce a hanging indent.

`Word-spacing` and `letter-spacing` define space between letters and words, respectively. Both quantities can take positive or negative values. Making large changes to letter spacing can quickly result in unreadable text.

The `text-decoration` property defines traditional text decorations. Allowed values are `underline`, `overline`, `line-through`, `blink`, and `none`. Not all browsers support all these values.

The `text-transform` property controls case within a selection of text, and can, for example, shift all letters to all uppercase. This can be very useful for headings.

The `vertical-align` property can align text with text or inline objects with text. This is useful for aligning inline images with text, or for creating superscripts and subscripts.

The `font` property is a shorthand for expressing the five various font-related properties, plus the line height, in a single declaration.

`White-space` controls the handling of whitespace characters within an element. Traditionally, whitespace (any combination of tab, space, carriage return, or line feed characters) is collapsed into a single space band. However, the value `pre` will force the browser to display all whitespace characters.

Chapter Exercises

The first exercise deals with contextual selectors. After reviewing the discussion of such selectors (and the examples provided in Table 4.1), practice using the contextual selectors by modifying the document in Figure 4.8, or by creating your own document. Create multiple selectors that apply to the same formatting element or elements, and note how the properties are applied when the document is rendered by a browser. Make sure that several of the test rules specify different values for the same property, and use this fact to determine which selectors have priority for different elements.

Figure 4.10 illustrates the use of the color, word, and letter-spacing properties. In this exercise, practice manipulating these selectors by duplicating 4.10 or by creating your own figure. Be sure to experiment with both positive and negative values for `word-spacing` and `letter-spacing`. Check to see how your browser responds to the `word-spacing` changes. You should also use `text-align` to check the behavior with left-aligned and fully justified text, and see how the word and letter-spacing properties interact with text alignment.

For the final exercise, using Figure 4.10, or your own figure, practice using the `vertical-align`, `line-height`, `text-indent`, and `text-align` properties. Try changing the font size in an inline element, and then use `vertical-align` to align the top or bottom of the enlarged text with the remaining text in the line. Also try using the percentage line height values to reposition elements vertically within the block of text. Notice how, no matter how far you vertically displace the element, the original space occupied by the non-displaced element is left empty.

Endnotes

1. The *compositor* is the person who actually composes the printed pages, based on the text content and the specified layout design.

2. The *designer* is the person who specifies the desired design for the book layout (e.g., fonts, line spacings, margins, heading styles, and the overall layout for the pages).

3. A *child* element is directly contained by its *parent:* For example, in the markup `<P> Paragraph <EM> text </EM> </P>` the **EM** element is the child of the parent **P** element.

5

Tutorial, Part 3: Formatting and Positioning of Elements

Chapters 3 and 4 introduced text-level formatting issues, and explained in detail how CSS can control text properties and formatting, including formatting within selections of text, such as line spacing and vertical alignment within a line. In a document that includes a collection of text blocks, such as paragraphs or headings, an author also wants to control the size and positioning of the blocks. For example, most authors want to:

- adjust the margins for blocks of text, to either narrow or widen the size of the displayed block, or to reposition the block, either vertically or horizontally

- add space around a block of text, to pad between the block and adjacent blocks

- place ruled borders around or alongside a block of text, to use as dividing borders (as in newspaper column dividers), or to denote the ends of blocks (as in horizontal rules)

- control list-item formatting, to change the bullets or position of the bullets relative to the text

- "hide" particular content from display (for example, a collection of sub-list elements that should be "hidden" in an overview of a list)

- "float" objects (e.g., images) or blocks of text on the page, such that the text of underlying non-floating elements flows around the floating object

These are the topics of this chapter. The chapter is divided into two sections. The first section presents an overview of the CSS Level 1 block formatting model—a simple "box" model in which each displayed element is treated as a rectangular box positioned on the display. This section introduces the main features of the box model, and describes the CSS properties that specify padding, borders, and margins associated with the formatting boxes. It also introduces the four different types of formatting elements supported by CSS—*block-level*, *list-item*, *inline*, and *floating*—and describes briefly the special formatting characteristics of each.

The second section looks in detail at the formatting characteristics of the four CSS formatting types. This section builds upon the model introduced in the first section, and introduces the details relevant to each of the formatting types. The features are illustrated with many example documents that illustrate the points made in the text, and that can also serve as templates for adapting CSS features into your own stylesheets.

Two caveats, however: First, several of the CSS formatting properties are not properly supported by Netscape Navigator 4 and Internet Explorer 3. Thus, although the CSS example documents are correct, some of the browser renderings given as figures illustrate common problems in element spacing or positioning. These problems are mentioned in the text, when they are particularly noticeable in the figures. However, to see how they really work with "current" browsers, you should obtain the example HTML documents from the book Web site (the location is given in the Preface) and view them yourself with your own CSS-aware browsers.

NOTE Known Problems with Current CSS Implementations

The CSS implementations in Navigator 4.0 and MSIE 3 have known problems related to element formatting and positioning. These problems fall into three categories: unimplemented features, implemented features that contradict the CSS specifications (in particular, percentage length values that are calculated relative to the browser canvas width, as opposed to the width of the parent element), and implemented features that are buggy, and behave inconsistently. This chapter attempts to document these problems within the text, and suggests workarounds where possible. In addition, the last section of the chapter outlines several particularly complex CSS formatting issues/problems.

Second, there are two new approaches to CSS element positioning, currently in the final stages of approval at the World Wide Web Consortium. These approaches allow for absolute control over element placement, and for control of element *z-indexing* (the order in which elements lie one atop the other). These new features are implemented in Netscape Navigator 4 and Microsoft Internet Explorer 4, and are described in Chapter 9.

Introduction to the CSS Formatting Model

CSS employs a very simple model for formatting HTML documents. In this model, every HTML element is transformed, on the display, into one or more rectangular boxes that contain the *markup content* of the element, which is either the text content of the element or the *object* referenced by the element (e.g., the inline image, applet, or form text input area). The CSS formatting block properties then control the layout, size, and positioning of these boxes, relative to the other boxes on the display.

Just as HTML elements can contain other elements, formatting boxes can contain other boxes. For example, a **DIV** element containing two **P** elements corresponds on the display to a **DIV** display "box" that contains two **P** display "boxes." An example of this is found in Figure 5.1, which illustrates the rendering of a simple HTML document (the different element "boxes" are marked by outlines) and the HTML element hierarchy defined by this document. Note how the element "tree" is effectively reproduced by the nesting of the formatting boxes. Note also that the top-level "box" that contains all the boxes corresponds to the **BODY** element: Every other box lies within this box, just as every displayed HTML element lies within the document **BODY**.

Also interesting in Figure 5.1 is how the **EM** element is transformed into not one but two formatting boxes. This is what was meant by the statement, at the beginning of the section, that an HTML element could be transformed into "one or more rectangular boxes." Elements such as **EM**

Figure 5.1 An illustration of the content layout model, here applied to an example HTML document. The document "tree" shows the hierarchical placements of the HTML elements. Each of these elements has been "boxed." Note how the nesting of the boxes follows the hierarchical structure. Note also how the EM element inside the P is transformed, on the display, into two formatting boxes, on adjacent lines.

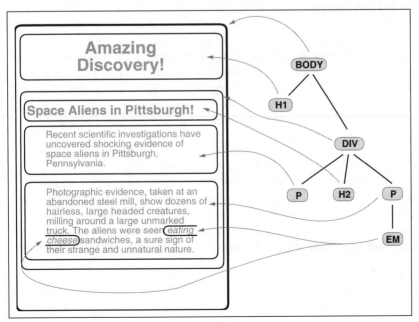

can span more than one line. In the CSS formatting model, each line resulting from the **EM** is treated as a separate formatting box. In CSS, such "multi-box" situations can only occur for non-empty inline HTML elements such as **EM**.

This element/box nesting model helps to justify property inheritance. Clearly it makes sense that a formatting box inherits the properties (font type and size, text color, etc.) of the box it is contained within. This model also helps explain why certain properties are not inherited. For example, background colors or images (properties related to these features are described in the next chapter) are not inherited because a child element, such as the **EM** within a **P**, can be thought of as lying "on top" of the underlying paragraph, and will simply let the paragraph background show through. Similarly, the properties width and height, which can define the width and height of an element, will also not be inherited, since the `width` and/or `height` of a box is not the same as (although it may be restricted by) the bounds of the parent element box. To see this, consider the **P** element inside the **DIV**: Obviously, the width of the paragraph could be adjusted independent of the width of the **DIV** it lies within.

As with HTML elements, not all CSS formatting elements/boxes are treated in the same way. For example, **P** defines a blocks of text that has well-defined breaks before and after the element, while **EM** defines an emphasized text string that would appear inline within a **P**. These are examples of two of the basic CSS formatting types: *block-level* (as in **P**) and *inline* (as in **EM**). The two other formatting types supported in CSS are *list-item* and *floating*. To understand the CSS model, it helps to understand these different formatting types, and the specifics of the box formatting model. These issues are discussed in the following section.

NOTE About Terminology

In the CSS specification, the different types of formatting boxes are called formatting *elements*. This is sensible, in that the items that are being formatted are markup elements, and there is usually a simple relationship between an HTML element and a formatting element. However, there are also cases where this relationship is not straightforward, since a CSS author can use the display property to *modify* the formatting type of an HTML element to whatever he or she wants, for example changing an **EM** element to be a block-level element instead of inline.

To reduce confusion, the discussion in the rest of this section refers to formatting *types*, as opposed to formatting elements. However, there are places where the words "formatting element" are used to avoid the annoying repetition of the word "type." In most cases, the meaning should be obvious. If the text seems confusing, try changing the word "element" to "type," and see if it makes more sense!

Formatting Types: Block-Level, Inline, and Floating

As mentioned previously, there are four main formatting types: *block-level*, *list-item*, *inline*, and *floating*. The *block-level* type represents blocks of text, such as paragraphs or headings, that are likely to occupy large blocks of the display window and that are typically preceded and followed by a line break. A typical example is the standard formatting of a **P** element: a block of text with line breaks before and after the text.

The *list-item* type corresponds to list-like items. Such items are formatted in a manner similar to block-level formatting, except that list items can take a graphic, bullet, or other decoration to mark the item. There are several properties specific to this type that control how the decoration is formatted with respect to the element content. These properties, and the special formatting issues relevant to this type of element, are described later in the section on list-item formatting (Example 12).

The *inline* type corresponds to blocks that appear inline within another block, and that can share space in a line with other inline blocks. The most typical examples are text highlighting/formatting elements such as **EM** or **STRONG**, which format strings of text within a block-level element such as a **P**. As mentioned earlier, non-empty inline HTML elements can yield multiple formatting blocks, since the element content can be broken across a line, and the CSS formatting model treats each line as a separate block.

By default, all HTML elements are treated as either block-level, inline, or list-item types. Table 5.1 lists the different formatting types, and those elements associated with these types by default.

Finally, the *floating* type corresponds to blocks that float to either the right or left margin of the element within which they are contained. Thus, an **IMG** element floated inside a **P** will float to the left or right inner edge of the **P**. There are no HTML elements that float by default; however, any HTML element can be transformed into a floating element via the `float` property. The supported values for `float` are `left` and `right`, which float the element to the left or right margin, respectively. In CSS, floating elements are treated as a special block-level formatting type. Formatting details associated with floating blocks are discussed near the end of this chapter.

Setting Formatting Type with the Display Property

The `display` property can turn any element into a block-level, list-item, or inline formatting type. More specifically, the declaration `display: block` creates a block-level element, `display: list-item` creates a list-item element, and `display: inline` creates an inline formatting element. Finally, the declaration `display: none` indicates that the associated element should not be displayed. If this latter property value is applied to an HTML element, the element and all of its content are ignored by the browser as the document is rendered, so that the content of the element is not displayed (although the text can be seen by viewing the document source).

The `display` property is supported by Navigator 4.0, although not all HTML elements accept the value `block`. This property is not supported by MSIE 3.

Replaced Elements

Some HTML elements are placeholders for non-text content; for example, an **IMG** element is a placeholder for an image file to be displayed with the document, while an **APPLET** is a placeholder for a software applet, and may be replaced by an applet's user interface component.

Such elements are called "replaced" elements, since they are replaced by the object referenced by the element. This is important to the CSS formatting model, as the size of the "box" required by these objects is often unknown until the object is loaded—for example, a browser does not know the size of an image until it arrives at the browser. In some cases the box size can be preset using CSS `height` and `width` properties (for example, to resize an image referenced by an **IMG** element). However, this is not always possible—for example, form **INPUT** fields cannot be resized. Table 5.1 lists those HTML elements that are "replaced" elements.

Display of Formatting Elements

As mentioned in the introduction, all CSS display types produce blocks of text on the display. In general, block-level, list-item, and floating elements yield a single box; for example, the box that defines the bounds of a paragraph or the box that outlines a floating image. With current browsers, adjacent block elements are separated vertically, with a margin of some sort between them. An example of this default rendering is shown in Figure 5.2, which illustrates the default formatting for two adjacent block-level formatting elements, one arising from an **H1** heading and the other arising from a **P**.

Block-Level Formatting Elements

All block-level formatting elements (in fact, all formatting elements) are surrounded by space defined by *padding*, *border*, and *margin* properties. It is this space that keeps elements separated one

Table 5.1 The Four CSS Formatting Groups and the HTML Elements That Belong to These Groups by Default

The CSS `Display` property can change the formatting group of any element.

Formatting Group	Default HTML Elements in Group
Block-level	ADDRESS, BLOCKQUOTE, BR, DD, DIR, DIV, DT, FORM, H1 to H6, HR, MENU, <u>MULTICOL</u>[a], OL, P, PRE, UL
Inline	A, APPLET, B, *BDO*, BIG, CITE, CODE, DFN, EM, EMBED, I, IMG, INPUT, KBD, *OBJECT*, *Q*, SAMP, SELECT, SMALL, *SPAN*, STRIKE, STRONG, SUB, SUP, TEXTAREA, TT, U, VAR

Other supported but non-recommended[b] inline elements are : BLINK, CENTER, FONT, <u>MARQUEE</u>, NOBR, *S*

List-item	LI
Floating	*(There are no default floating elements)*

Special Element Group

Replaced Elements	APPLET, EMBED, IMG, INPUT, *OBJECT*, SELECT, TEXTAREA

[a]There is no CSS equivalent to the Netscape <u>MULTICOL</u> element used to format multicolumn text.
[b]CSS recommends that authors avoid these elements, and that they instead use CSS properties to produce the desired formatting.

Figure 5.2 An illustration of the block formatting model as applied to the display of simple HTML elements: here a block-level formatting element (H1) followed by another block-level formatting element (P). The dashed lines show the inner box around the element content (here assuming that both elements have the same left and right *margins*). **Note how the elements do not overlap, and lie one above the other.**

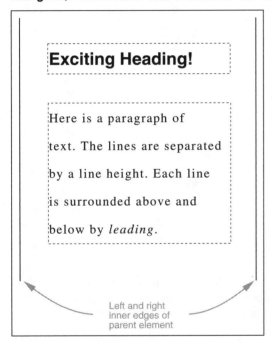

from another. A border is simply that—a border drawn around the element. Padding is extra space that is added just outside the formatting element and before any defined border. Margin spaces are added outside any border or padding space. The default size of padding and border spaces is zero. Most browsers provide positive default values for the margins above and below block-level elements, so that there are well-defined vertical separations between them. If margin, padding, and border properties were all zero, then elements would appear without any intervening space.

Inline Formatting Elements

Inline elements also produce formatting boxes. However, as discussed earlier, non-empty inline HTML elements can produce more than one formatting box, depending on how the text is laid out. This is because the boxes produced by such elements can be "broken" by the end of a formatted line, recommencing with a new box on the line below. An example of this is shown in Figure 5.3, which illustrates a block **P** element containing an inline **EM** element that is broken across two lines. Notice how the **EM** element is thus associated with two formatting boxes.

Figure 5.3 An illustration of the block formatting model as applied to the display of simple HTML elements: here a paragraph containing EM emphasized text. Note how the HTML EM element produces two formatting boxes on two adjacent lines.

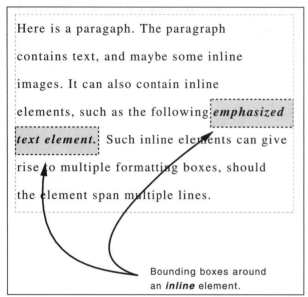

Here is a paragaph. The paragraph contains text, and maybe some inline images. It can also contain inline elements, such as the following *emphasized text element.* Such inline elements can give rise to multiple formatting boxes, should the element span multiple lines.

Bounding boxes around an *inline* element.

Empty elements, such as **IMG, APPLET,** or **INPUT,** are handled as inline formatting elements. Of course, such elements can produce at most one formatting block, since they cannot be broken across a line. At present, all "replaced" HTML elements are formatted as inline elements unless they are explicitly floated using the float property.

Padding, borders, and margins have little effect on the positioning of inline elements, and in particular should not affect the line spacing of the parent element. Thus, adding huge margins or padding space above or below an inline **EM** element within a paragraph will not affect the paragraph's line spacing. However, horizontal margins, padding, or border space may add space between the inline element and the surrounding text (the exact behavior depends on the browser).

"Floating" Formatting Elements

Floating elements produce boxes that "float" on top of the element within which they are contained. Consider, for example, a paragraph containing a left-floated **IMG.** The **IMG** element is floated on top of the paragraph element, but floats in such a way that it displaces any underlying inline content. An illustration of a floating element is shown in Figure 5.4.

The padding, border, and margin properties for "floating" formatting elements help to position the floated element with respect to the edges of the parent element, and to add space between the floated element and the surrounding text. Again, the details of how this is done are found in the second half of this chapter.

Figure 5.4 An illustration of the formatting of a floating element, here an IMG inside a P. Note how the floated image lies within the P, but *displaces* the text from the region underneath the floated image.

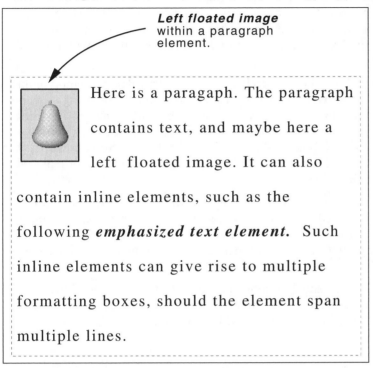

Formatting Details of the Formatting Box

The preceding text described briefly the formatting of the three main formatting types, illustrated in Figures 5.2 through 5.4. This text also introduced, in a rather vague manner, the idea that the formatted element is surrounded by extra space, where this space was defined by padding, margin, and border properties. The purpose of this section is to define these properties more precisely. In doing so we also need to introduce two properties, `height` and `width`, which define the actual size of the box containing the element content.

Height and Width

The height and width of an element are simply the dimensions of the bounding box surrounding the element content—that is, the space *inside* any margins, borders, or padding space. This box, also called the *inner bounding box*, is illustrated by the dashed line in Figure 5.5, here denoting the box for a paragraph element. Note how the box *inscribes* the element content as closely as possible. The height and width of the element are then simply the distances between these inner box edges.

In CSS, these two dimensions can sometimes be specified using `height` and `width` properties. Both properties can in principle take lengths as values, or they can take the keyword `auto`, which lets the browser adjust the dimensions as appropriate. `Width` can also take percentage values, in which case the width should be calculated as a percentage of the width of the parent element. The default value for both is `auto`. There are no current browsers that support `height`, while Navigator 4.0 and MSIE 4 support `width`. Also, all current browsers calculate such percentage values with respect to the full width of the browser canvas, and *not* with respect to the width of the parent element.

Not all formatting types support width or height specifications. In particular, non-empty inline formatting elements do not have a defined width or height. Recall how inline formatting elements can span multiple lines, yielding multiple formatting boxes of differing widths, and possibly differing heights. Thus `height` and `width` properties are irrelevant to these elements, and the browser instead uses the intrinsic dimensions of each box as obtained from the display. Note, however, that `height` and `width` can be used to resize inline **IMG** elements—the special handling of replaced elements is discussed near the end of the chapter.

In most cases, an author will not need to specify the height or width, as browsers by default adjust these properties to the values required by the element content. Indeed, problems can occur if an author tries to specify a fixed box size for a block-level element, since changes in the document content or in a related stylesheet property (e.g., font size) may cause the content to no longer fit inside the specified box.

However, for block-level or floating elements it is sometimes useful to specify one of these sizes—usually `width`—and let the other size vary such that the content fits inside the element's box. Some examples illustrating this are found in the second half of the chapter.

Padding Space

Padding space is space padded around the element content. Padding space is treated in many ways as part of the element, and is assigned the same background color or background image as the element content. Padding is often used to create a buffer region around the element content, and to create spacing between the element and adjacent elements, or between the content and an element *border* (borders are discussed in the next section). However, the effect of padding space on adjacent formatting elements depends strongly on the type of the element, as described later.

Padding length property values can be lengths or percentage values. Percentage lengths should be calculated with respect to the width of the *parent* element: However, all current browsers calculate percentage lengths with respect to the full width of the browser canvas. Values must be positive, as the value simply specifies the size of the padding region, which cannot be a negative. The default value for all padding lengths is zero. For obvious reasons, padding is not inherited. Figure 5.5 illustrates a paragraph formatted with padding space, while Figure 5.8 illustrates a paragraph without (bottom) and with (second from bottom) padding.

There are five properties for defining padding widths: four corresponding to the padding at the top, bottom, left, and right sides of the element, and one shorthand property for defining all widths at once. These properties and their meanings are defined in Table 5.2, while the handling of the shorthand property `padding` is described in Table 5.3. In this table, *len1* through *len4* are valid

Table 5.2 A Description of the Five Padding-Related Properties

Property	Values	Default Value	Description
padding-left	+, +%	0	Width of padding space at the left side of the element
padding-right	+, +%	0	Width of padding space at the right side of the element
padding-top	+, +%	0	Width of padding space at the top of the element
padding-bottom	+, +%	0	Width of padding space at the bottom of the element
padding	1–4 values, as above	*N/A*	Shorthand for padding widths; one to four values

Values Key	+	Positive length values
	+%	Positive percentage values
	N/A	Not applicable to shorthand properties

positive lengths or percentage values. Note that the shorthand border-width and margin properties use the same rules as outlined in Table 5.3 to relate listed lengths to the proper sides of the element.

Padding space can be applied to any formatting element. However, the effect of the padding space on the layout of adjacent formatting elements depends strongly on the formatting type of the element. With block-level or floating elements, the padding effectively "expands" outward from

Table 5.3 Meanings Associated with the Four Possible Padding Shorthand Property Values Here, len1 through len4 are any allowed padding length values, as described in the text.

Property Specification	Meaning
padding: *len1*	All four padding widths are of size *len1*
padding: *len1 len2*	Top and bottom padding widths are of size *len1*; left and right padding widths are of size *len2*
padding: *len1 len2 len3*	Top padding is of size *len1*, right and left padding are of size *len2*, bottom padding is of size *len3*
padding: *len1 len2 len3 len4*	Top padding is of size *len1*, right padding is of size *len2*, bottom padding is of size *len3*, left padding is of size *len4*

Figure 5.5 An illustration of padding space, borders, and margins around a formatting element, here a block-level element with a light gray background. Note how the padding space takes on the background properties of the element, while the border and margins do not. The margins (and any blank area in the border) instead are *transparent,* **and show through the content (background, and sometimes text or other content if the element has been moved using** `margin` **properties) of the underlying element.**

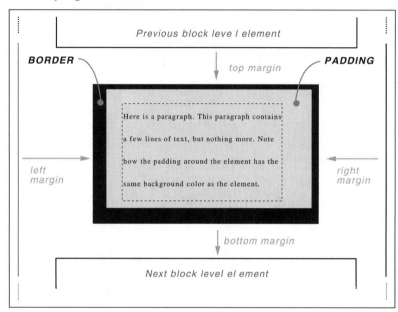

the element, and pushes the element away from the inner box edges of the parent element, or the outer edges of adjacent block-level or floating elements.

Borders

A border is a ruled line that lies outside the element content and padding space. An example of a very thick border is shown in Figure 5.5. The widths of the four borders are defined by the properties `border-left-width`, `border-right-width`, `border-top-width`, and `border-bottom-width`, or by the shorthand property `border-width`. Like padding widths, these properties can take length or percentage values, where percentage values should be calculated relative to the width of the parent element. However, all current browsers calculate such percentage lengths with respect to the full width of the browser canvas, and *not* with respect to the width of the parent element. Border width properties can also take any of the four keywords `thin`, `medium`, `thick`, or `none`, each having the obvious meaning. The default width specification is `medium`. Like padding spaces, border widths cannot be negative—clearly it is not sensible to talk about a border with a negative width! Table 5.4 summarizes the different CSS properties that affect an element border.

There are two properties for defining the nature of the border. `Border-color` specifies the color of the border, either as a name or as an RGB code. The default value is the same color as the

Table 5.4 A Description of the Eight Border-Related Properties

Property	Values	Default Value	Description
border-left-width	+, +%, thin, medium, thick, none	0	Width of border at the left side of the element
border-right-width	+, +%, thin, medium, thick, none	0	Width of border at the right side of the element
border-top-width	+, +%, thin, medium, thick, none	0	Width of border at the top of the element
border-bottom-width	+, +%, thin, medium, thick, none	0	Width of border at the bottom of the element
border-width	1–4 values, as above	*none*	Shorthand for border widths: one to four values, with side associations as described for the padding shorthand property (Table 5.3)
border-color	any valid color specification	text color in element	Color of border (default is color of text within the element)
border-style	*(see Table 5.5)*	none	Style or type of border (default is "none" for no displayed border)
border	*(see text)*	*N/A*	Shorthand for specifying same width, style, and color for all four borders

Values Key	+	Positive length values
	+%	Positive percentage values
	N/A	Not applicable to shorthand properties

text within the element. Border-style defines the type of the border. The allowed values and their meanings are listed in Table 5.5. The default value is none, which causes no border to be displayed, even if a width is given. Note that browsers do not necessarily support all styles, and will substitute the default style (solid) in place of a requested but non-supported choice.

NOTE Problems with Border Properties under MSIE 3 and Navigator 4.0

Borders are not implemented under MSIE 3, and are only partially implemented under Navigator 4.0. Navigator 4.0 does not support the eight edge-specific properties border-top, border-top-width, border-left, border-left-width, and so on. At the same time, the border-color property can take only one value, which specifies the color for all four borders. Border-width, on the other hand, can take from one to four values, to specify different widths for the four different borders. Border-style can also take from one to four values, to specify the styles for the four borders. However, the dashed and dotted styles are not supported, while the rendering of borders when multiple style values are specified is unpredictable. In particular, you cannot use the value none to eliminate single border edges: this keyword is ignored unless it is the only value assigned to the border-style property. If border-style: none, then the borders are drawn, but as *transparent* spacers: According to the CSS specifications, this declaration should instead cause the borders to not be drawn at all.

Finally, the border property can simultaneously set the width, style, and color of all four borders. The general form is

border width style color

where *width* is any allowed width specification, *style* is any allowed style specification, and *color* is any allowed color specification. These values can appear in any order, or can be absent, in which case the browser will assume the default. For example, the declaration

border thick red dashed

Table 5.5 The Nine Different Border-Style Property Values and Their Meanings

Property Value	Description
dashed	Draw the border as a dashed line; the line is drawn on top of the element background.
dotted	Draw the border as a dotted line; the line is drawn on top of the element background.
double	Draw the border as two thin lines (a double line), drawn on top of the element background. The distance between the inner edge of the inner line and the outer edge of the outer line is equal to the border width.
groove	Draw the border as a three-dimensional groove.
inset	Draw the border such that the element content looks like a depressed inset.
none	Do not display a border (the default).
outset	Draw the border such that the element content looks like a raised outset.
ridge	Draw the border as a ridge (a "raised" groove).
solid	Draw the border as a solid line.

calls for a thick, red, dashed border around the entire element, while the declaration

```
border: thin solid
```

calls for a thin solid-lined border using the color of the text within the element. Note that the declaration

```
border: thick red
```

does not produce a border, since the default border style is `none`.

Like padding space, borders can be applied to any formatting element. However, the effect of the border space on the layout of adjacent formatting elements depends strongly on the formatting type of the element. With block-level or floating elements the border effectively "expands" outwards from the element, and pushes the element away from the inner box edges of the parent element, or the outer box edges of adjacent block-level or floating elements.

Although `border` is often used to surround a block of text with a border, in principle, it can also be used to produce sidebars alongside blocks of text (for example, to illustrate certain sections) or to create a divider between adjacent blocks. This is not possible with MSIE 3 or Navigator 4.0.

Margins

A margin surrounds the element, its padding, and its border. The margin region is transparent, and will show through the background of the *parent* element. Thus if a **P** with a yellow background and a surrounding margin lies within a **DIV** taking a red background, then the margin region around the **P** will be red. Margin widths are specified by the four properties `margin-left`, `margin-right`, `margin-top`, and `margin-bottom`, or by the shorthand property `margin`, which can express the margins at the four sides of the element in a single declaration. The rules for these properties and their allowed values are shown in Table 5.6.

Margin sizes can be specified as lengths, percentage values, or by the keyword `auto`. Percentage values should be calculated with respect to the width of the parent element: However, all current browsers calculate such percentage lengths with respect to the full width of the browser canvas and not with respect to the parent element width. The keyword "auto" tells the browser to automatically determine the appropriate margin. The actual margin size produced by `auto` depends on the type of element (block-level, inline, floating) and on related margin, height, or width specifications—consequently, the details of how margins are processed are described later, when we go into the details of the different formatting types. As an example, however, consider the left margin produced by `margin-left: auto` applied to a block-level element. In this case, the actual left margin size will then depend on the size of the right margin, on the element's actual width, and on any intervening left or right padding space or borders.

For block-level or floating elements, the margin properties define both the *space* occupied by the formatting element and the *position* of the element relative to the parent element, or relative to adjacent elements above and below it. In CSS Level 1, the margin properties are the only mechanism for controlling the positioning of elements.

Table 5.6 A Description of the Five Margin-Related Properties

Property	Values	Default Value	Description
margin-left	+/-, (+/-)%, auto	0	Width and offset of margin at the left side of the element
margin-right	+/-, (+/-%), auto	0	Width and offset of margin at the right side of the element
margin-top	+/-, (+/-%), auto	0	Width and offset of margin at the top of the element
margin-bottom	+/-, (+/-%), auto	0	Width and offset of margin at the bottom of the element
margin	1–4 values, each as above	*none*	Shorthand for margins; one to four values, with side associations as described for the padding shorthand property (Table 5.3)

Values Key	+/-	Positive or negative length values
	(+/-)%	Positive or negative percentage values
	N/A	Not applicable to shorthand properties

The relative positioning model is of course not perfect, and in many cases an absolute positioning control is desired. This is not supported in CSS Level 1, but CSS extensions currently under development do allow for this type of detailed positioning control. This approach is discussed in Chapter 9.

Specifics of Element Formatting

As already mentioned, the effects of padding, border, margin, width, and height properties depend on the type of the element (block-level, inline, replaced) being formatted. For example, horizontal margins make a lot of sense for paragraphs, but how does the same concept apply to inline or floating elements? Similarly, how should the top and bottom margins of two adjacent block-level elements be combined, or how should vertical padding space of an inline element affect the line spacing of the parent block-level element?

The previous section introduced the basic terms and concepts used to describe layout. This second section looks to answer the following, more practical question: How do these concepts apply in the actual layout of the different formatting types, and to the actual layout of a document? This question is answered by looking at each of the different types of formatting elements, and examining, in detail and with examples, how the formatting model applies in each case.

Block-Level Formatting

The CSS layout model provides for a reasonable (if not terribly exciting) level of control over the positioning and dimensions of block-level elements. There are two distinct components. Horizontal positioning, controlled via several horizontal length properties, allows for the sizing and positioning of an element with respect to its *parent* element (e.g., a **P** positioned with respect to the borders of the parent **DIV**). Vertical positioning, controlled via several vertical length properties, supports the vertical positioning of an element relative to the block-level elements that precede and follow it. The formatting models for these two approaches are quite different, and are discussed separately in the following sections.

Note that block-level elements can also be transformed into floating elements via the `float` property. The formatting of floating elements is quite different from non-floating ones, and is described in a separate section near the end of this chapter.

Example 10: Horizontal Layout of Block-Level Elements

The horizontal position and size of a non-floating block-level element is determined by the seven properties `margin-left`, `border-left-width`, `padding-left`, `width`, `padding-right`, `border-right-width`, and `margin-right`. The CSS guiding principle for block-level elements is that the sum of these property values must be equal to the *width* of the parent element. That is:

margin-left + *border-left-width* + *padding-left* + *width* +

padding-right + *border-right-width* + *margin-right* = *width* (parent element)

This relationship between these property values is illustrated in Figure 5.6. The default value for the horizontal margin, padding, and border widths is zero, while the default for `width` is `auto`. In this default case (all paddings and borders set to zero, with margins set to auto) the browser will size the element width such that it fits just inside the `width` of the parent element, as illustrated by the first two displayed paragraphs in Figure 5.8 (the source for this HTML document is found in Figure 5.7).

Note that some of the element content will be empty, should the actual content not fill the entire region. This, for example, would be the case for a **P** element containing a short text phrase that does not span the full element width. Similarly, if padding and/or borders are added, then the element width will automatically shrink so that the content fits. These aspects of block-level element formatting are illustrated in the second and third paragraphs displayed in Figure 5.8. Note in the second paragraph how the box is filled out to occupy the available horizontal width. Note also how adding padding and border space to the third paragraph in Figure 5.8 reduces the actual width of the element. Finally, the fourth paragraph shows how left and right margins can reposition the margins for the element, as well as change the element width.

NOTE Left and Right Margin Restrictions under Netscape Navigator 4/MSIE 3

MSIE 3 supports left and right margins, but does not position margins properly: they are always positioned relative to the edges of the browser, instead of relative to the left and right edges of the parent element. Navigator 4 supports both left and right margins, but does not support negative right margin values, and does not support negative left margin values that would place the element content beyond the left edge of the browser window. In the latter case, the margin size is chosen such that the left edge of the element is aligned with the left edge of the display window.

NOTE `Background-Color` Problems with Netscape Navigator 4/MSIE 3

Unlike the situation shown in Figure 5.8, Netscape Navigator 4 and MSIE 3 do not completely color the area of a block element when a `background-color` is specified. Instead, these browsers highlight the text content with the specified color, and leave the remaining content untouched (and transparent). With Navigator 4, however, a specified `background-image` will fill the entire region. These (and other) background-related issues are discussed in Chapter 6.

Figure 5.6 Illustration of the relationship between the horizontal width properties for a block-level element. Note that the seven widths must sum to the `width` value of the parent element.

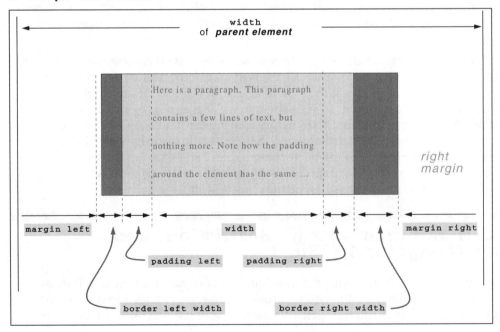

By default, horizontal margin widths are zero. Physically setting margin widths lets an author *reposition* the margins and/or *resize* the content between the margins. This is schematically illustrated in Figure 5.9, which shows how negative margins can in principle push the edges of the element outside the left and/or right boundaries set by the parent element. A simple CSS example is illustrated in Figures 5.10 and 5.11. The document in Figure 5.10 contains a **P** with zero margins, followed by a **DIV** with 20% margins on the left and right. The **DIV** in turn contains paragraphs with zero or negative left and right margins. To illustrate the bounds of the different elements, the **DIV** has been assigned a dark gray background color, and the **P** elements a light cyan (which appears in Figure 5.11 as light gray).

The first paragraph inside the **DIV** has left and right margins of zero: as a result, the left and right edges align with the edges of the **DIV** content, and are inset 20% with respect to the width of the **BODY** element. However, the second **P** inside the **DIV** has a left margin of -5%. Note how this paragraph extends to the left beyond the bounds of the enclosing **DIV**.

Note also that Figure 5.11 is retouched—the Navigator 4.0 browser used to create the figure does not properly handle the background colors of block elements such as **DIV** and P.

NOTE Margin and Background Behavior with MSIE 3 and Netscape Navigator 4.0

Netscape Navigator 4.0 and MSIE 3 do not properly render the background color for a block element: instead of filling the element "box" with the designated color, these browsers simply highlight the element text, and leave the remaining space transparent. Thus, Navigator 4.0 renders Figure 5.10 (the document that produces Figure 5.11) without a background for the space enclosed by parent **DIV**, and with the text in the two **P**s highlighted with the color specified in the CSS rule for paragraphs. Note, however, that if the element has a border, then Navigator 4.0 will properly paint the entire background using the specified background color!

NOTE Backgrounds and Margins in Navigator 4.0

With Navigator 4, if the parent element (e.g., the **DIV** in Figure 5.10) take a background *image*, then the full element background is tiled with this image. However, a background images for a parent element (for example, the **DIV** in Figure 5.10) disables negative margin values for all child elements. As a result, the second paragraph in Figure 5.11 can no longer pushes out to the left past the margin of the parent **DIV** (as requested by the negative `margin-left` property), and instead has a left margin aligned with the left edge of the parent **DIV**.

Display of Overlapping Elements By using negative margins to reposition a block element, it is possible to create block elements that overlap one another. So, how will these elements be displayed?

Figure 5.7 Example document illustrating horizontal padding space, borders, and margins as applied to block-level elements (here P). Stylesheet rules are in italics. Suggested browser rendering of this document is shown in Figure 5.8.

```
<HTML><HEAD><TITLE>Example of Auto-Adjusting Element Width</TITLE>
<STYLE>
<!--
P           { background: cyan;
              margin-left: 0;      /* set to 0 due to bug in NS4 Pre 3     */
              margin-right:0;}     /* set to 0 due to bug in NS4 Pre 3     */

P.padded    { padding:      1.5em;  /* a paragraph with padding and       */
              border-width:  thick;  /* borders.                          */
              border-style:  solid;
              }
P.margins  {margin-left: 25%;   /* Illustrates width adjustment due       */
             margin-right:10%;  /* to modified positive margins           */
             }
-->
</STYLE>
</HEAD><BODY BGCOLOR="#ffffff">
<H2>Example of Auto-Adjusting Element Width</H2>
<P>
   Here is a simple paragraph placed inside the <B>BODY</B> element.
   The paragraph width adjusts to fill the available space. The
   available space depends on the padding and border widths, and
   on the margins.</P>
<P>A tiny paragraph -- box padded so width fills parent.</P>
<P CLASS="padded">
   Here is a simple paragraph placed inside the <B>BODY</B> element.
   The paragraph width adjusts to fill the available space. The
   available space depends on the padding and border widths, and
   on the margins.</P>
<P CLASS="margins">
   Here is a simple paragraph placed inside the <B>BODY</B> element.
   The paragraph width adjusts to fill the available space. The
   available space depends on the padding and border widths, and
   on the margins.</P>
</BODY></HTML>
```

To know this, we need to know how elements are processed for display. In general, the browser proceeds sequentially through the document, and renders each element as it appears. Consequently, elements that occur later in the document are drawn *on top* of those that appeared earlier. If the element "on top" does not have any background properties (i.e., a color or a background image), then the content is simply drawn on top of the underlying content. However, if the element "on top" does have a

Figure 5.8 Rendering by the Netscape Navigator 4.0 browser of the document listed in Figure 5.7: The figure has been retouched so that the background color fills the entire "box" of each paragraph. The sums of the horizontal length measurements add up to the width of the parent element (the BODY). The result is that padding and border widths "shrink" the width of the element. Note how margin properties can reset the margin positions for the displayed text, thereby both repositioning it and resizing the width.

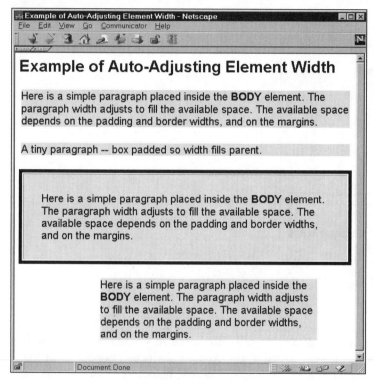

background, then this background is painted on top of the underlying element, and the element content is then drawn on top of the background.

The next generation of CSS supports a proper depth model for element rendering, which lets an author explicitly state the order of rendering for overlapping elements. This proposed model is described in detail in Chapter 9.

Limits on Element Positioning Most browsers impose limits on how elements can be repositioned, mostly to avoid complicated software problems when an element is moved outside a fixed boundary. For example, some browsers (e.g., Netscape Navigator 4.0) do not support negative margins that displace element content completely outside the display area, while most do not support

Figure 5.9 An illustration of how margins can horizontally position, shrink, or expand a block-level element relative to the parent element.

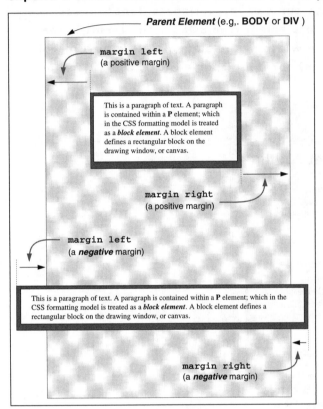

negative margins to reposition content outside of a table cell. Furthermore, some browsers simply ignore negative margins in these cases, while others "clip" the content at the cell border or at the edge of the browser window. At present, there is no consistency across browsers in their handling of such situations. The best advice is to avoid repositioning content off the display area (which is, in any event, sound advice!) and to avoid negative margins within table cells.

Using Auto or Fixed Margin/Width Sizes The preceding section assumed the default declaration width: auto. As a result, the margins could be freely adjusted (and padding or borders added), with the element width adjusting such that the sum of all the horizontal lengths added up to the parent element width. However, one can also set the left or right margins to auto, and fix the width at a particular size. This lets an author fix the width of the element, and reposition it from left to right. Note, however, that the height should not be fixed, since the browser will need to adjust the height so that the element content can fit in the prescribed horizontal space.

If only one of width, margin-left, or margin-right is set to auto, then the formatting is straightforward: The length that is auto is adjusted so that all seven lengths add up correctly. However, the situation is downright confusing when multiple lengths—or no lengths—are set to auto. CSS provides specific rules for handling these and other confusing cases. The rules are:

1. **Given no properties with value auto**—The browser assumes margin-right: auto, and adjusts the right margin to fit.

2. **Given only one property with value auto**—The property with value auto is automatically adjusted so that the sum of all seven widths adds up to the width of the parent element.

3. **Given margin-left: auto and margin-right: auto**—The left and right margins are set to equal values and are adjusted such that the sum of all property widths is equal to the width of the parent element. Note that this *centers* the element box within the parent element.

4. **Given width: auto and margin-left: auto**—This is not allowed. The browser will assume margin-left: 0 and adjust width to fit.

5. **Given width: auto and margin-right: auto**—This is not allowed. The browser will assume margin-right: 0 and adjust width to fit.

6. **Given that all three of width, margin-left, and margin-right are auto**—The browser sets margin-left: 0, margin-right: 0, and adjusts the element width to fill the available space.

Centering Block-Level Elements Rule 3 in the preceding list is useful for horizontally centering an element within another element. Suppose a document contains a **P** element that contains a sequence of five adjacent navigation icons, and that this paragraph should be centered on the page. The HTML markup for this paragraph might be:

```
<P CLASS="navbar">
    <IMG CLASS="navicon" SRC="nav1.gif" ALT="Access to Index"><IMG
        CLASS="navicon" SRC="nav2.gif" ALT="Site Directory"><IMG
        CLASS="navicon" SRC="nav3.gif" ALT="Contact Us"><IMG
        CLASS="navicon" SRC="nav4.gif" ALT="Free Software"><IMG
        CLASS="navicon" SRC="nav5.gif" ALT="Access to Infinite Wealth">
</P>
```

while the associated stylesheet rules that format the image and center the paragraph are:

```
IMG.navicon      { height:    auto;
                   width:     80px;
                   padding: 0;
                   margin:  0;              }
P.navbar         { width:          410px;
                   text-align:     center;
                   margin-left:    auto;
                   margin-right:   auto;  }
```

Figure 5.10. Example document illustrating negative block-element margins. Stylesheet rules are in italics. Suggested rendering for this markup is shown in Figure 5.11.

```
<HTML><HEAD><TITLE>Adjustable Margin Widths</TITLE>
<STYLE>
<!--
DIV        { background:    #999999;
             margin-left:   20%;
             margin-right:  20%
           }
P          { background:    #aaffff;   /* Default P properties           */
             margin-left:   0;   /* set to 0 due to bug in NS4 Pre 3     */
             margin-right:  0;   /* set to 0 due to bug in NS4 Pre 3     */
           }
P.negmarg  { margin-left:   -5%;  /* left margin moved left 5%;          */
             margin-right:  0;   /* do not move right margin.            */
           }
-->
</STYLE>
</HEAD><BODY>
<H2>Adjustable Margin Widths</H2>
<P>Here is a simple paragraph placed inside the <B>BODY</B> element.
   And outside the <B>DIV</B> that follows. Note the width of the
   <B>P</B> corresponds to the <B>BODY</B>. </P>
<DIV>
  <P>Here is a paragraph placed inside the <B>DIV</B> element.
     The paragraph width adjusts to fill the <tt>width</tt> of the
     <B>DIV</B>. The resulting paragraph width depends on the padding
     and border widths, and on the margins.</P>
  <P CLASS="negmarg">Here is a simple paragraph placed inside the
     <B>BODY</B> element. The paragraph has a left margin of -5%, which
     pushes the left side of the paragraph half way back to the left
     edge of the <B>BODY</B> (since the <B>DIV</B> margin was +10%).</P>
</DIV>
</BODY></HTML>
```

The first rule fixes the sizes of the images (the `auto` value for height ensures that the *aspect ratio* of the image—the ratio of width to height—remains unchanged should the `width` value cause the image to be resized), ensures that each image has no surrounding padding or margin space, and overrides any possible default values set elsewhere in the stylesheet. The second rule creates a block element 410 pixels wide (slightly greater than the combined widths of the five images within the element), with center-aligned content (so that the images are centered within the element), and with left and right margin widths set to `auto` (so that the **P** element is itself centered within the parent element).

Figure 5.11 Rendering, by Netscape Navigator 4 of the document listed in 5.10. Note how the light gray (light cyan, actually) P block-level elements extend out and overlap the edges of the parent DIV element (dark gray). This figure was retouched to color the region associated with the DIV, as Navigator 4 does not properly color the background for this element.

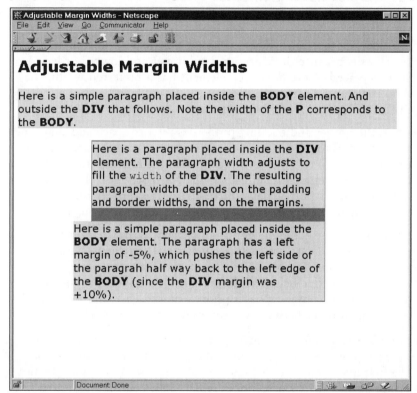

Note that most browsers define minimum permitted element widths; for example, a paragraph containing text may have a minimum width equal to the width of the font (otherwise the content would be entirely invisible). In these cases, the formatting software cannot reduce the width below this minimum value. If an author tries to specify a width smaller than this minimum, the browser will instead use the permitted minimum value.

Horizontal Formatting Characteristics of Navigator 4.0 and MSIE 3 Navigator 4.0 has a fixed minimum margin for all elements directly within the document **BODY**. This can be seen in Figure 5.8. where the heading and first three paragraphs have left and right margins of zero width. Note how there is remains a small margin space (approximately 10 pixels) between the element content and the window border. This is not the case, with MSIE 3 or 4, where zero-width left and/or right margins will indeed place content flush with the edge of the drawing canvas.

Also, Navigator 4.0 always leaves a small transparent padding space between an element border and the element content: this can be seen just inside the border surrounding the third paragraph in Figure 5.8. This space is always present, even if the padding space for the element is explicitly set to zero.

Example 11: Vertical Layout of Block-Level Elements

Vertical positioning and layout of block-level elements is controlled by seven properties: `margin-top`, `border-top-width`, `padding-top`, `height`, `padding-bottom`, `border-bottom-width`, and `margin-bottom`. Unlike the case for horizontal properties, there is no simple formula that relates these quantities. This is because there are no fixed upper and lower borders within which a formatting element is placed—note how each element has a preferred width (the width of the element it lies within), but can, in principle, expand to infinite length, since a displayed document is essentially a "scroll" of unspecified length.

As with the horizontal quantities, the border and padding properties refer to space added around the element "box," while the `height` refers to the height of the inner box containing the element content (see Figure 5.12). The default value for `height` is `auto`, so that the browser automatically chooses the height required to contain all the element content. In fact, for block-level elements, most browsers ignore `height` values other than `auto`. The default lengths for the vertical borders or padding space properties are zero, as was the case with the corresponding horizontal quantities.

Defining Block-Level Element Height The actual height of an element is measured between the top and the bottom inner edges of the element. This may seem a trivial statement, but it turns out to be a bit more complicated than it seems. For block-level elements that contain only text, the height is measured from the "bottom" of the line height at the last line in the block, to the "top" of the line height in the first line. This rather confusing description is more clearly illustrated in Figure 5.12, where the height is just the distance between the top and bottom dashed lines.

Things are somewhat more complicated given inline images or other replaced elements in the block-level element. In this case, the top of the element is either the top of the line height or the top of the replaced element in the first line, whichever is higher, while the bottom is either the bottom of the line height or the bottom of the furthest descending replaced element in the bottom line, whichever is lower. This is illustrated in Figure 5.13, which shows how the height of an element can be expanded by inline images.

As with the horizontal border and padding, vertical border and padding spaces are always positive, and simply define extra space added *outside* the inner box that contains the element content (and that defines the element *height*). However, adding extra vertical padding or border space usually does not affect the height of the *element*. This is because any added vertical space simply yields a longer document: Unlike the horizontal case where the document is restricted to lie between the left and right edges of the browser window, a document can grow to any length.

Vertical Margins The *vertical margin* is the vertical space left between two adjacent elements. In CSS, this distance is measured from the *outside bottom* (the line at the outside of any bottom padding and/or border) of an element to the *outside top* (the line at the outside of any top padding

Figure 5.12 An illustration of a block-level element's height. Note how the height is measured from the bottom of the line height for the bottom line and the top of the line height at the top line.

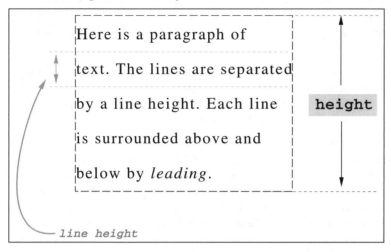

Figure 5.13 An illustration of a block-level element's height when the element contains both text and inline images. The height is measured from the bottom of the lowest image in the bottom line, to the top of the highest image in the top line.

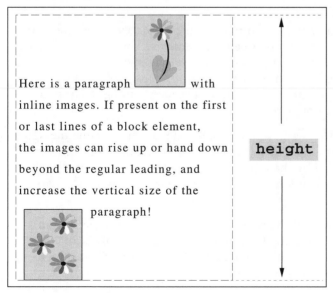

and/or border) of the element below it. Note, in particular, that if there are no borders or padding space between adjacent elements, then a zero margin brings the elements right into contact. However, if the elements have vertical padding spaces, then the elements will be separated by padding space, even if the margin is zero. This is illustrated in the example document in Figure 5.14, rendered in Figure 5.15. Note how the first two paragraphs have no spacing between them, while the bottom pair have intervening distance caused by the formatting element's top and bottom padding space.

Margins can be either positive or negative. A positive value increases the spacing between the top element and the bottom element, while a negative value brings the bottom element closer to the one on top. Indeed, a sufficiently negative margin will cause the two elements to overlap—a feature that can be used to introduce interesting typographic effects.

In CSS, the actual vertical separation between two elements is calculated from the `margin-bottom` value for the upper element and the `margin-top` value for the lower one. The CSS default values for the vertical margin properties are zero, although most browsers supply default `margin-top` and `margin-bottom` values to reproduce reasonable spacing between paragraphs and headings. Note that these properties can take either positive or negative values to indicate the direction of the margin offset. Values can be lengths (in any of the length units described in Appendix B), percentage values, or the keyword `auto`. Percentage values are calculated as a percentage of the parent element *width*—which is not terribly useful for determining heights, so that percentage units should be avoided. For vertical margins, the keyword `auto` is equivalent to a value of zero.

The actual vertical spacing is *not* calculated by simply adding these two margin property values. For example, if an element with a `bottom-margin` of 1cm is followed by an element with a `top-margin` of 2cm, the resulting vertical margin between the two is not 3cm. The rules by which the margins are determined vary depending on the sign of the margin values. The procedures used are as follows:

- **Bottom margin and following top margin are both positive**—Take the *maximum* of the two margin lengths, and use that value as the margin between the elements. Thus, if adjacent elements specified top and bottom margins of 2cm and 3cm, the resulting margin between the two elements would be 3cm. This is illustrated in the second pair of paragraphs in Figures 5.14 and 5.15: the bottom and top margins are each 1em, so that the resulting separation between the two paragraphs is 1em, and not 2em.

- **Positive margin and negative margin**—The margins are actually added. Move below the upper element a length equal to that specified by the positive margin, and then move back towards the upper element by the amount specified by the negative margin. Thus if adjacent elements specified top and bottom margins of -2cm and 3cm, the resulting margin between the two elements would be 1cm.

- **Both margins are negative**—Take the larger of the two margin lengths, and set the margin back from zero. Thus if adjacent elements specified top and bottom margins of -2cm and -3cm, the resulting margin between the two elements would be -3cm—that is, the second element would overlap the bottom 3cm of the first element.

Vertical Margins in MSIE 3 MSIE 3 supports the `margin-top` property, but does not support `margin-bottom`. MSIE 3 also assigns fixed default margins above and below all block-level elements *except* **ADDRESS, CENTER, DIV,** and **TABLE** (with these elements, the default top and bottom margins are of zero width: MSIE 3 also has a zero-width margin above a **FORM,** but a larger default margin below). These positive default margins *cannot* be set to zero using a `margin-top: 0` or other declarations: such a declaration has no effect on spacing around the elements.

Positive `margin-top` values have the expected effect, and increase the spacing between block elements. Negative values also have the expected effect, and bring the lower element (with the negative `margin-top` value) closer to (and perhaps on top of) the preceding block element.

Vertical Margins in Netscape Navigator 4.0 Netscape Navigator 4.0 supports both `margin-top` and `margin-bottom`, but with some oddities—these oddities are apparently designed to make Navigator 4 compatible with the behavior of MSIE 3. Like MSIE 3, Navigator 4.0 assigns fixed default margins above and below all block-level elements *except* **ADDRESS, CENTER, DIV,** and **TABLE** (with these elements, the default top and bottom margins are zero). These positive default margins *cannot,* in general, be set to zero using a `margin: 0` or other declaration: Such a declaration has no effect on spacing around the elements. However, there is one exception to this rule: the default top and bottom margins around a **P** element can be reduced to zero via the declarations `margin-top: 0` and `margin-bottom:0`.

Positive `margin-top` and `margin-bottom` values add extra spacing beyond that of the default margins. Similarly, negative `margin-top` values move an element up towards the preceding block element. However, negative `margin-bottom` values are not supported, and have no effect on element positioning.

TIP Use DIV Elements for Accurately Positioned Content

Since the default margins above and below a **DIV** are of zero width, it is easy to position these elements relative to a previous or subsequent **DIV**. Thus, if you wish to superimpose text blocks, these blocks should be placed inside **DIV**s.

The manner in which adjacent top and bottom margins are combined varies depending on the elements involved. If a **P, DIV, ADDRESS,** or **CENTER** element is above another **P, DIV, ADDRESS,** or **CENTER** element, then the margins are combined just as specified in the CSS specifications. However, if any other element is involved, then the resultant margin is the simple sum of the margin lengths defined by the margin properties of the top and bottom elements, plus the value of the default margin around the element. This complicates things very much for a page designer, since the default top and bottom margin values for most elements are unknown, so that it is hard to explicitly set the net vertical margin!

**Figure 5.14 Example document illustrating the different vertical spacings intro-
duced by adjacent padding and margin lengths. Stylesheet rules are in italics.
Note in Figure 5.15 how paddings combine additively, while margins do not, as
discussed in the text.**

```
<HTML><HEAD><TITLE>Illustration of Margins and Padding</TITLE>
<STYLE>
<!-
DIV            { margin-left:    0;   margin-right:    0; /* set defaults   */
                 margin-top:     0;   margin-bottom:   0;
                 padding:        0;   border-width:    0;
        }
DIV.paddingtop     { padding-bottom: 1em; }              /* Top paragraph    */
DIV.paddingbottom  { padding-top:    1em; }              /* Bottom paragraph */

DIV.margintop      { margin-bottom:  1em; }              /* Top paragraph    */
DIV.marginbottom   { margin-top:     1em; }              /* Bottom paragraph */
->
</STYLE>
</HEAD><BODY BGCOLOR="#ffffff">
<H2>Vertical Margins and Paddings</H2>
<DIV>This is the first paragraph with no padding or margins.
     This should be flush next to the following paragraph.</DIV>
<DIV>Here is the second paragraph with no padding or margins.
     This should be flush with the preceding paragraph.</DIV>
<HR>
<DIV CLASS="margintop"> This is the first paragraph with top
     and bottom margins of 1em. This margin should be combined
     with the 1em margin of the next paragraph.</DIV>
<DIV CLASS="marginbottom"> This is the second paragraph with top
     and bottom margins of 1em. This margin should be combined
     with the 1em margin of the previous paragraph.</DIV>
<HR>
<DIV CLASS="paddingtop"> This is the first paragraph with top
     and bottom paddings of 1em. This padding should be combined
     with the 1em padding of the next paragraph.</DIV>
<DIV CLASS="paddingbottom"> This is the second paragraph with top
     and bottom paddings of 1em. This padding should be combined
     with the 1em padding of the previous paragraph.</DIV>
<HR>
</BODY></HTML>
```

Netscape 4.0—Padding-Bottom and Paragraph Separation Last, we note that, under
Navigator 4.0, padding-bottom does not add space between two adjacent **P** elements. If a **P** is
followed by another **P**, any value of padding-bottom applied to the first paragraph is interpreted as having a value of zero. However, if a *border* is specified around the first paragraph, then this

Figure 5.15 Display of the document listed in Figure 5.14 by the Netscape Navigator 4 browser. Note how the first two paragraphs (actually DIV elements) are flush together, as the intervening margin is zero and there is no padding space between them. Padding space, however, keeps the last two paragraphs apart, even though the vertical margin is zero.

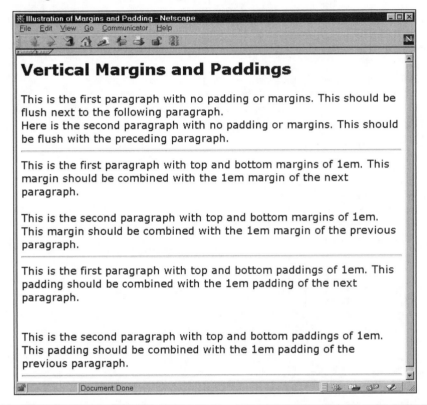

padding space magically reappears, and takes its rightful place between the bottom border and the inner bottom edge of the paragraph. This is likely a Navigator 4 bug, and not a feature!

Figure 5.16 uses vertical margins and indents to give a "shadowed" heading effect, by creating multiple, overlapping heading text strings. The various components of the "shadowed" text strings are created using the selectors .overlap0 through .overlap4. Notice how all the vertical margin and text indent property values are expressed in em units; this ensures the same relative offsets—and the same relative placement of the overlapping letters—independent of the font size or family. This is seen in Figure 5.17, which shows the same overlapped heading rendered in two different sized fonts.

Beautiful Document, or Stylesheet Abuse? Of course, the document in Figure 5.16 will present problems for browsers that do not properly understand CSS. If the interpretation of margin or

Figure 5.16 Document illustrating use of vertical margins and text indents to create shadowed heading text. Stylesheet content is in italics. The rendering of this document is found in Figure 5.17.

```
<HTML><HEAD><TITLE>Illustration of Overlapping Headings</TITLE>
<STYLE>
<!-
BODY  {font-family: "Comic Sans MS", sans-serif;    }
H1,H2 { padding:        0;      text-align: center;
        margin-bottom: 0;     margin-top: 0;         }
.overlap0  {color: #aaffff}
.overlap1  { margin-top: -1.5em; color: #99bbbb; text-indent: 0.1em}
.overlap2  { margin-top: -1.5em; color: #669999; text-indent: 0.2em}
.overlap3  { margin-top: -1.5em; color: #336666; text-indent: 0.3em}
.overlap4  { margin-top: -1.5em; color: #003333; text-indent: 0.4em}
->
</STYLE>
</HEAD><BODY BGCOLOR="#ffffff">
<H1 CLASS="overlap0">Heading Overlap Example</H1>
<H1 CLASS="overlap1">Heading Overlap Example</H1>
<H1 CLASS="overlap2">Heading Overlap Example</H1>
<H1 CLASS="overlap3">Heading Overlap Example</H1>
<H1 CLASS="overlap4">Heading Overlap Example</H1>
<BR><hr><BR><BR>
<H2 CLASS="overlap0">Heading Overlap Example</H2>
<H2 CLASS="overlap1">Heading Overlap Example</H2>
<H2 CLASS="overlap2">Heading Overlap Example</H2>
<H2 CLASS="overlap3">Heading Overlap Example</H2>
<H2 CLASS="overlap4">Heading Overlap Example</H2>
<BR><hr><BR><BR>
<H2>Heading Overlap Example</H2>
<H2>Heading Overlap Example</H2>
<H2>Heading Overlap Example</H2>
<H2>Heading Overlap Example</H2>
</BODY></HTML>
```

font sizes is incorrect (which currently is often the case), then the offsets will not work at different font sizes (for this reason, it is best to use **DIV** elements and pixel units for precise screen layouts). More importantly, if a browser does not understand stylesheets at all, then the reader sees five headings, one after the other (as illustrated at the bottom of Figure 5.17). This is confusing, to say the least! Also, if this document is read by a screen reader, then the listener will hear the same heading repeated over and over and over again. Once again, this is likely not the desired effect.

Special formatting such as this, however much it may be desired, is best avoided, since the special formatting requires extra HTML markup that makes the document unreadable without full

Figure 5.17 Display by Internet Explorer 4 beta 1 of the document listed in Figure 5.16. Note how the first two headings show the same pseudo-shadowed lettering, even though they are at different font sizes. The five headings at the bottom illustrate what is displayed by a browser that does not understand CSS—this is clearly *not* what you want your readers to see!

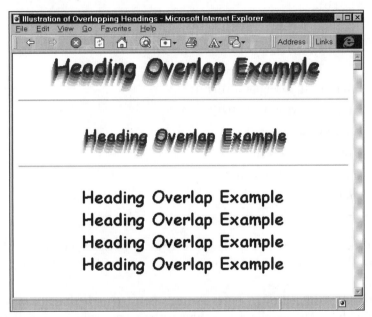

stylesheet support. If you are going to use CSS tricks such as this, it is best to serve the documents out using a Web server that can test for browsers that support CSS. Then, the full document can be delivered to browsers that fully support CSS, while an alternative document can be delivered to ones that do not.

Example 12: Special Formatting of List Item Elements

In terms of basic layout, list item elements (display: list-item) are treated as block-level elements. Thus the role of horizontal and vertical margins, padding space, and borders are handled in essentially the same way as just described. However, inside the list item "box," the content is preceded by a list item marker, and there are many ways in which this internal box layout can be controlled. For example, an author may wish to select the type of marker (bullet, number, etc.) for the list item, or substitute an inline graphic image in place of a standard bullet. Furthermore, there are several structural variants for list formatting; for example, embedding the bullet within the list item content (a compact list style) or placing the bullet alongside, and separate from, a box containing the list item content. These two formatting types are illustrated in Figure 5.18.

Figure 5.18 An illustration of the possible formatting within a list item box. The box to the left illustrates the effect of `list-style-position:inside`, **while the box to the right illustrates** `list-style-position:outside`. **The latter is the default list item format.**

```
                        list style position


              inside                      outside

    ┌─────────────────────┐    ┌─────────────────────┐
    │   Here is an example of list │    │   Here is an example of list│
    │ item text with the bullet │    │ item text with the bullet │
    │ embedded within the item. │    │ embedded within the │
    │ Note how the text wraps │    │ item. Note how the text │
    │ around the bullet. │    │ does not wrap around the │
    └─────────────────────┘    │ bullet. │
                                └─────────────────────┘
```

These formatting features are controlled in CSS by four properties. These properties, and their meanings, are listed in Table 5.7, while the meanings of the different `list-style-type` property values are summarized in Table 5.8.

Because list item properties are generally assigned to an entire list, it is best to apply these properties not to specific **LI** list items (although, of course, there is nothing to stop you from doing so!), but directly to **UL** or **OL** elements.

Browser Support for List Item Properties

MSIE 3 does not support any of these list item properties, while Navigator 4 supports only the `list-style-type` and related `list-style` properties.

Care must be taken when applying CSS rules to lists and list content. Rules applied to the entire list (i.e., to the **UL** or **LI** elements) are applied to the entire list and to all **LI** elements within the list. For example, one can use rules applied to **UL** or **OL** elements to: set the margins or padding above and below the list, or to change the color for the items (and bullets) within the list.

LI element CSS rules result in quite different formatting depending on the browser displaying the list. With MSIE 3 (and the beta version of MSIE 4) rules applied to **LI** elements affect the formatting of the entire element, including the text content and the item marker. Thus, changing the text color or size affects both the bullet and the text, while margins affect the margin above and below each item.

Table 5.7 A Description of the Four List Item-Related Properties

Property	Values	Default Value	Description
list-style-type	circle, decimal, disc disc, lower-alpha, lower-roman, none, square, upper-roman, upper-alpha		Specifies appearance/type of marker for list items
list-style-image	url(url-string),none	none	Specifies URL for image to use as list item marker; replaced marker specified by list-style-type
list-style-position	inside,outside	outside	Positioning of marker with respect to list content (*See Figure 5.18*)
list-style	1–3 values, each as above	*N/A*	Shorthand for list-item properties; one to three values taken from the style-type, style-image, and style-position properties.

Values Key url-string   Any valid URL
          N/A   Not applicable to shorthand properties

With Navigator 4.0, however, rules applied to **LI** elements affect only the list item bullet, and do not affect the text content of the element. Thus, changing the text color or size affects only the color or size of the list item number or bullet, but does not affect the **LI** element content. Similarly,

Table 5.8 List-Item-Type Property Values and Their Meanings

List Item Type	Description/Meaning
circle	An open circle
decimal	Decimal numbering of items (1, 2, 3, ...)
disc	A closed circle or disc
lower-alpha	Numbering of items with lowercase letter (a, b, c, ...)
lower-roman	Numbering of items with lowercase roman (i, ii, iii, iv, ...)
none	No bullet or number before item
square	Closed square
upper-alpha	Numbering of items with uppercase letter (A, B, C, ...)
upper-roman	Numbering of items with uppercase roman (I, II, III, IV, ...)

margin and padding properties can have unexpected effects. To summarize, the effects of the four possible margin and padding properties are:

Margin-top—affects the position of the entire list relative to the preceding element.

Margin-bottom—only positive values allowed. The effect is to reposition the content of each list item *downwards* relative to the list item marker.

Padding-top—adds padding space above the entire list.

padding-bottom—repositions the content of each list item *downwards* relative to the list item marker.

Example 13: Formatting of Inline Elements

In the CSS formatting model, all HTML elements are rendered on the display as one or more formatting boxes, which can, in turn, have borders, padding, and margins. However, as noted earlier, the interpretation of border, padding, and margin spaces, and indeed the way in which the HTML element is turned into a formatting box, is very different depending on the nature of the element.

In this context, the formatting of block-level elements is relatively straightforward. As described in the previous section, every block-level HTML element is turned into a single formatting box. The margins, padding, and borders are well defined and specify the size of the box, and the box's position relative to the parent element (horizontally) and relative to the preceding and following elements (vertically).

The situation is very different with inline elements. Since most inline elements are decomposable into one or more boxes, it no longer makes sense to define the element's "width," since there may be one or more boxes, each of a different width. As a result, the width property is not defined for inline elements. Similarly, the height of each of these boxes is fixed by the content of the box, and cannot be changed. Thus, height: auto simply prescribes the intrinsic height of the element, and any other height specification is ignored. These aspects (and several others) of inline element formatting are illustrated in Figure 5.19.

Inline elements can take padding and borders, defined in the same manner as for block-level elements. Vertical padding and border spacing *should not affect* the line spacing of the block-level element that contains the inline elements. Instead, the padding and/or border is added around the inline element box. As a result, if the vertical padding spaces or borders are large enough, the padding and/or border can actually overlap the text on adjacent lines, or the padding or border of other inline elements. In this latter case, the element that lies "on top" is the one that occurs later in the document. This point is illustrated in Figure 5.19.

Horizontal padding or borders, however, do add space between the inline element and the other text content inline with the element. This point is also illustrated in Figure 5.19.

Figure 5.19 Illustrations of inline formatting elements. The first inline element (with a white background) spans more than one line, and creates two formatting boxes— notice how the number and sizes of these boxes will depend on the parent element width. The second inline element (gray background, dark gray border) has large padding and border spaces, and overlaps with the previous inline element. Notice how the padding background of the later element overlaps those that come earlier. Notice also how the horizontal padding and margins add space inline around the element, while vertical padding, borders, and margins do not affect text positioning.

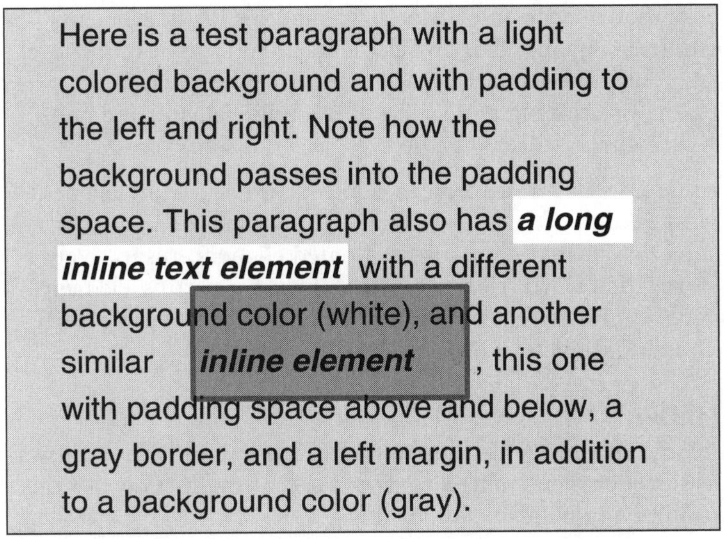

Here is a test paragraph with a light colored background and with padding to the left and right. Note how the background passes into the padding space. This paragraph also has *a long inline text element* with a different background color (white), and another similar *inline element* , this one with padding space above and below, a gray border, and a left margin, in addition to a background color (gray).

Inline elements can also take margins. Once again, vertical margins have no effect on line spacing or on formatting in general. Horizontal margins, however, will add spacing between the inline element and adjacent content in the line. This is also illustrated in Figure 5.19.

Inline Formatting by Current Browsers

There are no current browsers that properly format margins, padding space, and borders around inline elements. MSIE 3 totally ignores these properties for inline elements, while Netscape Navigator 4 formats them erratically—and incorrectly! With Navigator 4, non-zero bottom margin or padding values will introduce a line break just after the inline element, while non-zero left or right margin/padding values will cause the inline element to be repositioned towards the left edge of the parent element, superimposed on the content at that location. However, if the inline element takes a background image or a border, then it is treated as a block element: Line breaks are introduced before and after the element, and the margins and padding are applied to the element as if it were block-level. Early implementations of MSIE 4 were also unable to format these elements properly.

TIP Do not use Margins and Paddings with Inline Elements

Navigator 4.0 badly mishandles borders and paddings of inline formatting elements, and you are therefore advised to avoid padding, margin, or border properties in CSS rules that apply to such elements.

Floating Elements

"Floating" elements are formatting blocks that float to the left or right margins of the elements they lie within, displacing other text or inline elements. Floating elements are a type of block-level element, in that they are treated as a block and can displace adjacent content using margin, padding, or border properties. However, the positioning and sizing of floating elements are handled very differently from regular block elements, as discussed here.

HTML has no default floating elements. CSS can transform an element into a floating element via the `float` property. This property can take the values `left` or `right`, which float the element to the left or right inner edge of the element that contains the floated element, respectively. Both these values for `float` also transform the HTML element into a block formatting element, and override any `display` property value. In this sense, `float` is a generalization of the HTML **ALIGN**="left" or **ALIGN**="right" attribute as applied to **IMG** or **TABLE** elements.

Example 14: A Single Floated Element

The effect of the padding, border, and margin properties is illustrated in Figure 5.20, which shows a single left-floated image within a block-level element. This also assumes that the **IMG** is *not* the very first thing inside the block element, implying markup similar to:

```
<P> Here is a bunch of
    <IMG SRC="bigimg.gif" CLASS="left-align">
    paragraph text ..... </P>.
```

Figure 5.20 illustrates the positioning of a left-floated image. Here the image is positioned relative to the *left* inner edge of the parent element and below the *bottom* edge of the line of text preceding the image. (The nature of right-aligned images is equivalent—just reverse the words left and right!) Top and left padding or borders of the floated image simply push the element away from these edges, as will positive values for the top and left margin properties. Negative top or left margins can move the image *outside* the parent element, as was the case with regular block-level elements. Again, however, there may be browser-imposed constraints on the use of negative margins—for example, such that they cannot be moved outside a table cell.

The bottom and right properties control the space between a left-floated image and the remaining content of the parent element. The floated image can be thought of as floating *on top* of the parent element, and displacing any inline content. Right-hand borders, padding, or positive margin values push the text to the right of the image further away from the image. On the other hand, a

Figure 5.20 An illustration of the padding, border, and margin properties as applied to a left-floated element. The dashed lines denote the boundaries of the lines above and below the image, and the edge of the text to the right of the image. The same properties work with right-aligned images, except that here the right padding, border, and margin properties govern the placement of the IMG relative to the inner edge of the parent element.

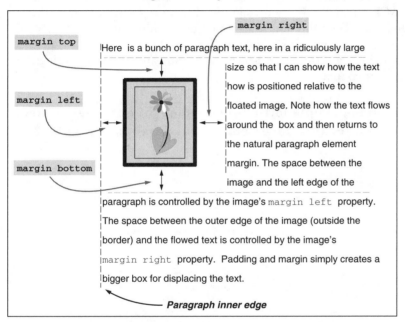

negative right margin can "pull" the text edge towards the floated element, and may bring it on top of the image (some browsers may, in fact, forbid this behavior). The distance from the right-hand inner edge of the floated element to the start of the text to the right of the floated element is determined by the floated element's right-hand side width properties, namely:

distance = padding-right + border-right-width + margin-right

(For right-floated elements, the distance between the flowed text and left-hand edge of the floated element is equivalent, with the word "right" everywhere replaced by "left.")

The bottom padding, border, and margin properties control the bottom boundary for the floated block; inline element content within the block can appear only below this border, and not above it. Notice that this means that the top of the inline text box (that is, the top of the line height for the line) must be below the floated element bottom border. This can lead to extra space below the floated element, as illustrated in Figure 5.22.

Figure 5.21 gives some simple examples of floated **IMG** elements. The document contains four paragraphs containing images: The first contains a left-floated image (no padding, border, or margins), the second a left-floated image with surrounding padding (top, left, and right) and positive margin (bottom); the third a left-floated image with negative left and top margins; and the fourth a left-floated image with negative right and bottom margins. Possible renderings are shown in Figure 5.22 (at the time this section was written, there were no browsers that properly supported padding and margin spacing around floating elements).

Notice in the second paragraph how the padding spaces and positive margins "expand" the bounds around the image, and push the inline text away from it. This is similar to the effect of the **IMG** element **HSPACE** and **VSPACE** attributes, but with significantly more control, as now the four sides can be treated independently. The third and fourth paragraphs illustrate the effect of negative margins; note how the left and top margins can reposition the floated element, while the bottom and right margins change the margins for the adjacent text, and can in principle bring the text in to overlap the floating element content.

Figure 5.21 A document containing simple left-aligned images. Stylesheet content is in italics. Suggested rendering for this document is illustrated in Figure 5.22.

```
<HTML><HEAD><TITLE>Floating Elements Test</TITLE>
<STYLE><!--
P              { background:       #dddddd;
                 margin:           0  5%; /* shade P, and add margin          */
               }
IMG            { border-width:     0;        /* Default IMG properties         */
                 padding:          0;
                 margin:           0
               }
IMG.flt        { float:            left; /* Float-left image                   */
               }
IMG.rtpad      { float:            left;
                 padding-left:     1em;      /* left side padded 2em           */
                 padding-right:    2em;      /* right side padded out 2em      */
                 padding-top:      1em;      /* image top padded out 1em       */
                 margin-bottom:    1em;      /* margin out bottom 2em          */
                 background:       green; /* Make background stand out!        */
               }
IMG.negflt     {float:            left;
                 margin-left:      -5em;     /* largish negative margins       */
                 margin-top:       -5em;
               }
IMG.neg2       {float:             left;
                 margin-right:     -2em;     /* Negative margins               */
                 margin-bottom:    -2em;
               }
--></STYLE>
</HEAD><BODY BGCOLOR="#ffffff">
<H2>Test of Floating Elements</H2>
```

Continued

Figure 5.21 *Continued*

```
<P><IMG CLASS="flt" SRC="icon3.gif"> Here is a paragraph element,
   containing a floated <B>IMG</B> element - the element is
   floated to the left. Note how the image is flush with the
   left edge of the paragraph it lies within, that the top
   of the image aligns with the top of the paragraph box,
   and that the text flows around the image.</P>
<P><IMG SRC="icon3.gif" CLASS="rtpad">
   Here is a similar paragraph with the same floated
   image, but this time with padding added to the image.
   Note how the padding "pads out" the region around
   the image, and displaces the adjacent paragraph content.
   A <TT>border</TT> would have the same effect.</P>
<P><IMG SRC="icon3.gif" CLASS="negflt"> Here is a similar
   paragraph with the same floated image, but now the image
   has negative top and left margins. This pulls the image
   outside the bounds of the parent element. It is not clear how the
   text should respond — ideally it should fill into the area,
   as shown here.</P>
<P><IMG SRC="icon3.gif" CLASS="neg2"> Here is a similar
   paragraph with the same floated image, but now the image
   has negative bottom and right margins. This should pull the
   text boundaries right under the floated image. The text would
   most likely be displayed on top of the image </P>
</BODY></HTML>
```

Example 15: Text Preceding Floating Elements

Text in the HTML markup that precedes a floated inline element strongly affects the placement of the floating element on the display. This is because a floated element cannot, by default (that is, without using negative margins to reposition it), appear *higher* than any preceding element or any preceding text content. Consider the example paragraphs in the document listed in Figure 5.23. These both contain floating **IMG** elements, but neither of these images can float upwards beyond the formatted line that contains the first five words of the paragraph, *Here is a paragraph element,* that preceded the **IMG** element in the HTML markup. The result is the rendering seen in Figure 5.24: The floated images rise up to the bottom of the *line box* (see Figure 4.3) that contains this text—which in this case corresponds to the first displayed line.

Consequently, a floating element must be the *very first* content inside the parent element if it is to be aligned with the top of the parent element content. Note how this was done in Figure 5.21.

Example 16: Multiple Floating Elements

A block element can, of course, contain more than one floating element. In general, a floating element will float to its assigned margin until it hits any previous element floated in that direction, whereupon it stops. An example is shown in Figure 5.25 and rendered for display in Figure 5.26.

Figure 5.22 Suggested browser rendering for the document listed in Figure 5.21. Note the effect of floating image padding (second paragraph), and negative margins (third and fourth paragraphs).

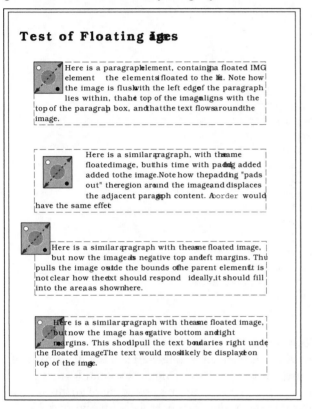

Figure 5.23 A simple document illustrating left-aligned images with text preceding the image. Stylesheet content is in italics. Typical rendering for this document is shown in Figure 5.24.

```
<HTML><HEAD><TITLE>Floating Elements — Text Before Element</TITLE>
<STYLE>
<!--
P           { background:      #cccccc;  /* light gray              */
              margin:          0  5%;    /* shade P, and add margin  */
            }
IMG         { border-width:    0;        /* Default IMG properties   */
              padding:         0;
              margin:          0; }
IMG.fltl    { float:           left;     /* Float-left image         */
            }
```

Continued

Figure 5.23 *Continued*

```
IMG.fltr  { float:            right; } /* Float-right image        */
-->
</STYLE>
</HEAD><BODY BGCOLOR="#ffffff">
<H2>Floating Elements — Text Before Element</H2>
<P>Here is a paragraph element, <IMG CLASS="fltl" SRC="icon3.gif">
   containing a right-floated <B>IMG</B> element. Note how the image
   is flush with the left edge of the paragraph it lies within, but
   does not float above the text line that precedes it.</P>
<P>Here is a paragraph element, <IMG CLASS="fltr" SRC="icon3.gif">
   containing a right-floated <B>IMG</B> element. Note how the image
   is flush with the right edge of the paragraph it lies within, but
   lies <EM>below</EM> the first line of text. This is because the
   first displayed line contains paragraph content that preceded
   the floating element.</P>
</BODY></HTML>
```

Figure 5.24 Rendering of the document listed in Figure 5.23 by the Netscape Navigator 4 browser. Note how the floated images do not rise above the line containing text that preceded the IMG elment inside the P.

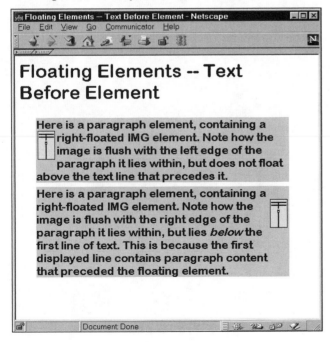

Note in the first paragraph how the two left-floated images align next to each other, with the text flowing around them.

Of course, these floated elements are still subject to the rule that they cannot appear before any text that precedes them in the HTML document. This point is illustrated in the third paragraph in Figures 5.25 and 5.26. Since the two left-floated images are separated by text (shown in bold italics), the second image must appear below the line containing this text, but still appears to the right of the previously left-floated image.

Borders and padding space should add up as expected, so that floating two images left, the first with a *right* padding of 1em and the second with a *left* padding of 2em, should result in a net 3em separation between the two. However, the MSIE 3, Navigator 4.0, and early beta versions of

Figure 5.25 Document illustrating multiple floating elements, here IMG elements inside a P. Stylesheet rules are in italics. Typical rendering for this document is shown in Figure 5.26.

```
<HTML><HEAD><TITLE>Multiple Floating Elements </TITLE>
<STYLE>
<!--
P          { background:    #cccccc url/gray.gif);
             padding-left:  1em;
             width:         100%;    }  /* Fixes a Netscape Bug ... */
IMG.fltl   { float:         left;
             border-width:  medium;
             border-style:  solid;    }
IMG.fltr   { float:         right;    }
-->
</STYLE>
</HEAD><BODY BGCOLOR="#ffffff">
<H2>Multiple Floating Elements</H2>
<P><IMG CLASS="fltl" SRC="icon3.gif"><IMG CLASS="fltl" SRC="icon.gif">
   Here is a paragraph element containing two left-floated
   images. The images all fit within the paragraph, and
   line up next to each other.</P>
<P><IMG CLASS="fltl" SRC="icon3.gif"><IMG CLASS="fltr" SRC="icon.gif">
   Here is a paragraph element containing a left-floated
   and a right-floated image. The images float to the
   opposing margins, and the text flows between them.  </P>
<P><IMG CLASS="fltl" SRC="icon3.gif">
   <STRONG><EM>Here is a second paragraph </EM></STRONG>
   <IMG CLASS="fltl" SRC="icon.gif">
   also with two left aligned images, but separated in the
   markup by text. The second image must appear below this
   text, and thus appears as </P>
</BODY></HTML>
```

Figure 5.26 Rendering of the document listed in Figure 5.25 by the Netscape Navigator 4 browser. Note how multiple floating elements can align next to each other, with their tops aligned (provided the positions are not modified via padding, border, or margin properties). Note also the gray border on the left side of all paragraphs: this is created by the paragraph element `padding-left: 1em` property.

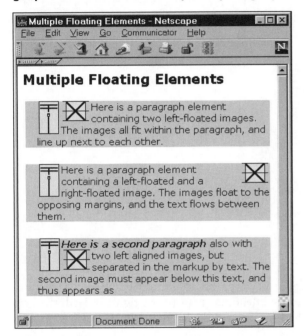

Internet Explorer 4 did not properly handle padding, borders, and margins around floating images, and did not produce this padding space.

Floating adjacent elements differently, one towards the left and one towards the right margin, is of course possible, an example being in the second paragraph of Figures 5.25 and 5.26. Note how the images simply float to their respective margins, with the text flowing between them. Of course, two images cannot be placed side-by-side if they are too big—floated images cannot overlap. If they are so big as to overlap, then the CSS formatting model states that the first floated element should be floated to its assigned edge, and that the second element should be moved down such that it can fit horizontally. A typical example is illustrated in Figure 5.27. The rendering will of course depend strongly on the size of the display window and on the sizes of the images—it is always a good idea to preview designs on both low- and high-resolution displays, to ensure that the formatting is acceptable in all cases.

Example 17: Floating Next to Block-Level Elements

Of course, an element can be floated next to other block elements, just as easily as within the content of a single paragraph. This is illustrated by the markup in Figure 5.28, rendered in Figure 5.29.

Figure 5.27 Schematic illustration of the result of floating large elements. If an element will not fit horizontally, it is moved down until it fits at the specified margin.

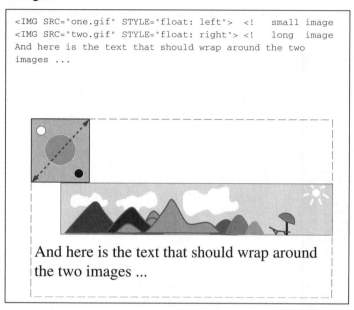

```
<IMG SRC="one.gif" STYLE="float: left">  <!  small image
<IMG SRC="two.gif" STYLE="float: right"> <!  long  image
And here is the text that should wrap around the two
images ...
```

And here is the text that should wrap around the two images ...

Here we have an image inside a **DIV**, left-aligned against two paragraphs and two headings. Notice how the image floats to the left, with the paragraphs and headings kept to the right. Indeed, the text content of the last two paragraphs wraps around the bottom of the left-floated image, as it should.

Figure 5.28 Document illustrating elements floated alongside other block-level elements. Stylesheet rules are in italics. The formatting of this document and a simple variant of this document are shown in Figures 5.29 and 5.30.

```
<HTML><HEAD><TITLE>Floating Next To Block Elements</TITLE>
<STYLE>
<!--
DIV        { width:       100%;         }
P          { background:  #cccccc url (gray.gif);      }
P.foo      { background:  transparent; }   /* Patch for Netscape bug       */
                                           /* (doesn't flow if colored     */
IMG.fltl   { float:       left;         }  /* Left floated image           */
-->
</STYLE>
</HEAD><BODY BGCOLOR="#ffffff">
<H2>Floating Adjacent Block Elements</H2>
```

Continued

Figure 5.28 *Continued*

```
<DIV>
  <IMG CLASS="fltl" SRC="iconlong.gif">
  <h3>Happy Faces Are Here Again!</h3>
  <P>Here is a long, left-floated image, containing four happy
     faces! Note how everything  (headings, and paragraphs) align
     next to it. Note also how left-floated icons
     <IMG CLASS="fltl" SRC="icon3.gif"> <EM>within</EM>
     the paragraph stay inside the paragraph (with its
     nice gray background). </P>
  <H3 CLASS="newsection">Three Cheers for Mr. Bean!</h3>
  <P CLASS="foo">Mr Bean is the first character of modern
     Television to express the true nihilism of modern TV
     programming. What is so truly remarkable, then, is that
     he has become one of the most popular characters in
     all media, actually out-drawing Claudia Shiffer at
     a recent Toronto public event. </P>
</DIV>
</BODY></HTML>
```

Figure 5.29 Rendering of the document listed in Figure 5.28 by the Netscape Navigator 4 browser. Note how the left-floated IMG floats to the left of the paragraphs and headings that are also inside the DIV.

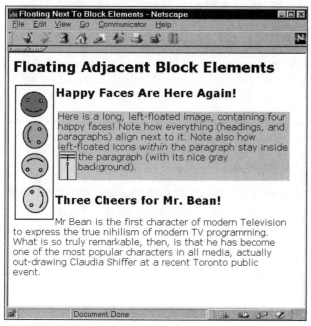

Example 18: Clearing below Floating Images

Of course, an author also wants control over the placement of other elements relative to the floating one. For example, in Figure 5.29 the author probably wanted the second heading, *Three Cheers for Mr. Bean!*, to start below the left-aligned image, and not alongside it.

In CSS, this formatting control is available through the `clear` property. This property, which can take the values "left," "right," "both," or "none," requests that the formatting of the associated element(s) start once the indicated margins are "clear"—that is, at a point in the display region where the element can be placed next to the specified edge of the parent element, or such that there is no floating element between the "cleared" element and the specified edge. Thus, positioning the Mr. Bean heading below the left-floated image would require the property declaration `clear:left` or `clear:both` applied to that heading. This can be done by adding the single CSS rule

```
.newsection   {float: left; }
```

since the document in Figure 5.28 came pre-prepared for this new rule. The result of this change is shown in Figure 5.30, where the heading and all subsequent text is cleared to follow the inline image.

Browser Problems with Floated Image Formatting   MSIE 3 does not support the `float` property, and can only process images that are floated using the HTML **ALIGN** attribute. Netscape Navigator 4 does support `float`, but provides little control over positioning of the floated element. For example, for a left-floated image, the only padding property that effects the rendering is `padding-left`, and this merely adds padding space to the left of the left-floated image (which is not terribly useful). Thus, this property cannot be used to add padding around the image: One must instead use the HTML **HSPACE** and **VSPACE** attributes.

More importantly, border properties cannot be reliably used to reposition a floated element. Indeed, there are some bugs in the Netscape rendering engine that can causes a repositioned, floated element to appear in quite unpredictable locations—indeed, one can often cause the image to jump from the left to the right side of the drawing canvas, simply by resizing the browser window! For now, the best advice is to avoid margin or padding properties.

Also, `border` properties cannot be used to draw a border around a floated image—Navigator 4 mis-formats the border, and will draw a box of an inappropriate size at an inappropriate place (usually a small box near the top corner of the floated image).

TIP Do Not Use Margin or Padding Properties along With Float

Navigator 4 does not properly handle margin, border or padding properties applied to floated elements, so you are best advised to avoid these properties with rules that specify the formatting for floated images.

Figure 5.30 Rendering of the document listed in Figure 5.28 but with the additional CSS rule `.newsection {clear: left;}`**. Note how the clear property clears the second heading to start alongside the left edge of the parent element and thus positions it to start after the left-floated element.**

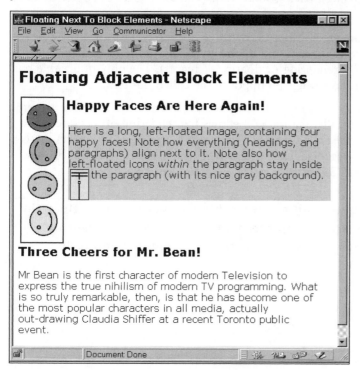

Example 19: Floating Non-IMG Elements

The previous examples have looked at floating images, which are indeed the most commonly floated elements. However, it is important to note that *any* element can be floated, and that floating non-image elements can lead to very useful formatting. The following is an example where a floated block element is used to create a call-out text box.

The goal here is to create a text *call-out*, which is a box adjacent the main flow of text that calls out an important point or feature in the text. Also called a *pull-quote*, this is a common feature of advertising or magazine copy layout. Such call-outs turn out to be easy to do in CSS, and the resulting document is also easy to read on browsers that do not support CSS.

For this example, we have chosen a default text layout that consists of a centered column with 20% margins on either side. The pull-quote should be placed to the left of this column, and inset into the column of text. Some possible CSS rules that provide this formatting, within an example document, are shown in Figure 5.31. The first CSS rule sets the desired margins for **P**, **H1**, **H2**, and **H3** elements. The second rule sets the default font for these headings to "Arial Black." The third rule generates the pull-quote, to be associated with any element of **CLASS**="pullq". The pull-quote is floated to the left, but has a left margin of 5% and a width of 30%, relative to the width of the parent element, which here is the document body—therefore, this block will start to the left of the regular text column, and will have a right margin that pushes into the regular text. The remaining properties set the text color (white), background color (white), and font properties (bold Arial) for the pull-quoted text element.

Figure 5.32 shows the resulting document as displayed by the Netscape Navigator 4 browser. Note how the formatting is quite close to that requested by the stylesheet (quite remarkable, really, considering all the bugs in Navigator 4.0's rendering of floating elements). The only noticeable bug is the missing margin for the first line in the paragraph opposite the called-out text.

An advantage of this approach is that it can gracefully degrade for browsers that do not support stylesheets, or that support them only partially. Figure 5.33 shows the rendering of this document by Netscape Navigator 3. This browser does not support stylesheets, but is still able to accurately render the content, if not with the same elegance. The same is true of a purely text-based browser, such as lynx, or of browsers such as MSIE 3 that only partially implement CSS.

Figure 5.31 Example document illustrating a floated block-level element. Here the floated element is used to generate a pull-quote next to the regular paragraph text. Stylesheet content is in italics. Rendering of this document is found in Figures 5.32 and 5.33.

```
<HTML><HEAD><TITLE>Floating Elements — Text Call-Out</TITLE>
<STYLE>
<!--
P,H1,H2,H3    { margin: 0.0em 20%;              } /* even columns          */
H1,H2,H3      { font-family:  Arial black;  }
.pullq        { float:        left;            /* left-aligned           */
                margin-left:  5%;              /* margins way to left    */
                width:        30%;
                color:        white;
                font-family:  arial;
                font-weight:  bold;
                background:    green;        }
-->
</STYLE>
</HEAD><BODY BGCOLOR="#ffffff">
  <H2>A Visit To Mars?</H2>
  <P>When I was younger, I believed that there was life on Mars.
     Now I don't mean this in the ordinary child's sense of believing
     in the fantastic. I really <em>believed</EM> that life existed
     there, and indeed that I had visited Mars at some point in
     my previous life.</P>
<!-- Note the FONT element, used to highlight the color for
     pre-stylesheet browsers -->
```

Continued

Figure 5.31 *Continued*

```
<FONT COLOR="red"><H3 CLASS="pullq">Boy Believes He Was
    On Mars!</H3></FONT>
<P>I dreamt about Mars.  Long, vivid, dreams of raised passageways
    and tunnels, of abandoned spaceports and stations, of strange
    smells and senses. I felt a deep longing for this place,
    and a deep kinship for the occupants who had apparently
    abandoned the place eons before, but still lived somewhere,
    if only I could find them.....</P>
<H3>What Did it Mean?</H3>
<P> Bla bla bla..... whadaya expect at 12?</P>
</BODY></HTML>
```

Figure 5.32 Rendering, by the Netscape Navigator 4 prerelease browser, of the document listed in Figure 5.31. Note the positioning of the left-aligned paragraph relative to the regular text paragraphs. There is a bug in Netscape Navigator 4: The first line of the paragraph adjacent to the floated paragraph is not properly adjusted to lie outside the floating region.

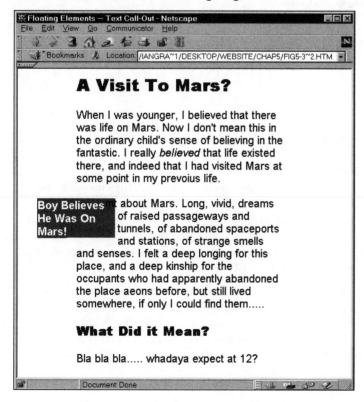

Figure 5.33 Rendering, by the Netscape Navigator 3 browser, of the document listed in Figure 5.31. This browser does not support stylesheets. However, the document is still clearly understandable, since the HTML markup preserves the logical structure of the text.

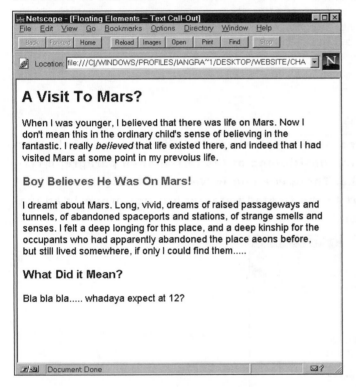

Example 20: Special Handling of Replaced Elements

As mentioned earlier, the `height` and `width` properties are rarely used, since for elements containing text, it is usually best to let the layout software determine the appropriate dimensions based on the layout and the positions of adjacent elements. However, `width` is on occasion used to specify a fixed width, with the `height` value left at "auto" to let the browser adjust the element height to accommodate the element content. By default, both property values are set to "auto," giving the browser maximum flexibility in laying out the element content.

The situation with replaced elements such as **IMG** or **APPLET** is somewhat different. With replaced elements, the resulting formatting element usually has a well-defined height and width, independent of the layout of the document on the display. For example, an **INPUT** element of **TYPE**="text", an embedded **APPLET**, and an inline **IMG** all have well-defined heights and widths. For these elements, the value `auto` for the `height` and `width` properties corresponds to these intrinsic dimensions.

For many replaced elements, these intrinsic dimensions are the only allowed width and height values: Any attempt to use property values to change these dimensions is ignored by the rendering software. However, some replaced elements can be resized, and in these cases the CSS `height` and `width` properties are used to specify the desired size. This is most commonly done with **IMG** elements, where an image can be resized to fit within the box specified by the `height` and `width` property values. This is analogous to using the **IMG** element **HEIGHT** and **WIDTH** attributes to specify a size, except that the CSS rules let the element be resized using document-specific units such as points, centimeters, em units, percentage units, and even pixels.

There are three ways in which the image can be resized:

1. **One of `height` or `width` is set to `auto`, the other set to a specific length**—The image is resized while preserving the *aspect ratio* (height-to-width ratio) of the image. This resizes the image without distorting it.

2. **Both `height` and `width` are set to `auto`**—The image retains its intrinsic dimensions.

3. **Both `height` and `width` are set to specific lengths**—The image dimensions are resized to the specified lengths. The image can be distorted, as the aspect ratio is not necessarily preserved.

There are several practical applications. First, the resizing can force an icon to fit into a specified box, so as not to affect the layout of related elements. For example, if the author wants red bullets as the leader for text, but wants the bullets to scale as text is resized, then the rule for these images could be:

```
IMG.iconstuff {height: 0.5em;  width: auto }
```

which ensures that the icons fit in the line (the icons are only 0.5em high) and that they are resized as the text size changes.

This particular example is illustrated in Figure 5.34, which is rendered for display by the Internet Explorer 4 browser in Figure 5.35. Notice how the images are resized proportional with the size of the font, as specified in the stylesheet rule.

NOTE Replaced Element Resizing Not Supported by MSIE 3 and Netscape Navigator 4.0

Neither MSIE 3 nor Navigator 4 support the use of `height` and/or `width` properties to resize an IMG (or other replaced) element. For best compatibility with older browsers, you should use the HTML HEIGHT and WIDTH attributes to specify approximate resizings, and then use the CSS `height` and `width` properties to specify the actual desired sizes—browsers that support CSS should take these CSS-specified properties and override the HTML-specified ones.

Figure 5.34 Example document illustrating the use of width properties to resize replaced elements. Stylesheet rules are in italics. Rendering of this document is found in Figure 5.35.

```
<HTML><HEAD><TITLE>Resizing Replaced Elements</TITLE>
<STYLE>
<!--
P.large        { font-size: large;   }
P.larger       { font-size: x-large; }
IMG.icon       { height:     0.8em;   } /* Scale with font size */
-->
</STYLE>
</HEAD><BODY BGCOLOR="#ffffff">
<P>Default icon is: <IMG SRC="bullet.gif">
<H2>Examples of Resized Replaced Elements </H2>
<P><IMG SRC="bullet.gif" CLASS="icon"> When I was younger, I
    believed that there was life on Mars....</P>
<P CLASS="large"><IMG SRC="bullet.gif" CLASS="icon"> When I was
    younger, I believed that there was life on Mars....</P>
<P CLASS="larger"><IMG SRC="bullet.gif" CLASS="icon"> When I was
    younger, I believed that there was life on Mars....</P>
</BODY></HTML>
```

Special Issues for TABLE Formatting

The formatting of **TABLE**s via CSS is one of the more difficult aspects of CSS. The problem is not with CSS itself: The mechanisms for linking CSS formatting to table blocks, rows and cells are straightforward. Instead, the problems lie in the browsers: All current browsers have severe limitations—and downright bugs—in their table formatting algorithms. This section attempts to describe the most important issues and problems, which should help you avoid (or at least recognize) these problems.

TABLEs and Property Inheritance

According to the CSS specifications, a **TABLE** should inherit properties from its parent in the same manner as other elements. However, The pre-CSS Navigator 3 browser did not inherit a number of formatting characteristics from the default properties for the document, and this annoyance has been inherited by the CSS parsing model in Navigator 4.0. The result is the following fact:

With Navigator 4.0, a TABLE element does not inherit any properties from its parent element.

Thus, if you set text colors or font styles, sizes, and so on for the **BODY** element or for an element (such as a **DIV**) that is a parent of a **TABLE**, then none of this information is passed down to the **TABLE** content. However, a **TABLE** will be physically constrained by the inner left and right margins of the parent element.

Figure 5.35 Rendering, by the Internet Explorer 4 (beta 1) browser of the document listed in Figure 5.34. Notice how the first three bullets are resized to the same size as the associated text.

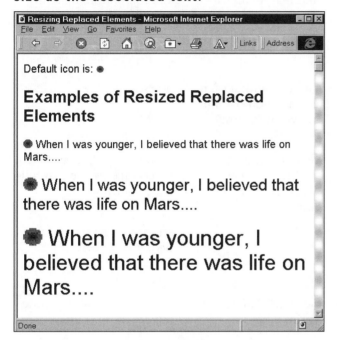

Even more annoying, text-formatting properties applied to **TABLE** or **TR** elements are not passed down to the actual cell content. Consequently, text formatting properties for table cells must be set in rules applied directly to **TD** and/or **TH** cells.

To help you keep track of this browser-dependent behavior, Tables 5.9 through 5.11 summarize the effect of the most common CSS properties on the MSIE 3, MSIE 4 (beta 1), and Navigator 4 browsers, when applied to **TABLE**, **TR**, and **TD/TH** elements. Test documents used to determine this behavior can be found at the book's supporting Web site.

Note in Tables 5.9 through 5.11 that Navigator 4 and MSIE 3 do not support height and width properties for table-related elements. However, both browsers do support **HEIGHT** and **WIDTH** attributes to the **TABLE**, **TD**, and **TH** elements,[1] and support both pixel and percentage units. For **TABLE**, percentage widths are calculated with respect to the width of the drawing canvas, while percentage heights are calculated with respect to the height of the drawing canvas. For **TD** or **TH**, percentage widths are calculated with respect to the table width: Thus, you must make sure that the widths of all the cells in a row sum to 100%. Similarly, percentage heights are calculated with respect to the table height.

Table 5.9 Effect of Some CSS Properties when Applied to TABLE Elements

Property	MSIE 3	Navigator 4	MSIE 4 (beta 1)
margin	add margin above **TABLE**, and add margin within first row of cells in the table	add margin above **TABLE**	add top/bottom margin to each cell
padding	no effect	padding within each cell and add padding above and below **TABLE**	no effect no effect
width	no effect (use **TABLE** element **WIDTH** attribute instead)	no effect (use **TABLE** element **WIDTH** attribute instead)	set table width as specified; percentages relative to full-width of canvas
height	no effect	no effect	set table height as specified; it is unclear how percentages values are calculated.
background	sets background for entire table	sets background for entire table	sets background for entire table
any text/ font property	sets text formatting properties for all cells	no effect	sets text formatting properties for all cells

Table 5.10 Effect of Some CSS Properties When Applied to TR Elements

Property	MSIE 3	Navigator 4	MSIE 4 (beta 1)
margin	add margin above **TABLE**, and add margin within first row of cells in the table	add margin above **TABLE**	add top/bottom margin to each cell
padding	no effect	padding with each cell and add padding above and below **TABLE**	no effect
width	no effect	no effect	set row width as specified; percentages relative to full width of canvas

Continued

Table 5.10 *Continued*

Property	MSIE 3	Navigator 4	MSIE 4 (beta 1)
height	no effect	no effect	set row width as specified; percentages relative to full width of canvas
background	no effect	sets background for a table row	sets background for a table row
any text/ font property	sets text formatting properties for all cells in row	no effect	sets text formatting properties for all cells in row

TABLE Formatting Bugs

From the previous discussion one might get the impression that compatibility problems between browsers could be resolved by applying explicit CSS rules to all **TD** and **TH** elements. Unfortunately, Navigator 4.0 has a number of severe bugs in **TABLE** parsing related to **TD** and **TH**-specific rules that make this approach difficult at best. These problems are illustrated by the example documents in

Table 5.11 Effect of Some CSS Properties when Applied to TD or TH Elements

Property	MSIE 3	Navigator 4.0 (*Buggy —see next section*)	MSIE 4 (beta 1)
margin	add margin to right and left of cell content	adds margin above, below and to left of cell content	add margin to all sides of cell content
padding	no effect	adds padding above, below and to left of cell content	no effect
width	no effect (*use TD/TH element WIDTH attribute instead*)	no effect (*use TD/TH element WIDTH attribute instead*)	set cell width as specified; percentages relative to full width of canvas
height	no effect (*use TD/TH element HEIGHT attribute instead*)	no effect (*use TD/TH element HEIGHT attribute instead*)	set cell height as specified; percentages relative to full width of canvas
background	sets background for cell	sets background for cell	sets background for cell
any text/ font property	sets text formatting properties for cell content	sets text formatting properties for cell content	sets text formatting properties for cell content

Figures 5.36. This figure shows a simple document consisting of a five paragraphs and a table, with two of the paragraphs and the table being enclosed inside a **DIV**. The CSS rules call for a default **BODY** font of "times new roman" (the browser default is Verdana), while the **DIV** rule calls for a large left margin and blue, center-aligned text. Finally, the **TD** rule calls for a gray background color around the table cells.

Figure 5.37 shows this document as displayed by Navigator 4.0—it is rendered as expected. But Figure 5.38 shows this same document, but with the browser window resized such that there is a line break inside one of the table cells. The result is irrevocably broken rendering of all text following the table!

Figure 5.36 Simple HTML document illustrating how CSS rules for TD elements can break the rendering of the document by Navigator 4.0. Example renderings are found in Figures 5.37 and 5.38.

```
<HTML><HEAD>   <TITLE>Simple Test of TABLE Formatting Bug</TITLE>
<STYLE>
<!--
BODY {font-family:      "times new roman"        }
DIV  {margin-left:      20%;
      text-align:       center;
      color:            #aaaaff;                  }
TD   {background:       #dddddd;                  }
-->
</STYLE></HEAD>
<BODY BGCOLOR="white">
<H2 ALIGN="center">An H2 Heading Outside The Table </H2>

<P>Here is some text before the DIV, and before the TABLE
</P>
<DIV>
  <P>Here is some text inside the table. Note how this text is
     blue, in italics, and in the times roman font. </P>
  <TABLE  BORDER>
  <TR>
    <TD> Here is the first cell </TD>
    <TD> Here is the second cell </TD>
  </TR>
  </TABLE>
  <P>Here is a paragraph that follows the table, but that is still
  inside the DIV. This is still centered... I hope!</P>
</DIV>
<P>And last, here is a final paragraph, outside the DIV.</P>
</BODY></HTML>
```

Figure 5.37 Rendering of the document listed in Figure 5.36 by the Netscape Navigator 4.0 browser. Note how the document is rendered just as requested by the stylesheet.

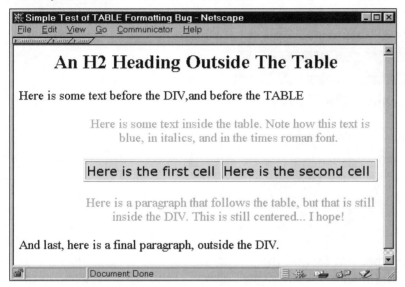

There are many similar problems, all largely related to CSS properties assigned to **TD** cells. To ensure universally functional documents, you should therefore avoid assigning CSS rules to **TD** or **TH** elements. The safe alternative is to:

- use the **BGCOLOR** attribute to assign background colors to **TD, TH,** or **TR** elements

- use **SPAN** elements within table cells to assign special text-level formatting to the cell content.

TIP Workaround For Netscape TABLE Bugs

Avoid CSS rules that assign formatting to TD or TH elements. Instead, use the BGCOLOR attribute to assign background colors to table cells (or rows), and use SPAN elements within table cells to assign special text-level formatting to the cell content.

Chapter Summary

In the CSS specification, the different *types* of formatting boxes are called *formatting elements*. Generally, there is a relationship between the HTML element and the formatting element; however, in CSS the author can use the display property to modify the formatting type of an HTML element to whatever he or she may choose.

Figure 5.38 Rendering of the document listed in Figure 5.36 by the Netscape Navigator 4.0 browser, here with the browser width reduced such that the text is broken within a table cell. Note how the document rendering is broken—all text subsequent to the table has "forgotten" the correct font family, while the paragraph following the table has "forgotten" its color.

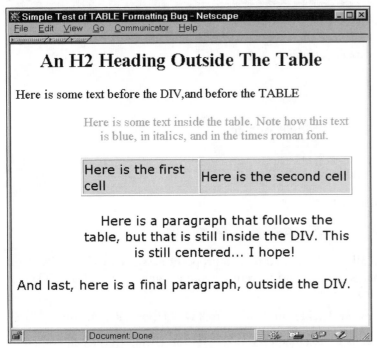

By default, all HTML elements are treated as either *block-level, inline,* or *list-item* types. These are outlined in Table 5.1. Some HTML elements are placeholders for non-text content. In some but not all cases, CSS `height` and `width` properties for boxes can be preset.

Typically a CSS designer does not have to specify `height` or `width`. However, for block-level or floating elements, it is sometimes convenient to specify the `width` so that the element fits in the desired space.

All block-level elements can be surrounded by space defined by various `padding-`, `border-`, and `margin-` properties. Margin spaces are added outside any border or padding space. The default size of padding and border spaces is zero.

Padding space is added just outside the element, and has the same background properties (e.g., color or background image) as the element. Padding lengths are always positive.

Borders are added just outside the padding space. Borders have specified widths, and can also be colored, or styled (e.g., `dashed`, `solid`, or `ridge`). Border lengths are always positive.

Margin space is added outside the border. Margins can be expressed in lengths, in percentages, or by the keyword `auto`. Margins can also be positive or negative. The handling of margins varies greatly depending on the nature of the element (block-level, inline, or floating) with the margin.

CSS provides for control over the *positioning* and *dimensions* of block-level elements. Horizontal positioning allows for the sizing and position of an element with respect to its parent element, whereas vertical positioning supports the vertical positioning of an element relative to the block-level elements that precede and follow it.

The horizontal position and size of a block-level element is determined by *seven* properties: `margin-left`, `border-left-width`, `padding-left`, `padding-right`, `border-right-width`, and `margin-right`. By default, margin widths are zero. Authors can reposition or resize the content by physically setting the margin widths. Negative margins can displace an element outside its parent element.

The vertical position and size of a block-level element is determined by *seven* properties: `margin-top`, `border-top-width`, `padding-top`, `height`, `padding-bottom`, `border-bottom-width`, and `margin-bottom`. Margin properties determine the spacing between subsequent block-level elements. Negative margins can be used to position elements one atop the other.

List items are treated as *block-level* elements. List items, however, also contain markers, and there are several properties for controlling the internal list-item box layout.

Inline elements produce formatting boxes; non-empty inline elements can produce multiple boxes. Empty elements such as **IMG**, **APPLET**, or **INPUT** are handled as inline formatting elements. Vertical margins, padding, and borders should not affect the layout of text around inline elements. Horizontal padding, borders, and margins should add space between the element and the surrounding text.

Floating elements produce boxes that "float" on top of the element within which they are contained. HTML has no default floating elements. Padding, border, and margin properties can dramatically affect the position of the element. A block element can contain more than one floating image. Any element can be floated.

Text in the HTML markup that precedes a floating element must appear *above* it. The floating image should be the very first content inside an element if it is to be aligned with the top of the element.

The `clear` property is used to *clear* elements so that they are positioned below left- or right-floated elements (or below both left- and right-floated elements).

Replaced elements usually have well-defined *heights* and *widths*. For some elements, these dimensions cannot be changed. However, some elements can be resized to fit within a box specified by `height` and `width` property values.

Chapter Exercises

Positioning and sizing elements on the display is without doubt one of the more complicated aspects of CSS, so you will be spending a lot of time working through positioning ideas. As a first exercise, work only with block-level elements. Starting with the example documents in Figures 5.7 and 5.10, experiment with the different margin, border, and padding properties and observe how they affect the size and positioning of an element. Try also modifying the document to add block-level elements within other block-level elements. You can then experiment with using "container" elements (such as **DIV**) to define blocks independent of other, sibling **DIV** elements.

The second exercise is to examine list-item elements. Construct a test document containing a list, and use the various `list-item` properties to specify formatting details for the list.

The next exercise is to practice with inline elements. Construct a test document containing inline elements, and add padding, borders, and margin spacing to some (or all) of these elements. You can use background colors to make the padding space visible. Observe how the different properties affect the rendering of the document.

Finally, you should experiment with floating elements. Take the example documents (Figures 5.23, 5.25, 5.28, and 5.31) and experiment with mixes of left- and right-floated elements, and with padding and borders applied to the elements. Try using negative margins to reposition the floated element—note that many browsers place hard limits on how a floating element can be repositioned. Also try using the `width` property to fix the size of floating elements. Try using margins to position one floating element on top of another floating element. This may not be possible, depending on the browser.

Endnotes

1. MSIE 4 (beta 1) supports a **HEIGHT** attribute for **TR** elements.

6

Tutorial, Part 4: Backgrounds, Miscellaneous Properties, and the Stylesheet Cascade

T his final tutorial chapter delves into document layout and CSS language details that were not discussed in the preceding three chapters. The chapter is divided into two sections. The first section examines the CSS properties that control element *back-grounds*, where a background is the color or image placed *behind* the content of a for-matting element. These properties are the obvious generalization of the **BODY** ele-ment **BACKGROUND** or **BGCOLOR** attributes, and allow for element-specific back-grounds, as well as for control over the placement and tiling of a background behind an element. This section includes examples to illustrate how this is done. Note that, given CSS's current limited ability to overlay one element on top of another (some-times called *z-indexing* or *layering* of content), backgrounds are the most reliable way of putting image content behind an element.

The second section covers CSS language issues glossed over in the preceding chap-ters. These issues include: referencing external stylesheets; the use of the `!important` parameter to raise the priority of a stylesheet declaration; and the details of the cas-cading rules that determine which properties are applied to a given element. Also dis-cussed is the way these mechanisms can be used to construct *stylesheet systems* for use across large collections of HTML documents. This section completes the tutorial on the CSS language, and in combination with the related material in Chapters 1 and 2, provides a complete overview of the CSS language structure, as well as a guide to the use of CSS for large document collections.

Browser Canvas and Element Backgrounds

HTML 3.2 supports background colors and/or images via the **BODY** element **BGCOLOR** and **BACKGROUND** attributes. Using these attributes, an author can specify a background color, or a background image, to tile over the entire display canvas. Although Microsoft introduced some HTML extensions to this model (table cell-specific backgrounds, for example), the approach is still rather limited, in that backgrounds are only possible with one or two HTML elements, while control over background positions and layout is nonexistent.

Of course, background effects are largely stylistic, so that it makes sense that control over such features is available in a stylesheet. Indeed, CSS has six properties for defining background properties such as background colors, background images, and background image positioning and tiling formats. These properties are described in the following sections.

Background Colors

The CSS `background-color` property defines a background color for the associated element or elements. The value for this property can be one of the sixteen supported named colors (e.g., "red" or "blue") or it can be an RGB color code using any of the four formats described in Chapter 8 and Appendix A. For example, the five different ways that the background color "aqua" (zero red, full intensities of green and blue) can be indicated are:

```
background-color: aqua;            /* Named color                  */
background-color: #00FFFF;         /* Hexadecimal RGB code         */
background-color: #0FF;            /* "Half-number" Hex RGB code   */
background-color: rgb(0, 255, 255) /* Integer RGB code             */
background-color: rgb(0, 100%, 100%) /* Percentage RGB code        */
```

The hexadecimal color intensities range from 00 (zero intensity) to FF (full intensity), for a total of 256 different levels. Thus the code #00FFFF corresponds to zero intensity red, full intensity blue, and full intensity green. The shorthand form #0FF is turned into a full hex code by doubling the digits: 0 becomes 00, F becomes FF, and so on. Integer RGB codes specify the color using integers ranging from 0 to 255, instead of hexadecimal numbers. Percentage codes use real percentage values, for example 65.23%, to express the intensity of the color. The browser converts these percentages into the appropriate integer intensities.

Background-color can be applied to any HTML element, including **IMG**. For block-level elements, the background color is applied to the region defined by the `height` and `width` of the element. For inline elements, the background region is defined horizontally, by the text range spanned by the element, and vertically, by the bounds of the line height. This is illustrated in Figures 6.1 and 6.2. The background properties, including the color, also extend into any padding space placed around the element. This is demonstrated by the padding spaces around the elements in Figure 6.1, as illustrated in Figure 6.2.

When you set a background color, the background for the element becomes *opaque*, and hides everything beneath it. However, if no background color (or image) is specified, then the background is transparent, and the underlying content shows through. In most cases, the underlying content is just the background of the parent element. However, the underlying content can also be the background *and content* of the element that happens to be behind it, should the "transparent" element have been repositioned on top of another element using negative margins. Some examples of repositioned elements overlapping other elements are found in Figures 6.3 and 6.4.

The `background-color` also becomes the background for any element lying on top of the background, including any specified background *image*. Thus, if an element has both a background color and a background image, the transparent pixels in the background image will display the color defined by the `background-color` property.

NOTE `Background-Color` **Not Properly Implemented on Current Browsers**

Both Netscape Navigator 4.0 and MSIE 3 do not implement `background-color` properly within block elements—these browsers simply use the background color to highlight the text, as opposed to using the color to paint the entire region enclosed by the element. This property is properly implemented by MSIE 4 (beta 1). Note also that MSIE 3 can only set background colors using the shorthand property `background`: it does not understand the explicit property `background-color`.

Background/Foreground Color Contrast
Background and foreground colors must be chosen together, to ensure that the displayed text is readable against the background—black text on a dark brown background is not going to be easy to read! This is important even if a background image is used, since if the reader of the document disables image loading, the text will be displayed against the specified background color. Consequently, even when a background color is designed to appear beneath a background image, the `background-color` and `color` property values should be chosen to provide sufficient contrast with each other.

Background Images
Element-specific background images are referenced using the `background-image` property. This property takes as its value the URL referencing the desired background image, for example:

```
background-image: url(http://www.backgrounds.com/puppies/labrador.gif);
background-image: url(../bgrounds/standard.gif);
```

By default, a background image is *tiled* under the element; that is, it is repeated across and down to fill the space occupied by the element and its padding space. An example of such a tiled background is shown in Figure 6.4, where the background image (shown as an inline image at the top of the page) is tiled to cover the region occupied by the **DIV** element. And yes, this is a rather ghastly background image—I have never claimed great ability as a graphics artist.

Figure 6.1 A simple document illustrating background colors applied to block-level and inline floating elements. The stylesheet content is in italics. Appropriate rendering of this document is illustrated in Figure 6.2. Note how the background color of an element is applied to the element's padding space.

```
<HTML><HEAD>
<TITLE> Example of Colored Backgrounds </TITLE>
<STYLE><!--
    /*
      Give DIV left and right margins and
      paddings, and a light gray color.
    */
DIV         { margin-left:      12pt;   padding-left:     6pt;
              margin-right:     12pt;   padding-right:    6pt;
              background-color: #cccccc;
            }
/* Ps, by default, have no padding or horizontal margins   */
P           { margin-left:  0;  margin-right: 0;  padding:  0;    }
/* This P has lef/right padding, and a purple background    */
P.one       { padding-left:     12pt;
              padding-top:      12pt;
              background-color: #ff77ff;
            }
/* EM elements have a cyan background                        */
EM          { background-color: #00ffff;   }
  /* This EM has padding all around it                       */
EM.padded   { padding-left:     12pt;    padding-right:    6pt;
              padding-top:      12pt;    padding-bottom:   12pt;
            }
--></STYLE>
</HEAD><BODY>
<H2> Example of Colored Backgrounds </H2>
<DIV>
<H3>Heading Inside Grayish DIV Element</H3>
<P CLASS="one">Here is the test paragraph, with an oddly colored
    background and with a 6pt border around it. Note how the color
    permeates the padded region. This paragraph also contains
    <EM CLASS="bg">inlined text</EM> with a different background
    color, as well as <EM CLASS="padded">inlined text</EM>
    with padding space in addition to a background color.
</P>
<P>And here is another P, but without special background
    properties.</P>
</DIV>
</BODY></HTML>
```

Figure 6.2 Suggested rendering of the document listed in Figure 6.1. Note how the background color applies to an element's padding space.

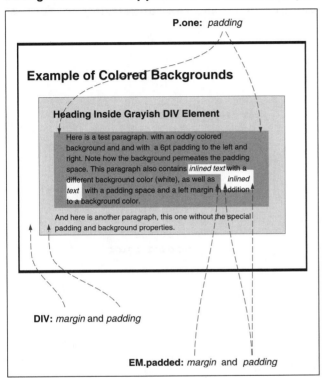

By default, the tiling should begin at the upper left-hand inner corner of the element. The tiling will then proceed throughout the element content and outwards into any padding space around the element. By looking at the tiling beneath the **DIV** element in Figure 6.4, you will see that Netscape Navigator 4 prerelease 4 does not do this properly—the tiling instead starts at the upper corner of the padding region.

The **DIV** in Figure 6.4 has a 1-em padding space on all sides, such that the **P** and **UL** elements appear to have margins, whereas, in fact, both elements start at the left edge of the **DIV** element, the apparent margins being the padding space of the **DIV**.

NOTE `Background-Image` Not Properly Implemented on Current Browsers

MSIE 3 does not understand the `background-image` property, but can set a background images using `background`. However, MSIE 3 does not tile the full area of a block element with a background image, and simply uses the image to highlight the text.

Figure 6.3 A simple document illustrating background color *opacity*. The stylesheet content is in italics. The appropriate rendering of this document is illustrated in Figure 6.4. Note how a defined background color means that underlying content is hidden by the opaque background.

```
<HTML><HEAD>
<TITLE>Background Transparency Example </TITLE>
<STYLE>
  <!--
  P.col      { background-color: #00ffff;            } /* colored P                  */

  DIV        { background-image: url(transp.gif);    /* DIV has background            */
               padding:          1em;                } /* pad to indent P's            */

  P.layer1   { background-color: #ff00ff;            /* b/g color - shift up          */
               margin-top:       -4.5em;             } /* to overlap with list         */

  P.layer2   { margin-top:       0 em;               /* P also overlaps               */
               color:            #337733;            /* no background color           */
               font-weight:      bold;               }
  --></STYLE>
</HEAD><BODY>
<H2> Background Transparency Test </H2>
<P><B>The background image is:</B> <IMG SRC="transp.gif"> </P>
<DIV>
  <P> Here is a paragraph with no background. Thus, the
      paragraph background is <EM>transparent</EM>, and
      shows through the background of the parent
      (<B>DIV</B>) element. </P>
  <P CLASS="col">Here is a paragraph with a background
     color. Since color is <em>opaque</em>, the background
     of the underlying <B>DIV</B> is now obscured. </P>
  <OL>
     <LI>Here is an ordered list</LI>
     <LI>This list has no background color, so
         that the background is transparent. </LI>
     <LI>Here is a third item.</LI>
     <LI>And now a fourth.</LI>
  </OL>
  <P CLASS="layer1">P after OL — moved to overlap</P>
  <P CLASS="layer2">P after P after OL — moved to overlap</P>
</DIV>
</BODY></HTML>
```

Netscape Navigator 4.0 does understand background-image, and tiles the full background region. However, Navigator 4.0 also adds a small margin space on all sides of an element that take background images (this is a bug). As a result, a document formatted with background images will have a somewhat different page layout than the same document formatted with background colors. Background-image is properly implemented by MSIE 4 (beta 1), such that page layout is identical with either background images or colors. However, margins are not obeyed for the background colors or tilings, and the backgrounds always extend to the left and right edges of the display.

Figure 6.4 Rendering of the document listed in Figure 6.3 by the Netscape Navigator 4 browser. Note how a defined background color obscures the underlying background and/or element content. The background image is tiled beneath the DIV element, as specified in Figure 6.3. Note, however, that the starting position for the first tiled image is incorrect.

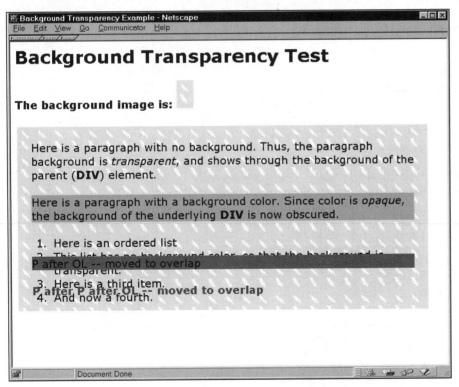

Controlling the Tiling Pattern

CSS supports a `background-repeat` property for controlling the way in which the element is tiled by a background image. This property can take four values. The default value is `repeat`, which causes the image to be tiled both horizontally and vertically, as illustrated in Figure 6.4. The remaining three values are demonstrated in Figures 6.5 and 6.6, where they are applied to the background tiling of single paragraphs. Notice how these paragraphs have no margins or padding; they have been given thin black borders so that the boundaries of the paragraphs are easy to see.

Figure 6.5 Example document illustrating the use of the `background-repeat` property to control the tiling of background images. The stylesheet content is in italics. Typical rendering of this document is shown in Figure 6.6.

```
<HTML><HEAD><TITLE>Background Tiling Test 1</TITLE>
<STYLE> <!--
/* Set default paddings/margins/borders                          */
  P          { margin: 0;          padding:0;
               border: 0;          margin-top: 0.1em;      }
/* NO TILING — 1 ONLY — put thin border around paragraph          */
  P.norep   { background-image:   url(top-tile.gif);
              background-repeat:   no-repeat;
              border:              solid thin black;       }
/* Tile HORIZONTALLY only — put thin border around paragraph       */
  P.horiz   { background-image:   url(top-tile.gif);
              background-repeat:   repeat-x;
              border:              solid thin black;       }
/* Tile VERTICALLY only — put thin border around paragraph        */
  P.vert    { background-image:   url(top-tile.gif);
              background-repeat:   repeat-y;
              border:              solid thin black;       }
/* Tile VERTICALLY only — put thin border around paragraph
   Pad text by 41px (width of img) so it does not lie over
   background                                                     */
  P.vpad    { background-image:   url(top-tile.gif);
              background-repeat:   repeat-y;
              border:              solid thin black;
              padding-left:        41px;                   }
  --> </STYLE>
</HEAD><BODY>
<H2> Background Tiling Test 1 </H2>
<P CLASS="norep">Here is a boring paragraph with a no-repeat
   background. Tiling patterns are controlled by the
   <CODE>background-repeat</CODE> property.</P>
<P CLASS="horiz"> Here is a paragraph with a background. The
   paragraph content is displayed on top of the background.
   Note how the background is <em>tiled</em>. Tiling patterns
```

Continued

Figure 6.5 *Continued*

```
    are controlled by the <CODE>background-repeat</CODE> property.</P>
<P CLASS="vert">Here is a paragraph with a background. The
    paragraph content is displayed on top of the background.
    Note how the background is <em>tiled</em>.  Tiling patterns
    are controlled by the <CODE>background-repeat</CODE> property.</P>
<P CLASS="vpad">Here is a paragraph with a background. The
    paragraph content is displayed on top of the background.
    Note how the background is <em>tiled</em>.  Tiling patterns
    are controlled by the <CODE>background-repeat</CODE> property.</P>
</BODY></HTML>
```

Figure 6.6 Rendering, by the Netscape Navigator 4 prerelease browser, of the document listed in Figure 6.5. This figure illustrates the use of the `background-repeat` **property to control background image tiling. Note that there should be no space between the background images (and each paragraph's content) and the borders drawn around the paragraphs; the small space left in the figure is due to a formatting error by Netscape Navigator 4.**

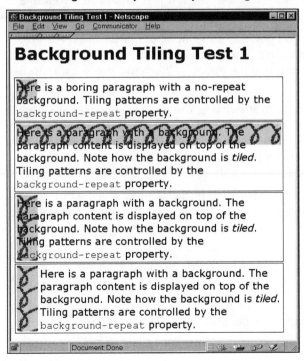

The value `no-repeat` turns off tiling—the background image is displayed only once, by default at the upper left-hand corner of the element. This is illustrated in the first paragraph in Figure 6.6 which corresponds, in Figure 6.5, to the stylesheet rule with selector `P.norep`. The value `repeat-x` causes the image to repeat only along the x-axis (horizontally), while the value `repeat-y` causes the image to repeat only along the y-axis (vertically). These patterns are illustrated in the second and third paragraphs shown in Figure 6.6. By default, this tiling starts from the upper left-hand corner of the element. As we will see, this starting location can be changed.

The `repeat-x` and `repeat-y` patterns are a convenient way of creating a horizontal or vertical border alongside some text. However, in this case a designer may wish to exclude text from the region containing the tiled border. This can be done by using padding space to push the edge of the text in, away from the tiled region—remember that, by default, tiling starts at the outer edge of the padding space region. This procedure was followed to create the fourth paragraph in Figure 6.6, which corresponds to the stylesheet rule in Figure 6.5 with selector `p.vpad`. This rule uses `padding-left: 41px` to ensure that the padding region takes up the vertically repeated background image (the image is exactly 41 pixels wide), so that the text starts just to the right of the background.

Specifying the Initial Location of the Background Image

As described in the previous section, background images are, by default, positioned to start at the upper left-hand inner corner of the element. If the image is then tiled, it is tiled starting from this starting location.

However, this is often not an appropriate starting point. For example, designers often wish to place a single, non-tiled background image at the center of an element, rather like a watermark. Such placement is only possible if there is a way to move the initial background image away form the default upper left-hand starting point.

CSS supports a `background-position` property for defining the starting point for the background. This property defines the position for the initial background image with respect to the upper left-hand corner of the image. The property value can be given in a multitude of different formats—given the simplicity of the idea, it is amazing how complicated the implementation actually is! In any event, the following description explains the different formats and their meanings.

If the background image is repeated, it will repeat starting from the location specified by `background-position`. Figure 6.7 illustrates, using light-gray replicas so that the rest of the figure is not obscured, how a repositioned background image would be repeated given the background-repeat value `repeat-x`.

Note that `background-position` applies *only* to block-level or replaced elements, since only those elements have well-defined boxes with respect to which a starting position can be defined.

Starting Position Using Two Length Coordinates The starting position can be specified using lengths in any of the standard units (em, ex, in, cm, mm, pc, pt, and px). The standard format is

```
background-position: lengthx lengthy
```

where *lengthx* and *lengthy* are the x and y offsets of the upper left-hand corner of the background image relative to the upper left-hand corner of the inner box around the element (that is, *not* with respect to the outer corner defined by the padding space region). This positioning is illustrated in Figure 6.7. Note how offsets are measured downwards and to the right of the upper corner of the element. Negative values are allowed, in which case the starting position can be outside the element. Note that the background cannot extend outside an element's padding space.

The default value for background-position is "0 0", which places the background image at the upper left-hand corner of the inner box of the element.

Starting Position Using One Length Coordinate If only one length is specified, it is taken as the horizontal offset of the background image. The vertical offset is then adjusted so that the image is in the middle of the element, halfway from both the top and bottom. This is equivalent to a vertical position of 50%. For example, the specification

```
background-position: 12em;
```

means that the background image is indented 12 ems from the left inner edge of the element, and is vertically centered within the element.

Figure 6.7 Use of lengths as background-position values to position a background image inside an element.

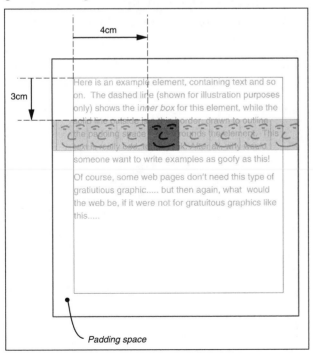

Starting Position Using Two Percentage Values The background-position property also supports percentage values, which position the background image within the element as a percentage of the element's width and height. The format for the expression is:

```
background-position: xx% yy%;
```

where `xx%` is the percentage position along the *x*-axis and `yy%` the percentage position along the *y*-axis. As when positions are given in length units, negative values are allowed—as are values greater than 100%.

The CSS specifications define these percentage positions as follows, using the x- (horizontal) axis to illustrate the approach. Consider a horizontal position of `30%`. This percentage means that the point on the background image that is `30%` in from the left-hand edge of the image is positioned such that it lies `30%` in from the left-hand inner edge of the parent element. Consequently, a value of 50% corresponds to a background centered within the parent element, while 0% corresponds to an element placed at the left-hand side, and 100% to a background placed flush with the right margin. This placement model is illustrated in Figure 6.8.

Alternatively, these percentage values can be thought of as defining the position of the *center* of the background image with respect to the box defined by the dashed line in Figure 6.9—the box

Figure 6.8 Description of percentage values indicating the positioning of a background image inside an element. Figure 6.9 provides an alternative interpretation.

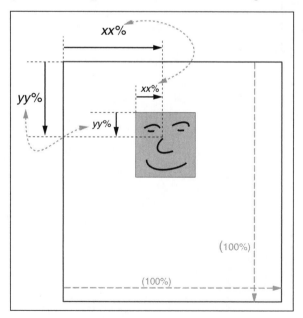

Figure 6.9 Description of percentage values indicating the positioning of a background image inside an element (Figure 6.8 provides an alternative interpretation of percentage values). The grayed "images" illustrate how the background will repeat, based on this starting location.

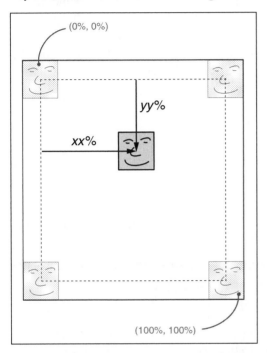

linking the centers of the background image when it is placed at the extreme edges of the parent element. Using this system, a percentage `background-position` value defines the location of the *center* of the background image relative to the minimum and maximum position of this element within the box, as illustrated in Figure 6.9.

Both interpretations of the positioning model are correct, and you can use whichever approach you find easiest to understand.

Starting Position Using One Percentage Value If only one percentage value is specified, it is taken as the horizontal offset of the background image, with the image also being vertically centered. This is equivalent to a vertical position of 50%. For example, the specification

```
background-position: 30%;
```

means that the background image is indented 30% in from the left inner edge of the element (as defined above), centered vertically within the element.

Mixed Percentage and Length Values Values for the background position can be a mix of percentage and length values, for example:

```
background-position: 70% 20px;
```

In this case, the top of the background image is lowered 20 pixels from the top of the element, while the image is positioned horizontally 70% in from the left side of the element, as discussed previously.

Starting Position Using Keywords In addition to length or percentage values, background position can also take the keywords `top`, `center`, `bottom`, `left`, and `right`. These keywords can appear alone or in pairs, with each distinct combination corresponding to a position defined using percentages. For example, the declaration:

```
background-position: right center
```

corresponds to a percentage position of "100% 50%", while the declaration

```
background-position: center
```

corresponds to a percentage position of "50% 50%". The possible keyword combinations and their meanings are illustrated in Figure 6.10, from which you can easily determine the corresponding percentage positions. Alternatively, the percentage positions are given explicitly in Table 8.6.

NOTE Several Background Properties Not Implemented on Current Browsers

Neither MSIE 3 or Netscape Navigator 4 support the `background-attachment` or `background-position` properties. Also, MSIE 3 does not support `background-repeat`. Navigator 4 does support `background-repeat`, but always starts the repeat pattern at the upper-left hand corner of the region defined by the box containing both the element and any padding space (according to CSS, it should start at the upper left-hand corner of the box that excludes the padding space). MSIE 4 (beta 1), does not yet support `background-repeat`, `background-position` or `background-attachment`.

NOTE Navigator 4.0 Problem with Transparent Background Images

When a background image is specified using the shorthand `background` property, Navigator 4.0 renders any transparent portions of a background image as black, thereby obscuring all text (yes, this is a bug!) The problem can be avoided by using the `background-image` property.

Figure 6.10 The placement of the background image for the indicated `background-position` **keyword values. The keyword values position the background at percentage offsets of 0%, 50%, or 100% along the horizontal and vertical axes, as illustrated.**

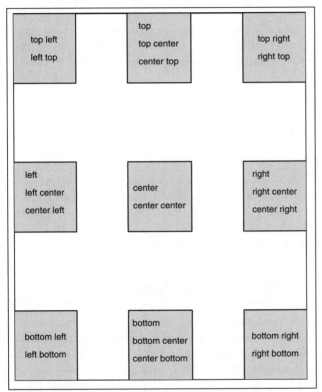

Scrolling or Fixed Backgrounds

Once a background is added, it is by default treated as *attached* to the document text or other content. Then, when the document is scrolled either horizontally or vertically, the background scrolls along with it.

This was the default behavior for most browsers, until Microsoft introduced non-scrolling backgrounds (using a special **BODY** element attribute). Non-scrolling backgrounds are *not* attached to the element content. Thus, when the document is scrolled, the background stays fixed on the display, with the content moving on top of it.

CSS uses the `background-attachment` property to define how the background should be attached to the element content. The value `scroll` (which is the default value) attaches the background to the element content, so that the background scrolls with the text. In contrast, the value `fixed` detaches the background from the element content, so that the background stays fixed on the display, with the element content scrolling on top of it. These are the only supported values.

Note that not all browsers support `fixed` background attachments, and that even when they do, they may support only fixed backgrounds for the **BODY** element (although this property is valid with all HTML elements, its meaning for non-**BODY** elements is unclear).

Shorthand `Background` *Property*

`Background` is a shorthand tool for specifying the values for the five background properties just described, in a single stylesheet declaration. The value for `background` is a string containing from one to five of the values supported by the other five background properties, in any order. Some examples of valid `background` declarations are:

```
background: red url(./bgrounds/std1.gif);
background: blue;
background: fixed center blue url(http://www.bgnds.com/yikes.gif) no-repeat
```

Background Property Examples?

You have probably noticed that this section included very few example documents employing background properties. Unfortunately, at the time this section was written, there were no browsers that properly supported the `background-position` or `background-attachment` properties, so that such examples were not possible. Example documents are provided at the book's Web site—please see the Preface to find the site's location.

External Stylesheets, and the Stylesheet Cascade

The preceding tutorial chapters outlined almost all the details of the CSS language syntax and structure. However, there remain two important issues to cover: (1) how stylesheet resources are associated with a given HTML document; and (2) how to handle the situation when more than one rule applies to the same element. These two issues are the subject of this section.

In the preceding chapters, stylesheet rules were always placed inside a document's **STYLE** element. This is convenient when working with a single document, but not so when developing stylesheets for many different documents. In this case, it is advantageous to keep the stylesheet rules in a separate file, which can be referenced by the documents that need it. HTML and CSS provide two ways for referencing such external stylesheets, as well as two ways of including stylesheet rules within an HTML document. These four mechanisms are described here in detail, and with examples.

Given multiple stylesheet sources (linked stylesheets, internal rules, etc.), there is a growing risk of rule conflict—that is, of having multiple stylesheet rules that apply to the same element, some coming from a linked stylesheet, and others coming from the stylesheet within the HTML document (rule conflict can also happen between rules inside a **STYLE** element). Consequently, there must be a mechanism for deciding which properties should be applied to a given element.

CSS defines this selection process through a procedure known as *stylesheet cascading*. The cascading rules determine which properties apply to a given element, and define the mechanisms by which an author can specify which rules should apply under a given set of circumstances. The second half of this section describes the details of this cascade mechanism, and the rules by which CSS rule conflicts are resolved.

Including Stylesheets in HTML Documents

There are four ways that style information can be included within, or associated with, an HTML document. Briefly, these are:

LINK element—An HTML **LINK** element can reference an external stylesheet. **LINK** can only appear in the document **HEAD**, and ahead of a **STYLE** element.

STYLE element—An HTML **STYLE** element contains stylesheet instructions to be applied to the HTML document. The **STYLE** element must be in the document **HEAD**.

@import "at rule" within a stylesheet—An HTML stylesheet can contain `@import` statements that import external stylesheet rules, referenced via a URL, into the existing stylesheet content. This is similar to a LINK element, but works within the stylesheet itself.

STYLE attribute—Most HTML elements support a **STYLE** attribute, the value of which is a collection of CSS properties to apply to the associated element.

As discussed in the next section, each mechanism has its own advantages and disadvantages. The best choice for an author will depend on how the stylesheet is being used.

LINK Element: Linking to an External Stylesheet

In this approach, the stylesheet is in a separate document, referenced using an HTML **LINK** element. The HTML markup is

```
<LINK REL="stylesheet" TYPE="mime/type" HREF="url">
```

where **REL**="stylesheet" indicates that the target resource is a stylesheet, the string `url` is the URL pointing to the stylesheet document, and `mime/type` is the MIME type for the stylesheet. The CSS stylesheet language has the MIME type `text/css`. Because of this choice for a MIME type name, most CSS stylesheet documents are given the filename extension *.css*. A typical example is then

```
<LINK REL="stylesheet" TYPE="text/css" HREF="../styles/mainpage.css">
```

A single document can contain more than one **LINK** element, each one referencing a different stylesheet. The browser will retrieve all the stylesheets, and will process the rules in the order in which they are retrieved. This processing stage is discussed in more detail later in this section.

The advantage of linked stylesheets is that a single, externally referenced stylesheet can be associated with any number of HTML documents, where each document simply links to the same external stylesheet using the **LINK** element. The disadvantage is that the stylesheet rules are, to some degree, "hidden" from the reader of the document—the browser "View Source" function shows only the content of an HTML document, and not the content of the linked stylesheet. This can be inconvenient when developing new stylesheets, or when trying to add "customized" styling on top of an existing collection of rules, since extra work is required to retrieve and view the external stylesheet.

STYLE Element: Stylesheets within the Document

Stylesheet content can be placed inside a **STYLE** element which, in turn, must be in the document **HEAD**. A simple example is:

```
<STYLE>
  BODY    { font-family:     times, serif;
            color:           black ;
            margin-left:     10%;
            margin-right:    10%;     }
/* more to follow.... of course ... */
</STYLE>
```

As far as document formatting is concerned, there is no difference between a stylesheet in a separate file or one in the **HEAD** of an HTML document, other than the order in which the rules are processed: A browser always treats **LINK**ed stylesheet content as coming *before* stylesheet rules placed in a **STYLE** element. This means that **STYLE** element content can be used to add local customization "on top" of the default rules specified by the **LINK**ed stylesheet(s).

Of course, this example **STYLE** element gives no indication of the stylesheet language being used. The stylesheet language should be indicated by a **TYPE** attribute, which takes as its value the MIME type for the language. For a CSS stylesheet, the appropriate start tag is then <STYLE TYPE="text/css">.

Hiding Stylesheets from Older Browsers Older browsers that do not understand stylesheets will try to interpret the stylesheet instructions as markup—needless to say, the results can be rather messy. To avoid this, the CSS specification lets an author place the entire stylesheet inside an HTML comment, thereby hiding the content from older browsers. For example, the stylesheet in the previous example would be hidden by using the markup (the HTML comment start and stop strings are in boldface):

```
<STYLE TYPE="text/css">
<!--
  BODY    { font-family:     times, serif;
            color:           black ;
            margin-left:     10%;
            margin-right:    10%;     }
 ... /* more rules below ... omitted from example */
-->
</STYLE>
```

These HTML comment strings are not relevant in a linked stylesheet document, and should be omitted. For example, if the content listed above were placed in an external stylesheet file, it would simply be:

```
BODY { font-family:  times, serif;
       color:         black ;
       margin-left:  10%;
       margin-right: 10%;     }
 ... /* more rules below ... omitted from example */
```

Importing within Stylesheets: The `@import` Statement

The CSS language supports an `@import` statement (also called an *at-rule*) for referencing external stylesheet instructions that should be loaded into the current stylesheet. Obviously, the value associated with an `@import` statement must specify the URL for the desired external stylesheet. The format is:

```
@import url(url_string);
```

where `url_string` is the URL being referenced. The actual URL can be placed in single or double quotes, if desired. Some examples are:

```
@import url(http://www.utoronto.ca/ian/styles/book1.css);
@import url( 'http://www.utoronto.ca/ian/styles/patch2.css' );
@import url( "dir1/blobby.css" );
```

The browser will load the referenced instructions, replacing the `@import` statement with the loaded instructions, and will use the resulting stylesheet to format the document.

NOTE The `@import` CSS Inclusion Mechanism Is Not Currently Supported

Neither MSIE 3 nor Netscape Navigator 4 support the `@import` CSS rule for including external stylesheet content. Indeed, `@import` rules can, under some circumstances, cause Navigator 4.0 to crash. For now, authors should therefore avoid `@import` rules, and should instead use HTML **LINK** elements to reference external stylesheets.

Handling of Partial URLs Partial URLs, such as the URL `dir1/blobby.css` in the preceding example, are evaluated relative to the URL of the *stylesheet* containing the `@import`, and *not* relative to the URL of the document that referenced the stylesheet. This is irrelevant if the `@import` is within a document's **STYLE** element. However, `@import` statements can also appear in a **LINK**ed stylesheet, in which case the URLs of the document and the referenced stylesheet, and hence the URLs referenced by the `@import` statements, can be very different. Consider the example illustrated in Figure 6.11. The two HTML documents in question are located at the URLs:

Figure 6.11 An illustration of how @import URLs are evaluated with respect to the location of the stylesheet, and not with respect to the location of the HTML document referencing the stylesheet. (A) illustrates the case when @import is used within a STYLE element, while (B) illustrates an @import in an equivalent, linked stylesheet.

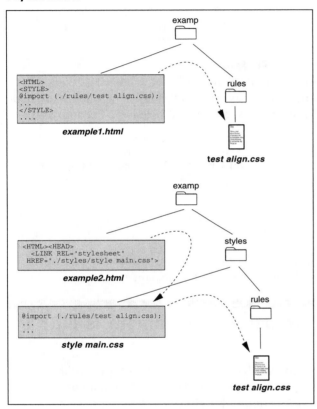

```
http://smaug.java.utoronto.ca/examp/example1.html        (Document A)
http://smaug.java.utoronto.ca/examp/example2.html        (Document B)
```

The first document (labeled (A) in Figure 6.11) uses a style element containing an @import statement, namely:

```
<STYLE>
<!—
@import (" ./rules/test-align.css")
H1, H2 {font-family: "Arial Black", Arial, sans-serif }
        /* and lots more rules .... */
</STYLE>
```

Consequently, the URL used to access the imported stylesheet is

```
http://smaug.java.utoronto.ca/examp/rules/test-align.css
```

Consider now the document in part (B) of this figure: This document uses a **LINK** element to reference this same stylesheet information. The element is:

```
<LINK REL="stylesheet" HREF="./styles/style-main.css">
```

but note how this stylesheet is located in a *different* directory than the HTML document. The file *style-main.css* contains the same stylesheet as before, namely:

```
@import (" ./rules/test-align.css")
H1, H2 {font-family: "Arial Black", Arial, sans-serif }
        /* and lots more rules .... */
```

which is the same content as in (A), but now in a separate file in a different directory. As a result, the stylesheet "imported" into this stylesheet via the @import statement is obtained using the partial URL evaluated relative to the location of the stylesheet document, namely:

```
http://smaug.java.utoronto.ca/examp/styles/rules/test-align.css
```

Ordering of Imported Stylesheets Note that @import statements must appear as the *first lines* in a stylesheet, and cannot appear after any stylesheet rule. Thus the stylesheet

```
@import url(http://joe.blow.com/test/style1.css)
@import url(http://joe.blow.com/optional/dummy.css)
H1 {color: blue}
H2 {color: green}
```

is valid, and requests that two external stylesheet documents be downloaded and placed *inline* with the local stylesheet, replacing the two @import statements. However, the stylesheet

```
@import url(http://joe.blow.com/test/style1.css)
H1 {color: blue}
@import url(http://joe.blow.com/optional/dummy.css)
H2 {color: green}
```

is invalid, since the second @import statement occurs after a locally specified rule. In this event, the browser *ignores* the second @import statement, and processes the stylesheet as if it contained:

```
@import url(http://joe.blow.com/test/style1.css)
H1 {color: blue}
H2 {color: green}
```

This syntax rule ensures that external stylesheets "come before" any rules defined explicitly within the document. The ramifications of this are discussed in more detail later, when we discuss the CSS cascading mechanism.

STYLE Attribute: Element-Specific CSS Properties

Versions of HTML that support stylesheets also support a new attribute, **STYLE**, used to include stylesheet instructions directly within an element start tag. The general syntax is:

```
<NAME STYLE="declarations"> ... </NAME>
```

where *NAME* is the element name, STYLE is the new attribute, and *declarations* is a semicolon-separated collection of CSS declarations to apply to the element. For example, the HTML markup

```
<EM STYLE="color:red; text-decoration: blink">locally
   applied style</EM>
```

means that the text inside this **EM** should be red and blinking. This mechanism lets an author place element-specific formatting right in the HTML markup, without using a **STYLE** element or linked stylesheets. The advantage is some added simplicity when marking up the document (there is no need for a **STYLE** element, for example) but at the expense of several disadvantages—such local style modifications can be hard to keep track of, and difficult to update and modify. One advantage, however, is *priority*—declarations present in a **STYLE** attribute value almost always *override* equivalent declarations arising from rules in a **STYLE** element or an external stylesheet.

For large collections of documents, and where maintenance is the main issue, an author should avoid **STYLE** attributes, and instead use stylesheet rules to specify formatting details.

META Specification of the Stylesheet Language

If there is no **STYLE** element, or if the **STYLE** element does not have a **TYPE** attribute, the browser will not know which stylesheet language is used within the **STYLE** attributes. The HTML language developers propose using special **META** elements to provide this information. The recommended form is:

```
<META HTTP-EQUIV="Content-style-type" CONTENT="type/subtype">
```

where *type/subtype* is the MIME type of the stylesheet language. For CSS, this is simply:

```
<META HTTP-EQUIV="Content-style-type" CONTENT="text/css">
```

Of course, most browsers currently ignore such **META** elements, just as they ignore the **TYPE** attribute of STYLE elements.

Importance of Specifying a Stylesheet Language

It is important to specify the stylesheet language, preferably using a **TYPE** attribute in a **STYLE** element. As discussed in Chapter 9, Netscape Navigator 4 actually supports two stylesheet languages: Cascading Stylesheets and JavaScript Accessible Stylesheets, or *JASS*. If the stylesheet type is not indicated, Navigator 4 will try and "guess" at the language, sometimes incorrectly. Explicitly indicating the stylesheet type ensures that this will never happen.

The CSS `!important` *Parameter* CSS properties can take an optional parameter, `!important`, to raise the priority of a declaration with respect to other declarations—a declaration that is `!important` will always override one that is not important. This parameter appears at the end of a declaration, just before the semicolon. An example is:

```
A  { text-decoration: underline !important; }
```

The parameter ensures, under almost all circumstances, that this property will be applied in place of any other text-decoration declaration associated with **A** elements.

The !important parameter is an important component of the CSS *cascading model* that determines which properties should be applied to a particular element, given multiple, conflicting declarations. This model is discussed in the next section.

NOTE The !important CSS Parameter Is Not Currently Supported

Neither MSIE 3 nor Netscape Navigator 4 support the !important parameter for raising the priority of a CSS declaration—indeed, MSIE 3 will discard any declaration that contains an !important. MSIE 4 (beta 1) also does not support !important.

Multiple Stylesheets and the CSS Cascade

One of the more complicated aspects of CSS is understanding how the rules are actually used to format a given HTML element. Each element is usually subject to many different rules and declarations, often with conflicting formatting requests. CSS resolves these conflicts via a set of *cascading rules*. Essentially, the cascading process means that the declarations for a given element take their default value unless overridden by a stylesheet declaration, which in turn can be overridden by a declaration coming from a rule that more specifically applies to the particular element.

Default, Author, and Reader Stylesheets

To understand cascading, it is important to understand the distinction between the three different actors who specify stylesheet rules: the *browser*, the *reader*, and the *author*. The first player is the browser, which defines a *default stylesheet*. This stylesheet consists of the rules that, in the absence of any other rules, define the default formatting layout for the browser. Usually this stylesheet defines formatting similar to that produced by pre-stylesheet browsers, such as Netscape Navigator 3. These rules have the lowest priority, and can be easily overridden by the other players. Note that default rules can never be !important.

The second player is the reader or user of the browser, who can define a *reader stylesheet*. This is a collection of rules, defined in some way by the user, that can override equivalent rules specified in the default stylesheet. The reader can also declare some declarations to be !important, and thereby ensure they are used regardless of other declarations for the same property. There are currently no browsers that support reader stylesheets, but the Internet Explorer 4 developers promise support for reader stylesheets in the final release of the browser.

The third and final player is the document author, who defines the *author stylesheet*, which is the stylesheet coming from all the rules and declarations embedded in the document or accessed by a document's **LINK** elements. The cascading rules let these author rules override the browser's defaults, and also override rules specified in the reader stylesheet—although this can be changed by the reader's use of the `!important` declaration.

The `!important` property is essentially a global override for the cascade procedure, Thus, a declaration declared `!important` by the *author* will override any author- or user-defined declarations that are not declared important. However, an `!important` declaration in a *reader* stylesheet *always* overrides author-defined declarations, even ones that are `!important`. This ensures that, by using `!important`, a reader always has the final say in specifying the formatting.

Evaluating the Stylesheet Cascade

The `!important` parameter is just one part of the cascading mechanism, and may seem a bit vague without a concrete example illustrating its role. Indeed, this book has yet to go into the details of the cascading mechanism, which is the way, within CSS, that the browser determines which declarations to apply when actually formatting a given element. The next five sections describe in detail the cascading mechanism, using a collection of stylesheet examples to illustrate the process.

The mechanism is complex, and somewhat tedious, so that this section may bear skipping on first reading. Indeed, most authors will be able to design perfectly functional stylesheets without knowing the details of the CSS cascade. However, if you are designing large CSS systems, consisting of many linked stylesheets, or have encountered a situation where the relationship between the CSS rules and a particular element's formatting instructions is unclear, then it is time to read this section and learn the gory details!

Step 1: Create the Full Document Stylesheet

The full stylesheet is the collection of rules applying to a document arising from the default, author, and reader-specified stylesheets. It is obtained by taking these parts and combining them in the following order:

1. **Rules from the browser's default stylesheet.** This is always the first collection of rules assumed by the browser, and is the specification for the default formatting of all documents. Quite often, this information is hidden within the browser (for example, in a configuration file) and is not accessible as a collection of CSS rules.

2. **Rules arising from the reader-specified stylesheet.** These are the CSS rules defined by the reader. Before adding these rules to create the complete document stylesheet, the reader stylesheet is fully expanded by inserting any content referenced by `@import` statements. The rules are then placed in the full document stylesheet according to the order in which they appear in the fully expanded author stylesheet.

3. **Rules arising from document LINK elements.** This is part of the author stylesheet. Before inserting these rules, each stylesheet must be fully expanded by replacing any `@import` statement

with the referenced content. The collection of rules is then placed in the full document stylesheet, according to the order of the corresponding **LINK** elements in the HTML document.

4. **Rules arising from any STYLE element in the document.** This is part of the author stylesheet. Before inserting these rules, the **STYLE** element is fully expanded by inserting any rules referenced by `@import` statements. The rules are then placed in the full document stylesheet, following the order in which they appear within the fully expanded **STYLE** element.

5. **Rules arising from declarations in HTML element STYLE attributes.** These are assumed to correspond to **ID**-based simple selector rules. For example, the markup `<P STYLE="color: blue">` ... `</P>` would correspond to the rule `#xyxxy {color: blue}` and the document markup `<P ID="xyzzy">` ... `</P>`.

To process this stylesheet, we must also keep track of the origin (default, reader, and author stylesheets) of the different rules, since cascading depend on this origin.

An example of this process is illustrated in Figures 6.12 and 6.13. Figure 6.12 lists an HTML document, its external, related stylesheets, and also a simple reader stylesheet defined by the user.

Figure 6.12 Source listing for the example HTML document *cascade.html* and the related stylesheet documents *list-styles.css* and *default.css*. Also listed are the CSS rules belonging to the *reader stylesheet*.

```
<HTML><HEAD>
  <TITLE> Cascading Properties Example </TITLE>
  <LINK REL="stylesheet" SRC="list-styles.css" TYPE="text/css">
  <STYLE>
    <!--
    @import url(default.css)
    UL LI UL {list-style-type: circle !important } /* An important rule  */
    LI        {font-family:    arial; sans-serif;} /* Try arial ...      */
    A         {text-decoration: overline; }        /* Line over anchors  */
    P EM      {color:          green; }
    -->
  </STYLE>
</HEAD><BODY>
<H1> Example of CSS Cascading </H1>
<P>This paragraph contains several exemplary <EM>list items</EM>.
The following is an example nested list:</P>
<UL>
  <LI>Here is an item in this example list.</LI>
  <LI>Here is another item in the list, containing a special
      <A HREF="flooby.html" ID="xyxxy">hypertext anchor</A>.</LI>
  <UL CLASS="special">
      <LI>Here is a second-level list item, inside a UL list with
          <B>CLASS</B>="special".</LI>
```

Continued

Figure 6.12 *Continued*

```
      <LI>The list should consequently be formatted in a special
          way</LI>
    </UL>
</UL>
</BODY></HTML>
```

list-styles.css

```
OL          { list-style-type: decimal; }    /* default decimal numbers    */
OL LI OL    { list-style-type: lower-alpha; } /* letters inside OL lists    */
UL LI OL    { list-style-type: lower-roman; } /* roman inside UL lists      */

UL          { list-style-type: disc;}         /* discs for UL lists         */
UL LI UL    { font-size: smaller;
              color:      #4444bb;
              list-style-type: square;         /* squares for UL inside UL   */
            }
UL.special  {color:      red;                  /* special lists are RED!     */
              list-style-type: disc; }
```

default.css

```
BODY        {color:             black;
             background-color:  white;
             font-family:       verdana, arial, sans-serif;
             margin-left:       2%;            /* black on white, with       */
             margin-right:      2%;            /* small margins all 'round   */
             margin-top:         1%;
            }
A:visited   {text-decoration: none; !important}
                                               /* no underline for visited links    */

H1,H2,H3    {font-family:  "Arial Bold", Arial, Helvetica, sans-serif;
             color:        #3333AA;            /* deepish blue for headings*/
P           {font-size:    normal;             /* Easy to read               */
             margin-left: 3%;
             margin-right: 3%;                 /* Paragraphs have margins    */
             text-align:   justify; }          /* And are justified!         */
P.leading   {text-indent:  5em; }              /* Indent leading Ps          */
P.columns   {font-size:    small;
             margin-left: 1em;                 /* P's in columns have        */
             margin-right: 1em; }              /* smaller font and smaller   */
                                               /* margins.                   */
```

Continued

Figure 6.12 *Continued*

```
EM          {color:       red;}            /* EM text is red          */
P EM        {color:       blue;}           /* but is blue inside P    */
```

Reader Stylesheet

```
A:link, A:visited, A:active  { text-decoration: underline !important ;}
BODY {font-size: large;}                /* Use larger fonts (bad monitor! */
UL    {list-style-type: circle;}
```

Figure 6.13 The full stylesheet associated with the document listed in Figure 6.12, indicating also which portions arise from the author and reader stylesheets.

Reader Stylesheet

```
A:link, A:visited, A:active  { text-decoration: underline !important ;}
BODY {font-size: large;}                /* Use larger fonts (bad monitor! */
UL    {list-style-type: circle; }
```

Author Stylesheet

```
OL          {list-style-type: decimal; }     /* default decimal numbers  */
OL LI OL    {list-style-type: lower-alpha; } /* letters inside OL lists  */
UL LI OL    {list-style-type: lower-roman; } /* roman inside UL lists    */

UL          {list-style-type: disc;}         /* discs for UL lists        */
UL LI UL    {font-size: smaller;
              color:      #4444bb;
              list-style-type: square;        /* squares for UL inside UL */
              }
UL.special  {color:      red;                 /* special lists are RED!   */
              list-style-type: disc; }

BODY        {color:              black;
              background-color: white;
              font-family:      verdana, arial, sans-serif;
              margin-left:      2%;           /* black on white, with    */
              margin-right:     2%;           /* small margins all 'round */
              margin-top:       1%;
              }

A:visited   {text-decoration: none; !important}
                                      /* no underline for visited links */

H1,H2,H3    {font-family:  "Arial Bold", Arial, Helvetica, sans-serif;
```

Continued

Figure 6.13 *Continued*

```
           color:        #3333AA;          /* deepish blue for headings*/
P          {font-size:   normal;           /* Easy to read          !    */
           margin-left: 3%;
           margin-right: 3%;               /* Paragraphs have margins   */
           text-align:   justify; }        /* And are justified!        */
P.leading  {text-indent: 5em; }            /* Indent leading paragraphs*/
P.columns  {font-size:    small;
           margin-left:  1em;              /* P's in columns have       */
           margin-right: 1em; }            /* smaller font and smaller  */
                                             /* margins.                */
EM         {color:        red;}            /* EM text is red            */
P EM       {color:        blue;}           /* but is blue inside P      */
UL LI UL {list-style-type: circle !important }    /* An important rule  */
LI         {font-family:   arial; sans-serif;}    /* Try arial ...      */
A          {text-decoration: overline; }          /* Line over anchors  */
P EM       {color:         green; }
```

For simplicity, this example ignores the browser's default stylesheet. Figure 6.13 shows the resulting "full stylesheet," with all the rules properly ordered and sorted according to their origins.

At the same time, pay attention to the structure of these stylesheets—notice how the linked and @imported stylesheets define global properties that quite probably would apply to many different documents, while the rules within the **STYLE** element are designed to provide local modifications, and override the global rules. This is indeed the intent of the CSS approach, and the rationale behind this design.

Step 2: Find Rule/Declarations Applying to a Given Element and Property

The next step is to take a specific formatting element in the HTML document and an associated CSS property, and find *all* the declarations that apply to this element and property. These should be listed as a collection of single-line CSS rules associated with the selected property, in the order in which they occur in the full stylesheet, complete with the *selector* associated with the declaration, and any !important parameter. The list must also note the *source* of the declaration: either the author, reader, or default stylesheet. All three pieces of information are needed to determine the priority of a declaration.

The result of this process is a grouped and ordered list of CSS rules pertaining to the chosen element, where each rule contains a single declaration (for the selected property), and where the origin of the rule is noted at the side.

Figure 6.14 shows the result of this process for three cases: the text-decoration property for "visited" A elements, the color property for **EM** elements inside paragraphs, and the list-style-type property for **UL** elements of **CLASS**="special" lying inside another **UL** list. In our example, there are only reader and author rules; the reader-defined rules are explicitly indicated (by the boldface comment string).

Figure 6.14 Rules extracted from the full document stylesheet that are relevant to the `text-decoration` property of visited anchor elements, the `color` property for EM elements inside P elements, and the `list-style-type` property for UL lists of CLASS="special" within UL lists. Rules derived from the reader stylesheet are noted with boldface CSS comment strings.

Visited Anchor Element

```
A:visited    { text-decoration: underline !important ;}    /* Reader! */
A:visited    { text-decoration: none;         !important; }
A            { text-decoration: overline; }
```

EM Element Inside a P Element

```
EM           {color:          red;}
P EM         {color:          blue;}
P EM         {color:          green; }
```

UL List of CLASS="special" Inside a UL List

```
UL           { list-style-type: circle;}                    /* Reader! */
UL           { list-style-type: disc;}
UL LI UL     { list-style-type: square;}
UL.special   { list-style-type: disc; }
UL LI UL     { list-style-type: circle !important }
```

Step 3: Use !important to Eliminate Rules

The third step is to take the list created at step 2 and use the `!important` declarations to eliminate multiple rules with the *same selector*. The procedure is as follows: If a rule is declared `!important`, then eliminate any rules with equivalent selectors that are not `!important`.

If multiple declarations in the stylesheet are `!important`, the above process may still yield more than one rule. In this case, the browser will first look at the rules arising from the *reader* stylesheet and use the *last* of the rules declared `!important`, discarding the others. If none of the reader-specified rules are `!important`, but there is one or more author-defined rule that is `!important`, then the browser selects the last such rule, and discards the rest.

These steps ensure that `!important` declarations always override non-important ones, and that declarations declared important by the reader *always override* equivalent declarations provided by the author.

Figure 6.15 shows the result of this stage of the process for the three cases considered in Figure 6.14, where the eliminated rules are shown in gray, with a line struck through the text. Of the three property/element combinations, only three are `!important`: one for **UL** lists and two for visited anchor elements. In the case of the **UL** list, the `!important` rule has the selector UL LI UL;

Figure 6.15 Rules for the text-decoration property of visited anchor elements, the color property for EM elements inside P elements, and the list-style-type property for UL lists of CLASS="special" within UL lists, after processing !important declarations. Rules to be dropped are in gray, and struck-through.

Visited Anchor Element

```
A:visited    { text-decoration: underline !important ;}    /* Reader! */
A:visited    { text-decoration: none;         !important;}
A            { text-decoration: overline; }
```

EM Element Inside a P Element

```
EM        {color:        red;}
P EM      {color:        blue;}
P EM      {color:        green; }
```

UL List of CLASS="special" Inside a UL List

```
UL           { list-style-type: circle;}                    /* Reader! */
UL           { list-style-type: disc;}
UL LI UL     { list-style-type: square;}
UL.special   { list-style-type: disc; }
UL LI UL     { list-style-type: circle !important }
```

consequently, all other rules with this selector are dropped, as illustrated in Figure 6.15. In the case of visited anchor elements, the two rules with selector A:visited are both !important. In this case, the reader-provided rule has priority over the author rule, so that the author rule is dropped.

Step 4: Eliminate According to Origin
The next step eliminates rules and declarations according to their origin from the browser, reader, or author stylesheets. The procedure is to take each remaining selector, and find all rules that employ that selector. Then, if there is a rule arising from the *author* stylesheet that uses this selector, discard all rules from the reader or default stylesheet that use the selector. This ensures, in the absence of !important declarations, that the author specifications have priority over the reader's.

Figure 6.16 illustrates this process when applied to the remaining rules in Figure 6.15. Here, only the UL selector has overlapping reader and author declarations, so that only one rule is eliminated at this step. The eliminated reader rule is shown, in Figure 6.16, in gray and with struck-through text.

Step 5: Eliminate Rules According to Selector Weight
At this point, there are likely several remaining rules for the same property, each rule having a different selector. The next step is to eliminate these rules according to *selector weight*. The guiding

Figure 6.16 Rules remaining from Figure 6.15 after eliminating dropped rules. This figure illustrates those rules now to be dropped due to their origin: Author-specified rules always override reader rules having the same selector, as described in the text. The eliminated rule is shown in dark gray and with struck-through text.

Visited Anchor Element

```
A:visited   { text-decoration: underline ! ;}
A           { text-decoration: overline; }
```

EM Element inside a P Element

```
EM          {color:        red;}
P EM        {color:        blue;}
P EM        {color:        green; }
```

UL List of CLASS="special" inside a UL List

```
UL          { list-style-type: circle;}                /* Reader! */
UL          { list-style-type: disc;}
UL.special  { list-style-type: disc; }
UL LI UL    { list-style-type: circle ; }
```

principle is *specificity*: Selectors that are *more specific* to the HTML element being formatted should override less specific ones.

In CSS, this is accomplished by calculating *weights* for each selector. Then, the rules with the highest weight are kept, and the others are discarded. The weight calculation algorithm is a bit complicated, but straightforward in practice. The procedure is as follows.

There are three different categories of weight, corresponding to **ID**, **CLASS**, and element name. We can call these categories **A**, **B**, and **C**, respectively. In CSS, **ID**-based selectors are treated as more specific (higher weight) than **CLASS**-based selectors, which are in turn treated as more specific than name-based selectors. Thus category **A** is "heavier" than category **B**, which is "heavier" than category **C**. The weights for each category are calculated as follows, with examples of the results of this process being shown in Figure 6.17 and Table 6.1.

1. Add a count of 1 to category **A** for each **ID** attribute value in the given selector. For example, the selector DIV#xp23 would yield a count of 1. Recall that properties associated with element **STYLE** attributes (e.g., <EM STYLE="color: red">) are treated as purely **ID**-based selectors, and are hence given a weight of 1 in this category. The larger the count in category **A**, the higher the priority. A selector with a count of 1 in category **A** has a higher priority than a selector with any number of counts in categories **B** and/or **C**.

2. Add a count of 1 to category **B** for each **CLASS** value in the selector, including pseudo-classes, such as :link. For example, the selector EM.special .open would yield a count of 2. Note that a selector with a count of 1 in this category has a higher priority than a selector with any number of counts in category **C**.

3. Add a count of 1 to category **C** for each *element name* in the selector, including any pseudo-element names, such as :first-line. For example, the selector EM.special .open would yield a count of 1.

Once this procedure is finished, it is time to determine the actual selector priority. The procedure is as follows:

1. Begin with category **A**, the highest priority category. Order the selectors according to the count in category **A**: The larger the count, the higher the priority.

2. Take the selectors with the highest weight in category **A** (i.e., the most **ID** values in the selector) and drop the rest. If there is more than one such selector, continue on to category **B**.

Figure 6.17 Rules remaining from Figure 6.16 after eliminating dropped rules. This figure illustrates those rules now to be dropped due to their weight: Higher weight rules override lower-weight ones, as described in the text.The eliminated rules are shown in dark gray and struck-through. The calculated weights are shown to the right, with the highest weights shown in boldface.

	Weights		
Visited Anchor Element	A	B	C
A:visited { text-decoration: underline;}			**2**
~~A { text-decoration: overline; }~~			1
EM Element inside a P Element			
~~EM {color: red;}~~			1
P EM {color: blue;}			**2**
P EM {color: green; }			**2**
UL List of CLASS="special" inside a UL List			
~~UL { list-style-type: disc;}~~			1
UL.special { list-style-type: disc; }		**1**	1
~~UL LI UL { list-style-type: circle }~~			3

Table 6.1 Example Weight Table for Selectors Relevant to an LI Element

Selector	Weights			Priority
	A	B	C	
LI			1	7
LI:first-letter			2	5
UL LI			2	5
UL.spec LI		1	2	3
UL LI.foo		1	2	3
UL.spec LI.foo		2	2	2
OL.enum LI#z23	1	1	2	1

Now, order these remaining selectors according to the count in category **B** (the number of **CLASS** attribute values in the selector), with the larger number corresponding to a higher priority.

3. Take the selectors with the highest count in category **B**, and drop the rest. If there is more than one such selector, move on to category **C**. Now, order the selectors according to the count in category **C** (the number of element names in the selector), with the larger number corresponding to a higher priority.

4. Take the selectors with the highest count in category **C**, and drop the rest. There may yet be more than one rule with the same selector and declaration. This case is handled at step 6.

Note how the definition of "specific" makes sense: **ID**-based selectors are more specific than **CLASS**-based selectors, which are in turn more specific than selectors based solely on element names.

Figure 6.17 illustrates the application of this process to the remaining rules in Figure 6.16. Note how there is still a selector (P EM) with multiple rules. This duplication is handled at step 6.

Determining "weights" is possibly the hardest aspect of the cascading procedure. To help illuminate how it works, Table 6.1 shows a few example selectors, alongside their weights.

Step 6: Eliminate According to Order in Stylesheet

At this last step there may yet be multiple rules using the same selector. These rules are now sorted by the *order* in which they appear in the stylesheet. The procedure is simple: The last specified rule overrides all preceding ones.

Figure 6.18 illustrates this procedure applied to the rules remaining from Figure 6.17. There are only two conflicting rules, with the selector P EM. This step means that we eliminate the first of these rules, and retain the second.

Figure 6.18 Rules remaining from Figure 6.17 after eliminating dropped rules. This figure illustrates those rules now to be dropped due to their position in the stylesheet: Later rules override earlier ones, all other criteria being equal. The eliminated rule is shown in dark gray and with struck-through text.

Visited Anchor Element

```
A:visited  { text-decoration: underline;}
```

EM Element inside a P Element

```
P EM        {color:              blue;}
P EM        {color:              green; }
```

UL List of CLASS="special" inside a UL List

```
UL.special { list-style-type: disc; }
```

The process is complete. Looking to Figure 6.18, you will see that there are now single declarations for each of the properties, and thus an unambiguous specification for the desired formatting.

MSIE 3 Mishandles Weights in Cascades

In the case of multiple properties with the same weight, MSIE 3 will mistakenly use the *first* specified property, instead of the last. This reflects the fact that MSIE was released prior to the completion of the CSS Level 1 specifications.

Stylesheet Design and Management

One of the purposes of the CSS model is to allow for well-designed reusable stylesheets—that is, stylesheets that can be used by many different documents, such that all the documents display the same basic design.

The first step is to create the stylesheet. But—a stylesheet is not created in isolation from the documents to which it will be applied. Therefore the two components—the overall markup design and the stylesheet—must be planned together. The following list of activities briefly outlines one possible approach.

- **Use HTML to structure the markup** into the appropriate logical and formatting-specific components. For example, if you have content that serves as a page header, place it inside a **DIV** of **CLASS**="header". You can now define stylesheet rules that depend on the selector `DIV.header` and that only apply here. This design can become a template that can be used to create other documents requiring the same style.

- **Create CSS rules that bind to the structure** defined by the HTML markup. If you specify the logical structure, and use **CLASS** attributes to define logical parts of the document, it is easy to create CSS rules that apply only to designated sections of the page. Note that *both* of these steps need to be done at the same time—you can't easily define the HTML structure without knowing the intended layout, and vice versa.

- **Use the STYLE element to develop and debug the stylesheet.** It often is easier to work on the stylesheet when it is embedded in the test document. Later, the stylesheet can be removed and placed in a separate file. When designing the stylesheet, try to group together the rules that belong together—for example, by placing all the rules associated with the "header" in one place, with the "footer" in another, and so on. Also, place all the generic rules—rules that apply to all elements regardless of their context— at the beginning of the stylesheet. This helps to keep the structure organized, and makes it easier to see which rules apply to a given element.

- **Document the stylesheet.** When the stylesheet is complete, and even while you are designing it, it is important to document how it works. A larger stylesheet will tend to become rather complicated, and no one else will be able to use it (including you in about three months, since by then you will have forgotten how it works!) unless there are detailed explanations of the purpose behind specific rules, and how they should be used. Thus, comments should be placed in the stylesheet itself, and should explain the purpose behind each formatting rule, and the appropriate application of the rule.

- **Remove the stylesheet from the document** and place it in an external stylesheet file. You should extract the stylesheet rules (excluding any HTML tags and the HTML comments that surround it) and save these rules in a file, typically with the filename extension *.css* (for example, *sheet.css*). This file will be the stylesheet for all your documents.

- **Use a LINK element to reference the stylesheet.** You now need to modify the test document to reference the external stylesheet; for example, `<LINK REL="stylesheet" HREF="styles/sheet.css">`. The stylesheet content can now be removed from the HTML document, since it is available via the **LINK**.

- **Create example HTML documents** that illustrate the use of the stylesheet. The stylesheet may be documented, but authors will be creating HTML documents, and not stylesheets. You thus need to prepare templates or example HTML documents that explain how the stylesheet works, and define how the different **CLASS** attribute values should be used. Authors can then use these example documents and the documentation in the stylesheet itself to create their own pages.

- **Use STYLE element content to provide local customization.** Sometimes, individual documents will require local customization. This can be entered into an HTML document within the (otherwise empty) **STYLE** element. Thus, stylish "flourishes" can be added to any document without the need to modify the stylesheet document itself.

The example stylesheets presented in Chapter 7 were largely developed using these principles. Of course, the proof is in the pudding—you will quickly find out that a structured approach to stylesheet design (such as the one presented above) will help you to design better and more useful stylesheets. Good luck!

Chapter Summary

The CSS `background-color` property defines a *background color* for the associated element. Colors can be defined by name, RGB color code, half-number RGB code, integer RGB code, and percentage RGB code, as described in Appendix A. Background colors for block elements are not properly rendered by MSIE 3 and Netscape Navigator 4.0.

An element's background becomes *opaque* when it is assigned a background color (or image). If no color or image is specified, the background is transparent.

Background and foreground colors should be chosen *together*, to ensure sufficient contrast between the text and background. If the contrast is poor, users will not be able to read the document!

The CSS `background-image` property defines a *background image* for the associated element. A background image is placed on top of any underlying background color. Thus, pixels that are transparent in the image will display this background color.

A background image is tiled *under* the element content. Tiling should begin at the upper left-hand corner of the element.

The `background-repeat` property controls the way the background is *tiled*. This property can take four values: `repeat`, `no-repeat`, `repeat-x`, and `repeat-y`. This property is not supported by MSIE 3.

The `background-position` property defines the *starting location* for the background image. If the image is repeated (see `background-repeat`), it is repeated from this starting location. This property is not currently supported.

The `background-attachment` property defines how the background should be *attached* to the element content. The values can either be `scrolled` or `fixed`. This property is not currently supported.

LINK elements can reference *external stylesheets*. The advantage of linked stylesheets is that the same stylesheet can be associated with any number of HTML documents.

An HTML STYLE element can contain stylesheet instructions to be applied to the HTML document. There is no difference between a stylesheet in a separate file and one in the **HEAD** of an HTML document.

The HTML attribute STYLE can include stylesheet instructions in *element start tags*. In general, authors should avoid STYLE attributes, and should use proper CSS rules instead.

HTML developers recommend using META elements to specify the stylesheet language. This ensures that browsers that support this feature will not need to guess at the language being used.

The CSS cascading scheme gives each declaration a *weight,* and uses the declaration with the highest weight when formatting an element. The rules for determining the "weight" are complicated, and are described in detail in this chapter.

Chapter Exercises

For the first exercise, copy the document in Figure 6.1 (or obtain it from the supporting Web site) and practice manipulating the color selectors. Use any of the color specification schemes described in Appendix A. Experiment with adjusting the background color of your figure. Try adjusting the text and background colors, and note how easy it is to make the text unreadable. Try using both background color and images, and with image loading disabled. Don't forget to add comments so that you can keep track of the changes you have made.

For the second exercise, copy the document in Figure 6.1 (or obtain it from the supporting Web site) and practice manipulating the background tiling. Try adding padding to the elements, and also try adjusting the position of the tiled image using `background-position`.

In the third exercise, you will need to collect, or prepare, some sample HTML documents with which to practice the various strategies for including stylesheet information. Review the methods presented in the section entitled "Including Stylesheets in HTML Documents." Try out the four different methods, and note the relative strengths and weaknesses of the different approaches.

For the fourth exercise, follow the stylesheet design and management strategy described in the last section of the chapter, and create a stylesheet or collection of stylesheets for one of your favorite HTML documents or document collections. Practice designing the HTML layout in combination with the CSS rules, and prepare example template documents that you would distribute to others who are to use these same stylesheets.

7

Example Stylesheet
Designs

The preceding four chapters provided a tutorial on the CSS language and on the basic use and functionality of the CSS formatting properties. Many examples were used to illustrate both the structure of the CSS language, and the effect of the different CSS properties on markup element formatting.

However, these were not complex examples, as they were designed to illustrate the details of each property, and not to demonstrate the use of multiple properties to define complicated page-level formatting. This chapter, on the other hand, looks precisely at this issue, and presents several examples of complex page layout using CSS. The examples give the explicit HTML markup and associated CSS rules, along with a detailed description of the design process that led to the given design.

The first section of this chapter is an overview of HTML design, with an emphasis on how HTML "should" be written to support stylesheets. This is followed by five examples where CSS is used to format specific HTML documents. The chapter concludes with some reference material for CSS *style galleries*—locations on the Web where you can view many different CSS examples, from which you can learn different CSS-based layouts and designs.

Appropriate HTML Markup Design

The goal of CSS is to separate layout details from the document markup. To use CSS properly, additional HTML markup is generally required, either to add the extra

NOTE Browser-Dependence of the Stylesheet Examples

The examples in this chapter were developed to take advantage of the latest CSS features as implemented by the Netscape Navigator 4.0 browser, and at the same time to create documents that function under browsers that do not support CSS. As a result, some of these examples do not render properly on other browsers that support CSS (namely MSIE 3 or MSIE 4 beta 1), and for two reasons: First, because the current Microsoft implementations of CSS are incomplete (MSIE 3) or incomplete and buggy (MSIE 4 (beta 1)); and second because Navigator 4 itself has a number of problems (e.g., fixed margins above and below heading elements) and CSS bugs that required browser-specific formatting rules to obtain the desired layout. However, these examples are available online at the book's supporting Web site (see the preface for the location) and the author will update this collection of example documents, such that the examples can serve as a guide to browser-independent CSS design.

structural markup necessary to distinguish the different parts of a document, or to add style-specific details to small selections within the document. This short section summarizes why this is necessary, and provides a set of simple design rules that help structure HTML documents in support of CSS.

Consider a document containing several basic groupings of content—for example, a page header, a page body (the bulk of the content), sidebars on the page, a page footer, and perhaps a navigation bar. In general, these sections will have their own formatting details, specific to their function. Before CSS, such details were inserted by adding formatting-specific tags (e.g., **FONT**, **BLINK**) or attributes (e.g., **ALIGN, HSPACE**) to the markup. The goal with CSS is avoid this formatting markup, and to use CSS rules that specify different formatting for the different parts.

However, to create CSS rules that attach formatting details to the different parts of a document, the parts must be grouped (so that they can be treated as a group) and distinguishable one from another (so that different rules can be specified for the different groups). The **DIV** element is the obvious tool of choice for accomplishing this goal. Using **DIV**, the document markup might become something like:

```
<DIV CLASS="header">
   ... header HTML content ...
</DIV>
<DIV CLASS="body">
   ... body HTML content ...
</DIV>
<DIV CLASS="footer">
   ... footer HTML content ...
</DIV>
```

where the **DIV** elements group the document into parts, and where the **CLASS** attributes (shown here in italics) label each part according to its function. As a result, stylesheet rules can use selectors such as `DIV.body` or `DIV.footer  TABLE` to specify formatting specific to the different parts of the document, without affecting the formatting of the other parts.

At the same time, elements within a group may also need to be subclassed. For example, The `DIV.body` division may contain multiple paragraphs, the first of which should be formatted in a special manner. This could be indicated with markup of the form:

```
<DIV CLASS="body">
   <P CLASS="first-par"> .... first paragraph content ... </P>
   <P> Remaining, default paragraphs ... </P>
   ...
</P>
```

where the **CLASS** attribute denotes the first paragraph's special nature.

In some cases, special formatting is desired within a regular HTML element—for example, special formatting for different parts of the text within a heading. This is precisely the place to use the **SPAN** element, since **SPAN** can specify formatting details that have no "structural" meaning. For example, to define special formatting for different portions of a heading, the markup could be:

```
<H1><SPAN CLASS="part1">Decorative</SPAN>
    <SPAN CLASS="part2">Heading</SPAN>
</H1>
```

where different formatting would be specified in CSS rules specific to the different classes of the **SPAN** element.

Of course, HTML still supports formatting-specific attributes (**ALIGN, BORDER**, etc.) that are in common use, and that must be present if a document is to be "reasonably" formatted by a browser that does not support CSS. A document author should include these attributes where necessary, but should also be sure to reproduce—or override—these formatting requests with appropriate CSS declarations. This ensures that the documents will be correctly formatted even if the author forgets the HTML attribute, or if the wrong value is assigned to the attribute (the stylesheet rules always override attribute-specified formatting properties).

To summarize, the design process for CSS-enabled HTML documents generally takes the following five steps:

1. Analyze the document design and use **DIV** elements to group logical document components (headers, sidebars, etc.) together, with **CLASS** attribute values to define the different groups.

2. Subclass any regular elements that need to be formatted differently from the default. For example, the main content of a document may contain several paragraphs, the first of which should be specially formatted (e.g., with special leading line emphasis). This first paragraph could be distinguished using a **CLASS** attribute.

3. If any special formatting is required for small spans of text within a traditional HTML element (e.g., spans within an **H1**, **P**, or **EM** element), use **SPAN** elements to span the text to be specially formatted.

4. Add any useful formatting-specific HTML attributes (e.g., **ALIGN**="center", **BORDER**="0", etc.) to the standard HTML elements. These rules will be used for formatting by browsers that do not support CSS.

5. Prepare the stylesheet rules that define the desired formatting. Make sure to include the declarations that override or reproduce any formatting instructions specified by HTML attributes. This ensures that the stylesheets will work, even if the document author forgets to include these HTML attributes, or includes the wrong values.

This process was used in the five example designs presented in the following sections.

Design Example 1: Title Page

This first example looks at headings, and at how headings can be specially formatted without affecting the underlying "heading-ness" of the markup. Thus, the goal is to add formatting instructions (and possibly formatting-specific HTML markup) that do not affect the logical structure of the element. The goal of this example is to reproduce the graphic design found on the cover of the book *The HTML Sourcebook, Third Edition*. Example HTML markup corresponding to the structure of this title page might be:

```
<H1 ALIGN="center">HTML</H1>
<H2 ALIGN="center">S o u r c e b o o k</H2>
<H3 ALIGN="center">Third Edition</H3>
<HR SIZE=4 NOSHADE WIDTH="40%">
```

where the items are centered so that the heading is acceptable on a pre-CSS browser, and where the extra space characters in the word "Sourcebook" are added to spread out the title. This added spacing is a common formatting trick (a better way to add such spacing is via the letter-spacing property, discussed later). Note also that the full title page has multiple **H3** elements (only one is shown here in the code), formatted in different ways, so we need a way of distinguishing these elements one from another.

The desired formatting is of course specified by the actual book cover, and is reproduced (using CSS) in the document displayed in Figure 7.2. The goal is to place the titles inside a light yellow box, bounded by a solid black line, with the first and third titles presented in a dark purple text (gray in this black-and-white picture) and with the word "Sourcebook" presented as white text on a black background, the background extending the full width of the surrounding box. Also, the tracking should be very loose on the letters in the word "Sourcebook," so that the word can spread out to fill the same horizontal space as the word "HTML" in the larger font above it.

Designing the HTML Markup

The obvious way to structure the heading markup is to treat the group of headings as a *block division*, and to place all the headings inside a **DIV** element. Indeed this makes eminent sense, since the headings really are a part of a special group, namely the group that makes up the heading or title page. At the same time, we noted that there were multiple **H3** headings in the original markup that need to be formatted differently (for simplicity, only one is shown here), so that we need a way of distinguishing amongst the different **H3** elements. The obvious tool is the **CLASS** attribute. The resulting modified markup is then (see also Figure 7.1):

```
<DIV CLASS="head">
  <H1 ALIGN="center">HTML</H1>
  <H2 ALIGN="center"> S o u r c e b o o k </H2>
  <H3 ALIGN="center" CLASS="edition">Third Edition</H3>
  <HR SIZE=4 NOSHADE WIDTH="40%">
</DIV>
```

where the style-related additions are shown in bold italics. The   non-breaking space characters were added to help adjust for a bug in Netscape Navigator 4, as discussed a bit later.

Now that we have the appropriate markup, the next step is to define stylesheet formatting rules specific to this collection of elements.

Creating Associated Stylesheet Rules

The first step is to establish the general rules that define the overall formatting for the document. Thus, our first rule sets the default font for all headings, namely:

```
H1,H2,H3,H4   {font-family:    "Garamond", "Times New Roman";    }
```

since we want this to be the default font for headings throughout the document. If we wanted this choice to be restricted to the **DIV** element, then the individual heading selectors would be `DIV.head H1`, and so on.

The next step is to define the formatting properties for the **DIV** element. Of course, we only need to set those properties that differ from the default (or inherited) values, and that are specific to this heading region. The **DIV** rule used in this example (see Figure 7.1) is:

```
DIV.head    {background:    rgb(255,204,0) url(yellowish.gif);
            color:         black;
            text-align:    center;
            border:        solid black medium;
            padding:       0;
            margin:        auto auto auto auto;
            width:         450px;    }
```

This rule contains several declarations. The first three specify the background color as an image file (or a color, should image loading be disabled on the browser), the default text color (black), and the text alignment within the block (centered). The next two rules specify the border and padding properties: a solid-line border around the block, and a padding space of zero. Padding should, by default, already be set to zero, but this declaration was required to compensate for a bug in Netscape Navigator 4, which otherwise improperly formatted the content. The last two declarations specify automatic left and right margins, and a fixed width for the element; here the width is fixed in pixels, with the size chosen to "just" contain the required text content, as defined by the remaining heading-related rules and the actual content of the headings. The "auto" properties on the left and right margins ensure that the **DIV** is centered on the canvas. Note that with margins set to "auto" you *must* specify a value for the element width, since the default width value ("auto") would cause the **DIV** to be sized as large as possible—and force both margins to zero width.

Rules for Individual Headings

The next step is to specify the formatting for the different headings within the division. The obvious way is via contextual selectors, since this restricts the rules to heading elements that lie inside the **DIV**. For the **H1** heading, the chosen rule is:

```
DIV.head H1   {
              text-align:         center;        /* Netscape bug */
              font-size:          72pt;
              color:              #772255;
              text-transform:     uppercase;
              padding:            0;             /* Netscape bug */
              margin-bottom:      0;     }
```

This specifies text in the specified color and in a (very large) 72pt font. Fixed point size fonts are used because the keyword-based sizes (xx-large, etc.) do not give sufficiently large sizes (and because, on early versions of Navigator 4, percentage font sizes did not work properly). Recall that the size ratio between each step of the keyword-based font sizes is only 1.5. Thus the largest font (xx-large) is only 3.375 times larger than the normal ("normal") size (e.g., 40pt compared with a "normal" size of 12pt). To get bigger fonts we need to turn to actual point sizes, or to large percentage values.

The padding and text-align properties are present because of a bug in early beta versions of Netscape 4, which improperly reset these properties to non-zero (padding) or the default values (text-align)—these declarations are otherwise redundant, as they simply repeat the proper default or, in the case of text-align, inherited values. These problems were fixed in the released version of Navigator 4.0.

The **H2** heading has a different but similar rule:

```
DIV.head H2   {font-family:       "Charter BT"    Garamond   serif;
              text-align:         center;         /* Netscape bug */
              font-size:          24pt;
              color:              white;
              background:         black;
```

```
letter-spacing:    12pt;
text-transform:    uppercase;
padding:           0;            /* Netscape bug */
margin-bottom:     0;
margin-top:      - 0.8em;   }
```

This rule again has the two declarations required due to bugs in early versions of Netscape. The remaining rules set the font family ("Charter BT", a slightly wider and heavier font than Garamond), font size (24pt, one third the size of the main heading), as well as background (black) and foreground (white) colors. Note also the negative top margin, which reduces the spacing between this heading and the previous element—large font sizes lead to large line heights, which in turn lead to large apparent spacing between adjacent elements, even with zero margin widths. Em units are used here to ensure that the size of the spacing changes proportionally if the font size is altered.

This rule also provides for an increased spacing between letters, through the declaration `letter-spacing: 12pt`. Unfortunately, this property is unimplemented on most browsers, including Netscape Navigator 4. It is because this property was not supported that the HTML markup included space characters between each letter in the word "Sourcebook." Such artificial spacing would not be necessary given support for the `letter-spacing` property.

The **H2** element should, when formatted, fully span the width of the parent **DIV**. However, we discovered that this does not happen, as Netscape Navigator 4 does not properly adjust the width of the background box for the heading element—instead, the black background box is clipped at the left and right edges that just enclose the text. According to CSS, the box should extend full width, from the left to right inner edges of the parent element (the **DIV**). This problem was compensated for by adding non-breaking space characters "around" the heading; that is:

```
<H2 ALIGN="center"> S o u r c e b o o k </H2>
```

Again, this trick should not be needed with browsers that properly support CSS.

We are now ready to format the third heading, the one of **CLASS**="edition". The associated stylesheet rule is:

```
DIV.head H3.edition   {
            text-align:       center;    /* Netscape bug */
            font-size:        16pt;
            color:            #772255;
            text-transform:   uppercase;
            padding:          0;          /* Netscape bug */
            margin-bottom:    0;
            margin-top:      -0.5em;  }
```

Again, the text alignment and padding declarations are required to fix a small browser bug. The text is once more in a smaller font (16pt) but is in the same purple color as the initial **H1** heading, and the top margin is negative so that the heading is brought closer to the preceding element.

The full HTML document corresponding to this example is shown in Figure 7.1. Figure 7.2 shows the rendering by Netscape Navigator 4—notice how the rendering obeys the specified formatting.

An important side effect of choosing point and em length units for all lengths, including element margins, line spacings, and widths, is *scalability*—if the font sizes are uniformly resized (and the **DIV** element width resized appropriately), then all lengths are scaled by the same ratios, so that both relative sizes and positions are unchanged. This is important because most browsers support font size adjustment menus or accelerator key sequences that shrink or expand the display by rescaling the font size. When this is done, all physical lengths in the document are rescaled to span a smaller or larger number of pixels. For example, shrinking a document might mean that a 12pt length that formerly spanned 16 pixels spans only 12 pixels after being resized. Consequently, if all lengths are expressed in points (or other absolute lengths), they are all resized by the same factor. An example is shown in Figure 7.3, which displays the same document shown in Figure 7.2 but resized by the procedure just mentioned. Notice that although the text is smaller, the relative positioning of all the components is unchanged.

In summary, by defining all the styling markup in CSS, the HTML document is kept simple, with the HTML markup accurately reflecting the underlying heading structure of the page. Indeed, if this same document is displayed by a browser that does not support CSS, the headings are reproduced in a less elegant but still understandable manner, as illustrated in Figure 7.4.

Figure 7.4 also illustrates why each of the heading start tags in the HTML document contained the **ALIGN**="center" attribute. The stylesheet also specifies center-aligned text, so that this attribute is actually unnecessary for a CSS-capable browser. But including this **ALIGN** attribute allows for HTML-based formatting by non-CSS-capable browsers. A more careful look at this aspect of HTML/CSS design is presented in the third example in this chapter.

Design Example 2: A Stylized Heading

The second example heading in Figure 7.1 is simply a stylized **H3** heading containing the text "*Catastrophic!*" I designed this example soon after recovering from a computer failure, and after thinking that the entire text for this book had been destroyed in a disk crash. The word that *really* came to my lips was perhaps inappropriate for a book example!

The desired formatting is shown at the bottom of Figure 7.2: a simple heading with a large, colored (actually a bluish-purple) script or *swash* character as the first letter. This leading character also is displaced downwards, such that it is vertically centered with the rest of the text, while the remaining text of the heading is shifted to the left so that it fits within the opening in the "C."

Structuring the HTML Markup

The text to format is contained within an H3 element, namely:

```
<H3>Catastrophic!</H3>
```

Since we actually want special formatting for the first letter, this would be an ideal place to use the :first-letter pseudo-element. Unfortunately, this pseudo-element is not supported by

Figure 7.1 Example HTML document illustrating the use of CSS to format headings. Stylesheet content is in italics. Renderings of this document are found in Figures 7.2, 7.3, and 7.4.

```
<HTML><HEAD><TITLE>Special Heading Formatting </TITLE>
<STYLE><!--
/* Examples of Heading Formattings   Ian Graham — 15 May 1997
    There are two Examples
    1) Reproduction of graphic on cover of "The HTML Sourcebook,
       Third Edition" (the vanity example)
    2) Special Leading Letter Emphasis on a regular heading.
    First, set the default heading font:
*/
H1,H2,H3,H4   {font-family:     "Garamond", "Times New Roman";     }

/**** EXAMPLE 1: HTML SOURCEBOOK Title page **********/
DIV.head      {background:      rgb(255,204,0) url(yellowish.gif);
               margin:          auto auto auto auto;
               width:           450px;
               color:           black;
               text-align:      center;
               padding:         0;
               border:          solid black medium;      }
DIV.head H1   {
               text-align:      center;
               font-size:       72pt;
               color:           #772255;
               font-weight:     normal;
               text-transform:  uppercase;
               padding:         0;
               margin-bottom:   0;                      }
DIV.head H2   {font-family:     "Charter BT";
               text-align:      center;
               font-size:       24pt;
               color:           white;
               background:      black;
               letter-spacing:  12pt;
               text-transform:  uppercase;
               padding:         0;
               margin-bottom:   0;
               margin-top:      -0.8em;                 }
DIV.head H3.edition    {
               text-align:      center;
               font-size:       16pt;
               color:           #772255;
               text-transform:  uppercase;
               padding:         0;
```

Continued

Figure 7.1 *Continued*

```
                margin-bottom:    0;
                margin-top:       -0.5em;        }
/********      Second example ————— **********/
SPAN.first    {font-size:         96pt;
               float:             left;
               color:             #3333aa;
               margin-bottom:     0.35em;
               font-family:       "Matura MT Script Capitals", fantasy;
                                                 }
SPAN.rest     {font-size:         32pt;
               color:             black;
               margin-left:       -1em;
               font-family:       "BernhardMod BT", serif;  }
-></STYLE></HEAD>
<BODY>
<DIV CLASS="head" >
  <H1 ALIGN="center">H T M L</H1>
  <H2 ALIGN="center"> S o u r c e b o o k </H2>
  <H3 ALIGN="center" CLASS="edition">Third Edition</H3>
  <HR SIZE=4 NOSHADE WIDTH="40%">
</DIV>
<H3><SPAN CLASS="first">C</SPAN><SPAN CLASS="rest">atastrophic!</SPAN></H3>
</BODY></HTML>
```

Navigator 4, the browser used to develop these examples. However, similar formatting can be created using **SPAN** elements, and this is the approach taken here.

Since the heading needs to be treated as two parts, the obvious choice is to group those two parts within two **SPAN** elements. The resulting markup is:

```
<H3><SPAN CLASS="first">C</SPAN><SPAN CLASS="rest">atastrophic!</SPAN>
</H3>
```

where the classes "first" and "rest" distinguish between the two **SPAN**s. Note that the heading must be treated as two parts because we want the first part (the letter "C") to be floated to the beginning of the heading, with the second part repositioned so that it overlaps the large leading "C." Consequently, we need to create formatting elements, within the parent **H3** element, for both heading parts.

Creating the Stylesheet Rules
The CSS rule defined for the first-letter formatting is:

```
SPAN.first    { font-size:       96pt;
                float:           left;
                color:           #3333aa;
                margin-bottom:   0.35em;
                font-family:     "Matura MT Script Capitals", fantasy;  }
```

Figure 7.2 Rendering, by Netscape Navigator 4, of the document listed in Figure 7.1.

Note again the enormous font size. This element is "floated" to the left; it must be floated because we want it on the left and because we also need to vertically reposition the letter relative to the other content of the **H3**. By default, the floated element will be aligned such that the *top* of the element aligns with the *top* of the adjacent non-floated element: namely, with the remaining line of text in the **H3**. The result is a large "C" that, by default, hangs down below the line of text, with the top of the "C" aligning with the top of the text.

The first-letter text can be moved upwards by adding a *positive* bottom margin to the floated element, which pushes the element up and away from the bottom edge of the parent **H3**. The length 0.35 em is measured relative to the font size of the letter, and was chosen to push the letter up to the desired position, given the selected font family ("Matura MT Script Capitals"). Note, however, that this alignment does not look as appropriate (or attractive) with other fonts, since, stylistically, the relative positioning depends strongly on the specific shape and style of the font.

Figure 7.3 Rendering, by Netscape Navigator 4, of the document listed in Figure 7.1, but with a reduced size font (rescaled to a smaller size). Note that the displayed content is simply a "reduced size" version of the page displayed in Figure 7.2.

The remaining text of the heading is formatted using the rule:

```
SPAN.rest        {font-size:      32pt;
                 color:           black;
                 margin-left:     -1em;
                 font-family:     "BernhardMod BT", serif;    }
```

This calls for a font one third the size of the large character, in black, and using the BernhardMod BT font. The negative left margin pulls the text to the left so that it overlaps the floating element.

Figure 7.1 lists these rules within an HTML document, while Figures 7.2 through 7.4 show browser renderings of this heading. Note how the use of absolute and font-size-related relative

Figure 7.4 Rendering, by Netscape Navigator 3, of the document listed in Figure 7.1. This browser does not support CSS, but is still able to intelligently display the document, since the markup reflects the true structure of the headings.

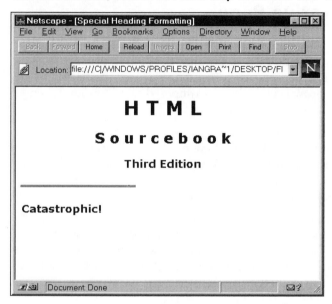

sizes means that the heading resizes properly if fonts are rescaled. Notice also how a CSS-incapable browser (Figure 7.4) can properly present the content as a heading, since all the formatting details were placed in **SPAN** elements, which are ignored by pre-CSS browsers like Netscape Navigator 3.

Alternative Sets of CSS Rules

As an alternative, the following two CSS rules "should" produce a similar leading-letter formatting. Deletions from the original rules are shown in gray, with a line struck through, and additions are shown in boldface italics.

```
SPAN.first { font-size:      96pt;
                           float:            left;
            vertical-align: -0.35em
             color:          #3333aa;
             font-family:    "Matura MT Script Capitals", fantasy; }
SPAN.rest  { font-size:      32pt;
             color:          black;
             margin-left:    -1em;
             font-family:    "BernhardMod BT", serif;                }
```

The only changes are in the formatting of the leading letter—the letter is not floated, but is instead vertically repositioned using the `vertical-align` property. In principle, these rules should give the same formatting as shown in Figure 7.2; unfortunately, the `vertical-align` property is not supported by any current browsers, so that this rule could not be tested.

Design Example 3: A Decorative Page

The third design example produces the page shown in Figure 7.5. The displayed content is just a paragraph, with stylesheet rules and **STYLE** elements used to produce the desired markup. The stylized arrows in the upper left- and right-hand corners are inline images placed inside anchor elements. The background is a speckled orange brown, with the superimposed text in bright green (small text) and black (large text).

In this example there are two goals: first, to provide a stylesheet and markup that produce Figure 7.5, and second, to include old-fashioned HTML formatting markup to reproduce, for older CSS-incapable browsers, some of the style features in Figure 7.5. Of course, it is impossible to reproduce all these features, but we can reproduce enough of them that a reader with an older browser can still see a page with some rather elegant styling content.

In this case, we will design the stylesheet rules and the markup together. Analysis of Figure 7.5 shows that there are three main parts: the background for the page, the navigation icons (the arrows to the left and right at the top of the page), and the text content. We will look at these three parts in sequence, and at the same time will show how to build the HTML markup and the associated CSS rules.

The Background

The background for the entire document can be specified as a **BODY** element stylesheet rule, namely:

```
BODY {background:  #c48400  url(bground1.gif) ;}
```

This specifies both a background color (an orange-brown) and a background image (the image is a slightly mottled textured surface with a base color similar to that specified by the background color RGB code). Choosing a background color close to that of the background image ensures that the text is readable even if the user disables image loading.

Essentially equivalent formatting can be specified for older browsers by using the **BODY** start tag:

```
<BODY BGCOLOR="#c48400" TEXT="#55ff55" BACKGROUND="bground1.gif">
```

which specifies the same background image and color, and also specifies the color for the text—we look at the CSS specification for the text color later in this example.

The Navigation Icons

We now want to define the navigation icons and the associated stylesheet rules. The appropriate HTML markup is simply

```
<DIV CLASS="navigate">
  <A HREF="prev.html"><IMG
```

```
      CLASS="left"  SRC="left-a.gif"></A>
  <A HREF="next.html"><IMG
      CLASS="right" SRC="right-a.gif"></A>
</DIV>
```

where the navigation buttons are placed in a **DIV** of **CLASS**="navigate" to indicate their function (this is informational only, as the stylesheet actually makes no use of this **CLASS**). The images inside the anchors are of **CLASS**="left" and **CLASS**="right". The CSS rules applying to these images are:

```
A:link IMG, A:visited IMG, A:active IMG { border:  none; }
IMG.left    {float: left;  }
IMG.right   {float: right; }
```

The first rule removes borders from **IMG** elements inside **A** elements (recall that the browsers will, by default, put a box around an image that is inside an anchor element), while the second and third rules float the images of the specified classes to the left and right margins, respectively.

We can use **IMG** element attributes to reproduce most of this behavior in older browsers. The required changes to the HTML markup are (with the additions noted in boldface italics):

```
<DIV CLASS="navigate">
<A HREF="prev.html"><IMG ALIGN="left"  BORDER="0"
   CLASS="left"  SRC="left-a.gif"></A>
<A HREF="next.html"><IMG ALIGN="right" BORDER="0"
   CLASS="right" SRC="right-a.gif"></A>
</DIV>
```

This aligns the elements as desired, and removes the borders from the images.

What happens if there is a conflict between the formatting requests of an HTML attribute and a related formatting request arising from a stylesheet property? The CSS specifications state that the CSS property should always have precedence over a formatting instruction specified by an HTML attribute. In essence, attribute-specified formatting is treated as having a much lower priority than formatting arising from CSS properties. Thus, in the above example, the CSS image alignment and border properties override any **IMG** element **ALIGN** and **BORDER** attribute values. Of course, browsers are not always consistent in following this rule, but it serves as a useful guide to mixed HTML and CSS design.

Formatting the Text Column

Ignoring the extra HTML introduced to support non-CSS browsers, the block of text marked up to produce the specially formatted text paragraph markup will simply be:

```
<DIV CLASS="column">
  <P><BR>Never fear to trust your mind, even if surrounded
    by <EM CLASS="outset">
    doubters</EM> who do not share your vision.
  </P>
</DIV>
```

Note how the block of text is placed inside a paragraph, while the enlarged text is marked up as an **EM** element of **CLASS**="outset". The paragraph is, in turn, placed inside a **DIV** element of **CLASS**="column"—this **DIV** defines the special columnar region of text. The **DIV** will impose the boundaries that define the column.

The stylesheet rule for the **DIV** element is:

```
DIV.column {margin-left:   70%;
            margin-right: 10%;
            font-family:  monospace;
            color:        #55ff55;
            font-size:    18pt;      }
```

This defines the narrow region for the column (20% of page width, starting 70% in from the left), and specifies a monospace font (such as Courier), an 18pt font size, and a greenish color.

The rule for the **EM** element is more complicated, namely:

```
EM.outset{
    display:      block;
    font-style:   normal;
    font-size:    144pt;
    font-family:"CaslonOpnface BT", Garamond,  "Times New Roman",  fantasy;
    line-height:  144pt;
    color:        black;
    margin-left: -320pt;
    margin-top:  -85pt;              }
```

The first declaration defines this as a *block*-level element. We define it thus so that we can use top and bottom margins to reduce the space between the **EM** element content and the paragraph text above and below it (note that the enlarged **EM** element content will create a large space between the **EM** text and the preceding and following paragraph text). We cannot control this spacing when the **EM** is an inline element, since CSS margins do not affect the positioning of inline content.

Declarations 2 through 6 set the font and text properties: the second resets the style to normal (inside an **EM** element, the default style is "italic") while the third and fourth select the desired size and family. The fifth declaration sets the line height, here exactly the same size as the font. This reduces the vertical size of the block occupied by the element, since the default line height is usually 1.5 times the font size.[1] Finally, the sixth declaration sets the color for the text to be black.

The final two declarations define the element positioning. The negative top margin moves the element up towards the preceding text, and ensures that the words "surrounded by" nestle comfortably on top of the letters "ers" that end the enlarged word. At the same time, the negative left margin of -320pt pulls the element sufficiently to the left that the letters "ers" are positioned underneath the text column. Note that we do not need to specify the width or the right margin, since they are automatically adjusted by the browser according to the formula given in Chapter 5.

HTML-Based Styling

For browsers that do not support CSS, we would now like to add HTML markup that reproduces some of this styling—and do this without affecting the CSS rendering of the document. A perfect equivalence is impossible, but we can add HTML-based styling that will give the page some of the characteristics of the desired page. Example markup is shown below, where the HTML-specified formatting additions are shown in boldface italics:

```
<FONT FACE="courier new" SIZE="7">
<DIV CLASS="column">
<P>Never fear to trust your mind, even if surrounded
    by <FONT COLOR="black" FACE="Arial Black"><EM CLASS="outset">
    doubters</EM> </FONT> who do not share your vision.
</P>
</DIV>
</FONT>
```

Note how a **FONT** element around the entire **DIV** is used to boost the size, while the **FONT** element placed around the **EM** element changes the color to black, and changes the font face to "Arial Black" (this font was chosen because the "CaslonOpnface BT" font does not look good when rendered in the same size as the regular text). The resulting rendering of the document by an older browser is shown in Figure 7.7. The document looks quite different from Figure 7.5, but still retains some of the characteristics of the original.

Appropriate Placement of FONT Tags

The HTML and CSS approaches work together in this example because of the placement of the HTML **FONT** elements. Note how the **FONT** elements are placed *outside* the HTML elements that have associated stylesheet rules. Thus, when formatting the document, the CSS parser first applies the formatting specified by the HTML **FONT** elements, and then *overrides* these settings using those properties set by the CSS rules. If, instead, the **FONT** tags were placed *inside* the **DIV** or **EM** elements, then the **FONT**-specified sizes and font families would override the CSS-specified values, leading to incorrect formatting.

Design Example 4: Chapter Cover Page

The next example represents an attempt to reproduce a book-style page design on a Web page. Of course, book design is often not appropriate for Web pages—and indeed, the layout illustrated in Figure 7.8 is missing some important features, such as navigation bars or hypertext anchors, that would be needed in a Web page. However, the page can be easily modified to provide full-blown Web functionality.

The goals in this example are twofold: (1) to reproduce the complex heading structure shown in Figure 7.8 using a single heading element, and (2) to reproduce the column of text using simple paragraph elements. The actual markup and stylesheet declarations are surprisingly simple, and degrade well for non-stylesheet-aware browsers. As always, this latter aspect is important, as we want this text page to be easily readable on all browsers.

Figure 7.5 A decoratively formatted page as rendered by the Netscape Navigator 4 prerelease 4 browser. The document leading to this rendering is shown in Figure 7.6, while the rendering of this same document by a pre-CSS browser is shown in Figure 7.7. The construction of the HTML markup and associated stylesheet rules is discussed in the text.

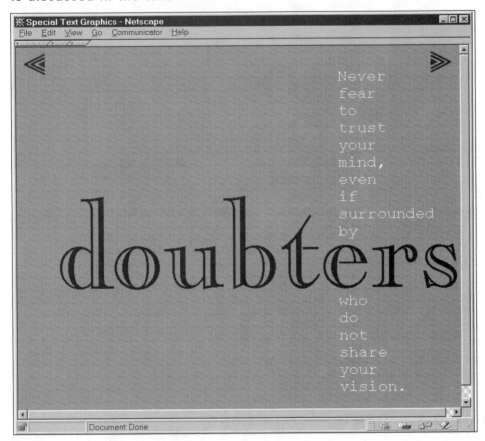

Page Markup Design

The basic HTML structure for this document is simply:

```
<H2>Chapter 7 ... Killer Rabbits From Hell </H2>
<P>A paragraph of the text flow .... </P>
<P>Another paragraph ...... </P>
```

This shows an **H2** heading for chapter titles (we can assume that somewhere else in the collection, **H1** is used for the book title) and **P** for the text paragraphs. The text is black-on-white, and

Figure 7.6 Example document leading to the pages displayed in Figures 7.5 (CSS-aware browser) and Figure 7.7 (pre-CSS browser). Stylesheet content is in italics. The stylesheet rules, and the HTML-specific formatting added to support pre-CSS browsers, are discussed in the text.

```
<HTML><HEAD><TITLE>Special Text Graphics </TITLE>
<STYLE><!--
BODY          {background:    #c48400  url(bground1.gif) ;    }
A:link IMG, A:visited IMG, A:active IMG {border:  none;    }
IMG.left      {float:         left;    }
IMG.right     {float:         right;   }
DIV.column    {margin-left:   70%;
               margin-right:  10%;
               font-family:   monospace;
               color:         #55ff55;
               font-size:     18pt;    }
EM.outset     {
  display:        block;
  font-style:     normal;
  font-size:      144pt;
  font-family:    "CaslonOpnface BT", Garamond, "Times New Roman", fantasy;
  color:          black;
  line-height:    144pt;
  margin-left:    -320pt;
  margin-top:     -85pt;        }
--></STYLE></HEAD>
<BODY BGCOLOR="#c48400" TEXT="#55ff55" BACKGROUND="bground1.gif">
<DIV CLASS="navigate">
  <A HREF="prev.html"><IMG ALIGN="left"  BORDER="0"
  CLASS="left"  SRC="left-a.gif"></A>
  <A HREF="next.html"><IMG ALIGN="right" BORDER="0"
  CLASS="right" SRC="right-a.gif"></A>
</DIV>
<FONT FACE="courier new" SIZE="7">
<DIV CLASS="column">
  <P><BR>Never fear to trust your mind, even if surrounded
     by <FONT COLOR="black" FACE="Arial Black,Arial"><EM CLASS="outset">
     doubters</EM></FONT> who do not share your vision. </P>
</DIV>
</FONT>
</BODY></HTML>
```

in an easy-to-read font. The advantage of this design is simplicity—these pages can be read by any browser, regardless of its support for CSS. In a sense, this represents the ideal of CSS design—one in which the stylesheet rules barely impact on the markup design.

Figure 7.7 Rendering of the document listed in Figure 7.6 by Netscape Navigator 3. This browser does not understand CSS, but does implement the FONT-element-based styling instructions and IMG element ALIGN attributes to reproduce some of the formatting seen in Figure 7.5.

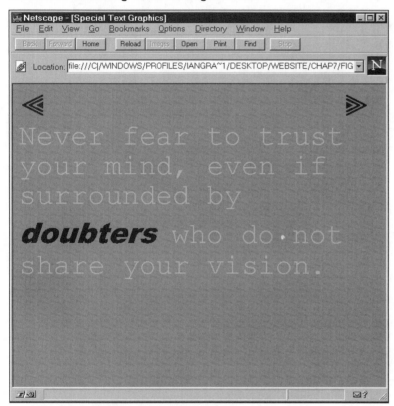

Stylesheet Rule Design

The first stylesheet rules will set the default properties for the document. The rules are:

```
BODY    { font-family: "Book Antiqua", "Bookman Old style", serif;
          background:  #ffffff }
P       { margin-left: 20%; margin-right: 5%; text-align: justify;}
```

The first rule selects the default fonts for the text, while the second rule sets the parameters for all paragraphs so that they will have a large left and a small right margin, and contain fully justified text.

The second task is to specify the heading element formatting. In practice, this could be accomplished by splitting the heading into two elements: one **H2** element containing the string "Chapter

7" and the other containing the rest of the title. Alternatively, however, we can use **SPAN** elements to specify formatting details, without changing the underlying HTML markup. This is the approach taken here.

The modified markup is:

```
<H2><SPAN CLASS="chapn">Chapter <SPAN CLASS="huge">7</SPAN></SPAN>
    <SPAN CLASS="chapt">... Killer Rabbits<BR> From Hell</SPAN>
</H2>
```

where the **SPAN** elements of class "chapn" (chapter number) and "chapt" (chapter title) denote the two parts of the heading. At the same time, the numeral part of the chapter number is inside a third **SPAN** element of **CLASS**="huge". This number is rendered in a much larger font than the word "Chapter," and the additional **SPAN** lets us create a CSS rule specific to this formatting feature.

The stylesheet rules associated with these elements are as follows:

```
SPAN.huge       {font-size:      200pt; }
SPAN.chapn      {display:        block;
                 text-align:     right;
                 color:          #dddddd;
                 font-size:      64pt;
                 font-family:    Arial, helvetica, sans-serif;  }
SPAN.chapt {
   display:             block;
   background-color:    transparent;
   text-align:         right;
   font-weight:        bold;
   margin-top:        - 180pt;
   margin-right:       66pt;
   padding-bottom:     70pt;
   font-size:          32pt;
   color:              black;
   font-family: "CaslonOpnface BT","TFMaltbyAntique","ShelleyVolante BT"; }
```

The first rule simply specifies a huge size (200pt) for the text inside the "huge" **SPAN** element—this is how we get the large chapter number.

The second rule, with selector SPAN.chapn, specifies the desired formatting for the **SPAN** element of **CLASS**="chapn"—note that this **SPAN** element will in turn contain the span element of **CLASS**="huge". This rule calls for a large Arial font text in a light gray, and also formats this as a block element, right-aligned inside the parent element. This will *not* align with the right margin of the paragraph text, but is instead right-aligned at the inner edge of the parent **BODY** element.

The next rule, with selector SPAN.chapt, specifies the formatting for the chapter title portion of the heading. This rule calls for a different font (color, font family, and font weight), and uses margin properties to position this element on top of the previous element, namely, the formatting

Figure 7.8 Example page for a Web "novel," based on a printed text formatting style, as rendered by the Netscape Navigator 4 prelease 4 browser. The listing for this document is shown in Figure 7.9. Other views of this same document are found in Figures 7.10 and 7.11.

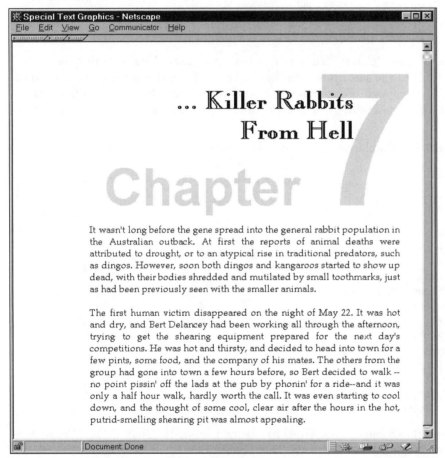

element containing the gray chapter number text. The -180pt negative top margin moves this block to overlay the large numeral 7, while the positive right margin pushes the right hand edge of the text away from the right margin of the page. Note that the text was right-aligned, so that it aligns appropriately on this displaced edge. Finally, the positive bottom padding ensures that the start of the first *paragraph* after the heading occurs well below the chapter title—recall that the top margin for the paragraph is calculated relative to the bottom edge of the preceding element, which in this case is the **SPAN** element containing the text "…Killer Rabbits From Hell." This text was shifted

Figure 7.9 Example document illustrating the special book-style chapter heading and paragraph formatting illustrated in Figure 7.8. Stylesheet content is in italics. The design of the document and the stylesheet is discussed in the text. Other views of this document by various browsers are found in Figures 7.10 and 7.11.

```
<HTML><HEAD><TITLE>Special Text Graphics </TITLE>
<STYLE><!--
BODY          {font-family:    "Book Antiqua", "Bookman Old style", serif;
              background:      #ffffff;
              font-size:       12pt;}
P             {margin-left:    20%; margin-right: 5%; text-align: justify;}
/* Two parts to the heading: "chapn" is the CHapter Number
                             "chapt" is the Chapter Title
 */
SPAN.chapn    {display:        block;
              text-align:      right;
              color:           #dddddd;
              font-size:       60pt;
              font-family:     Arial, helvetica, sans-serif;  }
SPAN.huge     {font-size:      210pt; }
SPAN.chapt    {display:        block;
              background-color: transparent;
              text-align:      right;
              font-weight:     bold;
              margin-top:      -180pt;
              margin-right:    72pt;
              padding-bottom:  72pt;
              font-size:       30pt;
              color:           black;
              font-family:     "CaslonOpnface BT", "ShelleyVolante BT"; }
--></STYLE></HEAD>
<BODY BGCOLOR="#ffffff">

<H2><SPAN CLASS="chapn">Chapter <SPAN CLASS="huge">7</SPAN></SPAN>
    <SPAN CLASS="chapt">... Killer Rabbits<BR> From Hell</SPAN>
</H2>

<P>It wasn't long before the gene spread into the general rabbit
  population in the Australian outback. At first the reports of animal
  deaths were attributed to drought, or to an atypical rise in
  traditional predators, such as dingos. However, soon both dingos
  and kangaroos started to show up dead, with their bodies shredded
  and mutilated by  small toothmarks, just as had been previously
```

Continued

Figure 7.9 *Continued*

```
    seen with the smaller animals.</P>
<P>The first human victim disappeared on the night of May 22.
    It was hot and dry, and Bert Delancey had been working all
    through the afternoon, trying to get the shearing equipment
    prepared for the next day's competitions. He was hot and thirsty,
    and ... (...rest deleted to save space ...) </P>
</BODY></HTML>
```

vertically, because a regular margin spacing between this element and a subsequent paragraph would cause the paragraph to itself be superimposed on the underlying chapter heading text.

The resulting formatting, using as an example an excerpt from my never-to-be published novel, *From Dolly to Bunny—Tales from the Genetic Underworld*, is shown in the document listed in Figure 7.9 and rendered for display in Figures 7.8, 7.10, and 7.11. Figures 7.8 and 7.10 show the same document, but with the overall font size rescaled to a smaller value. As in the first example in this chapter, the text rescales nicely.

Of course, a similar stylesheet can be constructed using em units. In this case, some approximately equivalent CSS rules are:

```
SPAN.chapn      {display:            block;
                 text-align:         right;
                 color:              #dddddd;
                 font-size:          4.25em;
                 font-family:        Arial, helvetica, sans-serif;  }


SPAN.huge   {font-size:      3em;  }

SPAN.chapt      {display:            block;
                 background-color:   transparent;
                 text-align:         right;
                 font-weight:        bold;
                 margin-top:         -12.5em;
                 margin-right:       5em;
                 padding-bottom:     2.5em;
                 font-size:          2em;
                 color:              black;
                 font-family:        "CaslonOpnface BT", "TFMaltbyAntique", "ShelleyVolante BT";}
```

where the modified length units are in boldface italics. Although em units are designed to make scalable documents easier to use, these units can sometimes be confusing, since they are calculated with respect to the font size in the parent element. For example, a 1-em unit for a **SPAN** element inside a **P** corresponds to a different (smaller) absolute length than a 1-em unit for a **SPAN** inside a heading, since the default rules for heading elements increase the font size inside the heading.

Figure 7.10 The same document as displayed in Figure 7.8 (the source listing is in Figure 7.9), but with the font size rescaled to a decreased size. Note how all the text is rescaled, but the relative lengths and positions stay the same.

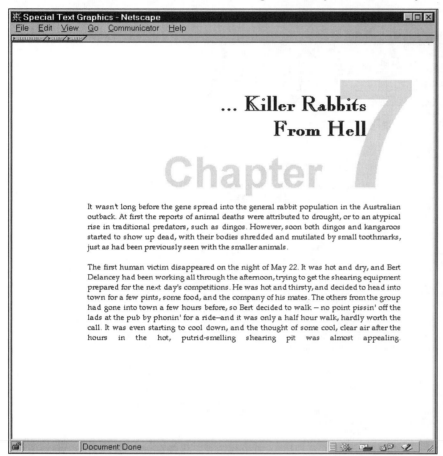

Finally, note that the chosen markup allows for intelligent rendering by browsers that do not support stylesheets. Figure 7.11 shows the display by the Netscape Navigator 3 browser. Note how the content is still easy to read, even though the design is lost.

Design Example 5: Newspaper Web Page

In the next example we look at creating the HTML and CSS rules for a collection of Web-based newspaper pages. The goal is to develop a *component-based* CSS design—that is, a design that

Figure 7.11 Display of the document listed in Figure 7.9 by the Netscape Navigator 3 browser. Although this browser does not support stylesheets, it is still able to intelligently render the document, since the document does not depend on the stylesheet to accurately communicate the content.

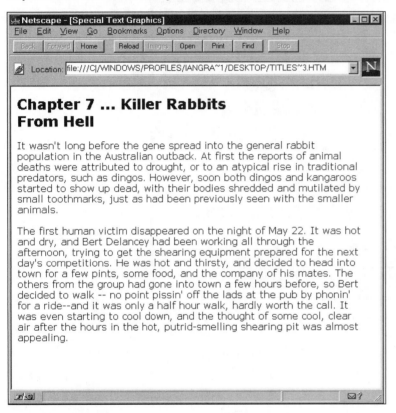

contains CSS components to be reused across a family of pages, each page styled in a similar way, with small variations according to the role of the page. For example, the different pages might be main home pages or sub-pages in the Web site hierarchy. Although these pages perform somewhat different functions, the look and feel of the pages can be preserved from page to page by using the same stylesheet rules.

A second goal is to produce pages that are usable in the absence of CSS support. This ensures that the pages are usable by older browsers, and also helps ensure that the HTML markup preserves the true structure of the document. This is important if the document is rendered by alternative means, such as in print or via a text-to-speech browser.

An example page from this newspaper Web site, illustrating the main layout components, is shown in Figure 7.12. There are four main displayed components:

1. The title or banner for the page—this is the banner containing the text *The Daily Blobby*, superimposed on a decorative background. There are likely also to be other, similar banners, for other section heading pages at the Web site.

2. The right-hand column of *Major News* items.

3. The navigation bar at the bottom of the page.

4. The block containing the main news article. This section includes the heading (*President is a Space Alien!*), several paragraphs, and a left-floated image.

Figure 7.12 An example page from *The Daily Blobby* newspaper Web site, as rendered by the Netscape Navigator 4 browser. The stylesheets and HTML document giving rise to this pages are listed in Figures 7.13 and 7.14 respectively. Construction of the document and stylesheet is described in the text.

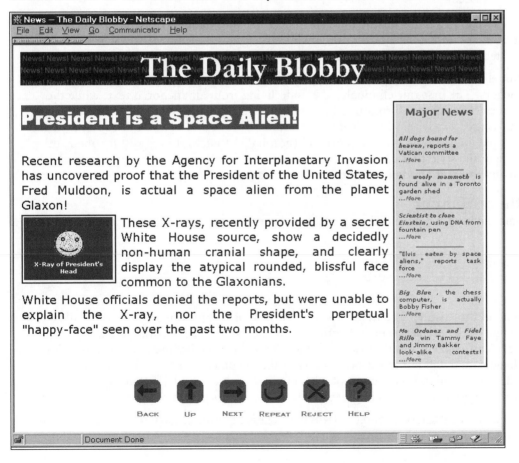

There is a fifth, non-obvious component, namely the standard default formatting properties that apply to all components and all pages. The following description presents each component, and describes how the desired HTML markup structure and associated CSS rules can be developed.

Default Stylesheet Rules

The default rules for these documents are simply:

```
BODY            { font-size:       10pt;
                  font-family:     Verdana, Arial, Helvetica, sans-serif;
                  width:           100%;
                  background:      white ;
                  color:           black;     }
A               { text-decoration: none;      }  /* No underlines         */
A:link          { font-style:      italic;       /* Italic/green- unvisited */
                  color:           #00aa00;   }
A:visited       { font-style:      normal;       /* Normal/gray for visited */
                  color:           #777777;   }
```

The **BODY** element rule sets the default font size (10pt) and family (Verdana or other sans-serif font) for the text, and calls for black text on a white background. All font sizes in other elements will be calculated using em units, to ensure that sizes will all scale uniformly.

The anchor element rules simply specify the desired text decoration and colors for the different hypertext anchors. The first rule eliminates the underlining from all anchored text, while the remaining two rules set special formatting for regular (:link), and previously visited (:visited) anchors. In this case, text within *unvisited* links should be green and in an italicized font, while text within visited links should be in a "normal" (non-italic) font, and in gray. Of course, other rules elsewhere in the stylesheet can override these settings, but these rules provide a standard style that will help give all text and links a common look and feel.

Page Title or Banner

The first component on the page is the title banner for the newspaper. A convenient markup model is:

```
<DIV ALIGN="center" CLASS="titlebanner">
   <H1 ALIGN="center">The Daily Blobby</H1>
</DIV>
```

This groups all the "banner" components inside a **DIV** of an appropriate class, and allows for future upgrading of the banner to include other components (such as decorative graphics, other headings, etc.). This also ensures that the CSS rules defined for the banner components will be specific to the banner, and will not affect other parts of the document. This is what we mean by *component*-based: Using a suitable collection of class attribute values and **DIV** elements, we can design the layout for each component largely independent of the others document parts.

Note also the use of **ALIGN**="center" attributes. These are unnecessary for the CSS stylesheet, but provide centering for non-CSS browsers.

The associated stylesheet rules are:

```
DIV.titlebanner        { width:          100%;  }
DIV.titlebanner H1     { width:          100%;
                         margin-left:    auto;   /* Fixes Netscape */
                         margin-right:   auto;   /* Bug .....        */
                         background:     black url(blackish.gif);
                         font-size:      2em;
                         font-family:    Garamond "Times New Roman", serif;
                         font-weight:    bold;
                         color:          white;
                         text-align:     center;  }
```

The first rule ensures that the **DIV** fully spans the available horizontal space. The second rule specifies the display of the H1 element inside this **DIV**. This **H1** is also of width 100%, but here the margin properties are set to "auto" to compensate for a bug in the browser used to develop the documents (the **H1** is improperly formatted unless the margins are explicitly set). The font size is twice the size of the parent font (2 em), and is in a bold Garamond font. Note, also, that the text is rendered in white on a background GIF image. The heading is also center-aligned in the element.

Major News Column

The right-hand column with the heading *Major News* must be styled as a floating element. The obvious HTML markup will place all the column content within an appropriately classed **DIV**. Markup approach for this component is then:

```
<DIV CLASS="rightcol">
   <H3>Major News</H3>
   <P><EM>All dogs bound for heaven</EM>, reports a
      Vatican committee<BR><A HREF="more.html">...More</A> </P>
   <HR SIZE=2  ALIGN="center" noshade>
   <P>A <EM>wooly mammoth</EM> is found ... </P>
   ... additional entries omitted ...
</DIV>
```

where the italicized string indicates text omitted to make the markup easier to follow. The structure of this **DIV** is obvious: The column heading is inside an **H3**, while each item in the news column is inside a **P**, with the items separated by **HR** elements. Notice how the hypertext anchors "...*More*" are always the last items in the paragraph, and are broken from the preceding paragraph text with a **BR**—this ensures that the anchor always appears as the first item in a line. There are no space characters between the preceding paragraph text and the hypertext anchor, to ensure that there is only one line break between the preceding text and the anchor.

Note that, within this **DIV**, none of the elements have **CLASS** attribute values. This is possible because contextual selectors can be used to specify the desired formatting for the elements inside the **DIV**.

We now look at the CSS rules associated with this block. The base rule is:

```
DIV.rightcol   { float:            right;
                 width:            20%;
                 margin:           0 0 0 0;
                 padding:          0.2em;
                 padding-bottom:   0.6em;   /* Fixes netscape bug */
                 border:           medium solid black;
                 background:       #ddddff;
                 font-size:        0.4em;
                 font-family:      Verdana, Arial, Helvetica, sans-serif;
                 text-align:       justify; }
```

which defines the properties for the specific **DIV**. This defines the **DIV** as a floating element that is 20% the width of the parent element, with no margins, a small 0.2-em padding on all sides (to space the text content away from the element border), with the bottom padding space then reset to a larger value of 0.6 em (which fixes a bug in the way Netscape assigns bottom padding to paragraphs). The next declaration calls for a solid black border, of medium thickness, around the element, followed by a declaration calling for a light blue background color.

The font characteristics are particularly important. The font size declaration reduces the font to 0.4 em of the default value, which ensures a much smaller font than that used in the rest of the document. This is particularly important given the `text-align:justify` declaration, since justified text looks very bad unless the font size is significantly smaller than the width available to the text. Finally, the font family specification simply ensures that this division will use the indicated fonts, even if the default **BODY** font is changed for some reason.

The second rule is:

```
DIV.rightcol H3   { font-size:        1.5em;
                    font-weight:      900;
                    color:            #ff0000;
                    text-transform:   capitalize;
                    text-align:       center;
                    margin:           0em;
                    padding:          0em;
                    margin-bottom:    0.7em;     }
```

which defines formatting for the **H3** heading element inside the column. The first three declarations call for a larger font (1.5 times the default font size) in as heavy a weight as possible, and in the color red. The next declaration states that the first letter of every word in the heading should be capitalized, while the fifth declaration states that the text content should be centered inside the heading element. Since the heading should span the full width of the parent **DIV**, the **H3** content will thus be centered on the column. The next two declarations remove any default padding or margin space that may exist around the element (default margin values are passed down from the browser's default stylesheet). We need to explicitly set these margins to zero to reduce the spacing between items in the column. The final declaration adds a small bottom margin, to space the heading slightly away from any subsequent text.

The next rule defines the formatting for **HR** elements inside the **DIV**. The rule is simply:

```
DIV.rightcol HR      { margin:             auto;
                       margin-top:         0em;
                       margin-bottom:      0em;
                       width:              80%;
                       padding:            0;    }
```

which calls for an **HR** that is centered within and 80% the width of the parent element, with no padding space or margins above and below. Unfortunately, Netscape Navigator 4 prerelease 4 does not properly handle margins between formatting (these declarations are ignored), which affects the rule for the **P** element, as discussed in the following.

The next rule defines paragraph formatting properties. This rule *should* be something like:

```
DIV.rightcol P       { padding:            0em;
                       margin-top:         0.2em;
                       margin-bottom:      0.2em;              }
```

The first declaration overrides any padding space that may be provided by a rule of lesser priority. The two margin properties should then yield a small margin above and below the paragraphs. Since the **HR** elements were assigned no borders or padding, this should result in a 0.2-em spacing between each paragraph and the preceding or following **HR**.

Unfortunately, as mentioned previously, with Netscape Navigator 4 **HR** elements always possess large and unchangeable vertical top and bottom margins. Thus, to produce a reasonable size for the margins, the actual stylesheet used the following margin property declarations (the changes are in boldface italics):

```
            margin-top:     -0.7em;
            margin-bottom:  +0.0em;
```

which serve to move each paragraph up towards the preceding **HR**, and which reduce the space left below an **HR**.

The final two rules specify special **A** and **EM** element formatting specific to this block. The rules are:

```
DIV.rightcol A       { font-variant:       small-caps;
                       font-weight:        bold;   }
DIV.rightcol EM      { color:              red;
                       font-weight:        bold;   }
```

The first rule requests that anchor element text be displayed in boldface and small-cap lettering, and helps to highlight the anchors in this block (note, though, that small-caps is not supported on Navigator 4). The second rule helps to highlight text inside **EM** elements, by formatting the text in boldface, and in red.

Navigation Bar

The third component is the navigation bar, which appears at the bottom of the page and consists of a horizontal sequence of navigation icons and associated text. The actual navigation bar is marked up as an HTML table—even with CSS, tables are the only reliable way to structure content horizontally, or both horizontally and vertically. The basic structure for the HTML markup is simply (omitted table content noted in italics):

```
<DIV CLASS="navbar" ALIGN="center">
  <TABLE>
    <TR ALIGN="center">
      <TD><A HREF="prev.html"><IMG BORDER=0
            SRC="left.gif"><BR>Back</A></TD>
      <TD><A HREF="http://www.utoronto.ca/"><IMG BORDER=0
            SRC="up.gif"><BR>Up</A></TD>
      ... more table cells ...
    </TR>
  </TABLE>
</DIV>
```

where **CLASS**="navbar" indicates the nature of this **DIV**. Note, in particular, the special structure of this table: Each table cell consists of an image (the navigation icon) followed immediately by a line break (**BR**), which is in turn immediately followed by a text string. These components are in turn enclosed within an anchor element. Also, the **DIV** and **TR** elements both take the attribute **ALIGN**="center", so that the content (the table itself, and the content of each cell in the table) will be centered by older browsers.

Let us look at the first two stylesheet rules associated with the navigation bar. These rules are:

```
DIV.navbar          { clear:        right;
                      width:        100%;  }


DIV.navbar TABLE    { margin-left:  auto;
                      margin-right: auto;
                      width:        800px; }
```

The first rule "clears" the **DIV** to start below any right-floated elements, thus ensuring that the navigation bar starts below the right-floated column. Setting the width to 100% simply ensures that the **DIV** occupies the entire available width (here the full width of the canvas). This is necessary because we wish to center the table on the display. We do this by centering the table within the **DIV** element, as indicated by the second of the two rules. However, the table will then be centered on the window *only* if the **DIV** actually occupies the full width of the browser canvas.

We now need to specify the formatting for the table cell elements. The rule is:

```
DIV.navbar TD {
    font-family:    "EngraversGothic BT", Arial, Helvetica, sans-serif;
    font-weight:    bold;
    font-size:      0.6em;
```

```
font-variant:  small-caps;
text-align:    center;
padding-left:  0.1em;
padding-right: 0.1em;  }
```

This rule is largely devoted to the text within the element. The requested font, "EngraversGothic BT," is a clean, small-caps font that works well for button labels; the font size is reduced to keep the text smaller than the icons, and is in boldface to make the text stand out. Small-caps lettering is requested to handle the case when the first requested font is not available. "EngraversGothic BT" is already a small-caps font, so that the declaration font-variant: small-caps; does not affect the rendering of this font. However, if this font is not available, the text transformation property can be applied to the alternative.

Finally the last rule associated with this block is:

```
DIV.navbar A      { text-decoration:   none;
                    font-style:        normal;  }
```

This rule is actually superfluous, as it simply re-declares the default anchor element properties. However, the rule was needed to compensate for some CSS rendering bugs in the early versions of Netscape Navigator 4.

Main News Article Page

The main news article section contains the rest of the document shown in Figure 7.14, namely the main headline, the text content, and the graphic figure. The basic markup for this block of text is:

```
<DIV CLASS="main">
  <H2>President is a Space Alien!</H2>
  <P>Recent research by the Agency for Interplanetary
     Invasion has uncovered proof that the President
     of the United States, Fred Muldoon, is actually
     a space alien from the planet Glaxon! </P>
  <P CLASS="figl"><IMG SRC="happy.gif"><BR>
     X-Ray of President's Head</P>
  <P>These X-rays, recently .. </P>
...
</DIV>
```

The entire block is contained within a **DIV** of **CLASS**="main", so that standard headings and paragraphs do not need special class attributes. However, left-aligned paragraphs (the figure box in Figure 7.14) are of the special **CLASS**="figl", while right-aligned paragraphs (none are present in this example) will be of **CLASS**="figr".

The first CSS rule is:

```
DIV.main        { margin-left:    0.2em;
                  margin-right:   0.2em;
                  padding-left:   0.0em;
                  padding-right   0.0em;  }
```

This sets the default parameters for the sections containing main news articles: small left and right margins, but otherwise no special margins or padding. The small left and right margins are used to add space between the **DIV** edge and any elements contained within it.

The remaining rules specify the formatting for each of the components inside this **DIV**. The first rule specifies **H2** heading formatting, and is simply:

```
DIV.main H2    { font-family:         "Arial Black", Arial, sans-serif;
                 padding-top:         0.2em;
                 padding-bottom:      0.2em;
                 background:          red;
                 color:               white;
                 text-align:          left;    }
```

Thus **H2** elements inside a **DIV** of **CLASS**="main" will be formatted in the "Arial Black" font using a white text on a red background. The extra padding added above and below the element simply widens the background color band, and makes the heading look more visually pleasing.

The next rule sets the default paragraph formatting properties. The rule is:

```
DIV.main P     { padding-top:         0em;       /* Reset from any    */
                 padding-bottom:      0em;       /* values set        */
                 margin-bottom:       0em;       /* in less-specific  */
                 margin-top:          0.2em;     /* rules.            */
                 text-align:          justify;   }
```

The padding and margin declarations override any padding or margin values that may have been set by other, less specific rules, and also set a small margin spacing (0.2 em) between subsequent paragraphs. The fifth declaration requests text justification for these paragraphs.

The last two rules specify the formatting for the left- and right-floated paragraphs. The two rules, shown side by side, are:

```
DIV.main P.figl {                          DIV.main P.figr {

   float:          left;                      float:          right;

   width:          20%;                       width:          20%;

   margin-left:    0;                         margin-right:   0;

   margin-top:     0.2em;                     margin-top:     0.2em;

   margin-bottom:  0.2em;                     margin-bottom:  0.2em;

   padding:        0.4em;                     padding:        0.4em;

   border:         medium black solid;        border:         medium black solid;

   background:     #333333;                   background:     #333333;
```

```
color:          white;              color:          white;

font-size:      0.4em;              font-size:      0.4em;

font-weight:    bold;               font-weight:    bold;

text-align:     center;      }      text-align:     center;      }
```

where the portions of the rules that are different are shown in boldface. The first two declarations define the width of the floated element (20% of the parent element width) and the positioning: "figl" paragraphs are floated to the left, "figr" to the right. The `margin-left` and `margin-right` properties are then set to zero appropriate to the floated direction of the element, which ensures that the outside border of the floated element is flush with the inner edge of the parent element, so that the edge of the image is aligned with the left edge of the paragraphs within the **DIV**.

The remaining properties define the formatting for the floated element. Margin properties ensure a minimum spacing above and below the element, `border` provides for a medium-thickness black line around the element, and padding adds padding between the content and the border. Inside the element, the background is dark gray and the text is white, with a font size of only 0.4 em. To make the text easier to read, the font is made boldface. Finally, the text is centered in the element (this will also center inline images that are alone on a line).

Assembling the Documents: External Stylesheets

Of course, a real newspaper Web site will have hundreds of pages, all requiring some (or all) of the styling specifications just described. Therefore, when building such a site, we do not want the stylesheet content inside the HTML documents. This is instead where **LINK** elements should be used to include CSS information from *external stylesheets*. Indeed, since the different formatting components (e.g., "right-col", "navbar", or "main") were designed to be separable, the styling details for each component can be placed in a separate stylesheet file, such that an HTML document contains links only to the required stylesheet components. Figure 7.13 shows the listings for five different stylesheet documents: *basic.css*, *titlebanner.css*, *main-art.css*, *navbar.css*, and *right-col.css*, which correspond to the five groupings of stylesheet rules described previously, while Figure 7.14 shows the HTML document that uses these stylesheets to produce the page displayed in Figure 7.12. In Figure 7.14 the **LINK** elements used to include the external stylesheets are shown highlighted in boldface.

Figure 7.13 Listings for the five external stylesheets *basic.css*, *titlebanner .css*, *main-art.css*, *navbar.css*, and *rightcol.css*. Figures 7.14 and 7.17 list HTML documents that reference these stylesheets.

***basic.css* (Base stylesheet—defines overall properties)**

```
/* Set default parameters for document: font size, family and
   body width. Also set the default colors and styles
   for hypertext anchors, and the default text color.
```

Continued

Figure 7.13 *Continued*

```
*/
BODY        { font-size:        10pt;
              font-family:      Verdana, Arial, Helvetica, sans-serif;
              width:            100%;
              background:       white ;
              color:            black;      }
A           { text-decoration:  none;       } /* No underlines          */
A:link      { color:            #00aa00;    }
A:visited   { font-style:       normal;     /* Normal/gray for visited */
              color:            #777777;    }
A:link      { font-style:       italic;     /* Italic/green- unvisited */
              color:            #00aa00;    }
```

titlebanner.css (Rules for the document title banner)

```
/* Now specify formatting for title banner --  should span full
   page width, with black background image, white text, and
   appropriate positioning
*/
DIV.titlebanner    { width:        100%;                      }
DIV.titlebanner H1 { font-size:    2em;
                     background:    url(blackish.gif);
                     font-family:   Garamond;
                     font-weight:   bold;
                     color:         white;
                     text-align:    center;
                     width:         100%;
                     margin-left:   auto;
                     margin-right:  auto;                     }
```

main-art.css (Rules for the main news articles)

```
/* Now specify formatting for main body article. Add some margins
   and paddings to the DIV to provide spacings. THen specify
   special formatting for the H2, P and floating P elements
   that can go inside.
*/
DIV.main        { margin-left:     0.2em;
                  margin-right:    0.2em;
                  padding-left:    0.0em;
                  padding-right:   0.0em;                  }
DIV.main H2     { font-family:     "Arial Black", Arial, sans-serif;
                  padding-top:     0.2em;
                  padding-bottom:  0.2em;
                  color:           white;
                  text-align:      left;
                  background:      red;                    }
```

Continued

Figure 7.13 *Continued*

```
DIV.main P        { padding-top:     0em;   /* Reset from any    */
                    padding-bottom:  0em;   /* values set        */
                    margin-bottom:   0em;   /* in less-specific  */
                    margin-top:      0.2em; /* rules.            */
                    text-align:      justify;               }
DIV.main P.figl   { float:           left;
                    width:           20%;
                    margin-right:    0;
                    padding-right:   0;
                    border:          medium black solid;
                    background:      #333333;
                    color:           white;
                    font-size:       0.4em;
                    font-weight:     bold;
                    text-align:      center;
                    margin-top:      0.2em;
                    margin-bottom:   0.2em;
                    padding:         0.4em;                 }
DIV.main P.figr   { float:           right;
                    width:           20%;
                    margin-right:    0;
                    padding-right:   0;
                    border:          medium black solid;
                    background:      #333333;
                    color:           white;
                    font-size:       0.4em;
                    font-weight:     bold;
                    text-align:      center;
                    margin-top:      0.2em;
                    margin-bottom:   0.2em;
                    padding:         0.4em;                 }
```

navbar.css **(Rules for the navigation bar)**

```
/* Now specify formatting for the Navigation bar. Note that
   much of the layout is also specified by TABLE element attributes,
   since stylesheeets has limited control over these properties
*/
DIV.navbar        { clear:           right;
                    width:           100%;                 }
DIV.navbar TABLE  { margin-left:     auto;
                    margin-right:    auto;
                    width:           800px;                }
DIV.navbar TD     { font-family:     "EngraversGothic BT", Arial, sans-serif;
                    font-weight:         bold;
                    font-variant:    small-caps;
```

Continued

Figure 7.13 *Continued*

```
                       text-align:        center;
                       font-size:         0.6em;
                       padding-left:      0.1em;
                       padding-right:     0.1em;                    }
DIV.navbar A         { text-decoration:   none;
                       font-style:        normal;                  }
```

rightcol.css **(Rules for the right column of short news headlines)**

```
/* Next specify formatting for right hand column of short news
   lead-ins. THis shold be floated right, and only 20% of the
   page width.  Note special formatting for H3, P, HR and A
   elements within this class of DIV.
*/
DIV.rightcol         { float:             right;
                       width:             20%;
                       font-size:         0.4em;
                       font-family:       Verdana, Arial, Helvetica, sans-serif;
                       margin:            0 0 0 0;
                       text-align:        justify;
                       padding:           0.2em;
                       padding-bottom:    0.6em;
                       border:            medium solid  black;
                       background:        #ddddff;               }
DIV.rightcol H3      { font-size:            1.5em;
                       font-weight:       900;
                       text-transform:    capitalize;
                       text-align:        center;
                       margin:            0em;
                       margin-bottom:     0.7em;
                       padding:           0em;
                       color:             #ff0000;               }
DIV.rightcol P       { margin-top:        -0.7em;
                       margin-bottom:     +0.0em;
                       padding:           0em;                   }
DIV.rightcol A       { font-variant:         small-caps;
                       font-weight:       bold;                  }
DIV.rightcol HR      { margin:            auto;
                       padding:           0;
                       border:            0;
                       width:             80%;
                       margin-right:      auto;                  }
DIV.rightcol EM      { color:             red;
                       font-weight:       bold;                  }
```

Figure 7.14 Listing for an HTML document that uses LINK elements to reference the stylesheet documents listed in Figure 7.13. The LINK elements are shown in boldface. Browser rendering of this document is shown in Figure 7.12.

```
<HTML><HEAD><TITLE>News --  The Daily Blobby</TITLE>
  <LINK REL="stylesheet" TYPE="text/css" HREF="./basic.css">
  <LINK REL="stylesheet" TYPE="text/css" HREF="./titlebanner.css">
  <LINK REL="stylesheet" TYPE="text/css" HREF="./main-art.css">
  <LINK REL="stylesheet" TYPE="text/css" HREF="./navbar.css">
  <LINK REL="stylesheet" TYPE="text/css" HREF="./rightcol.css">
</HEAD><BODY BGCOLOR="#ffffff">

<DIV ALIGN="center" CLASS="titlebanner">
  <H1 ALIGN="center">The Daily Blobby</H1>
</DIV>
<DIV CLASS="rightcol">
  <H3>Major News</H3>
  <P><EM>All dogs bound for heaven</EM>, reports a
     Vatican committee<BR><A HREF="more.html">...More</A>
  </P><HR SIZE=2  ALIGN="center" noshade>
  <P>A <EM>wooly mammoth</EM> is found alive in a Toronto garden
    shed<BR><A HREF="more.html">...More</A>
   </P><HR SIZE=2 ALIGN="center" noshade>
  <P><EM>Scientist to clone Einstein</EM>, using DNA from fountain
     pen<BR><A HREF="more.html">...More</A>
  </P><HR SIZE=2  ALIGN="center" noshade>
  <P>"Elvis <EM>eaten</EM> by space aliens," reports
     task force<BR><A HREF="more.html">...More</A>
  </P><HR SIZE=2  ALIGN="center" noshade>
  <P><EM>Big Blue</EM>, the chess computer, is actually Bobby
     Fisher <BR><A HREF="more.html">...More</A>
  </P><HR SIZE=2 ALIGN="center" noshade>
  <P><EM>Mo Ordonez and Fidel Rillo</EM> win Tammy Faye and
     Jimmy Bakker
     look-alike contests!<BR><A HREF="more.html">...More</A>
   </P>
</DIV>
<DIV CLASS="main">
  <H2>President is a Space Alien!</H2>
  <P>Recent research by the Agency for Interplanetary Invasion
     has uncovered proof that the President of the United States,
     Fred Muldoon, is actual a space alien from the planet Glaxon! </P>
  <P CLASS="fig1"><IMG SRC="happy.gif"><BR>
     X-Ray of President's Head</P>
```

Continued

Figure 7.14 *Continued*

```
<P>These X-rays, recently provided by a secret White House source,
    show a decidedly non-human cranial shape, and clearly display
    the atypical rounded, blissful face common to the Glaxonians.</P>
<P>White House officials denied the reports, but were unable
    to explain the X-ray, nor the President's perpetual
    "happy-face" seen over the past two months.</P>
</DIV>
<DIV CLASS="navbar" ALIGN="center">
  <TABLE><TR ALIGN="center">
    <TD><A HREF="prev.html"><IMG BORDER=0 SRC="left.gif"><BR>
        Back</A></TD>
    <TD><A HREF="http://www.utoronto.ca/"><IMG BORDER=0 SRC="up.gif"><BR>
        Up</A></TD>
    <TD><A HREF="next.html"><IMG BORDER=0 SRC="right.gif"><BR>
        Next</A></TD>
    <TD><A HREF="repe.html"><IMG BORDER=0 SRC="rot.gif"><BR>
        Repeat</A></TD>
    <TD><A HREF="reje.html"><IMG BORDER=0 SRC="not.gif"><BR>
        Reject</A></TD>
    <TD><A HREF="help.html"><IMG BORDER=0 SRC="quest.gif"><BR>
        Help</A></TD>
  </TR></TABLE>
</DIV></BODY></HTML>
```

Backward Compatibility

An important aspect of CSS-based design is that it allows for HTML documents that are understandable in the absence of CSS support. Figure 7.15 shows the bottom of *The Daily Blobby* page (Figure 7.14) as rendered by Netscape Navigator 3, a browser that does not use CSS. Although the page is not elegantly formatted, the text and figures are still understandable, given the structural nature of the markup. As mentioned before, by carefully adding **FONT** elements one can also add HTML-based styling, without affecting the stylesheet-based rendering.

For full compatibility, it is useful to check how a page looks when viewed by Internet Explorer 3—this browser supports a preliminary version of CSS, but does not support all CSS features, and indeed supports some features incorrectly. Figure 7.16 shows the rendering of the same document by MSIE 3. Once again the text is quite understandable, but only some of the styling has been applied. Thus, the stylesheets we have designed are usefully backwards-compatible, given the capabilities of earlier software.

Stylesheet Reuse

One of the key features of **LINK**ed stylesheets is their reusability by other documents. As an example, Figure 7.17 lists an HTML document that uses some of the stylesheets employed in Figure 7.14, plus a single new stylesheet, *details.css*, to specify formatting details specific to this style of page. This document can be thought of as a "detailed news" page (which, for *The Daily Blobby*,

Figure 7.15 Rendering of the document listed in Figure 7.14 by Netscape Navigator 3 (only the bottom portion of the document is shown). This browser does not support CSS. The rendered page should be compared with Figure 7.12 (full CSS support) and Figure 7.16 (partial CSS support).

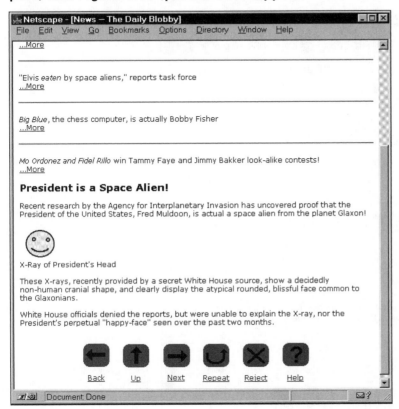

takes a stretch of the imagination!), with a different page layout and design. The new stylesheet contains the single rule

```
DIV.detailed-news   { margin-left:      25%;
                       margin-top:       0;
                       margin-bottom:    0;
                       padding:          0.5em;
                       margin-right:     0%;
                       font-family:      Garamond, "Times New Roman", sans-serif;
                       font-size:        0.75em;   }
```

which specifies a right-hand column of text, with a significantly reduced font size—this format would be good, for example, for an article to be printed for off-line reading. Note that this rule

Figure 7.16 Rendering of the document listed in Figure 7.14 by Microsoft Internet Explorer 3 (only the bottom portion of the document is shown). This browser only partially supports CSS. The rendered page should be compared with Figure 7.12 (full CSS support) and Figure 7.15 (no support for CSS).

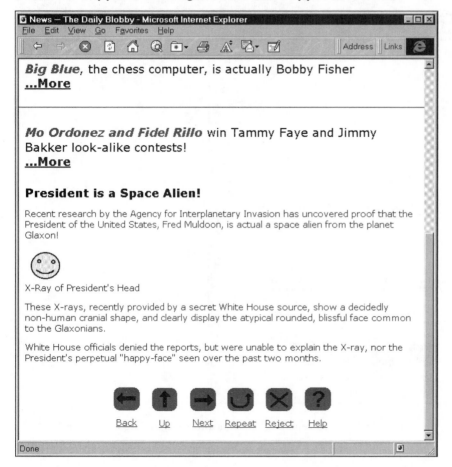

defines a new class of **DIV**, into which all other formatting elements (DIV.navbar, etc.) can be placed.

Figure 7.17 shows an example document that structures the page by placing the entire content (except for the title banner) inside this new class of **DIV**. Thus, the main article text and the navigation bar are all placed in the column at the right of the page, while the font size inside the main article text is significantly reduced.

The rendering of this page is shown in Figure 7.18. As expected, the styling as specified by the **CLASS**="main" and **CLASS**="navbar" **DIV** elements has been placed inside the new right-hand column, while the title banner appears at the top of the page, in the same style as shown in Figure 7.12. There is, however, one formatting error on this page: The navigation bar should be centered below the column of text, but is instead approximately aligned on the column. This is a result of incorrect parsing of the stylesheet by Netscape Navigator.

References: Additional CSS Designs

These five examples illustrated some basics of CSS design. By now you are probably realizing that although the language itself is quite straightforward, constructing large stylesheets can be quite complicated, since the CSS rules and properties interact with one another in complex ways. Thus, fine-tuning a design can be a time-consuming task, and is a procedure that takes experience to master.

The process of design is simplified somewhat if a designer can start from some good, and accurate, stylesheet examples. Like HTML markup, stylesheet listings are freely available over the Internet, either contained within retrieved documents, or as **LINK**ed resources from a document. Thus you can easily read example HTML documents and the associated CSS stylesheets, and study them to learn new design approaches.

There are a number of CSS "design gallery" Web sites to help you, including the companion Web site for this book: Some of these sites are listed at the end of this section. Be aware that many of these sites include designs that were originally designed for Microsoft's Internet Explorer 3 browser—the first browser to support stylesheets. Unfortunately, the CSS implementation in MSIE 3 was incomplete, and is also incorrect in several respects (this is not a criticism of the browser, but simply reflects the fact that the browser was released before the CSS specifications were finalized). Therefore, you should be careful when copying stylesheets, to make sure that the designs you borrow or learn from reflect the current language specification and accurate CSS design.

The companion Web site to this book contains several CSS design examples, including (but not limited to!) the ones presented in this chapter. Particulary, the companion site provides links to two versions of each example document: one containing the CSS rules, and one without. Viewing these two, related documents helps to illustrate how well (or how poorly) the design can function in the absence of proper CSS support.

Stylesheet Sourcebook Gallery
http://WWW.XXX.YY/ZZZZ/chap7/gallery.html A collection of stylesheet examples collected by the author. This also includes references to CSS example pages lying at other sites.

Microsoft CSS Gallery
`http://www.microsoft.com/truetype/css/gallery/entrance.htm` Note that many of these designs are optimized for MSIE 3.0, and thus do not support the latest CSS specification.

Generationweb.com CSS Gallery
`http://www.generationweb.com/gallery/css.htm` A small collection of CSS example pages.

Figure 7.17 A second HTML document making use of the stylesheets listed in Figure 7.13, plus the additional stylesheet *details.css* described in the text. The new LINK element is noted in boldface. For simplicity, some of the document text is omitted—omissions are noted in italics. Browser rendering of this document is shown in Figure 7.18.

```
<HTML><HEAD><TITLE>The Daily Blobby — Detailed News</TITLE>
  <LINK REL="stylesheet" TYPE="text/css" HREF="basic.css">
  <LINK REL="stylesheet" TYPE="text/css" HREF="details.css">
  <LINK REL="stylesheet" TYPE="text/css" HREF="titlebanner.css">
  <LINK REL="stylesheet" TYPE="text/css" HREF="main-art.css">
  <LINK REL="stylesheet" TYPE="text/css" HREF="navbar.css">
</HEAD><BODY>
<DIV ALIGN="center" CLASS="titlebanner">
    <H1 ALIGN="center">The Daily Blobby</H1>
</DIV>
<DIV CLASS="detailed-news">
 <DIV CLASS="main">
  <H2>President is a Space Alien!</H2>
  <P>Recent research by the Agency for Interplanetary Invasion has
     uncovered proof that the President of the United States, Fred
     Muldoon, is actual a space alien from the planet Glaxon! </P>
  <P CLASS="figl"><IMG SRC="happy.gif"><BR>
     X-Ray of President's Head</P>
  <P>These X-rays, recently provided by a secret White House source,
     show a decidedly non-human cranial shape, and clearly display the
     atypical ... omitted text ...</P>
  <P class="figr"><IMG SRC="globe.jpg"><BR>Proposed Park Logo</P>
  <P>Our white house agents have recovered evidence of  an
     interplanetary ... omitted text ... the earth's
     position as the third planet from the sun ... </P>
  </DIV>
  <DIV CLASS="navbar" ALIGN="center">
    <TABLE><TR ALIGN="center">
      <TD><A HREF="prev.html"><IMG BORDER=0 SRC="left.gif"><BR>
         Back</A></TD>
      <TD><A HREF="http://www.utoronto.ca/"><IMG BORDER=0 SRC="up.gif">
         <BR>Up</A></TD>
      ... omitted TD table cells ....
  </TR></TABLE>
  </DIV>
</DIV>
</BODY></HTML>
```

Figure 7.18 Rendering of the document listed in Figure 7.17 by the Netscape Navigator 4 browser. The formatting of this document is specified by the stylesheets in Figure 7.13, plus an additional stylesheet document (*details.cs*) described in the text.

Endnote

1. The line height can also be specified as `line-height: 1em;`—however, this declaration was not properly processed by the Netscape Navigator 4 browser used to develop these examples.

CSS Language
Reference

T his chapter provides a detailed reference to the Cascading Stylesheets Level 1 (CSS1) language, and of all the CSS properties. The descriptions are very brief and succinct—you should look at Chapters 3 through 6 for details of how to use these properties. Chapter 8, the last section, provides a tabular summary of all properties, pseudo-classes and pseudo-elements, and indicates whether or not they are supported by current CSS-capable browsers.

CSS Syntax

A CSS stylesheet consists of *rules* that specify formatting instructions to associate with particular elements in a document; in general, a stylesheet contains many such rules. An example is:

```
H1 {font-weight: bold;}
```

Each CSS rule begins with a *selector* (e.g., H1) that specifies the element or elements to which the rule should be applied, followed by one or more *declarations* (e.g., font-weight: bold) that specify formatting properties for the element. The above rule is particularly simple, and has only one declaration.

Each declaration has two parts: the *property*, (e.g., font-weight) which defines the formatting property being specified by the declaration, and the *value* (e.g., bold) assigned to the property. The colon character (:) is the separator between the property and the associated value. The colon is a special character in declarations, and cannot appear as part of a value.

The collection of declarations associated with a selector is contained within curly brackets: the left curly bracket ({) marks the start of the collection, and the right curly bracket (}) denotes the end. Each declaration is terminated by a semicolon—that is, the semicolon denotes the end of one declaration, and the possible beginning of another. The semicolon is optional if there is only a single declaration; multiple declarations are more common for CSS rules, as in:

```
H1 { font-family: arial, helvetica, sans-serif;
     left-margin: 5%;   color: blue; }
```

In this case, the semicolons are mandatory, as the parser otherwise does not know where one declaration ends and the next begins.

Comments in Stylesheets

In CSS, comments are delimited by the starting string /* and the ending string */. All text between and including these two strings is treated as a comment by a CSS parser, and is ignored. Comments cannot nest, and cannot overlap.

Case Sensitivity

In general, CSS rules are case-*insensitive*, which means that element names (in the selectors), property names, and most of the property values can be entered in either uppercase or lowercase. Thus the rules

```
BODY { font-family: verdana, arial, helvetica, sans-serif
       font-weight: normal }
```

and

```
body { FONT-FAMILY: verdana, arial, helvetica, sans-serif
       FonT-WeiGHt: noRMaL }
```

are equivalent. Note, however, that some property values, such as font family names, URL strings, or **CLASS** or **ID** attribute values, are *not intrinsic* to the CSS specification, and are sometimes case-*sensitive*. The best plan is to capitalize all element names, use lowercase for all CSS property names and defined property values, and ensure that any class or **ID** values used in the stylesheet have the same case as the HTML attribute values in the document associated with the stylesheet.

Property Inheritance

CSS properties always have a value—if not otherwise specified, this is the default value, as given by the CSS specifications. In many cases, properties defined within one element are passed on to, or *inherited* by, child elements of the given element. For example, consider the HTML markup:

```
<STYLE> <!--
  DIV {font-family: arial, sans-serif;}
--> </STYLE>
```

```
......
<DIV>
   <H3>Example Division</H3>
   <P>This is the first paragraph in this DIV. Not terribly
      exciting, but then it is often <EM>hard</EM> to find
      good examples at 3:00AM. </P>
   <P>For my second paragraph, I will quack like a duck! </P>
</DIV>
```

Here the single stylesheet rule states that **DIV** content should be displayed using the Arial font. The **P** and **H3** elements then *inherit* the font-family property value from the parent **DIV**, while the **EM** element inherits the font from the **P** within which it is contained, which in turn inherits the font from **DIV**.

This inheritance approach is logical, and is in keeping with one's general expectations of what will happen: The display properties will inherit some overall characteristics unless changed by the stylesheet.

However, not all properties inherit values from the parent element. Properties such as background-image, vertical-align, and margin do not inherit property values, because inheritance is not sensible. For example, an element does not inherit a background image property value, since the element is simply displayed above the background of the parent element, so that inheritance is irrelevant. Similarly, margins are not inherited, since each element's margins are unique and independent of the parent.

The property specifications that appear in the second half of this chapter explicitly state whether or not a property inherits its value from the parent element.

CSS Selectors

This CSS rule *selector* defines the collection of elements to which the rule applies. There are several types of selectors for rules specific to a generic element, a specific class of an element, or even to elements contingent on their place within a document. The seven basic types (not to be confused with sins) are:

Simple selectors—Selectors based solely on element name.

Class-based simple selectors—Selectors based on the **CLASS** attribute value of an element; may also be based on the element name.

Pseudo-class-based simple selectors—Selectors based on the *pseudo-class* properties of an element, and which may also be based on the element name.

Pseudo-element-based simple selectors—Selectors that apply to a particular subset of a given element, such as the leading line of a paragraph, or the leading letter of a line.

ID-based simple selectors—Selectors based on the **ID** attribute value of an element, and which may also be based on the element name.

Contextual selectors—Selectors based on a simple selector and the context of the selector; for example, a selector that applies only to **EM** elements inside an **H1**.

Grouped selectors—Groupings of selectors, such that the same rule is applied to all selectors in the group.

The different types of selectors were described in detail in Chapters 3 and 4, and are only briefly reviewed here.

Simple Selectors

Simple selectors reference a single HTML element by name, and specify formatting instructions specific to the indicated element type. An example is found in the rule:

```
P {text-align: left; text-indent: 5em}
```

Simple selectors are useful for defining overall properties that apply to all elements of a given type. Other selectors, such as class-based ones, can provide formatting instructions specific to a subset of these elements.

Class-Based Simple Selectors

Class-based selectors associate stylesheet rules with a particular *class* of HTML elements, where elements are assigned a class via the **CLASS** attribute, as described in Chapter 2. In a selector, a class name is indicated by placing a period in front of the class name, as in the rule:

```
.intro { font-size: larger;  font-weight: bolder}
```

This selector then references *any and all* elements of the specified class, regardless of element type. Class-based selectors can be associated with a specific type of element by appending the class name to the element, separated by a period. For example, the rule:

```
P.intro { font-size: larger;  font-weight: bolder}
```

applies only to paragraphs of **CLASS**="intro".

A selector can contain, at most, one class value. Thus, expressions such as `P.cl1.cl2` are not allowed.

CLASS is allowed with almost all body content elements, the exceptions being those elements that are not displayed with the document (**AREA, MAP, PARAM,** and **SCRIPT**) and those that are formatting-specific and destined to be entirely replaced by stylesheet rules (**CENTER** and **FONT**).

CLASS attribute values can be name tokens—that is, they can contain any of the characters A–Z or a–z, the numbers 0–9, or a hyphen (-)—but they must begin with a letter and not a number or a hyphen. They can also contain any Unicode character in the decimal range 161–255 (these are the same as the characters in the upper half of the ISO Latin-1 character set). However, within a CSS stylesheet, this latter group of characters must be entered as a hex code sequence that encodes the location of the character. The code consists of a backslash (\) followed by hexadecimal digits (0-9A-F) corresponding to the position of the character. For example, the character Ê (capital E with a circumflex) would be entered as \CA, as it is the 202nd character (hexadecimal CA) in the character set. Consequently, if a document contained the expression **CLASS**="Êgale", then the corresponding CSS selector rule would use the suffix .\CAgale.

Pseudo-Class-Based Simple Selectors

Pseudo-class-based selectors are like class-based ones, except that the class-like information comes from the browser itself, and reflects information about the status of the browser, or the status of particular elements in the displayed document. CSS Level 1 defines only three pseudo-classes: link, to denote hypertext anchors that are unexplored by the user; visited, to denote hypertext anchors that were previously visited by the user; and active, to indicate active links—links that are currently selected by the user.

CSS pseudo-classes are denoted by a leading colon (:), for example :link or A:visited. Pseudo-class and regular class names can be combined in a single selector using the general form:

NAME.class:pseudoclass

where *NAME* is the element name, *class* is the class name, and *pseudoclass* is the pseudo-class name. Note that the class name must appear first, followed by the pseudo-class.

A selector cannot contain multiple pseudo-classes—thus the selector A:link:active is forbidden.

Pseudo-classes are generally applicable only to certain HTML elements—the three currently defined pseudo-classes are valid only with anchor elements.

Pseudo-Element-Based Simple Selectors

Pseudo-element selectors define rules that apply to a *specific subset* of a formatting element, where this subset can depend on the element content, or on the configuration of the browser displaying the document. CSS Level 1 defines two pseudo-element selectors, both of which apply only to block-level elements. These are first-line, which references the first displayed line in the element, and first-letter, which references the first displayed letter of the element. Like pseudo-classes, pseudo-elements are denoted by a leading colon (:), for example :first-line or P:first-letter.

First-line references the first displayed line of the element—that is, the first line of text as displayed by the browser. The selected text is essentially treated as inline text (i.e., like **EM** element content) but with several restrictions—in particular, you cannot apply the float property to a first-line pseudo-element, nor can you modify the margins, padding, or border properties. Table 8.1 lists the properties that *can* be applied to a first-line pseudo-element.

First-letter references the first letter in the element. By default, the first-letter content is treated like a floating element (for example, so that a drop-cap leading letter can float to the start of the element). This behavior can be changed by applying the float property to the pseudo-element.

The text affected by the first-letter pseudo-selector will vary depending on language and on punctuation. For example, if a first-letter selector is applied to an element beginning with a quotation

Table 8.1 CSS Properties That *Can* Be Applied to a First-Line Pseudo-Element.

background	background-attachment	background-color	background-image
background-position	background-repeat	clear	color
font	font-family	font-size	font-style
font-weight	font-variant	letter-spacing	line-height
text-decoration	text-transform	vertical-align	word-spacing

mark, such as: *"I thought the king had more affected the Duke of...,"* then the first-letter pseudo-element will consist of both the quotation mark and the first letter (i.e., *"I"*). There are many language-specific rules for selecting characters to include as part of a first-letter pseudo-element.

Almost all properties can be applied to a first-letter pseudo-element. Table 8.2 lists those properties that *cannot* be applied, or that can be applied only in restricted ways.

Combining Class and Pseudo-Element Selectors A pseudo-element and a regular class selector can be combined, using the general form:

NAME.class:pseudoelem

where *NAME* is the element name, `class` is the class name, and `pseudoelem` is the pseudo-element name.

Browser Support for Pseudo-Elements

Support for pseudo-elements is not a core feature of CSS. Current browsers ignore pseudo-elements completely.

Table 8.2 CSS Properties That *Cannot* Be Applied to a First-Letter Pseudo-Element

display	height
letter-spacing	list-style-type
list-style-image	list-style-position
list-style	text-align
text-indent	vertical-align (but allowed if `float:  none` is also applied)
white-space	width
word-spacing	

ID-Based Simple Selectors

ID-based selectors allow for stylesheet rules related to a particular ID-labeled element. Such selectors are indicated by prepending a hash character (#) to the **ID** value. For example, to specify formatting specific to **H1** elements with **ID**="x23", the CSS selector would be:

```
H1#x23
```

while to specify a rule specific to any element with this **ID** value, the selector would be:

```
#x23 { font-face: Arial; }
```

ID values are name tokens, as described in the previous selection on class-based selectors.

Note that the HTML specification requires that **ID** values be *unique* in a document; thus there can be at most one **ID**="x23" label. However, most current browsers do not complain if there are multiple elements with the same **ID** value; they usually just apply the stylesheet instructions to the first element having the given **ID** value.

ID is supported with almost all body content elements, the exceptions being those elements that are not displayed with the document (**AREA**, **MAP**, **PARAM**, and **SCRIPT**) and those that are formatting-specific and destined to be entirely replaced by stylesheet rules (**CENTER** and **FONT**).

Contextual Selectors

Contextual selectors specify rules that depend on the *context* of the element within the element hierarchy of the document. Such rules are thus contingent on the *position* of a selected element: that is, on both the element and its parent element. For example, to specify special formatting for **EM** elements that lie somewhere within a **UL** that, in turn, lies somewhere within a **DIV** of **CLASS**="blobby", the contextual selector would be:

```
DIV.blobby UL EM
```

There is no limit to the number of selectors that can be in a contextual selector; the selectors are simply separated by whitespace. Note that contextual is not the same as parent-child, as discussed in Chapter 4.

It is possible for rules with different contextual selectors to apply to the same element. The cascading rules of CSS define how a browser chooses which properties from these different rules apply to the element. Cascading is summarized later in this chapter, and is discussed in detail in Chapter 6.

Grouped Selectors

Grouped selectors let an author specify a single rule that applies to multiple selectors. This is done by separating the individual selectors by commas. An example is:

```
H1, H2, H3, H4 {font-family: Arial, Helvetica, sans-serif }
```

In essence, this is simply a shorthand way of expressing the four rules:

```
H1 {font-family: Arial, Helvetica, sans-serif }
H2 {font-family: Arial, Helvetica, sans-serif }
H3 {font-family: Arial, Helvetica, sans-serif }
H4 {font-family: Arial, Helvetica, sans-serif }
```

The individual selectors in a grouped selector need not be simple—they can be anything up to and including a contextual selector, for example:

```
H1 EM, P.intro EM,  EM.red {color: red}
```

Including Stylesheets in HTML Documents

There are three ways that style information can be included within, or associated with, an HTML document:

LINK element—An HTML **LINK** element can reference an external stylesheet. **LINK** is a **HEAD**-level element, and can appear only in the document **HEAD**.

STYLE element—The HTML **STYLE** element can contain CSS stylesheet instructions to be applied to the HTML document. The **STYLE** element must be in the document **HEAD**.

STYLE attribute—Most HTML elements support a **STYLE** attribute, the value of which is a collection of CSS properties to apply the associated element.

LINK Element: Linking to an External Stylesheet

In this approach, the stylesheet is in a separate document, referenced using an HTML **LINK** element. The relevant markup is

```
<LINK REL="stylesheet" TYPE="mime/type" HREF="url">
```

where the value **REL**="stylesheet" indicates that the target resource is a stylesheet, *url* is the URL pointing to the stylesheet document, and *mime/type* is the MIME type for the stylesheet. The CSS stylesheet language has the MIME type `text/css`.

STYLE Element: Stylesheets within the Document

Stylesheet rules can be placed inside a **STYLE** element which, in turn, must be placed in the document **HEAD**. As far as formatting is concerned, there is no difference between placing the stylesheet in a separate file or in the **HEAD** of an HTML document. The advantage of the former, of course, is that the same stylesheet can be used by many different files, without the need for duplicating the information in the **HEAD** of every document.

The **STYLE** element should take a **TYPE** attribute to specify the stylesheet language, where the value is the appropriate MIME type. For a CSS stylesheet, the appropriate value is "text/css".

Hiding Stylesheets from Older Browsers Older browsers that do not understand stylesheets may try to interpret the stylesheet instructions as HTML markup. To avoid this problem, the entire content of a STYLE element can be placed within an HTML comment, thereby hiding the stylesheet from older browsers. Thus, typical content for a **STYLE** element would be (the HTML comment markers are shown in bold italics):

```
<STYLE TYPE="text/css">
<!--
  BODY { font-family: times, serif; }
  /* ... more rules to follow ... */
-->
</STYLE>
```

STYLE Attribute: Element-Specific Property Specifications
The **STYLE** attribute includes stylesheet declarations directly within an element start tag. The syntax is:

```
<NAME STYLE="declarations"> ... </NAME>
```

where *NAME* is the HTML element name, STYLE is the new attribute, and *declarations* is a semicolon-separated collection of declarations to be applied to the element. An example is:

```
<EM STYLE="color:red; text-decoration: blink">locally ... </EM>
```

The CSS recommends placing rules in a **STYLE** element, and avoiding the use of **STYLE** *attributes.*

META Specification of a Default Stylesheet Language If there are no **STYLE** or **LINK** elements, then there is no way of knowing the language used in **STYLE** attribute values. CSS proposes that **META** elements provide this information. The default document stylesheet language is then specified by:

```
<META HTTP-EQUIV="Content-style-type" CONTENT="type/subtype">
```

In the absence of this element, a browser may guess at the language, with unpredictable results.

Note that this implies that the default type can be indicated by an HTTP response header field of the form

```
Content-style-type: type/subtype
```

At present, there are no browsers that understand this particular HTTP header field, or the associated **META** element.

Importing Stylesheets: The `@import` Statement
CSS supports an `@import` statement (also called an *at-rule*) for referencing external stylesheet instructions to be loaded into the stylesheet. An `@import` statement must specify the URL for the desired external stylesheet. An example is:

```
@import url(http://www.utoronto.ca/ian/styles/book1.css)
```

The browser will load the referenced external instructions, replacing the @import statement by the loaded instructions, and will use the resulting stylesheet to format the document.

Note that @import statements must appear as the *first lines* in a stylesheet, and cannot appear after any stylesheet rule. This ensures that any external stylesheets are loaded before any styling information specified in the document. Any @import statements appearing *after* a stylesheet rule are ignored. At present, there are no browsers that support @import.

Increasing Declaration Importance with !important

In CSS, the relative importance of a declaration can be increased using the !importance parameter. This parameter appears at the end of the declaration and indicates that the declaration is of higher importance than other declarations in the same rule:

```
margin-left: 5% !important;
```

The !important declaration is used by the browser when determining which rules actually apply. In general, a stylesheet will contain many different rules that apply to the same element or elements. The CSS *cascading rules* define which rule, and which declarations within those rules, should actually be used to format a given element. Cascading is summarized later in this chapter, and was discussed in detail in Chapter 6. At present, there are no browsers that support !important declarations.

Processing CSS Rules: Error Handling

CSS parsers should ignore declarations that contain errors. Thus, if a rule contains four declarations, but one has an error (for example, a missing colon, or an illegal property value), then this declaration will be ignored, but the other three declarations will be processed.

The most common error is omitting the semicolon from the end of a property declaration. This will probably cause the browser to ignore this declaration in addition to the next one (or sometimes all the remaining declarations in the rule), since the software only knows that the declaration has ended upon encountering the next semicolon, or the next curly bracket that ends the rule.

Of course, if there is an error in the selector, the software will ignore the entire rule.

Processing CSS Rules: The Cascade

One of the more complicated aspects of preparing CSS stylesheets is figuring out which rules and declarations are actually used to format a given element—each element is usually subject to many possible rules and declarations, with conflicting formatting requests. CSS defines how this is done via a set of *cascading rules*. Essentially, "cascading" means that the declarations for a given element take their default value unless overridden by a stylesheet declaration, which in turn can be overridden by a declaration coming from a rule that more specifically applies to the given element.

The rules for how this sequence of *cascading selection criteria* is applied are rather complex, and are only briefly summarized here. Please see the second half of Chapter 6 for a detailed discussion of cascading.

Start with the complete collection of property declarations that apply to a given element—including declarations assumed by the browser's default settings, any declarations arising from a user-specified stylesheet (called *reader declarations*), and finally any declarations arising from the document's own stylesheet (*called author declarations*). The selection criteria are:

- **The declared importance of a declaration**—Declarations containing the `!important` parameter are given a higher weight than all other declarations with the same selector. A reader declaration declared `!important` always has a higher weight than a corresponding author declaration. An author declaration declared `!important` always has a weight higher than a reader declaration that is *not* marked `!important`. This ensures that the reader's choices can always override the author's, but that an author can always override a reader's "unimportant" rules.

- **Where the rule comes from**—In general, author-specified stylesheets (i.e., external stylesheet information obtained from **LINK** elements, internal stylesheets within a **STYLE** element, or stylesheet instructions within **STYLE** attributes) have precedence over browser- or user-specified stylesheets. This lets a stylesheet override the browser's default settings.

- **The specificity of the rule**—A selector that is more specific to a given element overrides a less-specific one. CSS supports a weighting formula for calculating how specific a given rule is—the higher the weight, the more specific the rule. The weighting algorithm is as follows:

  - **ID**-based selectors always have a higher weight than ones that do not contain an **ID** value. Add 1 to the **ID**-based weight for each **ID** value in the selector (the highest number has the highest weight).

  - **CLASS**-based selectors (including pseudo-classes) always have a higher weight than selectors that do not contain **CLASS** values. Add 1 to the **CLASS**-based weight component for each **CLASS** value in the selector (the highest number has the highest weight).

  - *Element name*-based selectors have the lowest weight. For each name (including pseudo-element names) add 1 to the name-based weight component.

- **The order in which the rule occurs in the document**—Sort the properties by the order they appear in the stylesheet. If two declarations have the same weight, then the one that appears later in the stylesheet overrides the one that appears earlier. Note that stylesheet content included via **LINK** elements is treated as coming *before* the content of the **STYLE** element. This ensures that rules specified in a **STYLE** element will override any rules specified in an external stylesheet.

Please see Chapter 6 for a more detailed description of the application of this algorithm.

Length Units

CSS supports several different length measurement units, described in detail in Appendix B. There are two main categories of units: (1) *absolute* units such as inches or centimeters, and (2) *relative* units such as em or ex units. Pixel units are also supported, but are not recommended.

In CSS, lengths are given by a string containing a two-letter suffix indicating the units of measure preceded by a number, with no space between the two—for example, `1.23in`, corresponding to 1.23 inches. Supported length units and the corresponding CSS suffices are: em units (em), ex units (ex), inches (in), centimeters (cm), millimeters (mm), points (pt), picas (pc), and pixels (px). Positive and negative lengths are possible, although some properties support only positive lengths. Lengths of zero can be given simply as the digit 0, since length units are irrelevant in this case.

Color Units

CSS supports several ways to specify a color. These can be divided into two categories: color names, and RGB color specifications. The two mechanisms, and color in general, are discussed in more detail in Appendix A. The following is a brief summary of the mechanisms used in CSS declarations.

Named Colors

CSS supports sixteen different symbolic color names, corresponding to the sixteen colors of the Windows VGA color palette: aqua, black, blue, fuchsia, gray, green, lime, maroon, navy, olive, purple, red, silver, teal, white, and yellow. Note that CSS does not officially support the extended list of named colors supported by the **FONT** and **BGCOLOR** attributes of Netscape Navigator 3/4 and Internet Explorer 3/4. However, these extended color names are widely supported.

RGB Color Codes

RGB color codes specify a color in terms of the mixture of the three primary colors, red, green, and blue. In general, such codes use eight bits to represent the intensity of each of the three primary colors, so that 24 bits are required to specify any color; thus, this is commonly called the 24-bit color system. There are, of course, some tricky details, most of which are discussed in Appendix A.

CSS lets an author specify RGB color codes in four different ways: two using hexadecimal codes (as currently possible in HTML **BGCOLOR** attribute values), one way as integer color levels, and one way as percentage intensities. The details of the four notations are:

#rrggbb—Where rr, gg, and bb are the hexadecimal codes for the intensity of each color, ranging from 00 (zero) to FF (hexadecimal for the integer 255).

#rgb—Where r, g, and b are "abbreviated" forms of the 24-bit color codes. Such codes are converted into proper 24-bit notation by doubling each color value; for example, the code #A15 would be converted to the full RGB code #AA1155.

rgb(red, green, blue)—Where red, green, and blue are the integer intensities of the red, green, and blue colors, ranging from 0 to 255. This is a decimal equivalent of the #rrggbb notation.

rgb(red%, green%, blue%)—The color is expressed as an RGB code, but the intensity of each RGB component color is expressed as a percentage of maximum intensity. Fractional percentage values are allowed. Note that this percentage must be converted by the browser to the appropriate integer value. Percentages greater than 100% are truncated.

URLs as CSS Values

The `background-image` property and the `@import` directive take URLs as their value. In CSS, URLs are expressed using any of the following three notations:

```
url(url-string)
url('url-string')
url("url-string")
```

where *url-string* is the URL being referenced, and where an author can, if desired, add extra whitespace between the brackets and the URL inside the brackets. For example, the above could also be written as:

```
url( url-string)
url('url-string' )
url( "url-string" )
```

The use of quotation marks (single or double) is at the discretion of the author. Because the single quote, double quote, left bracket, and right bracket are specially parsed in this situation by the CSS parser, these characters must be *escaped* if present as part of the URL itself. This can be done in two ways. The preferred mechanism is to replace these characters by their *URL encodings*—this is the accepted URL mechanism for including special characters in a URL. Alternatively, CSS lets an author *escape* the characters by adding a leading backslash character. These two options are illustrated in the following chart:

Character	URL Encoding	CSS Escape Sequence
"	%22	\"
'	%39	\'
(	%40	\(
)	%41	\)

Here are some example URL references:

```
url(http://www.splunge.com/stuff.gif)
url( "http://styles.mycompany.com/media/2/style\'.css" )
url( "http://styles.mycompany.com/media/2/style%39.css" )
```

The last two references are equivalent, but use different special character encodings.

Full and Partial URLs

URLs within CSS stylesheets can be either full or partial. Note in particular that partial URLs are evaluated relative to the URL used to retrieve the *stylesheet*, and not relative to the URL used to retrieve the document. These two URLs are the same if the style information comes from a **STYLE** element inside the HTML document. They may not be the same, however, if a stylesheet is included via a **LINK** element.

When creating a stylesheet, the author often starts with style instructions within the HTML document, and then later moves the instructions to a separate file. In doing so, an author must be careful not to break the partial URL references.

CSS Property Specifications

Organized in alphabetical order, the following section provides brief, detailed specifications of all the properties defined in CSS Level 1. Descriptions of the use of each property are found in Chapters 3 through 6, and references to the appropriate chapters are included, where applicable.

Each section includes a property overview, which defines the property name and purpose; the default value for the property; the allowed values for the property; the elements to which the property can be applied; and the *inheritability* of the property—that is, whether or not the property is inherited from the parent element. An example illustrating this overview is given in Figure 8.1.

Figure 8.1 Example property overview, showing the different components.

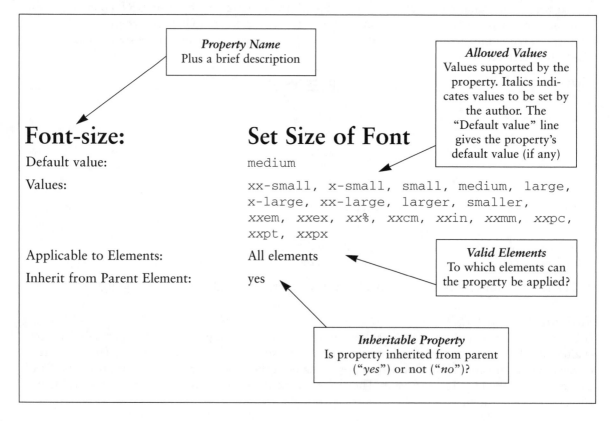

Allowed property values are listed in the *Values* line, and are given in a monospace font (courier), while the default value for the property is given by the *Default value* line, at the top of the property overview. Non-italicized values indicate property values that are fixed by the CSS specification—for example, the value small for the property assignment font-size: small. Value strings set in italics indicate values that can be selected by the stylesheet author, usually subject to a rule associated with the type of value. For example, the value *xx*cm means that the string *xx* is set by the author, but the context (cm) indicates that the value *xx* must be a real or integer number corresponding to a length specified in centimeters. Table 8.3 summarizes the meanings of all the italicized values that appear as property values.

The *Applicable to Elements* line indicates which elements the property can be applied to. With CSS, most properties can be applied to most **BODY**-content elements, but there are some cases where the rules only apply to *block-level* formatting elements (elements that define blocks of text), *inline* formatting elements (elements that appear inline within a block element, such as **EM** or **IMG**), list-item elements (**UL**, **OL**, or **LI**), or *replaced* elements (elements that are replaced by objects of unknown size, such as **APPLET** or **IMG**).

Table 8.4 summarizes the HTML elements that, by default, fall into these four categories. New elements introduced as part of the HTML standards process are in italics, while proprietary HTML extensions (e.g., Netscape/Microsoft) are underlined. Note also that the display property can *change* the formatting type for a given HTML element, as discussed in Chapter 5.

Table 8.3 Description of Shorthand Notation Used in Property Value Specifications

Property Value	Description
url(*urlstring*)	An arbitrary partial or complete URL, where *urlstring* is the URL.
cname	Any of the 16 color names specified in Appendix A.
#*rrggbb*	An arbitrary 24-bit RGB code, where *rr*, *gg*, and *bb* are the hexadecimal values for the intensity, in the range 00–FF, for the red, green, and blue channels, respectively.
#*rgb*	An arbitrary 24-bit RGB code, where *r*, *g*, and *b* are hexadecimal digits, in the range 0–F, corresponding to the intensity for the red, green, and blue channels, respectively. The full 8-bit color for each channel is created by "doubling" the specified digits; that is, #6FA is transformed into the full 24-bit color specification #66FFAA.
rgb(*red, green, blue*)	An arbitrary 24-bit RGB code, where *red*, *green*, and *blue* are the integer values of the intensity, in the range 0–255, for the red, green, and blue channels, respectively.
rgb(*red%, green%, blue%*)	An arbitrary RGB color code, where *red%*, *green%*, and *blue%* are the real percentage values of the intensity, in the range 0–100%, for the red, green, and blue channels, respectively.

Continued

Table 8.3 *Continued*

Property Value	Description
xx% or *yy%*	Arbitrary, real percentage value. Can be a positive or, depending on the property, a negative value.
length, lengthx, or *lengthy*	An arbitrary length, specified in any of the relative (em, ex) or absolute (cm, mm, in, pc, pt, px) length units. Can be a positive or, depending on the property, a negative value.
*xx*em or *xx*ex	Arbitrary *relative* length, in em or ex units respectively. Can be a positive or, depending on the property, a negative value.
*xx*cm, *xx*in, *xx*mm, *xx*pc, *xx*pt, *xx*px	Arbitrary absolute length, in centimeters, inches, millimeters, picas, points, and pixels, respectively. Can be a positive or, depending on the property, a negative value.

Table 8.4 HTML Elements and Their Groupings As Understood by Cascading Stylesheets Level 1
Underlined elements are proprietary elements introduced by browser vendors (see Chapter 2). Italicized elements are new elements, introduced subsequent to HTML 3.2.

Formatting Group	HTML Elements in Group
All elements	All below plus **HTML**.
Block-level elements	**ADDRESS, BLOCKQUOTE, BODY, CENTER, DD, DIR, DIV, DT, FORM, H1** to **H6, HR, LI, MENU, <u>MULTICOL</u>, OL, P, PRE, TABLE, TD, TH, TR,** and **UL.** Also, any element with property `float:left` or `float:right`, or `display: block` or `display:list-item`. **CENTER** should be avoided in new documents. **<u>MULTICOL</u>** is Netscape-specific.
Inline elements	**APPLET, <u>BLINK</u>, B,** *BDO,* **BIG, CITE, CODE, DFN, EM, <u>EMBED</u>, FONT, I, IMG, INPUT, KBD, <u>MARQUEE</u>, <u>NOBR</u>,** *OBJECT, Q,* **S, SAMP, SELECT, SMALL,** *SPAN,* **STRIKE, STRONG, SUB, SUP, TEXTAREA, TT, U, VAR.** Also, any element with property `display:inline`. **APPLET, BLINK, <u>EMBED</u>, FONT, <u>MARQUEE</u>,** and **<u>NOBR</u>** are deprecated, and should be avoided in new documents.
List item elements	**OL, UL, MENU, DIR, LI,** or any element with property `display:list-item`.

Continued

Table 8.4 *Continued*

Formatting Group	HTML Elements in Group
	MENU and DIR are deprecated, and should be avoided in new documents.
Replaced elements	APPLET, <u>EMBED</u>, IMG, INPUT, *OBJECT*, SELECT, TEXTAREA

Background: Shorthand for Background Properties

Default value:	*no default value*
Values:	One to three values, specifying the background color (as per `background-color`), image (as per `background-image`), repeat specification (as per `background-repeat`), scrolling property (as per `background-attachment`), and position (as per `background-position`)
Applicable to Elements:	All elements
Inherit from Parent Element:	no

This is a shorthand property for specifying the background properties `background-color`, `background-image`, `background-repeat`, `background-attachment`, and `background-position` within a single declaration. The value is a space-separated collection of values allowed by these five background properties, given in any order. An example is:

```
background: scroll gray url(../bgrounds/tiles.gif) repeat-y
```

Please see the individual background properties for descriptions of the allowed values.

Background-attachment: Scrolling Properties of Background Images

Default value:	`scroll`
Values:	`scroll`, `fixed`
Applicable to Elements:	All elements
Inherit from Parent Element:	no

This property specifies how a background image is fixed to the window; that is, whether or not the image scrolls with the page content. There are two values: `scroll` (the default) indicates that the background image should scroll with the content (the traditional behavior of most pre-stylesheet browsers), while `fixed` indicates that the background should be fixed, and should not scroll as the window display region is scrolled.

Note that `fixed` is not widely supported—many browsers treat it as equivalent to `scroll`.

Background-color: Set Background Color/Transparency

Default value:	`transparent`
Values:	`cname`, `#rrggbb`, `#rgb`, `rgb(red, green, blue)`, `rgb(red%, green%, blue%)`, `transparent`
Applicable to Elements:	All elements
Inherit from Parent Element:	no

This property specifies the background color for an element. The default value is `transparent`, in which case the background for the element is transparent, so that the element shows through the background or content of the parent element.

The value can be the keyword `transparent`, a color name (`cname`), or an RGB color code, in any of the three supported formats, as discussed in Appendix A. Note that `background-color` is *not* inherited from a parent element. However, elements are rendered *on top of* their parent element, and will thus display the background color of the parent element, provided their own background is "transparent."

A stylesheet author must be careful to choose background and foreground (text) colors that contrast strongly—otherwise, there will be many users who cannot read the text against the background.

Background-image: Specify Background Image

Default value:	`none`
Values:	`url(urlstring)`, `none`
Applicable to Elements:	All elements
Inherit from Parent Element:	no

This property specifies a background image to display beneath the elements associated with the rule. The default value is `none`, for no background image. The other allowed value is a URL reference to the desired background image. If the referenced image is smaller than the area occupied by the element, then the background image can be *tiled* onto the area. Tiling properties are controlled by `background-repeat`.

When loaded, a background image appears *on top* of any specified background color, so that if the image uses transparency, the transparent pixels will display this background color.

Both `background-color` and `background-image` should be specified, to handle the situation when users disable image loading.

Background-position: Initial Position for Background

Default value:	`0 0`
Values:	`top`, `top center`, `top left`, `top right`, `left`, `left center`, `center`, `center center`, `right`, `right center`, `bottom`, `bottom center`, `bottom left`, `bottom right`,
	`xx%`, `length`,
	`xx% yy%`, `lengthx lengthy`, `xx% lengthy`, `lengthx yy%`
Applicable to Elements:	Block-elements and replaced elements
Inherit from Parent Element:	no

This property specifies the *initial* position for the background image relative to the upper left-hand corner of the inner box of the associated block-level element. There are several ways this position can be specified, and the rules for doing so are rather complicated.

`xx% yy%`—Specifies the horizontal (`xx%`) and vertical (`yy%`) position of the image within the associated element, where `0%` aligns the left or topmost edge of the image with the left or top edge of the area, and `100%` aligns the right or bottom edge of the background with the right or bottom edge of the associated element region (see Figures 6.8 or 6.9). Thus the position `50% 50%` corresponds to a background image centered within the associated element. Note that negative percentages are permitted, as are percentages greater than `100%`. Such values will position the starting location for the background outside the area of the element.

`xx%`—A single percentage specifies the horizontal position of the background image, as per the algorithm described above. The vertical position is taken as `50%`—the background image is vertically centered within the element.

`lengthx lengthy`—Specifies the position of the upper left-hand corner of the background image with respect to the upper left-hand corner of the element area—note that this is quite different from the percentage positions described earlier. Negative values are allowed, in which case the upper left-hand corner of the image lies outside the element. The values can be in any of the CSS-supported length units.

`length`—A single length specifies the horizontal position of the background image, as per the algorithm described previously. The vertical position is assumed to be `50%`—that is, the background image is vertically centered within the element.

`xx% lengthy`—Specifies the horizontal position as a percentage value and the vertical position as an absolute length, using the algorithms described above.

`lengthx yy%`—Specifies the horizontal position as an absolute position and the vertical position as a percentage value, using the algorithms described above.

In addition to these length and percentage specifications, the property also supports the keyword values, each with a well-defined percentage equivalent. These are listed in Table 8.5, and are illustrated in Figure 6.10.

Background-repeat: Background Image Tiling Rule

Default value:	`repeat`
Values:	`no-repeat`, `repeat`, `repeat-x`, `repeat-y`
Applicable to Elements:	All elements
Inherit from Parent Element:	no

This property specifies how a background image should be *tiled* onto the area occupied by the associated element, and is thus only relevant if the background image is smaller than the element's area. The initial position for the tiling is defined by `background-position`, the default being to start with the image in the upper left-hand corner of the element. There are four supported values:

`repeat` (default value)—Repeats the image both horizontally and vertically, to fully tile the region.

`no-repeat`—The background image appears only once, and is not repeated.

`repeat-x`—Repeats the background image horizontally only.

`repeat-y`—Repeats the background image vertically only.

Table 8.5 Keyword Values Supported by the `Background-Position` Property

Values	Percentage equivalent	
`top, top center, center top`	50%	0%
`top left, left top`	0%	0%
`top right, right top`	100%	0%
`left, left center, center left`	0%	50%
`center, center center`	50%	50%
`right, right center, center right`	100%	50%
`bottom left, left bottom`	0%	100%
`bottom, bottom center, center bottom`	50%	100%
`bottom right, right bottom`	100%	100%

Border: Shorthand for All Border Properties

Default value:	*no default value*
Values:	one to three values, specifying the same border width (as per `border-left-width`), border style (as per `border-style`), and border color (as per `border-color`) for all four borders
Applicable to Elements:	All elements
Inherit from Parent Element:	no

This is a shorthand property that defines identical properties for all four borders of the associated elements. `Border` can take from one to three values, with these values specifying: the width of all four borders (as per `border-left-width`), the style for all four borders (as per `border-style`), and the color for all four borders (as per the `border-color`). If one of the specification values is absent, the browser will assume the default values, or the values set by other edge-specific border properties. The following are some simple examples:

`border: thick red`—Draw all four borders as thick red lines, using the default style (or whatever styles were set in other, edge-specific border properties).

`border: medium blue dashed`—Draw all borders as dashed blue lines of medium thickness.

Border-bottom: Shorthand for Bottom Border Properties

Default value:	*no default value*
Values:	one to three values, specifying the bottom border width (as per `border-bottom-width`), the border style (as per `border-style`), and the border color (as per `border-color`)
Applicable to Elements:	All elements
Inherit from Parent Element:	no

This is a shorthand property for defining the properties of the bottom border. It can take from one to three space-separated values, with these values specifying: the width of the border (as per `border-bottom-width`), the style for the right border (as per `border-style`), and the border color (as per `border-color`). If any of the values is absent, the browser will use the value set by any border property that might apply to the bottom border (i.e., from `border-bottom-width`, `border-width`, `border-color`, `border-style` , or `border`). If no value is specified by any such property, the browser will assume the appropriate default value. For example:

`border-bottom: thick red`—Draw the bottom border as a thick red line, using the default style (or whatever style was set by a `border` property). Note that the default style is `none`, which means that the border would not be displayed.

`Border-bottom: medium blue dashed`—Draw the bottom border as a dashed blue line of medium thickness.

Border-bottom-width: Set Border Width at Bottom of Element

Default value:	`medium`
Values:	`medium`, `thick`, `thin`,
	xx`em`, *xx*`ex`, *xx*`cm`, *xx*`in`, *xx*`mm`, *xx*`pc`, *xx*`pt`, *xx*`px`
Applicable to Elements:	All elements
Inherit from Parent Element:	no

This property defines the width of the bottom border for any element associated with the rule (see Chapter 5 for a description of borders and border formatting). The default value is `medium`, corresponding to a medium-sized border (as determined by the browser). Note, however, that if the rule *does not contain* a `border-bottom` (or other) property assignment to set the *style* of the border, then the border is not displayed, since the default style is `none`. If the width is nonzero, the color and design of the border are controlled by the `border-style` and `border-color` properties, which affect the entire border of the element, or by the `border-bottom` property, which can affect only the bottom border. By default, the border takes the same color and properties as the text within the element.

The value can be specified in two ways: using the keywords `medium`, `thick`, and `thin` (the actual width is determined by the browser), or by a length specification. Lengths must be greater than zero, as border widths must be positive. In the case of length specifications, em and ex units are calculated relative to the size of the font inside the element taking the border.

Border-color: Shorthand Border Color Specifications

Default value:	*no default value*
Values:	One to four color specifications
Applicable to Elements:	All elements
Inherit from Parent Element:	no

This property lets an author set border color specifications for all four borders. An author need not specify colors for all four borders, as CSS lets the browser infer the missing values from those that are actually present. For example, specifying a single color value implies that all four borders are of the specified color. Table 8.6 illustrates the different possible ways the `border-color` property can specify the different border colors.

Border-left: Shorthand for Left Border Properties

Default value:	*no default value*
Values:	one to three values, specifying the top border width (as per `border-left-width`), the border style (as per `border-style`), and the border color (as per `border-color`)
Applicable to Elements:	All elements
Inherit from Parent Element:	no

This is a shorthand property for defining the properties of the left-hand borders. It can take from one to three space-separated values, with these values specifying the width of the border (as per `border-left-width`), the style for the left border (as per `border-style`), and the border color (as per `border-color`). If any of the values is absent, the browser will use the value set by any border property that might apply to the left-hand border (i.e., from `border-left-width`, `border-width`, `border-color`, `border-style` , or `border`). If no value is specified by any such property, the browser will assume the appropriate default value. Some examples are:

Table 8.6 The Four Possible Ways That `Border-color` **Can Specify Border Colors Here,** `c1`, `c2`, `c3`, **and** `c4` **are arbitrary color specifications, as per the** `color` **property specification.**

Border-color property value	Color assignments
`border-width: c1`	all border colors set to $c1$
`border-width: c1 c2`	top and bottom border colors set to $c1$, right and left border colors set to $c2$
`border-width: c1 c2 c3`	top border color set to $c1$, right border color set to $c2$, bottom border color set to $c3$, left border color set to $c2$
`border-width: c1 c2 c3 c4`	top border color set to $c1$, right border color set to $c2$, bottom border color set to $c3$, left border color set to $c3$

`border-left: thick dashed red`—Draw the left border as a thick, dashed red line.

`Border-left: blue dashed`—Draw the left border as a dashed blue line with thickness as specified by other border-related properties, or as per the default.

Border-left-width: Set Border Width to Left of Element

Default value:	`medium`
Values:	`medium`, `thick`, `thin`,
	`xxem`, `xxex`, `xxcm`, `xxin`, `xxmm`, `xxpc`, `xxpt`, `xxpx`
Applicable to Elements:	All elements
Inherit from Parent Element:	no

This property defines the width of the left border for any element associated with the rule (see Chapter 5 for a description of borders and border formatting). The default value is `medium`, corresponding to a medium-sized border (as determined by the browser). Note, however, that if the rule *does not contain* a `border-left` (or other) property assignment to set the *style* of the border, then the border is not displayed, since the default style is `none`. If the width is nonzero, the color and design of the border are controlled by the `border-style` and `border-color` properties, which affect the entire border of the element, or by the `border-left` property, which affects only the left border. By default, the border takes the same color as the text within the element.

The value can be specified using the keywords `medium`, `thick`, and `thin` (the actual width is determined by the browser), or by a length specification, where lengths must be greater than zero, as border widths must be positive. In the case of length specifications, em and ex units are calculated relative to the font size within the element taking the border.

Border-right: Shorthand for Right Border Properties

Default value:	*no default value*
Values:	one to three values, specifying the top border width (as per `border-left-width`), the border style (as per `border-style`) and the border color (as per `border-color`)
Applicable to Elements:	All elements
Inherit from Parent Element:	no

This is a shorthand property for defining the properties of the right border. It can take from one to three space-separated values, with these values specifying the width of the border (as per `bor-`

der-right-width), the style for the right border (as per border-style), and the border color (as per border-color). If any of the values is absent, the browser will use the value set by any border property that might apply to the bottom border (i.e., from border-right-width, bor-der-width, border-color, border-style , or border). If no value is specified by any such property, the browser will assume the appropriate default value. Some examples are:

border-right: thick red—Draw the right border as a thick, red line, using the default style (or whatever style was set by a border property). Note that the default style is none, which means that the border would not be displayed.

Border-right: medium blue dashed—Draw the right border as a dashed, blue line of medium thickness.

Border-right-width: Set Border Width to Right of Element

Default value:	medium
Values:	medium, thick, thin, xxem, xxex, xxcm, xxin, xxmm, xxpc, xxpt, xxpx
Applicable to Elements:	All elements
Inherit from Parent Element:	no

This property defines the width of the right border for any element associated with the rule (see Chapter 5 for a description of borders and border formatting). The default value is medium, corre-sponding to a medium-sized border (as determined by the browser). Note, however, that if the rule *does not contain* a border-right (or other) property assignment to set the *style* of the border, then the border is not displayed, since the default style is none. If the width is nonzero, the color and design of the border are controlled by either the border-style and border-color prop-erties, which affect the entire border of the element, or the border-right property, which affects only the right border. By default, the border takes the same color as the text within the element.

The value can be specified using the keywords medium, thick, and thin (the actual width is determined by the browser), or as a length specification, where lengths must be greater than zero, as border widths must be positive. In the case of length specifications, em and ex units are calculat-ed relative to the font size inside the element.

Border-style: Set Formatting for Border Lines

Default value:	*no default value*
Values:	One to four space-separated values, where those values can be: dashed, dotted, double, groove, inset, none, outset, ridge, or solid

Applicable to Elements: All elements

Inherit from Parent Element: no

This property defines the style for the borders drawn around the associated elements. `Border-style` can take from one to four values: A single value defines the border style for all borders, while four values assign different border styles to the four different borders. The meanings of the four possible forms are described in Table 8.8. The default value for each border is `none`, in which case the border is not drawn, regardless of the specified width or color. The different named values and their meanings are summarized in Table 8.7.

NOTE Not All Border Types Are Supported

Some browsers may interpret some or all of these border types (except for the type `none`) as `solid`. For example, Navigator does not understand the `dashed` or `dotted` styles, and uses `solid` in their place.

Table 8.7 The Border Style Keyword Values and Their Meanings

Style Keyword	Description
dashed	The border is a dashed line on top of the background color of the associated element.
dotted	The border is a dotted line on top of the background color of the associated element.
double	The border is a double line on top of the background color of the associated element. The inner and outer lines are drawn on the inner and outer edges of the border width region.
groove	The border is a three-dimensional groove on top of the background color of the associated element (as with an **HR** element).
inset	The border is a drawn such that the element content appears inset into the page.
none	No border is drawn. This is the default value.
outset	The border is drawn such that the element content appears depressed into the page.
ridge	The border is drawn as a raised ridge.
solid	The border is a solid line. The color is set by the `border-color` property or is inherited from the color property of the associated element.

Table 8.8 The Four Possible Ways That Border-style Can Be Used to Specify Border Styles

Here, s1, s2, s3, and s4 are style specifications, as described in Table 8.7.

Border-style property value	Border style assignments
border-style: *s1*	all border styles set to *s1*
border-style: *s1 s2*	top and bottom border styles set to *s1*, right and left border styles set to *s2*
border-style: *s1 s2 s3*	top border style set to *s1*, right border style set to *s2*, bottom border style set to *s3*, left border style set to *s2*
border-style: *s1 s2 s3 s4*	top border style set to *s1*, right border style set to *s2*, bottom border style set to *s3*, left border style set to *s4*

Border-top: Shorthand for Top Border Properties

Default value:	*no default value*
Values:	one to three values, specifying the top border width (as per border-top-width), the border style (as per border-style), and the border color (as per border-color)
Applicable to Elements:	All elements
Inherit from Parent Element:	no

This is a shorthand property for defining the properties of the top border. It can take from one to three space-separated values, with these values specifying the width of the border (as per border-top-width), the style for the top border (as per border-style), and the border color (as per border-color). If any of the values is absent, the browser will use the value set by any border property that might apply to the top border (i.e., from border-top-width, border-width, border-color, border-style, or border). If no value is specified by any such property, the browser will assume the appropriate default value. For example:

border-top: solid—Draw the top border as a solid line, using the width and color set by the border-top-width, border-style, border-color, or border properties, if so specified, or by using the default values for these properties, if no alternative values are given.

Border-top-width: Set Border Width at Top of Element

Default value:	medium
Values:	medium, thick, thin,

*xx*em, *xx*ex, *xx*cm, *xx*in, *xx*mm, *xx*pc, *xx*pt, *xx*px

Applicable to Elements:	All elements
Inherit from Parent Element:	no

This property defines the width of the top border for any element associated with the rule (see Chapter 5 for a description of borders and border formatting). The default value is `medium`, corresponding to a medium-sized border (as determined by the browser). Note, however, that if the rule *does not contain* a `border-top` (or other) property assignment to set the *style* of the border, then the border is not displayed, since the default style is `none`. If the width is nonzero, the color and design of the border are controlled either by the `border-style` and `border-color` properties, which affect the entire border of the element, or by the `border-top` property, which affects only the top border. By default, the border takes the same color as the text within the element.

The value can be specified in two ways: using the keywords `medium`, `thick`, and `thin` (the actual width is determined by the browser), or by a length specification. Lengths must be greater than zero, as border widths must be positive. In the case of length specifications, em and ex units are calculated relative to the size of the font inside the element taking the border.

Border-width: Shorthand Border Width Specifications

Default value:	*no default value*
Values:	one to four border width specifications, each width as per `border-width-top`, etc. See Table 8.9 for associated meanings.
Applicable to Elements:	All elements
Inherit from Parent Element:	no

This property lets an author set multiple border-width specifications (left, bottom, etc.) in one declaration. An author need not specify all the `border-width` widths or heights, as CSS lets the browser infer the missing values from those that are given. For example, specifying a single `border-width` value implies that all four borders are of the specified size. Table 8.9 illustrates the different possible ways the `border-width` property can specify the border widths.

Table 8.9 The Four Possible Ways That `Border-width` Can Be Used to Specify Border Widths

Here, xx, yy, zz and ww are arbitrary width specifications, as per the `border-width-top` property specification.

Border-width Property Value	Border width assignments
`border-width:` *xx*	all border widths set to *xx*

Continued

Table 8.9 *Continued*

Border-width Property Value	Border width assignments
`border-width: xx yy`	top and bottom border widths set to *xx*, right and left border widths set to *yy*
`border-width: xx yy zz`	top border width set to *xx*, right border width set to *yy*, bottom border width set to *zz*, left border width set to *yy*
`border-width: xx yy zz ww`	top border width set to *xx*, right border width set to *yy*, bottom border width set to *zz*, left border width set to *ww*

Clear: Specify Placement Relative to Floating Elements

Default value:	`none`
Values:	`both`, `left`, `none`, `right`
Applicable to Elements:	All elements
Inherit from Parent Element:	no

This property controls the positioning of elements with respect to adjacent, floated elements; it can be used to reposition an element such that it is cleared to start below a floated element, and not beside it. Clearing is done with respect to the block-level element that contains an element (and that contains the floating element); thus, if an element lies within a **TD** table cell, it will be cleared with respect to the edges of the table cell. The four allowed values are:

`both`—The element is moved down so that there are no floating elements between the cleared element and the left and right inner edges of the parent block-level element. In essence, the element is *cleared* to both the left and right.

`left`—The element is moved down below any element that has floated to the left. That is, the element is *cleared* to the left.

`right`—The element is moved down below any element that has floated to the right. That is, the element is *cleared* to the right.

`none` (*default value*)—The element is not moved—there can be floating elements to either the left and right of the element. This is the default.

`Clear` is a generalization of `<BR CLEAR="...">` HTML elements. However, this property can be applied to any element, eliminating the need for purely formatting-specific **BR**s. Example 18 in Chapter 5 illustrates the use of `clear`.

Color: Set the Text Color

Default value:	depends on browser (usually black)
Value:	cname, #rrggbb, #rgb, rgb(red, green, blue), rgb(red%, green%, blue%)
Applicable to Elements:	All elements
Inherit from Parent Element:	yes

This property sets the text color for the referenced element. This is often called the *foreground* color, to distinguish it from the *background* color of the window. Text color is inherited from the parent element, as one would expect. Note, however, that background color is not inherited (see the background-color).

Color can be specified in several ways. These include: named colors (*cname*), 24-bit hexadecimal RGB codes (#*rrggbb*, or #*rgb*), decimal integer RGB codes (rgb[*red, green, blue*]) or as percentage RGB code (rgb[*red%, green%, blue%*]). The meanings of these codes are described briefly in Table 8.4, and in detail in Appendix A.

Note that although a 24-bit RGB system can representing 16,777,216 different colors, many computers are only capable of 256 (8-bit color). This can cause problems if the color requested cannot be displayed on the local system—in this case, the computer either will replace the requested color by one that is available (color *substitution*) or will *dither* the requested color using a mixture of the supported colors. See Appendix A for more details.

Display: Specify How Element Is Processed

Default value:	block
Values:	block, inline, list-item, none
Applicable to Elements:	All elements
Inherit from Parent Element:	no

Display specifies the *formatting type* for the associated HTML elements, and can be used to override the default formatting types listed in Table 8.3. The default value is block, although for non-block elements this is overridden by the browser's default stylesheet. The four possible values are:

block (*default value*)—Formats the element as a block-level formatting element.

inline—Formats the element as an inline formatting element.

`list-item`—Formats the element as a list-item formatting element.

`none`—Does not display the element. The element, and all of the elements contained within it, will not be displayed by the browser.

`Display` is not inherited, but using `display:none` to hide an element will naturally hide all the elements contained within it. Note that some browsers ignore `display` and instead use the default HTML element formatting types set by the browser.

Float: Float Element to Side of Parent Element

Default value:	`none`
Values:	`left`, `none`, `right`
Applicable to Elements:	All elements
Inherit from Parent Element:	no

This property lets a stylesheet author specify *floating* positioning for an element. A floated element floats either to the left or the right of the parent element, with subsequent content of the parent element flowing around the floated element. This is similar to using **ALIGN**=“left” or “right” attributes with **IMG** elements to float an image to the edge of the parent element. However, `float` can be applied to any element, including one containing text.

There are three possible values for `float`:

`left`—Float the element to the left-hand inner edge of the parent element.

`right`—Float the element to the right-hand inner edge of the parent element.

`none` (*default value*)—Do not float the element.

Note that the values `left` and `right` turn the affected element into a block-level element, although margin properties are handled differently than for non-floated block-level elements. See Chapter 5 for details.

Font: Shorthand for Font and Line Spacing Properties

Default value:	*no default value*
Value:	one to six values, in any order, specifying the font family (as per `font-family`), the font size (as per `font-size`), the font style (as per `font-style`), the font variant (as per `font-variant`), the font weight (as per `font-weight`), and the line height (as per `line-height`). These are combined as per the description below.

Applicable to Elements:	All elements
Inherit from Parent Element:	yes

This is a shorthand for specifying the line spacing plus the five font-related property values. The value is a space-separated collection of the different values, except that the font-size and line-height properties must be combined using the form

`size/height`

where *size* is any valid `font-size` value, and *height* is any valid `line-height` value. The line height can be given without the font size, or vice versa, in which case the forms are:

Size only	*size*
Line height only	*/height*

An example `font` property declaration is:

`font: bold 80%/1.5 Arial, Helvetica, sans-serif italic`

Font properties are described in detail in Chapter 3, while the `font` property is discussed in Chapter 4.

Font-family: Selector for Font or Font Family

Default value:	Depends on browser; often Times Roman
Values:	Comma-separated list of *font names* or generic *font families*
Valid HTML Elements:	All elements
Inherit from Parent Element:	yes

This property specifies the font *face* or *family* desired within the associated elements. The value is a comma-separated list of the desired fonts, given in decreasing order of preference. A browser will look through this list of fonts, and will choose the first font available on the browser. For example, the declaration

`font-family: "gill sans", arial, helvetica, sans-serif`

specifies three alternative fonts, the preferred one being "gill sans." If a font name consists of more than one word, then the name must be enclosed in single or double quotation marks, as shown in this example.

The last entry in a list of fonts should be a *generic font name*. In CSS, generic names request a generic type of font. This is important for handling the case when none of the specifically request- ed fonts are available. The five generic family names, along with an example from each family, are:

Generic Family Name	Example Font
serif	Times New Roman
sans-serif	Helvetica
cursive	*Shelley Volante BT*
fantasy	**Bragadoccio**
monospace	`Courier`

Most computers do not have cursive or fantasy fonts installed, in which case these generic fami- ly names are of no use. If none of the listed fonts are available, the browser will default to the font employed by the parent element.

Font-size: Set Size of Displayed Font

Default value:	`medium`
Value:	`xx-small, x-small, small, medium, large, x-large, xx-large, larger, smaller, xxem, xxex, xx%, xxcm, xxin, xxmm, xxpc, xxpt, xxpx`
Applicable to Elements:	All elements
Inherit from Parent Element:	yes

This property specifies the desired size for the font within the associated element. The size can be specified either as an absolute size (using length measures or specific keywords) or as a size rela- tive to the font size of the parent element. Even within these two categories, there are a number of ways (perhaps too many!) of specifying size. The allowed values are:

xxcm, xxin, xxmm, xxpc, xxpt, xxpx—Specify the font size as an *absolute* size using any of the CSS- supported length units.

`xx-small, x-small, small, medium, large, x-large, xx-large`—Specifies the font size as an absolute size, relative to a table of seven sizes maintained by the browser. The actual sizes corresponding to these values will vary from browser to browser. CSS recommends that each step in this size scale corre- spond to a size ratio of 1.5. Note that there is no guarantee that all seven sizes will be available on all browsers.

xx%—Specifies the font size as a percentage of the font size of the *parent element*.

*xx*em, *xx*ex—Specifies the size relative to the font size of the *parent element*.

larger, smaller—Specifies font size relative to the font size of the *parent element*. CSS recommends that each change correspond to a font size ratio of 1.5.

See Chapter 3 for details of this and other font properties. Note that, although the default size is medium, this property is inherited—inheritance will override the default value. One result of this fact is that setting a specific font size for the document **BODY** will cause all heading elements to have the same font size as regular body content.

Font-style: Selector for Font Style

Default value:	normal
Values	normal, italic, oblique
Applies to Elements:	All elements
Inherit from Parent:	yes

This property specifies the desired italic nature of the font, the default value being the non-italicized form. The three possible values are:

normal (*default value*)—The normal or upright version of the font.

italic—The italicized version of the font.

oblique—The slanted or oblique version of the font.

Not all fonts come in both italic and oblique forms. If the CSS rule requests italic, the browser will first look for an italic variant of the font. If one is not available, it will look for an oblique version. If an oblique version is not available, it will use the normal variant of the preferred font. On the other hand, if the CSS rule requests oblique, the browser will first look for an oblique version, and failing that will look for an oblique version of the next font specified in the font-family specification, and proceed through the entire list of specified fonts. If no oblique form is found, the browser will substitute a normal version of the original font. See Chapter 3 for details of this and other font properties.

Font-variant: Selector for Small-Caps Lettering

Default value:	normal
Values:	normal, small-caps

Applicable to Elements: All elements

Inherit from Parent: yes

This property specifies variants of a font, excluding those variants due to italic styling or weight. CSS currently supports only two values for font-variant: `normal` for the regular style of the font, and `small-caps` for small-caps styling, the default value being `normal`. `Small-caps` requests that both upper- and lowercase letters be displayed using an uppercase font, with a slightly smaller font being used for the lowercase letters. See Chapter 3 for details of this and other font properties.

Font-weight: Set Weight for Font

Default value: `normal`

Values: `bolder`, `lighter`,

`normal`, `bold`, `100`, `200`, `300`, `400`, `500`, `600`, `700`, `800`, `900`

Applicable to Elements: All elements

Inherit from Parent Element: yes

This property sets the weight, or thickness, for the font. Since there are many non-standardized ways of naming weights, CSS chose a numerical scale, ranging from 100 (lightest weight) to 900 (heaviest weight) in steps of 100. On this scale, the "normal" weight for a given font is 400, while a "bold" weight is 700. Note that the absolute weight corresponding to a particular number varies significantly from font family to font family.

Of course, not all fonts come in nine different weights. CSS guarantees that the numeric scale will always produce font weights that are ordered such that 100 is always lighter than or equal to 200, 200 is lighter than or equal to 300, and so on. CSS also supports four weight keywords, with associated meanings:

`normal`—The normal weight for the current font (a weight of 400).

`bold`—A weight that is characteristically bold for the current font (a weight of 700).

`lighter`—The font version with the next lighter weight. The resulting weight depends on the font and on the weight inherited from the parent element. If a lighter weight font is unavailable, the browser will use the inherited weight.

`bolder`—The font version with the next heavier weight. The resulting weight depends on the font and on the weight inherited from the parent element. If a higher weight font is unavailable, the browser will use the inherited weight.

CSS does not support any other weight descriptions (medium, demibold, heavy, etc.) commonly used in font descriptions, since these words have meanings that vary significantly from font to font. Additional details about these issues (and difficulties!) are found in Chapter 3.

Height: Set Height of the Element

Default value:	`auto`
Values:	`auto`, *xx*em, *xx*ex, *xx*%, *xx*cm, *xx*in *xx*mm, *xx*pc, *xx*pt, *xx*px
Applicable to Elements:	Block level and replaced elements
Inherit from Parent Element:	no

This property (closely related to `width`) sets the height for the inner box containing the associated element. The details of how this property is used are found in Chapter 5, and also in Chapter 9. `Height` is most useful with replaced elements, such as **IMG** or **OBJECT**, which are replaced by downloaded data with an intrinsic size (e.g., a 300-by-243 pixel image) that is unknown until the data arrive. In these cases, `height` can set the height for the region displaying the element. For **IMG**, the image dimensions can also be rescaled (shrinking or expanding) to fit the specified box. For other types of replaced data, this may not be possible.

If applied to a block-level element, `height` specifies the height of the box into which the content should be placed. This may mean adding space above and/or below the text (if the content is smaller than the allocated region), or adding scrollbars to allow viewing of non-visible text (if the content is larger than the allocated region). Note, however, that most browsers do not support `height` properties for block-level elements, and use browser-determined height values instead.

`Height` can take several values. The keyword `auto` means that the height size is automatically scaled, either to the actual size of the element, or such that the height/width ratio of the object is kept constant. Heights can also be given as absolute or relative lengths, in any of the standard units. Relative lengths are determined relative to the font size of the *parent* element. Percentage values should be relative to the height of the parent element.

Letter-spacing: Adjust Default Spacing between Letters

Default value:	`normal`
Values:	`normal`, *xx*em, *xx*ex, *xx*cm, *xx*in *xx*mm, *xx*pc, *xx*pt, *xx*px
Applicable to Elements:	All elements
Inherit from Parent Element:	yes

This property allows for adjustment of the default spacing between adjacent characters. The value can be either the keyword `normal`, which references the default spacing algorithm for the font, or a positive or negative length in any of the supported length units. A positive length increases the letter spacing, while a negative value decreases it. Specifying a letter spacing should also disable the use of *ligatures* (pairs of characters that are physically joined when typeset), and should stop the browser from adjusting letter spacing when trying to justify text flow. In contrast, the keyword `normal` lets the browser support ligatures or adjust letter spacing as desired.

Note that the default letter spacing is affected by the choice of text alignment (see `text-align`), since full text justification can lead to adjusted letter spacing in the associated text.

Most current browsers ignore letter-spacing values other than `normal`.

Line-height: Alignment of Text within an Element

Default value:	`normal`
Values:	`normal`, *xx*,
	xx%, *xx*em, *xx*ex, *xx*cm, *xx*in *xx*mm, *xx*pc, *xx*pt, *xx*px
Applicable to Elements:	Block-level elements
Inherit from Parent Element:	yes

This property sets the line spacing within an element. As discussed in Chapter 5, this also defines the top and bottom inner edges of the block element, which in turn define a block element's height. Within a block element, the line height is also equivalent to the spacing between two subsequent text baselines.

There are a number of possible values for this property. These are:

`normal`—Lets the browser select a spacing appropriate to the font being used.

*xx*em, *xx*ex—Specifies the line height relative to the size of the font within the element (*not* relative to the size in the parent element).

*xx*cm, *xx*in *xx*mm, *xx*pc, *xx*pt, *xx*px—Specifies the line height using any of the absolute length units.

xx%—Specifies the line height as a percentage of the size of the font in the element.

xx—Specifies the line height as a ratio relative to the current font size. This value changes the way line height is inherited (see discussion).

In general, line height is inherited as an absolute length; thus, if the font size is 12pt and the line height is 150%, then the resulting line height is 18pt, and this length is passed down to any child elements. However, if the line height is specified as a number (e.g., 1.5), then the child element inherits this ratio, and will multiply the font size of the parent element by this ratio to determine the local line height. See Chapter 4 for more details.

List-style: Shorthand for List Item Properties

Default value:	*no default value*
Values:	one to three values, in any order, specifying the list style type (as per `list-style-type`), the list style image (as per `list-style-image`), and the list style position (as per `list-style-position`)
Applicable to Elements:	List-item elements
Inherit from Parent Element:	yes

This is a shorthand property for setting the type properties for list-item decorations or markers. The property can take up to three space-separated values, corresponding to the values allowed by the `list-style-type`, `list-style-image`, and `list-style-position` properties. List-item formatting is discussed in detail in Chapter 5.

List-style-image: Specify Image for List Item Marker

Default value:	none
Values:	url(*urlstring*), none
Applicable to Elements:	List-item elements
Inherit from Parent Element:	yes

This property specifies an image file to use as a list item marker, in place of the marker specified by the `list-style-type` property (or the default marker). The value none indicates that no image should be used, and that the browser should use the decoration indicated by `list-style-type`. There are no current browsers that support this property.

List-style-position: Set Positioning for List Item Markers

Default value:	outside
Values:	inside, outside
Applicable to Elements:	List-item elements
Inherit from Parent Element:	yes

This property specifies the placement for list-item markers (either default bullets or numbers, or images specified by `list-style-image`). The value `outside` (the default) places the marker outside the box containing the list item text, while the value `inside` places the marker within the box containing the list item text. These two forms are illustrated in Figure 5.18. There are no current browsers that support this property.

List-style-type: Set Decoration for Items in Lists

Default value:	`circle`
Values:	`circle`, `disc`, `none`, `square`, `decimal`, `lower-alpha`, `lower-roman`, `upper-alpha`, `upper-roman`
Applicable to Elements:	All items with display value of `list-item`
Inherit from Parent Element:	yes

This property specifies the type of marker to use with items in a list. The default value for this property is `circle`, although the browser's own stylesheet will override this to set numbered items for **OL** ordered lists. The supported values have largely self-evident meanings; detailed descriptions are found in Table 5.8.

Note that a marker image specified by `list-style-image` will override the decoration specified by `list-style-type`, provided the image is actually loaded by the browser. Thus if image loading is disabled, the items will be decorated as indicated by the `list-style-type` property. If images are then loaded, the decorations will be replaced by the specified image.

Margin: Shorthand Margin Specifications

Default value:	*no default value*
Values:	One, two, three, or four margin width specifications, each as per `margin-top`. The meanings of the four variants are given in Table 8.10.
Applicable to Elements:	All elements
Inherit from Parent Element:	no

This shorthand property lets an author specify multiple margin widths within the same margin assignment. An author need not specify all the margin widths, as CSS lets the browser infer the missing widths from the values that are actually present. For example, specifying a single value implies that all four margins are of the specified size. Table 8.10 illustrates the different ways the margin property can be used to specify the margin widths.

Table 8.10 The Five Possible Ways That Margin Can Be Used to Specify Margin Widths

Here, xx, yy, zz, and ww are arbitrary width specifications, as per the `margin-top` property specification.

Margin property value	Margin assignments
margin: *xx*	all margins set to *xx*
margin: *xx yy*	top and bottom margins set to *xx*, right and left margins set to *yy*
margin: *xx yy zz*	top margin set to *xx*, right margin set to *yy*, bottom margin set to *zz*, left margin set to *yy*
margin: *xx yy zz ww*	top margin set to *xx*, right margin set to *yy*, bottom margin set to *zz*, left margin set to *ww*
margin: auto	browser automatically determines appropriate margin widths

Margin-bottom: Set Bottom Margin for Element

Default value:	0
Values:	auto, *xx*em, *xx*ex, *xx*%, *xx*cm, *xx*in *xx*mm, *xx*pc, *xx*pt, *xx*px
Applicable to Elements:	All elements
Inherit from Parent Element:	no

This property sets the length/offset of the bottom margin for the element associated with the rule, relative to the top of the subsequent formatting element in the display. The space defined by the margin is transparent, and the content of the parent element shows through. The size of the margin can be specified in absolute (inches, picas, etc.), or relative (em or ex) length units, as a percentage, or via the keyword auto. The default value is 0, which implies no margin. Relative lengths are determined relative to the font size of the element (which is inherited from the parent if the element does not contain any text), while percentage values should be calculated relative to the parent element *width*. Note, however, that all current browsers actually calculate percentage margins relative to the full width of the display canvas. The keyword auto lets the browser determine a (hopefully) appropriate margin size.

Note that margin lengths can be either positive or negative: Negative margins can position formatting elements on top of (or underneath) other formatting elements. Also, the effect of the keyword auto varies depending on the type of formatting element (block-level, inline, floating) the margin is applied to, as does the way margins are combined between adjacent elements. Please see Chapter 5 for a detailed discussion of these issues.

Margin-left: Set Left Margin for Element

Default value:	0
Values:	auto, *xx*em, *xx*ex, *xx*%, *xx*cm, *xx*in *xx*mm, *xx*pc, *xx*pt, *xx*px
Applicable to Elements:	All elements
Inherit from Parent Element:	no

This property sets the length/offset of the left margin for the element associated with the rule, relative to the left inner edge of the parent element (if a block-level element) or possibly the right side of a previously left-floated element (if the element is itself floated to the left). The margin space is transparent, and any underlying content shows through. The size of the margin can be specified in absolute (inches, picas, etc.) or relative (em or ex) length units, as a percentage, or via the keyword auto. The default value is 0, which implies no margin. Relative length units are determined relative to the font size of the current element (which is inherited from the parent if the element does not contain any text), while percentage value should be calculated relative to the parent element width (current browsers actually calculate this relative to full width of the browser canvas). The keyword auto lets the browser determine a (hopefully) appropriate margin size.

Note that margin lengths can be either positive or negative: Negative margins can position formatting elements on top of (or underneath) other formatting elements. Also, the effect of the keyword auto varies depending on the type of formatting element (block-level, inline, floating) the margin is applied to, as does the way margins are combined between adjacent elements. Please see Chapter 5 for a detailed discussion of these issues.

Margin-right: Set Right Margin for Element

Default value:	0
Values:	auto, *xx*em, *xx*ex, *xx*%, *xx*cm, *xx*in *xx*mm, *xx*pc, *xx*pt, *xx*px
Applicable to Elements:	All elements
Inherit from Parent Element:	no

This property sets the length/offset of the right margin for the element associated with the rule, relative to the right inner edge of the parent element (if a block-level element) or possibly the left side of a previously right-floated element (if the element is itself floated to the right). The margin space is transparent, and any underlying content shows through. The size of the margin can be specified in absolute (inches, picas, etc.) or relative (em or ex) length units, as a percentage, or via the keyword auto. The default value is 0, which implies no margin. Relative length units are determined relative to the font size of the current element (which is inherited from the parent if the element does not contain any text), while percentage value should be calculated relative to the parent element *width* (current browsers actually calculate percentage margins relative to the full width of the browser canvas). The keyword `auto` lets the browser determine a (hopefully) appropriate margin size.

Note that margin lengths can be either positive or negative: Negative margins can position formatting elements on top of (or underneath) other formatting elements. Also, the effect of the keyword `auto` varies depending on the type of formatting element (block-level, inline, floating) the margin is applied to, as does the way margins are combined between adjacent elements. Please see Chapter 5 for a detailed discussion of these issues.

Margin-top: Set Top Margin for Element

Default value:	0
Values:	`auto, xxem, xxex, xx%, xxcm, xxin xxmm, xxpc, xxpt, xxpx`
Applicable to Elements:	All elements
Inherit from Parent Element:	no

This property sets the length/offset of the top margin for the element associated with the rule, relative to the bottom of the preceding formatting element in the display. The margin space is transparent, and any underlying content shows through. The size of the margin can be specified in absolute (inches, picas, etc.) or relative (em or ex) length units, as a percentage, or via the keyword `auto`. The default value is 0, which implies no margin. Relative length units are determined relative to the font size of the current element (which is inherited from the parent if the element does not contain any text), while percentage value should be calculated relative to the parent element *width* (current browsers actually calculate percentage margins relative to the full width of the browser canvas). The keyword `auto` lets the browser determine a (hopefully) appropriate margin size.

Note that margin lengths can be either positive or negative: Negative margins can position formatting elements on top of (or underneath) other formatting elements. Also, the effect of the keyword `auto` varies depending on the type of formatting element (block-level, inline, floating) the margin is applied to, as does the way margins are combined between adjacent elements. Please see Chapter 5 for a detailed discussion of these issues.

Padding: Shorthand Padding Specifications

Default value:	*no default value*
Values:	One, two, three, or four padding widths specifications, each as per `padding-top`. The meanings of the four variants are given in Table 8.11.

Applicable to Elements:	All elements
Inherit from Parent Element:	no

This property lets an author set multiple padding space specifications (left, bottom, etc.) within the same declaration. An author need not specify all the padding space widths or heights, as CSS lets the browser infer the missing widths from the values that are actually present. For example, specifying a single padding space implies that all four margins are of the specified size.

Table 8.11 illustrates the different possible ways the margin property can be used to specify the margin widths. Please see the `padding-bottom` property (and Chapter 5) for a detailed description of padding and padding properties.

Table 8.11 The Four Possible Ways That Padding Space Can Be Used to Specify Padding Space Widths

Here, xx, yy, zz, and ww are arbitrary width specifications, as per the `padding-bottom` **property specification.**

Padding Property Value	Padding assignments
`padding:` *xx*	all padding spaces set to *xx*
`padding:` *xx yy*	top and bottom padding space set to *xx*, right and left padding space set to *yy*
`padding:` *xx yy zz*	top padding space set to *xx*, right padding space set to *yy*, bottom padding space set to *zz*, left padding space set to *yy*
`padding:` *xx yy zz ww*	top padding space set to *xx*, right padding space to *yy*, bottom padding space set to *zz*, left padding space set to *ww*

Padding-bottom: Height of Bottom Padding Space

Default value:	0
Values:	*xx*em, *xx*ex, *xx*%, *xx*cm, *xx*in *xx*mm, *xx*pc, *xx*pt, *xx*px
Applicable to Elements:	All elements
Inherit from Parent Element:	no

This property sets the height of the bottom padding space for the element associated with the rule. The value can be specified in absolute (inches, picas, etc.) or relative (em or ex) length units or as a percentage. Em and ex units are determined relative to the size of the font contained within the element (or the inherited font size, for elements that do not contain text). Percentage values should be evaluated with respect to the *width* of the parent element (current browsers actually calculate percentage padding lengths relative to the full width of the browser display canvas). The default value for this property is zero, corresponding to no padding space. Padding lengths cannot be negative—obviously, a padding space of zero width is as small as it can get!

Padding space acts as a "spacer" around the element content. Background properties applied to an element, such as background color, will affect the region marked out by the padding properties. Background images tile onto the padding area, subject to the `background-repeat` and `background-position` property values.

Padding is discussed in depth in Chapter 5, and you are referred there for details.

Padding-left: Width of Left-hand Padding Space

Default value:	0
Values:	*xx*em, *xx*ex, *xx*%, *xx*cm, *xx*in *xx*mm, *xx*pc, *xx*pt, *xx*px
Applicable to Elements:	All elements
Inherit from Parent Element:	no

This property sets the width of the left padding space for the element associated with the rule. The value can be specified in absolute (inches, picas, etc.) or relative (em or ex) length units or as a percentage. Em and ex units are determined relative to the size of the font contained within the element (or the inherited font size, for elements that do not contain text). Percentage values should be evaluated with respect to the *width* of the parent element (current browsers actually calculate percentage padding lengths relative to the full width of the browser display canvas). The default value for this property is zero, corresponding to no padding space. Padding lengths cannot be negative—obviously, a padding space of zero width is as small as it can get!

Padding space acts as a "spacer" around the element content. Background properties applied to an element, such as background color, will affect the region marked out by the padding properties. Background images tile onto the padding area, subject to the `background-repeat` and `background-position` property values.

Padding is discussed in depth in Chapter 5, and you are referred there for details.

Padding-right: Width of Right-hand Padding Space

Default value:	0
Values:	*xx*em, *xx*ex, *xx*%, *xx*cm, *xx*in *xx*mm, *xx*pc, *xx*pt, *xx*px
Applicable to Elements:	All elements
Inherit from Parent Element:	no

This property sets the width of the right padding space for the element associated with the rule. The value can be specified in absolute (inches, picas, etc.) or relative (em or ex) length units, or as a percentage. Em and ex units are determined relative to the size of the font contained within the element (or the inherited font size, for elements that do not contain text). Percentage values should be evaluated with respect to the *width* of the parent element (current browsers actually calculate percentage padding lengths relative to the full width of the browser display canvas). The default value for this property is zero, corresponding to no padding space. Padding lengths cannot be negative—obviously, a padding space of zero width is as small as it can get!

Padding space acts as a "spacer" around the element content. Background properties applied to an element, such as background color, will affect the region marked out by the padding properties. Background images tile onto the padding area, subject to the `background-repeat` and `background-position` property values.

Padding is discussed in depth in Chapter 5, and you are referred there for details.

Padding-top: Height of Top Padding Space

Default value:	0
Values:	`xxem, xxex, xx%, xxcm, xxin xxmm, xxpc, xxpt, xxpx`
Applicable to Elements:	All elements
Inherit from Parent Element:	no

This property sets the height of the top padding space for the element associated with the rule. The value can be specified in absolute (inches, picas, etc.) or relative (em or ex) length units, or as a percentage. Em and ex units are determined relative to the size of the font contained within the element (or the inherited font size, for elements that do not contain text). Percentage values are evaluated with respect to the *width* of the parent element. The default value for this property is zero, corresponding to no padding space. Padding lengths cannot be negative—obviously, a padding space of zero width is as small as it can get!

Padding space acts as a "spacer" around the element content. Background properties applied to an element, such as background color, will affect the region marked out by the padding properties. Background images tile onto the padding area, subject to the `background-repeat` and `background-position` property values.

Padding is discussed in depth in Chapter 5, and you are referred there for details.

Text-align: Alignment of Text within Element

Default value:	browser-specific; usually `left`
Values:	`center, justify, left, right`

Applicable to Elements:	Block-level elements
Inherit from Parent Element:	yes

This property specifies the alignment of text within the element, and thus applies only to block-level elements. There are four possible values, the default value usually being `left`, for left-aligned text (this may vary, depending on language). The four values are:

center—Centers the text between the left and right inner edges of the element .

justify—Fully justifies the text between the left and right inner edges of the element. Justification may require that the browser adjust the word spacing and letter spacing of the text content. These characteristics the can be affected by the `word-spacing` and `letter-spacing` properties.

left—Aligns the text along the left inner edge of the element; the right text margin is ragged.

right—Aligns the text along the right inner edge of the element; the left text margin is ragged.

Note that some browsers cannot fully justify text, and use either left or right justification instead.

Text-decoration: Special Text Decoration Properties

Default value:	none
Values:	blink, line-through, none, overline, underline
Applicable to Elements:	All elements
Inherit from Parent Element:	no

This property defines special text formatting, and thus is relevant only to elements that contain text. It is not relevant to non-text elements (e.g., **IMG**) nor to non-text content of an element (e.g., an **IMG** inside an **EM**).

The supported values are:

blink—Renders the text as blinking.

line-through—Draws the text with a line struck through the words.

none (*default value*)—Applies no decoration to the text.

overline—Draws the text with a line above it.

underline—Draws the text with a line underneath it.

A declaration can specify multiple values, as a space-separated list. Any displayable text decoration, such as a horizontal line, should take the same color as the text content of the element. Note that `text-decoration` is not inherited, but that the decoration should be displayed "through" any child elements. This means that the text decoration will retain the same vertical position/color specified in the parent element, even if the text color or font size is changed in the child. Please see Chapter 4 for more details.

Text-indent: Indent of First Line of Text

Default value:	0
Values:	`xxem, xxex, xx%, xxcm, xxin xxmm, xxpc, xxpt, xxpx`
Applicable to Elements:	Block-level elements
Inherit from Parent Element:	yes

This property specifies the indent for the first line of text within the element. This property is typically used with paragraph elements to define a paragraph indent. The value can be a length in any of the relative (em, ex), or absolute (picas, inches, cm, etc.) units, or it can be a percentage, which is evaluated with respect to the width of the parent element. Child elements inherit the calculated absolute indent, and not the percentage value.

Text indents can be negative, to create "hanging" indents; note that this results in the text starting outside the box of the element.

Since this property is inherited, defining an indent for a **DIV** will cause this same absolute indent to be implemented for all **P** elements inside the **DIV**.

Text-transform: Perform Case Transformations of Text

Default value:	`none`
Values:	`capitalize, lowercase, none, uppercase`
Applicable to Elements:	All elements
Inherit from Parent Element:	yes

This property defines special case conversion transformations desired before the element text is rendered for display. The default value is `none`, to indicate that no transformation is required. The allowed values are:

`capitalize`—Converts the leading letter of each word to uppercase.

`lowercase`—Converts all letters in the element to lowercase.

none (*default value*)—No text transformation. Although this is the default, bear in mind that this property is inherited.

uppercase—Converts all letters in the element to uppercase.

Text transformation is relevant only to characters that have both upper- and lowercase forms. Many languages have characters that do not have these two forms, in which case this property is meaningless. This property is described in more detail in Chapter 4.

Vertical-align: Define Vertical Alignment of Element

Default value:	baseline
Value:	baseline, bottom, sub, super, top, text-top, middle, text-bottom, *xx%*
Applicable to Elements:	Inline elements
Inherit from Parent Element:	no

This property defines the vertical positioning of the element. This position can be expressed in three ways: with respect to the parent element; with respect to the entire line on which the text appears; or as a percentage of the *line height* of the surrounding text. This property is often used to align images within a line of text—for example, to align images containing text or mathematical expressions with the regular text with which they are associated. It can also be used to create text superscripts or subscripts. Note, however, that the super/subscripted text will have the same font size as the parent element.

Vertical-align can take eight keyword values, in addition to percentage values. Six keyword values define alignment with respect to the parent element. These are:

baseline (*default value*)—Aligns the baseline of the element with the baseline of the parent element. If the "aligned" element does not have a baseline (for example, if it is an **IMG**), aligns the bottom of the element with the baseline of the parent element.

middle—Aligns the vertical midpoint of the element with the middle of the parent element. The middle of the parent element is defined as the position of the baseline plus half the height of the letter "x." This is typically used to align an image with preceding text.

sub—Displays the element as a subscript of the parent element.

super—Displays the element as a superscript of the parent element.

text-top—Aligns the top of the element with the top of the parent element's text content. This will have no effect if aligning text with text and if the two text segments use the same font family and size.

`text-bottom`—Aligns the bottom of the element with the bottom of the parent element's text content. This will have no effect if aligning text with text and if the two text segments use the same font family and size.

The remaining two keyword values define alignment with respect to the content of the line within which the element is embedded:

`top`—Aligns the top of the element with the top of the tallest element in the line.

`bottom`—Aligns the bottom of the element with the bottom of the lowest element in the line.

Note that the use of `top` and `bottom` can lead to problems if more than one element in a line is top-aligned and another is bottom aligned, since it may not be possible to unambiguously satisfy both alignment conditions. These and other alignment issues are discussed in Chapter 4.

Finally, percentage values ($xx\%$) determine the position of the element baseline (or bottom if there is no baseline) as a percentage of the line height relative to the baseline of the parent element. Thus a value of 100% will raise the element to lie at the baseline of the next line of text, while a value of -100% will lower the element to lie on the baseline of the next line of text. There are no current browsers that support percentage values.

White-space: Specify Handling of Whitespace

Default value:	`normal, nowrap, pre`
Values:	`normal`
Applicable to Elements:	Block-level elements
Inherit from Parent Element:	yes

This property specifies how the browser should handle extra whitespace within the document text, where whitespace is any combination of space, tab, carriage-return, or linefeed characters. There are three possible values:

`normal` (*default value*)—The browser should collapse multiple whitespace characters into a single word space, and should insert line breaks where appropriate for formatting the text. This is the default behavior for all HTML elements except **PRE**.

`nowrap`—The browser should collapse multiple whitespace characters into a single word space, but line breaks can only occur at explicit **BR** elements. This is similar to the behavior of the **NOBR** element. This value is not supported by current browsers.

pre—The browser should preserve all whitespace characters and space the text out accordingly. Thus, space and tab characters will introduce horizontal spacings, while carriage return and linefeed characters will cause line breaks in the formatted text. If the chosen font is a monospace font, this will lead to formatting equivalent to that within the standard HTML **PRE** element.

Width: Set Width of the Element

Default value:	auto
Values:	auto, *xx*em, *xx*ex, *xx*%, *xx*cm, *xx*in *xx*mm, *xx*pc, *xx*pt, *xx*px
Applicable to Elements:	Block-level and replaced elements
Inherit from Parent Element:	no

This property (closely related to height) sets the width for the box containing the associated element. This is most useful with replaced elements, such as **IMG** or **OBJECT**, which are replaced by downloaded data that will have an intrinsic size (e.g., a 300-by-243 pixel image) that is unknown until the data arrive. In these cases, width (and height) can set a fixed size for the region displaying the element. For **IMG**, the image can be rescaled (shrinking or expanding) to fit the specified box. For other types of replaced data that cannot be resized, such as spreadsheets, this may mean attaching scrollbars to the data viewer (to allow hidden portions to be viewed) or adding space around the object should the replaced data be smaller than the allocated space. Note that many browsers cannot handle resizing of such data and instead use the intrinsic size of the object, ignoring any specified height and width values.

If the element corresponding to this rule contains text and is resizable, width simply specifies the width of the box into which the text should be placed. This may again mean adding space on either side of the text , should the content be smaller than the allocated region.

Width can take several possible values. The keyword auto means that the width size is automatically scaled, although the way this scaling takes places very much depends on the type of element (see Chapter 5). In particular, width has no meaning for inline elements. Width values can also be absolute or relative lengths; relative lengths are determined relative to the font size within the element (or inherited from the parent element, should the element not contain text). Finally, width (unlike height) values can be specified as percentage values, which should be calculated as a percentage of the width of the parent element. Current browsers, however, calculate percentage widths relative to the full width of the browser canvas.

Please see Chapter 5 for a detailed description of how width and height control element formatting and layout.

Word-spacing: Adjust Default Spacing between Words

Default value:	normal
Values:	normal, *xx*em, *xx*ex, *xx*cm, *xx*in *xx*mm, *xx*pc, *xx*pt, *xx*px
Applicable to Elements:	All elements
Inherit from Parent Element:	yes

This property allows for adjustment of the spacing between adjacent words. The value can be a positive or negative length in any of the supported relative or absolute length units, where a positive value increases the word spacing, a negative value decreases it. Relative lengths (em, ex) are calculated relative to the font size within the element. Note that percentage values are not allowed. The default value for this property is the keyword normal, which references the default word spacing selected by the browser.

Note also that the default spacing is affected by text justification (text-align:justify), since justification adjusts (usually adds) spacing between words to produced justified text flow. If justification is enabled, word-spacing may adjust the average spacing between words in the justified region. Word-spacing is not widely supported.

Status of CSS Support in Current Browsers

This last section summarizes the status of CSS support in current browsers. The details of support are discussed elsewhere in the book, particularly in Chapters 3 through 6. However, Table 8.12 provides a succinct check for property support, and is a quick way of knowing if a property has known problems. This is a useful first reference when trying to diagnose CSS stylesheet problems.

Table 8.12 Summary of CSS Support for Currently Released Browsers
In this table the letter "n" indicates that the property, pseudo-class, or pseudo-element is not supported, while "P" indicates partial support (with a description, if a simple description of the partial support exists), and "B" indicates relatively severe bugs in the implementation (with a description, should there be a simple description of the problem).

Property	MSIE 3	Navigator 4
Background		**P B** (mishandles transparent portion of transparent images)
Background-attachment	**n**	**n**
Background-color	**n**	

Continued

Table 8.12 *Continued*

Property	MSIE 3	Navigator 4
Background-image	n	**B** (adds spurious margin around element)
Background-position	n	n
Background-repeat	n	
Border	n	
Border-bottom	n	n
Border-bottom-width	n	
Border-color	n	
Border-left	n	n
Border-left-width	n	
Border-right	n	n
Border-right-width	n	n
Border-left	n	n
Border-left-width	n	
Border-style	n	**P** (no dashed or dotted; cannot specify different styles for different sides)
Border-top	n	n
Border-top-width	n	
Border-width	n	
Clear	n	**B** (doesn't always clear properly)
Color		
Display	n	
Float	n	
Font	**P B**	
Font-family		
Font-size	**P**	
Font-style	**PB**	

Table 8.12 *Continued*

Property	MSIE 3	Navigator 4
Font-variant	n	n
Font-weight	PB	
Height	n	P
Letter-spacing	n	n
Line-height	n	B (numerical values not properly inherited)
List-style	n	P (only list-style-type)
List-style-image	n	n
List-style-position	n	n
List-style-type	n	
Margin	P (percent only)	P B (many elements have fixed margins)
Margin-bottom	P (percent only)	
Margin-left	P (percent only)	B (cannot set properly to zero)
Margin-right	P (percent only)	B (cannot set properly to zero)
Margin-top	P (percent only)	
Padding	n	B (some paddings not properly set)
Padding-bottom	n	
Padding-left	n	B (right padding not properly set)
Padding-right	n	B (right padding not properly set)
Padding-top	n	

Continued

Table 8.12 *Continued*

Property	MSIE 3	Navigator 4
Text-align	**P** (no justify)	
Text-decoration	**P** (no blink or overline)	**P** (no overline)
Text-indent		
Text-transform	**n**	
Vertical-align	**n**	**P** (no percentage; no sup or sub)
White-space	**n**	**P** (no nowrap)
Width	**n**	**B** (problems specifying full width of parent element)
Word-spacing	**n**	**n**
Pseudo-Classes		
:link		
:visited	**n**	**B** (not reliably detected by browser)
:active	**n**	**n**
Pseudo-Elements		
:first-letter	**n**	**n**
:first-line	**n**	**n**

Advanced Features/
Future Developments

This final chapter looks at some advanced and upcoming CSS features, and at some Web software issues related to CSS and document formatting. Some of these features are being implemented in current browsers, while others are more speculative but are likely to be implemented in the near future. Certainly you are advised to take everything in this chapter with a grain of salt—and some sections require more salt than others. The text is careful to point out which content is less reliable, and which can largely be trusted to reflect true browser behavior.

There are six main sections in this chapter. The first section covers CSS extensions for positioning and depth indexing of elements. This covers a collection of seven newly proposed CSS properties for positioning formatting elements on the display, and for controlling the placement of elements on top of each other. These extensions to CSS are relatively stable at this point, with support for them already integrated into Navigator 4 and Internet Explorer 4.

The second section reviews the application of scripting languages to CSS. Both Microsoft and Netscape support (in Navigator 4 and Internet Explorer 4, respectively) script access to stylesheet properties, which allows for significant control over the presentation of a document by a script. However, the mechanisms for this are implemented differently—and incompatibly—by these two companies.

The third section discusses font-related issues. CSS may in the future support property values that "describe" generic information about a font; this information can be used to find the "best" replacement for a requested, but unavailable, typeface. The section also describes the new Bitstream *dynamic font* technology. This technology, implemented in Netscape Navigator 4, lets a browser download font description files from a server, for use when displaying a document. The technology thus lets authors design documents using whatever fonts they wish, since the browser can download the required font files from the server, and use them to display the documents. Microsoft is taking a different approach, which they refer to as *font embedding*. Both approaches are discussed.

The fourth and fifth sections look at proposed, but as yet unimplemented, extensions to CSS. The fourth section looks at aural cascading stylesheets—a proposed new dialect of CSS appropriate for text-to-speech rendering of a document. The fifth section looks at proposed CSS extensions to support standard properties required when printing documents, such as widow and orphan control, or the insertion of forced page breaks. Both of these issues are under active debate, and the proposed CSS extensions are still very preliminary.

The sixth section takes a brief look at some existing CSS-related software. This encompasses document management, conversion tools, and HTML editors, as well as Web browsers not mentioned previously in the book. Finally, the last section is a detailed list of references where the reader can find up-to-date information on these subjects. No book can be current on such rapidly changing issues, and if you are interested in finding out more, you will find these URL references a valuable starting point for doing so.

Positioning and Z-Ordering of Elements

Two of the conspicuous weaknesses of CSS Level 1 were the lack of control over positioning, and an inability to specify element depth-indexing. In Level 1, it is very difficult to control the absolute or relative placement of elements on the display, or to control which elements should appear on top of (or below) each other. The latter issue is important for deciding if a floated element should appear "on top" or "below" other elements, while both issues are important for dynamic HTML pages containing graphical interface components that depend on positions to define meaning. For example, a dynamic HTML document may contain twelve different HTML segments, representing twelve different options on the same product to be purchased. A designer may want all twelve of these segments to appear at the same place on the page, with the user able to dynamically "reveal" one of the items while hiding the rest. This requires the ability to position the elements one on top of another (so that they appear at the same place), and the ability to change the order in which they appear, so that each, in turn, can be "popped" to the top, "hiding" the ones lying beneath it.

Because of these needs, the World Wide Web Consortium has developed a draft specification for CSS extensions that permits control over positioning and "z-indexing" of formatting elements. This proposal includes seven new properties—`clip`, `left`, `overflow`, `position`, `top`, `visibility`, and `z-index`—for defining the position and depth of an element on the display, and some modifications to the `height` and `width` properties that define the sizes of elements. This section outlines these proposed changes, and uses examples to show them in practice—both Netscape Navigator 4 and Microsoft Internet Explorer 4 support these new CSS properties.

CSS Level 1 implicitly supports a single positioning model, by which every element appears in the document according to its position relative to parent elements (e.g., inline element inside a paragraph) or the preceding elements (e.g., a paragraph following another paragraph). Floating elements are also supported but only within this outline. To distinguish this model from newer approaches, this is referred to as "static" positioning, since the positions or the elements are essentially static, and cannot be altered.

The new positioning specification proposes two new positioning models, either of which can be selected using the new CSS `position` property. *Absolute* positioning lets a stylesheet author specify the absolute position of an element, relative to a well-defined upper left-hand corner (which is the upper left-hand corner of the browser window if no other origin is specified). The second model is called *relative* positioning, This approach positions an element relative to the location it would occupy if it were otherwise not moved—that is, the position it would have if it were not repositioned. Examples will be presented later to make this concept clearer. In both cases, the new `top` and `left` properties specify the translated location for the positioned element.

Absolutely positioned elements can also be placed inside an absolutely or relatively positioned parent element. In this case, the positions of the child elements are determined relative to the upper left-hand corner of the parent. Again, examples will be given to illustrate how this works.

As mentioned, the new `top` and `left` properties define the location of the repositioned element. At the same time, the `z-index` property defines the relative "depth" of elements; for example, if multiple elements are positioned one on top of another, the `z-index` value tells which are on top and which are below.

In most cases, the `height` and `width` properties define the dimensions for a positioned element. However, sometimes an element cannot fit inside the specified height and width. The `overflow` property then determines how the browser should handle the situation—for example, "clip" the content, provide scrollbars to scroll through the content, or do nothing and let the content overflow the specified dimensions.

The new `clip` property defines a clipping box for a displayed element, and defines how the element's presentation should be clipped.

Finally, the `visibility` property can hide or expose an element by making the entire element transparent. An element that is hidden still occupies space on the display—it is just not seen by the user, and appears as a transparent box (or boxes). Thus, an invisible paragraph with nothing under or on top of it simply appears as a large blank space on the display. Note that this differs from `display: none`, which causes an element to be ignored when the document is rendered to the display.

You should be aware that the following descriptions and specifications are based on a preliminary positioning draft, so that the actual syntax and allowed values may change slightly before the final specification. You are encouraged to visit the W3C Web site for the latest specifications.

Absolute Positioning

Absolute positioning, resulting from the declaration `position: absolute`, defines a rectangular box element's absolute position relative to a well-defined upper left-hand corner. The property `top` measures the distance down from this upper left-hand corner to the top of the positioned element, while the property `left` measures the distance to the right from the upper left-hand corner to the left edge of the positioned element, and can be either positive or negative in value. The properties `height` and `width`, if present, define the size of the positioned element.

If an element with property `position: absolute` is *not* within another absolutely (or relatively) positioned element, then the absolute position is determined relative to the upper left-hand corner of the browser drawing area. An example of such positioning is shown in Figures 9.1 and 9.2, which illustrate four absolutely positioned elements. Note how these elements are positioned relative to the upper left-hand corner of the browser window. You can use the lines on the background to determine the coordinates of the positioned elements: The solid lines are spaced 100 pixels apart, with the dashed lines occurring at 50-pixel intervals. Note also how Navigator 4 does not properly fill the element box with the designated background color.

Positioned out of Regular Flow

Figure 9.2 illustrates an important aspect of absolutely positioned elements—such elements are positioned *independently* of the regular flow of content on the display. Thus, the paragraph that follows the four absolutely positioned paragraphs ignores the existence of those four paragraphs, and simply starts below the page heading. Similarly, the absolutely positioned paragraphs are positioned on top, and independent of the regular text flow. The relative positioning model allows for an easier mixing of absolute and static positioning approaches, as discussed later.

Top and Left Properties

The `top` and `left` properties specify the location of the positioned element. The value for each can be a length specified in any of the standard CSS length units, or it can be a percentage value. In the case of percentages, the value is calculated as a percentage of the containing element width (`left`) or height (`top`). In the case of Figure 9.1, the containing element is the **BODY**, so that the width and height would simply be the dimensions of the browser display area. The value `auto` is also supported, and corresponds to the element's "normal" position in the flow—generally this means a value of zero for both `top` and `left`, which places the element at the upper left-hand corner of the container.

The listing in Figure 9.1 gives the `top` and `left` values for the four positioned elements (measured in pixels). These positions can be verified measuring the positions of the elements in Figure 9.2, noting that the background solid lines are 100 pixels apart, with the dashed lines at 50-pixel intervals.

Depth or Z-index of an Element

Figures 9.1 and 9.2 also illustrate the use of the z-index property to "stack" elements on the display. By default, elements are stacked in the order in which they occur in the HTML markup—that is, later elements are drawn on top of earlier ones. However, In Figures 9.1 and 9.2 the second pair of "absolutely" positioned elements use z-index values to reverse this order. The first element has a z-index of 2 and the second a value of 1, so that the first element is displayed on top of the second.

Z-index actually defines the stacking order for *sibling* elements (those elements that are child elements of the same parent, such as a collection of **P** elements within the same **BODY**, as in Figure 9.1), as well as the stacking of an element with respect to its parent. According to the draft specifications, a group of elements with *positive* z-index values are stacked one above the other according to these values, and, as a group, are stacked *above* the parent element. Similarly, a group of elements with *negative* z-index values are stacked one above the other according to these values (larger on top of smaller—for example, -1 on top of -2), and as a group are stacked *beneath* the parent element.

Clipping an Absolutely Positioned Element

Absolutely positioned elements can be *clipped*—that is, the region displayed to the user can be clipped such that only a portion of the element is displayed, the remainder being treated as transparent. For traditional text and image-based Web pages, this is not a terribly useful feature. However, Navigator 4 and Internet Explorer 4 both support significant multimedia capabilities through scripting interfaces to the document, and using this interface can dynamically modify the clipping area around an element. This allows for such presentation features as "wipe in" text, or the slow reveal of images.

In CSS, clipping is controlled using the clip property, which can be applied only to absolutely positioned elements. The default value is auto, which clips the element at its outer edge (this is essentially no clipping). Alternatively, the clipping box can be set using the expression:

```
clip: rect(top, right, bottom, left);
```

where *top*, *right*, *bottom*, and *left* are the positions, relative to the upper left-hand corner of the element being clipped, of the top, right, bottom, and left edges of the rectangular clipping region, respectively. The values for *top*, *right*, *bottom*, and *left* can be any absolute or relative length measure (but not percentage units), or the keyword auto. The auto keyword causes the corresponding edge of the clipping region to be positioned such that, in that edge's direction, there is no element content outside the clipping region.

Figures 9.3 and 9.4 show an example of clip in action. The figure contains two identical absolutely positioned paragraphs, the only difference being the vertical displacement (top) to keep them separated on the display. The second paragraph, however, takes the property:

```
clip:        rect(0px,150px, 150px, 50px);
```

This clips the paragraph with a box having the top edge at 0 pixels, the right edge at 150 pixels in from the right, the bottom edge 150 pixels down from the top, and the left edge 50 pixels in from the left. Figure 9.4 shows the resulting effect. Note how all content outside the clipped region is transparent, and shows the underlying content on the page.

Figure 9.1 An example of absolute positioning relative to the browser window. Also illustrated is the property `z-index`. For simplicity, some of the text in the "default" paragraph (the gray text in the background of Figure 9.2) is omitted. Browser rendering of this document is shown in Figure 9.2.

```
<HTML><HEAD><TITLE>Example of Absolute Positioning </TITLE>
<STYLE><!--
/* First set up default properties for page                    */

BODY       {background-image: url(100px.gif);  font-size: 14pt;    }
H1         {font-size:  18pt; text-align: center; color: green;    }
.default   {margin-top: 0px;; color:  #e0e0e0;                        }
/
* All absolutely positioned elements are 300 pixels wide
  The following are the CSS rules for the four positioned
  elements
*/
.absolute1 {top:        100px;        /* 100 pixels down   */
            left:       200px;        /* 200 pixels in     */
            width:      300px;
            position:   absolute;  background: #ffff77;    }
.absolute2 {top:        150px;        /* 150 pixels down   */
            left:       300px;        /* 300 pixels in     */
            width:      300px;
            position:   absolute;  background: #77ff77;    }
.absolute3 {top:        350px;        /* 350 pixels down   */
            left:       200px;        /* 200 pixels in     */
            width:      300px;
            z-index:    2;
            position:   absolute;  background: #ffff77;    }
.absolute4 {top:        400px;        /* 400 pixels down   */
            left:       300px;        /* 300 pixels in     */
            width:      300px;
            z-index:    1;
            position:   absolute;  background: #77ff77;    }
--></STYLE></HEAD><BODY>
<H1>Example of Absolute Positioning</H1>
<P CLASS="absolute1">
   This paragraph is <B><I>200</I></B> pixels across and <B><I>100</I></B>
   pixels down from the upper left-hand corner of the window.</P>
<P CLASS="absolute2">
   This paragraph is <B><I>300</I></B> pixels across and <B><I>150</I></B>
   pixels down from the upper left-hand corner of the window.</P>
<P CLASS="absolute3">
   This paragraph is <B><I>200</I></B> pixels across and <B><I>350</I></B>
   pixels down from the upper left-hand corner of the window.</P>
```

Continued

Figure 9.1 *Continued*

```
<P CLASS="absolute4">
  This paragraph is <B><I>300</I></B> pixels across and <B><I>400</I></B>
  pixels down from the upper left-hand corner of the window.</P>
<P CLASS="default">
  Two of the clear weaknesses of CSS Level 1 were the lack of control
  over positioning and depth-indexing: in Level 1 it is very difficult
..( text deleted)... </P>
</BODY></HTML>
```

Controlling Element Overflow

With absolutely (and relatively) positioned elements of fixed `height` and `width`, it is possible that the actual element content does not fit inside the specified region. In this case, the `overflow` property defines how the browser should handle the overflow. The value `none` (which is the default) lets the browser display the overflowed content, and lets the element overflow its allocated space.

Figure 9.2 Rendering, by Netscape Navigator 4, of the document listed in Figure 9.1. Note how the four absolutely positioned elements are positioned on top of the regular text flow, and are unaffected by this text. The solid lines drawn on the background are 100 pixels apart, with the dashed lines at 50-pixel intervals.

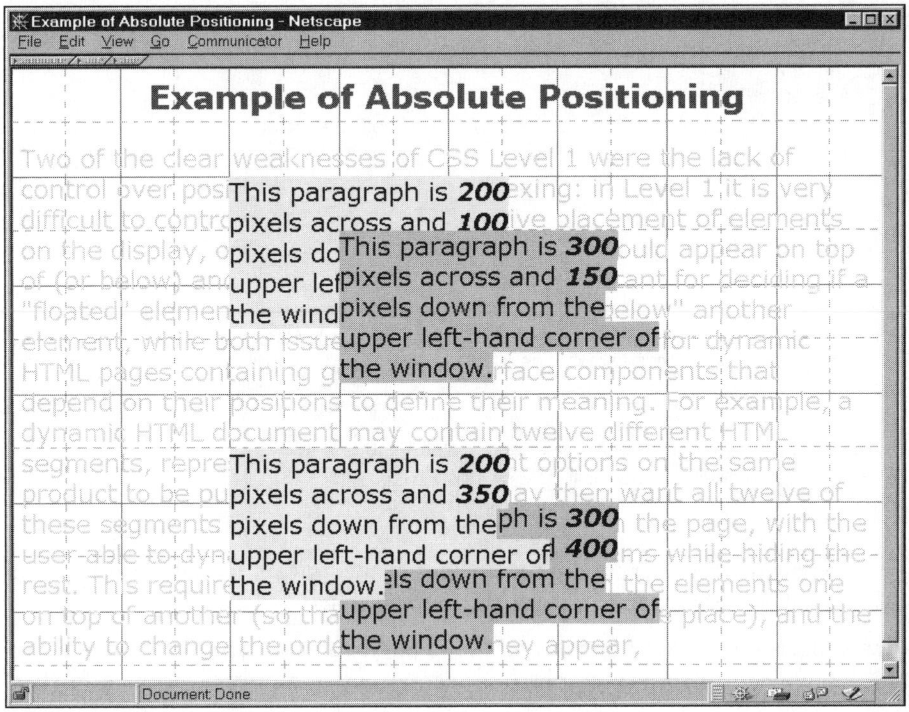

Figure 9.3 An example document and stylesheet illustrating the `clip` property. The second paragraph (of class `absolute2`) uses this property to clip the display area of the element, while the first paragraph is not clipped. Browser rendering of this document is shown in Figure 9.4.

```
<HTML><HEAD><TITLE>Example of Element Clipping </TITLE>
<STYLE><!--
/*
  First set up default font and "grid" background
  Then put title in green and larger font.
*/
BODY       {background-image: url(100px.gif);  font-size: 14pt;  }
H1         {font-size:  18pt; text-align: center; color: green;  }
/*
   Now format two absolutely positioned elements. The
   second ("absolute2") will be "clipped"
*/
.absolute1 {top:         100px;
            left:        200px;
            width:       300px;
            position:    absolute;
            background: #ffff77;       }
.absolute2 {top:         250px;
            left:        200px;
            width:       300px;
            position:    absolute;
            clip:        rect(0px,150px, 150px, 50px); /* Clipped region */
            background: #77ff77;       }
--></STYLE>
</HEAD><BODY>
<H1>Example of Element Clipping </H1>

<P CLASS="absolute1">
  This paragraph is <B><I>200</I></B> pixels across and <B><I>100</I></B>
  pixels down from the upper left-hand corner of the window.</P>

<P CLASS="absolute2">
  This paragraph is <B><I>200</I></B> pixels across and <B><I>250</I></B>
  pixels down from the upper left-hand corner of the window.</P>
</BODY></HTML>
```

Alternatively, the value clip tells the browser to clip the content at the bottom or right-hand edge of the element, so that no displayed content extends outside the defined space.

The effect of overflow is illustrated in Figures 9.5 and 9.6. The document listing in Figure 9.5 shows two identical, absolutely positioned paragraphs (the second one is simply positioned further

Figure 9.4 Rendering, by the Netscape Navigator browser, of the document listed in Figure 9.3. Note how the second paragraph is clipped according to the boundaries specified by the associated clip **property.**

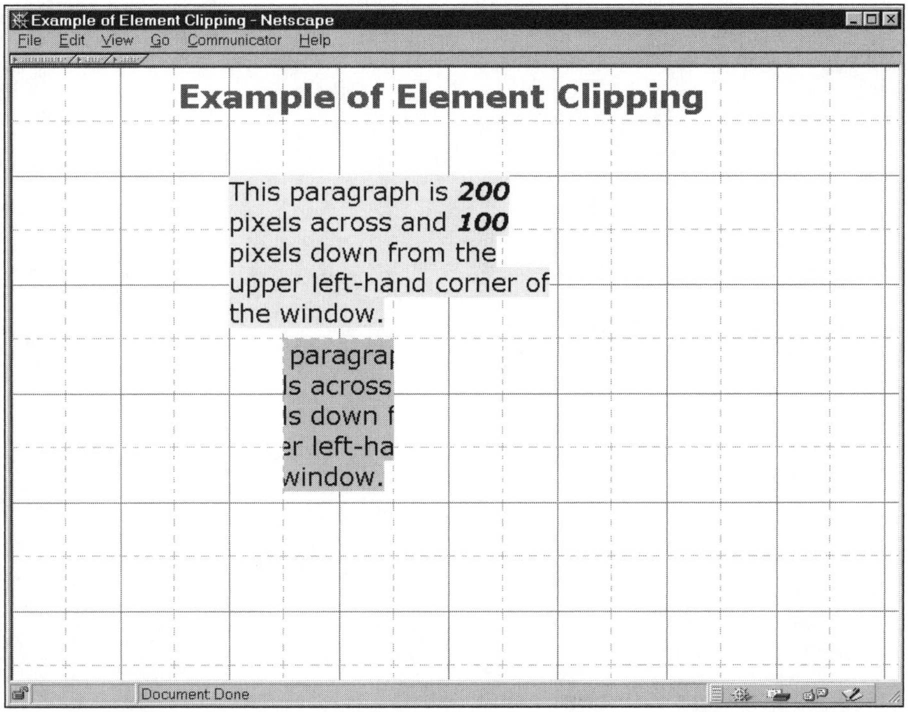

down on the display), both with properties width: 300px and height: 100px. However, the rule associated with the second paragraph also has the declaration overflow: clip. Note how in Figure 9.6 the first paragraph overflows the defined region for the element, since the default clip value (none) is assumed. However, clipping is applied to the second paragraph, such that the text is arbitrarily cut off 100 pixels down from the top of the element, since 100 pixels is the specified element height.

Relative Positioning

The new positioning model also supports *relatively* positioned elements, created using the declaration position: relative. By default (that is, when top and left are set to auto or to zero), relatively positioned elements appear inline with the regular statically positioned elements, as illustrated in the first displayed paragraph in Figure 9.8 (the associated document is listed in Figure 9.7). Note how the relatively positioned elements appear inline with the regular paragraph text, and are not positioned separate from them—this is entirely different from the case with absolutely positioned content.

Figure 9.5 An example document and stylesheet illustrating the `overflow` property. The second paragraph (of class `absolute2`) uses this property to restrict the overflow of the element, while the first paragraph does not. Browser rendering of this document is shown in Figure 9.6.

```
<HTML><HEAD><TITLE>Example of Overflow</TITLE>
<STYLE><!--
/*
   First set up default font and "grid" background
   Then put title in green and larger font.
*/
BODY        {background-image: url(100px.gif);  font-size: 14pt;       }
H1          {font-size:  18pt; text-align: center; color: green;       }
/*
    Now insert two absolutely positioned elements. The
    second will be clipped using the "overflow" property
*/
.absolute1 {top:          100px;
            left:         200px;
            width:        300px;
            height:       100px;
            position:     absolute;
            background: #ffff77;       }
.absolute2 {top:          300px;
            left:         200px;
            width:        300px;
            height:       100px;
            position:     absolute;
            overflow:     clip;        /* Element can't overflow    */
                                       /* Defined height and width */
            background: #77ff77;       }
--></STYLE>
</HEAD><BODY>
<H1>Example of Element Overflow </H1>

<P CLASS="absolute1">
  This paragraph is <B><I>200</I></B> pixels across and <B><I>100</I></B>
  pixels down from the upper left-hand corner of the window.</P>

<P CLASS="absolute2">
  This paragraph is <B><I>200</I></B> pixels across and <B><I>300</I></B>
  pixels down from the upper left-hand corner of the window.</P>
</BODY></HTML>
```

In the case of relatively positioned elements, the `top` and `left` properties reposition the element relative to the "normal" position it occupies in the text flow. This is illustrated in the second dis-

Figure 9.6 Rendering, by the Netscape Navigator 4 browser, of the document listed in Figure 9.5. Note how the second paragraph does not overflow the defined bounds of the element, as specified by the associated `overflow` property.

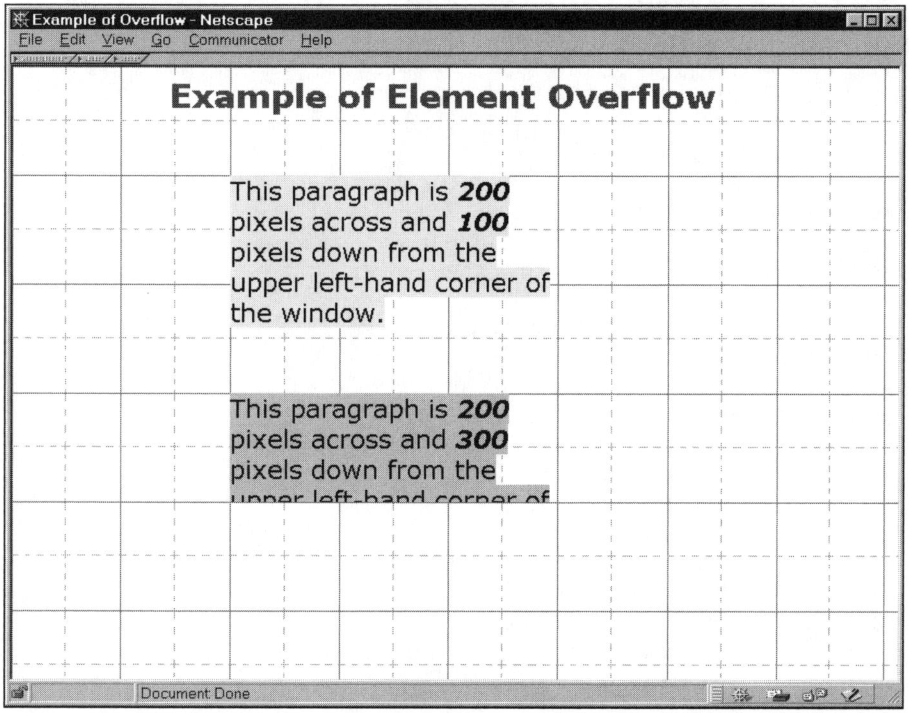

played paragraph in Figure 9.8, where the two relatively positioned elements (both **EM** elements inline within the **P**) are displaced from their "normal" positions. The first element (consisting of two inline boxes) is positioned 50 pixels to the left and 12 pixels upwards, while the second element is positioned 20 pixels downwards and zero pixels to the right, which in both cases is relative to its "normal" position. Notice how this does *not* affect the regular flow of text—the element may be moved, but the space occupied by the element in its "normal" position is simply left blank.

Absolute Positioning within Another Element

In a preceding section, we illustrated how an absolutely positioned element is, by default, positioned relative to the upper left-hand corner of the browser window. However, this origin for absolutely positioned elements can be changed by placing an absolutely positioned element as a *descendent* of an absolutely or relatively positioned element. For example, if an absolutely positioned **EM** element is within a **P** that, in turn, is within an absolutely positioned **DIV** element, then the position of the **EM** is determined relative to the upper left-hand corner of the absolutely positioned **DIV**.

Figure 9.7 An example document and stylesheet illustrating relatively positioned elements. The first paragraph contains two relatively positioned EM elements within a P, both elements in their normal (unmoved) positions. The second paragraph uses the `top` and `left` properties to translate these elements to new positions relative to their default locations.

```
<HTML><HEAD><TITLE>Example of Relative Positioning </TITLE>
<STYLE><!--
/*      First set default formatting properties                */

BODY    {background-image: url(100px-2.gif);  font-size: 12pt;     }
H1      {font-size:  16pt; text-align: center; color: green;        }
DIV     {margin-left: 92px; margin-right: 42px; margin-top: -14px; }


EM      {position:   relative;  /* All EM's relatively positioned */
         color:      #ff0000;
         background: #dddddd;  }
/* Two relatively positioned EM elements,displaced a different
   amount - */
.relm1  {left:     -50px;      /* Relative positioning:  */
         top:      -12px  }    /* 50px to the left         */
                              /* 12px upwards            */


.relm2  {left:      0px;       /* Relative positioning:  */
         top:      20px; }     /* 0px to the right        */
                              /* 20px downwards          */
--></STYLE>
</HEAD>
<BODY>
<H1>Example of Relative Positioning</H1>

<DIV CLASS="container">
  <P CLASS="default">
    Here is a paragraph of text containing two <EM>sequences
    of EM emphasized</EM> text. In the first paragraph, these are
    relatively positioned but placed  at their default positions,
    while in  the second, they are <EM>repositioned</EM>
    using the top and left properties.</P>
  <HR NOSHADE SIZE=5>
  <P CLASS="default">
    Here is a paragraph of text containing two <EM CLASS="relm1">sequences
    of EM emphasized</EM> text. In the first paragraph, these are
    relatively positioned but placed at their default positions, while in
    the second, they are <EM CLASS="relm2">repositioned</EM>
    using the top and left properties.</P>
</DIV>
</BODY></HTML>
```

Figure 9.8 Rendering, by the Netscape Navigator browser, of the document listed in Figure 9.7. Note how the EM elements in the second paragraph are repositioned relative to their "normal" locations, as per the `top` and `left` property values shown in Figure 9.7. Note also how moving these elements does not change the flow of the remaining text.

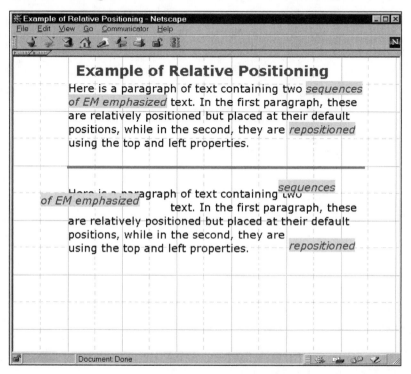

This specific case is illustrated in Figures 9.9 and 9.10. Figure 9.9 shows a single, absolutely positioned **DIV** element positioned to begin 200 pixels down and 100 pixels in from the upper left-hand corner of the browser window. This **DIV** contains a paragraph that, in turn, contains an **EM** element that is absolutely positioned to begin 150 pixels down and 100 pixels in from the defined origin. In this case, the defined origin is the upper left-hand corner of the **DIV** element that contains the **EM**. Inspection of Figure 9.10 shows that, indeed, the **EM** element is positioned with respect to the origin of the **DIV** (recall that the underlying grid lines are drawn at 50-pixel intervals).

Similarly, an absolutely positioned element can be placed within a *relatively* positioned one. In this case, the origin for the absolutely positioned element is just the upper left-hand corner of the relatively positioned element that contains it. This is illustrated in Figures 9.11 and 9.12. Figure 9.11 lists a simple document containing three paragraphs, the second of which is relatively positioned. However, this paragraph is not itself moved—instead, it contains an absolutely positioned

Figure 9.9 An example document and stylesheet illustrating an absolutely positioned element EM contained within another absolutely positioned element. According to the CSS draft, the EM element should be positioned 150 pixels down and 100 pixels in from the upper left-hand corner of the DIV. Figure 9.10 shows the rendering of this document by the Netscape Navigator 4 browser.

```
<HTML><HEAD><TITLE>
Absolute Positioning within an Absolutely  Positioned Element
</TITLE>
<STYLE><!--
/*
    Absolutely position and EM element within a
    relatively positioned P.
*/
/* Default properties */
BODY        {background-image: url(100px.gif);  font-size: 12pt;  }
H1          {font-size:  18pt; text-align: center; color: green;  }

/* Absolutely positioned P and absolutel positioned EM */
DIV.absd    {position:      absolute;
                top:           200px;      left:          100px;     }

EM.abse     {position:      absolute;
                top:           150px;      left:          100px;
                color:         white;      background:    blue;      }
--></STYLE></HEAD>
<BODY>
<H1>Absolute Positioning within an Absolutely Positioned Element</H1>

<DIV CLASS="absd">
  <P>Here is a standard paragraph containing regular text.
     This paragraph lies within an absolutely positioned <B>DIV</B>
     element. The paragraph also contains an absolutely positioned
     <EM CLASS="abse"><B>150PX DOWN; 100PX IN</B> </EM> <B>EM</B>
     element, that is absolutely positioned relative to the upper
     left-hand corner of the <B>DIV</B>.
  </P>
</DIV></BODY></HTML>
```

EM element which is positioned relative to the upper left-hand corner of the **P** such that it lies just to the left of it (left: -100px), but top-aligned (top: 0px). Notice how the display property is used to transform this **EM** into a block-level element—this allows the text to be "poured" into a box of the specified width (85 pixels). Finally, the declaration overflow: clip ensures that the element content cannot overflow outside the specified box, so that text from the "sidebar" cannot overflow with the regular paragraph text. Figure 9.12 shows the results of this specified rendering.

Figure 9.10 Rendering, by the Netscape Navigator 4 browser, of the document listed in Figure 9.9. Note how the EM element in the paragraph is positioned relative to the upper left-hand corner of the containing DIV element.

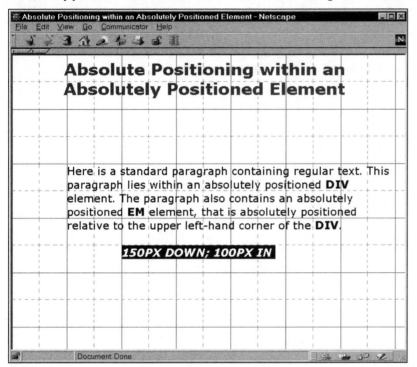

The use of absolutely positioned elements within other absolutely or relatively positioned elements gives enormous control over the placement of content on the page. Such control is particularly important for dynamic documents generated by scripting programs. In the case of Netscape Navigator 4 and Microsoft Internet Explorer 4, scripting languages can move absolutely positioned objects across the display—while the user is watching—to create simple forms of multimedia using HTML elements and dynamic control over the CSS positioning properties. These issues are briefly touched upon in a later section on "Scripted Stylesheets and the Document Object Model."

Visibility of Elements, and Element Transparency

The new CSS draft also supports a new property, `visibility`, which can "hide" an element without actually removing it from the rendered flow. For example, if an **EM** element within a paragraph were subject to `visibility: hidden`, then the **EM** text region would simply be replaced by a blank, transparent region. Thus, the `visibility` property values `hidden` and `visible` (display the element—this is the default value) can toggle the text content in and out of the display, without affecting the rendering of the surrounding or parent elements.

Figure 9.11 An example document and stylesheet illustrating an absolutely positioned element EM contained within a relatively positioned P. Note how this P is not repositioned, and occupies its default location. The EM element is positioned 100 pixels to the left of the P, and is aligned with the paragraph top (`top: 0px;`). Note, also, how the rule `display: block-level` transforms the EM into a block element. Thus the EM element can have a defined width—here 85 pixels. Figure 9.12 shows the rendering of this document by the Netscape Navigator 4 browser.

```
<HTML><HEAD>
<TITLE>Absolute Positioning within Relative Positioning</TITLE>
<STYLE><!--
/*
    Absolutely position and EM element within a
    relatively positioned P.
*/
/* Default properties */
BODY       {background-image: url(100px-2.gif);  font-size: 12pt;  }
H1         {font-size:  18pt; text-align: center; color: green;    }
DIV        {margin-left: 142px;  margin-right: 21px;               }

/* Positioned Elements  */
P.rel    {position:    relative;   background: #dddddd;    }
EM.note  {position:    absolute;
          display:     block-level;
          width:       85px;
          font-family: "EngraversGothic BT", sans-serif;
          font-style:  normal;
          font-weight: bold;
          overflow:    clip;
          top:         0px;       left:        -99px;
          color:       #ff0000;  background:   #ddddff;   }
--></STYLE>
</HEAD><BODY>
<H1>Absolute Positioning within Relative Positioning</H1>

<DIV>
  <P>Here is a standard paragraph that is statically positioned —
  no funny stuff here!</P>
  <P CLASS="rel">Here is a standard paragraph containing regular text,
    but this paragraph is <EM>relatively</EM> positioned. The paragraph
    in turn contains an EM element that is converted, by the
    associatd CSS rule, into an absolutely positioned block-level
    element, positioned to lie outside the paragraph, and to the
    left.  <EM CLASS="note">Never trust a Wookie!!</EM>
```
Continued

Figure 9.11 *Continued*

```
  </P>
  <P>Finally, here is another standard paragraph, statically
  positioned — no funny stuff here either!</P>
</DIV>
</BODY></HTML>
```

The `visibility` property is illustrated in Figures 9.13 and 9.14. The left and right columns (contained within a table) each contain three one-line paragraphs—in fact, the text content of the two columns is identical. However, the second paragraph in the right-hand column has the associated CSS declaration `visibility: hidden`. Note, in Figure 9.14, that this paragraph is hidden, but that the space occupied by the paragraph is not collapsed.

Figure 9.12 Rendering, by the Netscape Navigator 4 browser, of the document listed in Figure 9.11. Note how the EM element in the paragraph is positioned to the left of the P, and has the specified 85-pixel width.

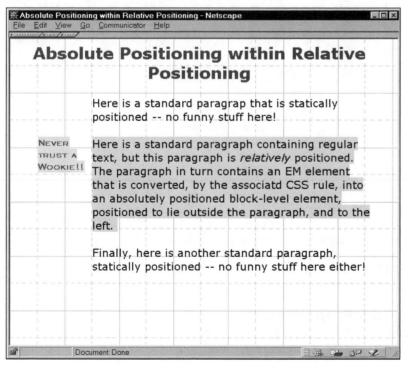

Figure 9.13 An example document and stylesheet illustrating the use of the visibility **property to "hide" elements. Both columns in the table contain three one-sentence paragraphs. However, the second paragraph in the second column has the associated CSS declaration** visibility: hidden, **which hides the content from view. Browser rendering of this document is shown in Figure 9.14.**

```
<HTML><HEAD><TITLE>Example of Visibility Property</TITLE>
<STYLE><!--
/*
   Use visiblity to turn a paragraph "transparent"
*/
BODY        {background-image: url(100px-2.gif);  font-size: 12pt;    }
H1          {font-size:  18pt; text-align: center; color: green;     }
/*
     Attach CLASS "hide" to a "hidden" element. Use this to
     Hide the second paragraph in the second table column.
*/
.hide { visibility: hidden;   }
--></STYLE>
</HEAD><BODY>
<H1>Example of Element Visibility</H1>

<DIV ALIGN="center">
  <TABLE WIDTH="80%" BGCOLOR="#dddddd"><TR>
  <TD VALIGN="top">
    <P>First Test paragraph. </P>
    <P>Second Test paragraph.</P>
    <P>Third Test paragraph. </P>
  </TD>
  <TD>
    <P>First Test paragraph.</P>
    <P CLASS="hide">Second Test paragraph.</P>
    <P>Third Test paragraph.</P>
  </TD>
  </TR></TABLE>
</DIV>
<P>In the above table, the second paragraph on the right hand
   column should be <EM>invisible</EM>, as it has the associated
   stylesheet property "<TT>visibility: hidden;</TT>".</P>
</BODY></HTML>
```

Review of Positioning CSS Properties

The following sections summarize the changes and additions to the CSS property specifications given in Chapter 8. The notation is the same as in Figure 8.1, and you are referred there for details.

Figure 9.14 Rendering, by an early beta version of Microsoft Internet Explorer 4, of the document listed in Figure 9.13. Note how the second paragraph in the second table column is "hidden" from view. This is accomplished using the `visibility` **property, as illustrated in Figure 9.13.**

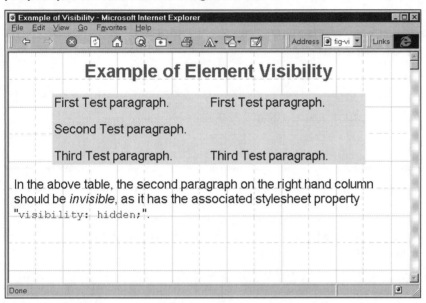

Clip: Specify Element Display Clipping Properties

Default value:	auto
Values:	auto, rect(*ltop, lright, lbot, lleft*)
Applicable to Elements:	"Absolutely" positioned elements
Inherit from Parent Element:	no

This property, valid only with absolutely positioned elements, specifies the *clipping box* to be applied around the element. The content of the clipping box is visible, while the element content outside the clipping region is *hidden*—this region is rendered as transparent, and displays any underlying content. The default value is the keyword `auto`, which causes the clipping region to cover the bounds of the entire element, including any border or padding, or any child elements that may be positioned outside the element.

The value can specify a rectangle using the notation rect (*ltop, lright, lbot, lleft*), where the four user-specified quantities *ltop, lright, lbot,* and *lleft* refer to the position of the top, right, bottom, and left edges of the clipping rectangle, respectively, measured relative to the upper left-hand inner corner of the element. These values can be positive or negative. Percentage values are not allowed. Each of these four lengths can also take the keyword `auto`, which moves that edge of the clipping region to the outer edge of the element, including any border or padding space, or any child elements that have been positioned outside the parent. Figures 9.3 and 9.4 show an example of the `clip` property in action.

Height: Specify Height of Element

Default value:	auto
Values:	auto, *xx*em, *xxx*ex, *xx*cm, *xx*in, *xx*mm, *xx*pc, *xx*pt, *xx*px, *xx*%
Applicable to Elements:	Block-level, replaced, and "absolutely" positioned elements
Inherit from Parent Element:	no

This property specifies the *height* of the element. The use of `height` with statically positioned elements is unchanged from CSS Level 1. `Height` is also used with relatively positioned elements, in the same manner as with statically positioned ones. Thus, the only important change relates to the use of `height` with absolutely positioned content, where it specifies the height of the box that contains the absolutely positioned content.

The default value for `height`, as in other positioning models, is `auto`. In this case, the height of the element is automatically adjusted (consistent with the element width) so that the element just contains its content. Note that the element may then be clipped by the parent element, should the resulting height be larger than the space made available to it by the parent—recall that the parent element may have a fixed height.

`Height` can be given in absolute or relative length units, or as a percentage value—percentage values are calculated relative to the *height* of the parent element. Percentage values are *undefined* should the parent element itself be formatted with `height: auto`. Thus, authors should not use percentage values in this case.

Left: Specify Position of Left Edge of Element

Default value:	auto
Values:	auto, *xx*em, *xx*ex, *xx*cm, *xx*in, *xx*mm, *xx*pc, *xx*pt, *xx*px, *xx*%
Applicable to Elements:	"Absolutely" or "relatively" positioned elements
Inherit from Parent Element:	no

This property defines the initial position for the left edge of the element, relative to a well-defined coordinate system. Consequently, this property does not apply to "statically" positioned elements. The position can be specified using any of the defined absolute or relative length units, or it can be a percentage value, in which case the percentage is calculated relative to the width of the parent element. Percentage values are undefined if the parent element `width` was set to `auto`. Negative values are allowed. Finally, the position can be specified using the keyword `auto`—in most cases, this is equivalent to a value of zero.

The meaning of `left` varies depending on the positioning type. The two cases are:

Absolutely Positioned Elements—`Left` determines the position relative to the left inner edge of the "nearest" element that is itself absolutely or relatively positioned. For example, given an absolutely positioned **P** inside a statically positioned **BLOCKQUOTE,** that is, in turn, inside a **DIV** that is relatively positioned, then the "left" edge of the **P** is positioned with respect to the top left-hand corner of the relatively positioned **DIV,** independent of the position of the **BLOCKQUOTE.** This point was illustrated in Figures 9.9 and 9.10.

Relatively Positioned Elements—`Left` determines the position relative to the "normal" position of the element—that is, the position it would have if unmoved. Relatively positioned elements appear inline with regular "statically" positioned text, and, by default, appear in the normal "statically" positioned locations (corresponding to a `left` value of zero). `Left` can then horizontally move the element from this default location. An example is shown in Figures 9.7 and 9.8.

Overflow: Specify Handling if Box Is Smaller than Content

Default value:	`none`
Values:	`none, clip, scroll`
Applicable to Elements:	"Absolutely" or "relatively" positioned elements
Inherit from Parent Element:	no

This property, illustrated in Figures 9.5 and 9.6, defines the desired handling for element rendering, should the content not fit within the specified height and width. The are three possible values. These are:

`clip`—The displayed content is be clipped at the defined edges of the element. Any content outside the element will not be displayed.

`none` (*the default*)—The displayed content is not clipped, and overflowed content is displayed.

`scroll`—The displayed content should be clipped at the defined edges of the element, as per `clip`. However, the browser should (if possible) provide scrollbars on the element to let the user scroll to view the clipped content.

Position: Specify Type of Element Positioning

Default value:	static
Values:	absolute, relative, static
Applicable to Elements:	All elements
Inherit from Parent Element:	no

This property defines the positioning model for the associated HTML elements. There are three possible keyword values. The value static, which is the default, is equivalent to the positioning model in CSS Level 1—that is, the element cannot be positioned other than through margin properties, or by floating the element using the float property. The value absolute refers to absolute positioning with respect to the upper left-hand corner of the browser canvas, or with respect to the origin of another absolutely or relatively positioned element that contains the given element. In this case, the properties left and top give the position of the upper left-hand corner of the "positioned" element, measured from the top of the containing element (top), and in from the left-hand inner edge of the containing element (left). The value relative refers to relative positioning with respect to the "normal" position of the element in the regular flow of text. In this case the properties left and top refer to the displacement of the element from this normal position.

Top: Specify Position of Top of Element

Default value:	auto
Values:	auto, xxem, xxex, xxcm, xxin, xxmm, xxpc, xxpt, xxpx, xx%
Applicable to Elements:	"Absolutely" or "relatively" positioned elements
Inherit from Parent Element:	no

This property defines the initial position for the top of the element, relative to a well-defined coordinate system. Consequently, this property does not apply to "statically" positioned elements. The position can be specified using any of the defined absolute or relative length units, or it can be a percentage value, in which case the percentage is calculated relative to the actual width of the parent element. Percentage values are undefined if the parent element height was set to auto. Negative values are allowed. Finally, the position can be specified using the keyword auto—in most cases, this is equivalent to a value of zero.

The meaning of top varies depending on the positioning type. The two cases are:

Absolutely Positioned Elements—Top determines the position relative to the top edge of the "nearest" element that is itself absolutely or relatively positioned. For example, given an absolutely positioned **P**

inside a statically positioned **BLOCKQUOTE** that is, in turn, inside a **DIV** that is relatively positioned, then the "top" of the **P** is positioned with respect to the upper edge of the relatively positioned **DIV**, independent of the position of the parent **BLOCKQUOTE**.

Relatively Positioned Elements—Top determines the position relative to the "normal" position of the element—that is, the position it would have if unmoved. Relatively positioned elements appear inline with regular "statically" positioned text, and by default appear in the normal "statically" positioned locations (corresponding to a top value of zero). Top can then vertically move the element from this default location.

Visibility: Specify Initial Display State for Element

Default value:	inherit
Values:	hidden, inherit, visible
Applicable to Elements:	All elements
Inherit from Parent Element:	yes if value is inherit; no otherwise

This property, which applies to all elements independent of the positioning model, defines the visibility of an element. The value visible makes the element visible, and is the standard behavior of the **BODY** element. The value hidden hides the element by making it transparent; however, the element is left in the displayed document, and the document is formatted as if the content exists. Thus, the effect of "hiding" an element is to display a blank space in the document in place of the hidden content. This is illustrated in Figures 9.13 and 9.14.

The third value, inherit, is the default. This causes an element to inherit the visibility of its parent. Thus if a paragraph is hidden, any contained, inline elements are also hidden. This inheritance can be overridden by specifying explicit visibility for an element. For example, an **EM** element inside a paragraph could be declared visible, such that if the paragraph is hidden, all text disappears except for the text within the designated **EM**.

Width: Specify Width of Element

Default value:	auto
Values:	auto, *xx*em, *xx*ex, *xx*cm, *xx*in, *xx*mm, *xx*pc, *xx*pt, *xx*px, *xx*%
Applicable to Elements:	Block-level, replaced, and "absolutely" positioned elements
Inherit from Parent Element:	no

This property specifies the *width* of the element. The use of width with statically positioned elements is unchanged from CSS Level 1. Width is also used with relatively positioned elements, in the same manner as with statically positioned ones. Thus, the only important change relates to the use of `width` with absolutely positioned content, where it specifies the width of the box that contains the absolutely positioned content.

The default value for `width` is `auto`. In the case of absolutely positioned elements, this positions the left edge of the element to lie immediately inside the right inner edge of the parent element (the edge inside any padding or border). Note that if an element is significantly repositioned, the element's right edge may be to the left of the left edge. In this case, the `width` is set to zero.

`Width` can be given in absolute or relative length units, or as a percentage value—percentage values should be calculated relative to the width of the parent element. Percentage values are *undefined* should the parent element be itself formatted as `width: auto`. Thus, authors should avoid percentage values in this case.

Z-index: Specify Stacking Order of Element

Default value:	`auto`
Values:	`auto, nn` (*integer value*)
Applicable to Elements:	"Absolutely" or "relatively" positioned elements
Inherit from Parent Element:	no

This property specifies the stacking order for an element relative to the parent element, or relative to other "sibling" elements (elements that are children of the same parent element) that may occupy the same position on the display. This lets an author specify the order in which elements lie one on top of another.

The value for `z-index` is a positive or negative integer (including zero), where elements with larger z-index values lie on top of elements with smaller values. For example, an element with a `z-index` value of 2 lies on top of an element with a value of 1. Furthermore, elements with positive `z-index` values lie on top of the parent element, while elements with negative values lie below it.

Each of these superimposed elements can, in turn, contain child elements which can be stacked above or below it, according to the `z-index` values. The result of this process is stacked as a unit relative to its own parent and sibling elements.

Scripted Stylesheets and the Document Object Model

A stylesheet language, such as CSS, simply specifies the desired static layout for the content of a Web page—once the page is displayed, the rendering is in principle fixed until the document is reloaded, or a new page accessed.

Given the dynamic nature of the Web, and the growing use of Web browsers as interfaces to dynamic tools such as databases, this "static" nature was perceived by both Netscape and

Microsoft as a major limitation of the stylesheet approach. Both companies, therefore, began to look for ways to affect the styling and rendering of a document, and to allow for dynamic modification and update of content required by database- or multimedia-driven applications.

The results were two highly incompatible technologies, both of which are misleadingly called the same thing: "Dynamic HTML." The Netscape approach, incorporated into the Navigator 4 browser, is based on an extension to the JavaScript language known as *JavaScript Accessible Stylesheets*. This approach includes support for the element positioning model described in the CSS positioning draft, and defines a JavaScript-based software interface to these properties. Microsoft, on the other hand, is defining a software interface to all elements on an HTML page, with the intent of developing a general-purpose programming interface to these elements that can be accessed by any scripting language (e.g., JavaScript or VBScript) or by a downloaded Java applet or Active-X plug-in. This approach is built into Internet Explorer 4, and has a number of features not presently available via the Netscape approach.

Both approaches are exciting, but they are, unfortunately, completely incompatible—documents written to use the Netscape approach will not work on MSIE 4, and vice versa. Fortunately, both companies have agreed to fully support CSS, so that by limiting yourself to plain CSS, you can guarantee universally usable documents, at the expense of a few (albeit, rather exciting) bells and whistles.

In the long run, the two browser vendors will converge on a common *document object model*—the model by which script software can interact with the underlying formatting elements on a Web page. This should, in turn, unify the approach to script-controlled formatting, and eliminate the incompatibility between the two approaches.

Netscape's JavaScript Stylesheets

Prior to the adoption of cascading stylesheets by all browser vendors, Netscape began developing its own approach to document styling, called *JavaScript Accessible Stylesheets* (also known as *JASS* or *JSSS*). The idea behind JASS was that, just as JavaScript can interact with HTML elements such as hypertext anchors or HTML FORM input elements, the language could also be modified to interact with any HTML element in the document, and modify its formatting or presentation parameters. Thus was born JASS—a set of extensions to the JavaScript language that lets an author write JavaScript programs that can access each HTML element and set the formatting properties for those elements.

At its simplest level, JASS is simply an alternative to CSS—that is, every styling detail that can be specified in CSS can also be specified using JASS. The advantage lies is the *scripting* capability, which allows the style of a page to be modified on-the-fly as the page is rendered. Indeed, using JASS stylesheets, it is possible to dynamically "hide" and "reveal" sections of a document by turning the `display` property on and off. However, for the most part, JASS-based styling is quite static. For example, once a color is selected for a particular element (for example, a heading), the color is then fixed, and can only be changed by reloading the entire document.

JavaScript Stylesheet Overview

This overview assumes some familiarity with the JavaScript object model, and with JavaScript programming in general. If you are not familiar with these concepts, you may wish to skip this section.

The JavaScript Stylesheet approach introduces several new classes and methods to the JavaScript language. First, HTML elements become *object properties* of the document object, as do element **CLASS**es and **ID**s. These objects can take other properties that define the formatting characteristics of the element—these properties are exactly equivalent to the CSS formatting properties. For example, to reference **H3** elements and place an underline under the text content, the JavaScript statement is

```
document.tags.H3.textDecoration = "underline" ;
```

which is exactly equivalent to the CSS rule `H3 {text-decoration: underline}`. Similarly, to specify a particular text color for all elements of **CLASS**="blobby", the JavaScript statement would be

```
document.classes.blobby.all.color = "#a3f5dd";
```

where `all` is a special property that refers to all elements. To specify the color for only **P** elements of this class, the expression would be:

```
document.classes.blobby.P.color = "#a3f5dd";
```

The CSS equivalents to these two expressions are, respectively:

```
 .blobby   {color: #a3f5dd; }
P.blobby   {color: #a3f5dd; }
```

ID values are similarly treated. The JavaScript expression for requesting a specific font weight for an element of **ID**="xp23" is just:

```
document.ids.xp23.fontWeight = "bold";
```

Contextual selectors are possible using the new JavaScript `contextual()` method. An example is:

```
contextual(tags.UL, tags.UL, classes.special.LI).color = "yellow"
```

which is equivalent to the CSS rule:

```
UL UL LI.special {color: yellow; }
```

In principle, you can also include JASS stylesheet instructions within **STYLE** attribute values for specific stylesheet elements. In this case, the statement inside the **STYLE** value does not need to specify the properties implicit due to the location of the element in the document (just as with CSS). For example, to specify a line spacing and text color for a particular paragraph element, the markup could be:

```
<P STYLE="lineHeight='1.5'; color='red'"> .... </P>
```

Note how single quotes are used inside the stylesheet expression. Note, also, that the document now must have, somewhere in the document **HEAD**, a **STYLE** element that specifies **TYPE**="text/javascript", as otherwise the browser will assume CSS stylesheets, which is incorrect.

The preceding few short paragraphs provided a very brief summary of the JavaScript language additions introduced by Netscape in support of the JavaScript stylesheets approach. Additional details are found in the references at the end of this chapter. Again, as JASS is only supported by Netscape, and as essentially equivalent formatting is available via CSS, you are best advised to use CSS unless there is some special, dynamic aspect to your pages that requires JASS.

Including JavaScript Stylesheets in HTML Documents

JavaScript stylesheets are included in HTML documents either as part of a program script (within a **SCRIPT** element) or by placing them within a **STYLE** element, as per cascading stylesheets. If the latter is done, the **TYPE** of the script must also be specified, since the browser must be told which type to expect. The appropriate specification for JavaScript stylesheets is

```
<STYLE TYPE="text/javascript">
... javascript stylesheet content ....
</STYLE>
```

where the MIME type for the stylesheets, `text/javascript`, is shown in boldface. Note that a server delivering JavaScript stylesheets must indicate this MIME type in the HTTP message that contains the document. Typically, JavaScript programs and JavaScript stylesheets have the filename extension *.jss*.

The Microsoft Approach

Microsoft, of course, does not support JASS. Instead, Microsoft chose to start from the ground up, by developing an object model for the entire HTML document, along with a defined set of object properties, as well as a set of methods to interact with those objects. This is a similar idea to JASS, but grander in scope, since JASS only allows (at least for now) for limited modification of the underlying document and associated styling, whereas the Microsoft approach potentially allows for much greater interaction, and for browser-based software control over every aspect of a document's content and presentation.

The Document Object Model

The Microsoft approach is based on what is now known as the *Document Object Model*, or *DOM*. The idea behind DOM is that the document can be treated as a nested collection of formatting objects, each object being created by an underlying HTML element. The object model then defines methods and properties associated with these objects. For example, a **P** element would have properties for the parent formatting element, the different stylesheet "properties" of the element, and the element content. By accessing these properties (for example, via a VBScript or JavaScript program), software can access the specific properties of the element (e.g., to retrieve the specific content of an element) and modify the properties (e.g., replace the content of a paragraph with new text). This is more powerful than Netscape's original version of JASS, in that the Microsoft model gives software access to the actual text content of an element, whereas the JASS model can only access an element's styling properties.

In addition to being able to access properties of an element, the DOM also supports methods by which software can dynamically interact with a formatting element, and change its formatting style, or even change the text content. This can all be done dynamically, so that a DOM-based system can redraw the content of the screen in real time as the user clicks on the anchors or modifies form input elements.

The DOM methods and properties are still being specified. The approach is designed to be language-independent, so that scripts in JavaScript or VBScript or any other language can access the DOM methods and manipulate the underlying elements.

Of course, the main weakness of this approach is its proprietary nature—the DOM approach works *only* on Microsoft Internet Explorer 4, and does not work on any versions of Netscape Navigator or any other browser. Thus, it is difficult to write DOM documents that work properly on browsers other than Microsoft's. This is an important point to consider if you are trying to make your documents accessible to the widest possible audience.

Although DOM was a Microsoft "invention," the World Wide Web Consortium recently formed a working group to develop a standards-based DOM, with the intent of defining a standard version for all Web browsers. With luck, the establishment of a "standard" DOM will eliminate the incompatibilities between the Netscape and Microsoft approaches, and once again lead to platform-independent documents.

Additional information about Microsoft's Dynamic HTML approach and the DOM is available at the Microsoft Web site. Some URLs that serve as useful starting points are given in the References section at the end of this chapter.

Font Downloading and Dynamic Fonts

One of the greatest limitations of CSS design is the lack of fonts—a Web browser can display only fonts that are present on the user's computer. Thus, although Web page designers can *specify* all sorts of wonderful fonts in their designs, most browsers will not be able to display them, since they are not present on the local computer.

Resolving this problem is both technically and politically complicated. The technical solution is relatively straightforward, and comes in two parts:

1. Provide *font matching* information—the browser downloads the Web page, but the page contains information that specifies *general characteristics* of the desired font. If the font is unavailable, the browser can look at the general characteristics of the desired font, and substitute the available font that is most similar to the desired choice.

2. Provide *downloadable* fonts—the browser downloads the Web page, and also downloads the fonts needed in the page.

However, this two-part solution assumes that there is a standard format for describing the general characteristics of a given font, and that there is a standard format for *downloadable* fonts.

Neither of these statements is entirely accurate. There are several proposed font description systems, but no accepted universal scheme. The most popular of these is the PANOSE system. PANOSE font match works reasonably well, and provides good font matching under most circumstances. As discussed below, there are recent proposals to use the PANOSE system within CSS to specify the characteristics of the desired font. However, matching is useless if there are no similar fonts on the computer, which returns us to the original problem.

Font downloading is an even more useful approach, as it in principle resolves all the "missing font" problems. However, this solution suffers from some other important problems. As noted in Chapter 3, there are many different and entirely incompatible font formats (PostScript Type 1, PostScript Type 3, TrueType, etc.). At the same time, these formats are not compact—some TrueType fonts, for example, require 100KB files to store the font information. Obviously this will cause grief on the Web, where file sizes need to be kept small if pages are to be displayed quickly, although compression can solve some of this problem. Last, there are legal problems—most fonts are purchased under the agreement that they will not be redistributed, or will only be redistributed in such a way that they cannot be reused. By making a TrueType or PostScript font available for downloading, a document author is essentially giving the font away for free, in violation of this contract with the font developer. Technical solutions to these legal issues are only now being developed.

Netscape Dynamic Fonts

Netscape is attempting to deliver downloadable fonts using a new technology from Bitstream, known as *TrueDoc*. TrueDoc combines a font format and font distribution technology in a single package, and is designed explicitly for contexts such as Web or other electronic document publishing. Netscape has incorporated TrueDoc technology into its browser, Netscape Navigator 4, and its HTML authoring tool, Netscape Composer. The browser includes software, called the *displayer* or *character shape player*, that can read the TrueDoc font format (known as a *portable font resource*, or *PFR*) and render the font symbols to the display. Netscape Composer comes equipped with portable font resource creation software, called the *character shape recorder*, that can take the fonts employed in a document and dynamically create TrueDoc font files for them.

The implementation is as follows. When creating a document, an author can use any of the fonts available on the local computer, in any supported format (bitmap, TrueType, PostScript, or other). When the document is created, the fonts are referenced using appropriate CSS `font-family` properties, with the value being the one used by the selected font.

When the author *saves* the document to disk, the TrueDoc system (which must be incorporated into the editor) takes each of the fonts used in the document, dynamically examines the font's characters, generates a portable font resource description for the font, and stores this information in a PFR file. This file is the TrueDoc equivalent of the original font. These files store font information in a highly compressed format (often less than 20KB), so that they can be quickly transported over the Internet. Also, each file is encrypted, and can be used only with documents coming from the Web site at which the document was created. Thus, the font files cannot be copied and used with other applications or other Web pages, thereby protecting the copyright of the original fonts.

Referencing External Font Files

To use these external fonts, an HTML document must reference the required font resource files. The HTML editor that creates these external font files will create these references automatically. There are two ways to reference external fonts: via **LINK** elements, or via a new CSS extension that supports external font file references.

With **LINK**, the appropriate format is:

```
<LINK REL="fontdef" HREF="URL-to-fontdesc.pfr">
```

where the attribute **REL**="fontdef" indicates that the **LINK** references a font description file, and where the value of HREF is the URL pointing to the desired font file.

External fonts can also be referenced from within a stylesheet, using a CSS language extension proposed by Bitstream and Netscape. The format for the extension is not finalized, but will look something like the following:

```
@font-face {
    font-family: family-name;
    src:         url(PFR-file-url);
    font-weight: default-weight;
}
```

where *family-name* is the family name for the font stored in the referenced PFR file, *PFR-file-url* is the URL pointing to the associated PFR file, and *default-weight* is the weight for the default font (usually "normal"). Note, however, that the World Wide Web Consortium has not finalized the CSS syntax for external font specifications so that the format in the example is unlikely to be the specified syntax. Please see the W3C Web site (*http://www.w3.org*) or the book Web site for up-to-date information on this subject.

Elsewhere in the stylesheet, the font is referenced using `font-family` and the appropriate font name, just as before. For example, if a stylesheet contains the following external font reference:

```
@font-face  {
    font-family:   "ShelleyVolante BT";
    src:           url(./fonts/svolante.pfr);
    weight:        normal;
}
```

then elsewhere in the stylesheet this font can be referenced using the `font-family` property as per the standard mechanism:

```
H1 {font-family: "ShelleyVolante BT", cursive;
    font-size:    1.5em;
    font-weight:  bold;  }
```

This is clearly backward-compatible with older browsers—older software simply ignores the `@font-face` rules, is unable to use the downloaded font, and uses the standard CSS mechanisms to find an acceptable font.

MIME Type for PFR Files

Of course, the Web server delivering the documents must be configured to send the correct MIME type when it downloads a portable font resource file. As mentioned above, the default filename extension for such files is *.pfr*. The correct MIME type is

```
application/font-tdpfr
```

where the substring `tdpfr` refers to "TrueDoc Portable Font Resource."

Microsoft Font Embedding

Microsoft is proposing a method for font downloading that differs significantly from the Netscape/Bitstream approach. Instead of using a new font format, Microsoft plans to use its existing TrueType *embedded font* technology. With embedded fonts, a document contains (in a compressed format) the actual TrueType font specification, which can then be used by the application viewing the font. The application can then use a TrueType displayer (Windows 3.1/95/NT have such displayers integrated into the operating system) to display these fonts within the document. In its current format, the embedded font technology actually places the fonts within the file containing the document text (for example, a Word document). It is not yet clear how this will work on the Web, although most likely the font information will be placed in a second file (or files), referenced from within the document as described previously for the TrueDoc approach.

The advantage of this approach is that the delivered fonts are exactly those used to produce the document, so there are no concerns that the fonts were degraded in some way (some have argued that the TrueDoc fonts are only a poor copy of the original). This is also a disadvantage, however, since the downloaded fonts are just standard TrueType fonts, and can, in principle, be reused by any TrueType-capable application, thereby violating the copyright of the font. Microsoft is actively developing encryption and security technology to prevent this from happening.

A major perceived disadvantage is the limitation to TrueType fonts—the embedded font approach only works with TrueType fonts, not with PostScript or other font formats. This is a big limitation, since most professional typography and layout is done using PostScript fonts, and not TrueType. Microsoft and Adobe are working on a new font specification, called *OpenType*, which will be the successor to TrueType and which will merge the PostScript and TrueType formats under a new, universal format. However, this format is still being defined, and will not be deployed in the near future.

It is unclear how the "font wars" will play out, or which format (or formats) will dominate in the next few years. The Bitstream, Microsoft, and Netscape Web sites provide much interesting—and biased—commentary on these issues.

Font Matching and PANOSE Numbers

Another idea is to specify the general characteristics of the font in the stylesheet—then, if the browser does not have the specified font, it can use this information to choose an available font that is as "close" to the desired font as possible. Doing so requires two things: a *scheme* for describing the generic characteristics of a font, and a *guarantee* that all fonts available on the local system will be characterized by this scheme, so that the software can find the best available font.

The most common scheme of this type is known as the PANOSE typeface matching system. This is a de-facto industry standard, owned by Hewlett-Packard, that uses integer numbers to characterize ten main characteristics (such as family type, serif style, contrast, mid-line position, etc.) of the font. The system then employs a "closeness" algorithm, by which PANOSE-aware software can determine which available font has a PANOSE number "closest" to a given PANOSE specification.

There is as yet no defined way for including PANOSE information in a stylesheet. One possible syntax is

```
font-family: "Times New Roman", "Times Roman", serif #2263545234;
```

where the number after the # is the PANOSE number for the desired font. A PANOSE-aware browser would use this number to locate the preferred local font, should the specified "Times New Roman" font not be available.

Hewlett-Packard has also developed software that can dynamically generate a font based on the PANOSE numbers. Known as INTELLIFONT, this technology can take the PANOSE codes and generate a plausible version of the desired font. The resulting characters are, of course, never as good as the desired font. Nevertheless, this approach does provide for a last-gasp attempt at finding an appropriate font, should all other avenues (substitution, font downloading etc.) be exhausted.

There are, of course, limitations to the PANOSE scheme. For example, the scheme was designed with Western European languages and relatively standard fonts in mind, and is not easily adapted to languages with more complex writing systems, such as Chinese. Efforts are underway to extend PANOSE to cover these cases.

At present, there are no Web browsers that support PANOSE numbers for font substitution.

Fonts and Character Sets

Finally, it is important to recognize that a font is *not* the same thing as a character set. A character set defines a relationship between computer binary codes and characters, or letters, while a font simply defines a set of symbols that should be used for a given set of characters or letters. For example, the "Times New Roman" font defines 224 font symbols, conveniently chosen to be appropriate for the 224 characters defined in the ISO Latin-1 character set. Indeed, most fonts designed for use with Western European languages are designed to work with the 8-bit ISO Latin-1 character set.

For non-European languages, this situation is a bit more complicated. However, most non-European languages now use their own special 8-bit character sets (e.g., for Greek, Cyrillic, or Arabic) and define fonts appropriate to this character set. Thus, if a document is written using the eight-bit ISO 8857-2 character set (for Eastern European languages), then the stylesheet would simply request a font designed to work with this character set.

At present, the distinction between character sets and fonts is not important, since, in most cases, there is a simple relationship between character sets and fonts, such as for the cases outlined in the previous paragraphs. For example, given the ISO Latin-1 character set an author would use one set of fonts, and given ISO 8857-2 would use another set. This works, but has the limitation that the character sets cannot be mixed in the same document—thus one cannot easily mix English and

Arabic in the same document. Similarly, it requires that each user's computer store literally hundreds of different character sets, and then many different fonts for these different character sets.

This distinction between character sets and fonts will soon be very important. This is because the Web has recently adopted the *Unicode* character set as the default set for the Web. Unicode supports many tens of thousands of characters, instead of the less than 256 characters supported by 8-bit character sets such as ISO Latin-1. Moreover, Unicode supports many different *types* of characters (Roman, Arabic, Japanese, Cyrillic) within this character set. In this sense, Unicode is designed to be a *universal* character set—one that can contain all characters from any language, such that any document in the world can be written using a single character set, Unicode.

With Unicode there is no longer a simple relationship between character set and font—obviously it does not makes sense to talk about a single "Times Roman" font for a Unicode document, since this font only applies to the characters of (at best) Western European languages, and not to the thousands of other characters from other languages. Thus, a document written in the Unicode character set can take a number of different fonts, with each font applied to the different group or *range* of characters appropriate to that font.

Clearly, CSS needs to support this aspect of Unicode. The mechanism for doing so is still being developed, but in general will involve specifying *both* the desired *font* and the *range* of characters in the Unicode character set to which the font should be applied. For example, to apply the "Times New Roman" font to the first 256 characters of the Unicode character set (this is the part of Unicode that supports these characters), the CSS markup might be

```
@font-face {
    font-family:      "Times New Roman", "Times Roman", serif;
    unicode-range:    0000-00FF;
    panose:           2263545234;
}
```

where the new at-rule `@font-face` groups together the information about a specific font and range of characters in the character set (there is as yet no specification for this format—the above is purely the invention of the author!). This rule specifies three things: the desired font, the range of characters in the Unicode character set that should be presented using this font—here the zero'th to the 255th (hexadecimal FF) character in the Unicode character set, and finally the PANOSE number for the font. As described earlier, the latter declaration helps the browser substitute a replacement font, should the requested font not be available.

Such CSS details are under current development, and you are encouraged to visit the World Wide Web Consortium Web site for up-to-date information on this interesting topic.

Aural Cascading Stylesheets

One of the advertised strengths of stylesheets is the ability to provide different stylesheets appropriate to different display devices. Of course, this concept is useless without stylesheet languages appropriate to these other devices.

The first proposal for an alternative presentation language has been put forward by Chris Lilley of the World Wide Web Consortium and T. V. Raman of Adobe, who have developed an initial draft for an *aural* stylesheet language, formally known as *Aural Cascading Stylesheets*, or *ACSS*. ACSS provides formatting instructions relevant to the aural or spoken presentation of text—which obviously requires instructions distinctly different from a screen-based approach.

There are many possible applications for an aural approach. Some examples (based on a short list given in the ACSS preliminary draft) are:

Audio interface in vehicles—A driver may use the Web to check for road information or search for hotels. Obviously it would be inappropriate to read Web pages while driving!

Hands- and eye-free documentation systems—A technician (or medical doctor) may want to call up important Web-based information relevant to the task at hand, but may not be free to leave or look away from the task.

Mixed media presentations—A Web document could contain text to be read, along with text to be narrated. ACSS would let both forms of content appear as regular text in the same document.

Home entertainment—Web-based games could have audio instructions (or dialog text related to game characters) that should be rendered to speech while the users are playing.

Illiteracy—Some people can't read, so that an audio interface gives them access to Web resources that are otherwise inaccessible.

Visual (or other) impairment—Some people have significant visual impairments, or may have perceptual disorders (e.g., dyslexia) that make reading difficult or impossible. Aural presentation gives these users access to otherwise inaccessible resources.

Note that, although there is a moral imperative in providing aural access to Web resources, the imperative is not entirely altruistic—as we all age, we run an increasing risk of developing visual impairments that affect our ability to read comfortably, or at all. Technologies such as ACSS will therefore in the long run benefit all of us.

ACSS is based on the CSS language syntax, and is designed to work with CSS, so that a document can contain some content to be displayed on a graphics display, and some to be spoken out loud. The current ACSS draft proposals define approximately twenty properties for specifying how elements should be spoken when rendered into speech. The following are some example properties, with brief descriptions:

`volume`—Sets the volume for the spoken text.

`pause-before`—Sets the time delay before speaking the selected text.

`elevation, azimuth`—Specifies the *position* of the speaker (to allow for different apparent sources of the spoken text).

`voice-family`—Specifies the type of voice—for example, "feminine," "masculine," or more detailed descriptions such as "announcer" or "comedian."

`stress`—Specifies the level of stress or emphasis for the voice.

The ACSS specification is undergoing rapid development, and should soon evolve into a standard. Full details about ACSS are available on the W3C Web site, at the URL:

`http://www.w3.org/pub/WWW/TR/NOTE-ACSS`

Printing and Other Alternate Media

Of course, one of the original claims of the Web was that it would reduce the need for printed pages—after all, if material is accessible online, why would anyone want to print it? The truth, of course, is that this transformation did not happen, and indeed it is unlikely to happen in the foreseeable future. If anything, the Web has led to an *increase* in printed pages, since readers often want to "take away" copies of the individual pages they have read, or want printable copies of longer document collections for reading off-line, and at their leisure.

At present, the Web offers poor support for print-format presentation. Browsers do let users print pages, but the quality of the printed output—the placement of headings with respect to subsequent text, the proper scaling of images to the printed page, the setting of font sizes, and many other features—are all poorly implemented. Indeed, as discussed at the end of Chapter 5, many current CSS-enabled documents simply can't be printed! There are two reasons for this situation. First is the fact that browser developers have placed relatively little emphasis on printing, concentrating their efforts on the online component—printing was more or less an afterthought. More fundamentally, however, is the lack of any way to customize printing properties separate from the properties appropriate to the graphical display; for example, the desired page size and margins for printed (as opposed to online pages), possible alternating "left" and "right" page formatting, and the specification of page breaks. Such concepts are critical to proper printing of documents, but are irrelevant to the online display. Finally, there is a need for "alternative" renderings, so that something meaningful can be printed in place of multimedia or other dynamic content that cannot be printed.

This is an obvious role for a stylesheet language, and indeed a recent CSS draft proposes several CSS printing extensions. In particular, the language proposes a new at-rule, `@page`, used to define *page*-specific properties as opposed to markup element-specific ones. For example, a CSS stylesheet might contain the rule

```
@page { size: landscape;
        margin: 5%;    }
```

which also introduces a proposed new property, `size`, for specifying the desired size of the paper. Some other proposed properties include `page-break-before`, for setting page breaks before an element, and `page-break-after`, for setting a page break after an element. In addition, the new pseudo-elements `:left` and `:right` allow for page properties that apply only to left-hand or right-hand pages, for example

```
@page :left  {margin: 5%  5%  5% 10%}
@page :right {margin: 5% 10%  5%  5%}
```

to specify different left and right margins for left-hand or right-hand pages.

Alternate Media Types

Of course, print and online presentations may call for other differences in formatting—for example, an author may wish to use a larger Verdana font for online presentation, but a smaller Garamond font for printing. Similarly, we noted earlier that ACSS lets an author specify rules appropriate for aural presentation, as opposed to an online or printed one. Associating all these options with a given document means that there needs to be a way of selecting different sets of stylesheet rules for the different presentation media.

There are recently proposed CSS and HTML mechanisms for defining such alternatives. Within CSS, the proposed `@media` at-rule, combined with a number of predefined media types, allows for stylesheet rules that apply for different presentation modes. For example, the stylesheet

```
@media screen {
       BODY  {font: 12pt Verdana }
}
@media print  {
       BODY  {font: 10pt Garamond }
}
@media screen,print {
       P {margin-left: 5%; line-height: 1.4; }
}
```

contains three blocks of rules, the first and third applying to on-screen presentations, and the second and third to print. The content of an `@media` rule can be any collection of CSS rules, so that many alternative-media stylesheets can be contained within the same CSS.

Alternate Media and LINK Elements

Alternatively, media-specific stylesheets can be included in an HTML document via **LINK** elements. The relevant syntax is simply

```
<LINK REL="stylesheet" TYPE="text/css"  MEDIA="media-type" HREF="url">
```

where *media-type* is a comma-separated list of media types (for example, "print, screen" for rules that apply to both printed and online formats) and `url` is the URL referencing the stylesheet document. There are currently six proposed media type values:

all (*default value*)—Applies to all presentation media types.

aural—For aural presentation, such as synthesized speech—this is the type particularly relevant for aural cascading stylesheets.

braille—For Braille devices (note that there are as yet no Braille-specific CSS properties).

print—For printed output (or for a browser's "Print Preview" mode).

projection—For projected presentations.

screen—For presentation on a computer screen.

Others will no doubt be added to support other presentation modes. Note that these are the same media type values used by the CSS @media at-rules.

Alternate Media and STYLE Elements

At the same time, the **STYLE** element must be able to specify the media to which the style element content applies. Under this proposed extension to HTML, the **STYLE** element can also take a **MEDIA** attribute to specify the media type. The format is then

```
<STYLE TYPE="text/css" MEDIA="media-type">
..... stylesheet content ...
</STYLE>
```

where, once again, *media-type* is a comma-separated list of media types. If **MEDIA** is absent, a browser will assume the value all.

Alternative Stylesheets and the TITLE Attribute

In many cases, it would be nice to give readers a choice of alternative styles that they can apply to the same document—for example, a user may wish to switch between "screen" view, when previewing a document, and "presentation" view when making a presentation using the document. The "HTML and Stylesheets" draft from the World Wide Web Consortium proposes using the **LINK** element **TITLE** attribute to provide alternative stylesheets, and a mechanism for users to select between these alternatives. The format is simply

```
<LINK REL="stylesheet"           TITLE="sheet-title1" HREF="url">
<LINK REL="alternate stylesheet"  TITLE="sheet-title2" HREF="url">
```

where *sheet-title1* and *sheet-title2* are the titles associated with the stylesheets, and where the **REL** value "alternate stylesheet" has the obvious meaning. The first of these two **LINK** elements references the default stylesheet—this is the one that will be used by default, but the fact that it has a **TITLE** means that it can be replaced by an "alternate stylesheet," should the browser support this feature.

An HTML document might then contain the following sequence of **LINK** elements:

```
<LINK REL="stylesheet"           HREF="url">
<LINK REL="stylesheet"           TITLE="Presentation Mode" HREF="url">
<LINK REL="alternate stylesheet" TITLE="Compact Outline"   HREF="url">
<LINK REL="alternate stylesheet" TITLE="Annotation Mode"   HREF="url">
```

This contains three alternative stylesheets, with associated titles. A browser that supports this feature would let the user select (for example, using a pull-down menu) which of the three optional stylesheets he or she wishes to use, with the text in the **TITLE** providing a description of the stylesheet. The default stylesheet would be the one with attribute **REL**="stylesheet."

Note that this example contains a **LINK** element that lacks a **TITLE**. Such **LINK** elements as this reference *persistent stylesheets*: Such stylesheets are *always* applied to the document, and cannot be deselected.

Additional information about printing and other media support is found in the CSS Printing and Style drafts mentioned in the References section.

CSS-Aware Software

There are already several browsers that support some or all of CSS Level 1, while there are also several document editors that have implemented support for CSS. The following is a brief summary of some such software. Additional lists of software are found at:

```
http://www.w3.org/pub/WWW/Style/#software
```

HotDog
http://www.sausage.com/ HotDog Professional, from Sausage Software, is a popular commercial and shareware HTML editor. The latest version advertises support for CSS, and lets an author create styling as the document is written.

HoTMetaL Intranet Publisher (HiP)
http://www.softquad.com/hip/ HiP, from SoftQuad Inc., is a sophisticated Intranet Web site development and management system, built on top of SoftQuad's known expertise in SGML. The latest version of HiP has support for CSS, and lets authors create custom stylesheets and deliver them with their documents.

WebMaker
http://www.harlequin.com/webmaker WebMaker, from The Harlequin Group Ltd., is a tool for converting Adobe FrameMaker documents into HTML. The latest version of WebMaker (version 3.0) has advertised support for CSS in this process—WebMaker will take the styling information in the FrameMaker document and convert it into the closest CSS equivalent.

Homesite Version 2.5
http://www.allaire.com/products/homesite/overview.cfm Homesite, from Allaire Corp., is an integrated Web site management and document creation system, based on the Allaire Cold Fusion script-

ing language for building dynamic documents. The system includes an HTML editor and document management tool, and this tool has some support for CSS.

JoyHTML

http://www.abc.se/~m8974/joyframe.htm JoyHTML is a shareware HTML editor, written in Swedish, so that learning how to use the software is a useful way to learn some Swedish. The editor has built-in controls for adding styling information to documents as they are edited.

HoTaMaLe

http://www.adobe.com/prodindex/framemaker/exportpi.html HoTaMale, from Adobe Inc., is an export filter for Adobe FrameMaker. This filter can export HTML documents, and can convert FrameMaker-format styling information into its closest CSS equivalent.

QuickSite 2.0

http://www.deltapoint.com/qsdeved/index.htm QuickSite, from DeltaPoint Inc., is an integrated Web site creation and management suite. The package is advertised as having built-in support for cascading stylesheets.

Amaya

http://www.w3.org/pub/WWW/Amaya/ Amaya is the W3C's testbed software for Web client development. It is a combination of browser and editor, and in both roles has support for some aspects of CSS. It is available for downloading at the indicated URL.

References

CSS References, Drafts, and Notes
http://www.w3.org/pub/WWW/Style/ (W3C Stylesheets overview)

http://www.w3.org/pub/WWW/TR/WD-positioning (W3C CSS Positioning draft)

http://www.w3.org/pub/WWW/Style/css/Speech/NOTE-ACSS (W3C Aural Cascading Stylesheets note)

http://www.w3.org/pub/WWW/TR/WD-print (W3C CSS Printing extensions draft)

http://www.w3.org/pub/WWW/TR/WD-style (W3C HTML and Style draft)

Fonts, Dynamic Fonts, and Font Matching
http://www.w3.org/pub/WWW/Fonts/ (W3C Notes on fonts and the Web)

http://fonts.verso.com/main.html (Studio Verso Pages on fonts and the Web)

http://www.w3.org/pub/WWW/Printing/Workshop_960425.html (W3C Workshop on fonts and printing)

http://www.fonts.com/hp/fontech.htm (PANOSE font matching system) http://www.fonts.com/hp/infinifont/index.htm (INFINIFONT font generation system)

http://www.w3.org/pub/WWW/Printing/stevahn.html (PANOSE and the Web)

http://www.Bitstream.com/w3/ (Bitstream TrueDoc font format)

http://www.bitstream.com/world/index.htm (Netscape TrueDoc/Dynamic font information)

http://home.netscape.com/flash1/comprod/products/communicator/index.html (Netscape dynamic font information)

http://www.microsoft.com/truetype/web/plans/default.htm (Microsoft's plans for Fonts on the Web)

http://www.truetype.demon.co.uk/ttparam.htm (Parametric TrueType information)

http://www.microsoft.com/truetype/embed/embed2.htm (Embedded TrueType fonts)

http://www.microsoft.com/truetype/tt/tt.htm (OpenType and TrueType specifications)

http://www.truetype.demon.co.uk/opentype.htm (OpenType font format information)

Javascript Accessible Stylesheets
http://developer.netscape.com/library/documentation/communicator/stylesheets/jssindex.htm (JavaScript Accessible Stylesheets)

Dynamic HTML
http://www.w3.org/pub/WWW/MarkUp/DOM/ (W3C Document Object Model information)

http://developer.netscape.com/library/ (Netscape developer information)

http://developer.netscape.com/library/documentation/htmlguid/dynamic_resources.html (Netscape Dynamic HTML documentation)

http://www.microsoft.com/ie/ie40/browser/dynamic.htm (Microsoft Dynamic HTML overview)

http://www.microsoft.com/workshop/author/dynhtml/ (Microsoft Dynamic HTML technical reference)

Color, Color Codes,
and Color Names

Computer display colors are usually defined using a scheme known as RGB (Red-Green-Blue) color codes. This scheme expresses each color as a mixture of the primary colors red, green, and blue (this scheme was chosen because these are the colors of the three phosphors used on most computer monitors). Usually, the intensity of each color ranges from a value of 0 (no intensity) to 255 (as bright as possible). As a result of this choice, the strength of each of the three primary colors can be expressed in a single byte (an 8-bit code can store $2^8 = 256$ different numbers). Therefore, any color can be expressed as a 24-bit sequence containing the intensity of the red, green, and blue components. This is why high-resolution graphics systems are often said to support "24-bit color."

RGB colors are often expressed as numbers in the hexadecimal numbering system. In this system, a complete color specification looks like:

RRGGBB

where *RR* is the hex code for the red intensity (ranging from 00 to FF), *GG* is the hex code for the green intensity (ranging from 00 to FF), and *BB* is the hex code for the blue intensity (you get the idea). For example, the code 000000 corresponds to black, FFFFFF corresponds to white (as bright as possible), and AAAAAA corresponds to a rather light shade of gray.

The CSS color scheme is based on the RGB color system, although there are some important implementation details that need to be understood to use the scheme successfully. The next section outlines the CSS mechanisms for naming colors, while the subsequent section discusses these implementation issues.

Color Specification In CSS

CSS supports several ways for specifying colors, all of which are based on the RGB system. These can be divided into two main categories: color names, and RGB color codes. These two mechanisms are discussed in the following sections.

CSS Named Colors

CSS supports 16 different symbolic color names, corresponding to the 16 colors of the Windows VGA color palette. For example, to specify text in the color "fuchsia" (a pinkish-purple), a CSS author can use the declaration

```
color: fuchsia;
```

in place of the specific RGB code corresponding to this color.

The 16 color names supported in CSS, alongside their RGB equivalents, are listed in Table A.1. As mentioned, these colors are defined as part of the standard Microsoft Windows colormap, and are consequently never *dithered* by Microsoft Windows systems that support only 8-bit color (*dithering* is discussed later in this appendix). Figure A.1 lists an HTML test document illustrating the use of these names. For obvious reasons, we do not bother displaying a black-and-white rendering of this document! The document can be retrieved from the book's supporting Web site.

Table A.1 The 16 Defined CSS Color Names and Corresponding RGB Hex Codes

Color Name	RGB Code (Hex)
aqua	00FFFF
black	000000
blue	0000FF
fuchsia	FF00FF
gray	808080
green	008000
lime	00FF00
maroon	800000
navy	000080
olive	808000

Continued

Table A.1 *Continued*

Color Name	RGB Code (Hex)
purple	800080
red	FF0000
silver	C0C0C0
teal	008080
white	FFFFFF
yellow	FFFF00

Figure A.1 The HTML document colortst.html that illustrates the 16 different named colors supported by CSS Level 1.

```
<HTML><HEAD>
<TITLE> Test of CSS Named Colors</TITLE>
<STYLE> <!--
BODY      {background: #eeeeee }
DIV       {text-align: center  }
TD.aqua   {background: aqua;    }
TD.black  {background: black;   color:white} /* Note named colors */
TD.blue   {background: blue;    color:white}
TD.fuchsia{background: fuchsia;color:white}
TD.gray   {background: gray;    color:white}
TD.green  {background: green;   color:white}
TD.lime   {background: lime;    }
TD.maroon {background: maroon;  color:white}
TD.navy   {background: navy;    color:white}
TD.olive  {background: olive;   color:white}
TD.purple {background: purple;  color:white}
TD.red    {background: red;     color:white}
TD.silver {background: silver;  }
TD.teal   {background: teal;    color:white}
TD.white  {background: white;}
TD.yellow {background: yellow;  }
--> </STYLE>
</HEAD><BODY>
<H1> Test of CSS Named Colors </H1>
<DIV>
<TABLE WIDTH="60%" CELLPADDING="5" CELLSPACING=4>
<TR>
  <TD CLASS="aqua">Aqua</TD>   <TD CLASS="black">Black</TD>
  <TD CLASS="blue">Blue</TD>   <TD CLASS="fuchsia">Fuchsia</TD>
</TR><TR>
  <TD CLASS="gray">Gray</TD>   <TD CLASS="green">green</TD>
  <TD CLASS="lime">Lime</TD>   <TD CLASS="maroon">Maroon</TD>
```

Continued

Figure A.1 Continued

```
</TR><TR>
  <TD CLASS="navy">Navy</TD>      <TD CLASS="olive">Olive</TD>
  <TD CLASS="purple">Purple</TD> <TD CLASS="red">Red</TD>
</TR><TR>
  <TD CLASS="silver">Silver</TD> <TD CLASS="teal">Teal</TD>
  <TD CLASS="white">White</TD>   <TD CLASS="yellow">Yellow</TD>
</TR>
</TABLE>
</DIV></BODY></HTML>
```

Extended Named Colors

In addition to the 16 color names defined in the CSS specifications, the CSS implementations under Netscape Navigator 4, MSIE 3, and MSIE 4 also support the 124 color names listed in Table A.2. An example document illustrating these colors is found at the book's supporting Web site. Note that these colors are not part of the Windows colormap, and thus will be dithered or substituted on computers with 8-bit color displays.

Table A.2 The 124 Colors of the Extended Color Names, and Corresponding RGB Hex Codes. Note That the Color "Aliceblue" Is Not Supported on Netscape Navigator 4

Name	RGB Code (Hex)	Name	RGB Code (Hex)
aliceblue	F0F8FF	antiquewhite	FAEBD7
aquamarine	7FFFD4	azure	F0FFFF
beige	F5F5DC	bisque	FFE4C4
blanchedalmond	FFEBCD	blueviolet	8A2BE2
brown	A52A2A	burlywood	DEB887
cadetblue	5F9EA0	chartreuse	7FFF00
chocolate	D2691E	coral	FF7F50
cornflowerblue	6495ED	cornsilk	FFF8DC
crimson	DC1436	cyan	00FFFF
darkblue	00008B	darkcyan	008B8B
darkgoldenrod	B8860B	darkgray	A9A9A9
darkgreen	006400	darkkhaki	BDB76B
darkmagenta	8B008B	darkolivegreen	556B2F

Continued

darkorange	FF8C00	darkorchid	9932CC

Table A.2 *Continued*

Name	RGB Code (Hex)	Name	RGB Code (Hex)
darkred	8B0000	darksalmon	E9967A
darkseagreen	8FBC8F	darkslateblue	483D8B
darkslategray	2F4F4F	darkturquoise	00CED1
darkviolet	9400D3	deeppink	FF1493
deepskyblue	00BFFF	dimgray	696969
dodgerblue	1E90FF	firebrick	B22222
floralwhite	FFFAF0	forestgreen	228B22
gainsboro	DCDCDC	ghostwhite	F8F8FF
gold	FFD700	goldenrod	DAA520
greenyellow	ADFF2F	honeydew	F0FFF0
hotpink	FF69B4	indianred	CD5C5C
indigo	4B0082	ivory	FFFFF0
khaki	F0E68C	lavender	E6E6FA
lavenderblush	FFF0F5	lawngreen	7CFC00
lemonchiffon	FFFACD	lightblue	ADD8E6
lightcoral	F08080	lightcyan	E0FFFF
lightgoldenrodyellow	FAFAD2	lightgreen	90EE90
lightgrey	D3D3D3	lightpink	FFB6C1
lightsalmon	FFA07A	lightseagreen	20B2AA
lightskyblue	87CEFA	lightslategray	778899
lightsteelblue	B0C4DE	lightyellow	FFFFE0
limegreen	32CD32	linen	FAF0E6
magenta	FF00FF	mediumaquamarine	66CDAA
mediumblue	0000CD	mediumorchid	BA55D3

Continued

mediumpurple	9370DB	mediumseagreen	3CB371

Table A.2 *Continued*

Name	RGB Code (Hex)	Name	RGB Code (Hex)
mediumslateblue	7B68EE	mediumspringgreen	00FA9A
mediumturquoise	48D1CC	mediumvioletred	C71585
midnightblue	191970	mintcream	F5FFFA
mistyrose	FFE4E1	moccasin	FFE4B5
navajowhite	FFDEAD	oldlace	FDF5E6
olivedrab	6B8E23	orange	FFA500
orangered	FF4500	orchid	DA70D6
palegoldenrod	EEE8AA	palegreen	98FB98
paleturquoise	AFEEEE	palevioletred	DB7093
papayawhip	FFEFD5	peachpuff	FFDAB9
peru	CD853F	pink	FFC0CB
plum	DDA0DD	powderblue	B0E0E6
rosybrown	BC8F8F	royalblue	4169E1
saddlebrown	8B4513	salmon	FA8072
sandybrown	F4A460	seagreen	2E8B57
seashell	FFF5EE	sienna	A0522D
skyblue	87CEEB	slateblue	6A5ACD
slategray	708090	snow	FFFAFA
springgreen	00FF7F	steelblue	4682B4
tan	D2B48C	thistle	D8BFD8
tomato	FF6347	turquoise	40E0D0
violet	EE82EE	wheat	F5DEB3
whitesmoke	F5F5F5	yellowgreen	9ACD32

Explicit RGB Color Codes

CSS supports four ways of encoding explicit RGB color codes as a CSS property value. Two of these mechanisms allow for hexadecimal codes for the colors, as described previously. The remaining two mechanisms allow for color codes using decimal or percentage notations. These different forms are summarized in the following.

Full RGB Color Code—#*RRGGBB*

Here *RR*, *GG*, and *BB* are the hexadecimal codes for the intensity of each color, ranging from 00 (zero) to FF (hexadecimal for the integer 255). For example, black is #000000, white is #FFFFFF, and blue is #0000FF. The hex codes are case-insensitive, so that #00af3d is equivalent to #00AF3D.

Short Form Hexadecimal Code—#*RGB*

Here *R*, *G*, and *B* are "abbreviated" forms of the 24-bit color codes. Such codes are converted into proper 24-bit notation by doubling each color value; that is, the code #*ABC* is converted into the code #*AABBCC*. For example, the code #A15 would be converted to the full RGB code #AA1155.

Decimal Code—rgb(*red*, *green*, *blue*)

Here *red*, *green*, and *blue* are the integer intensities of the red, green, and blue colors, ranging from 0 to 255. This is simply a decimal equivalent of the hexadecimal notation. For example, black is rgb(0,0,0), white becomes rgb(255,255,255), and blue is rgb(0,0,255).

Percentage Code—rgb(*red%*, *green%*, *blue%*)

The color is expressed as an RGB code, but the intensities of each color are given as a percentage of the maximum intensity, with values ranging from 0% (no intensity) to 100% (maximum intensity). Fractional percentage values are allowed, so that color specifications such as rgb(123.23%, 65.2% 82%) are valid. On an actual computer, color intensities are expressed as integers, and the CSS software thus converts the percentage values to the closest system-supported integer. Percentages greater than 100% are simply truncated; thus, a value of 120% is equivalent to 100%. The advantage of this system is that it is not restricted to 24-bit color, since the percentage values in principle allow for unlimited precision in color specification.

Note that, although a 24-bit RGB system is capable of representing 16,777,216 different colors, many computers are capable of displaying only a few colors at the same time, often as few as 256 (8-bit color). This can cause problems if the color requested by a color property assignment cannot be displayed on the local system—in this case, the computer will replace either the requested color by one that is available (color *substitution*) or will *dither* the requested color using a mixture of the supported colors.

Limited Numbers of Colors: The Colormap

To display arbitrary 24-bit RGB colors, a computer must have 24 bits of memory for each pixel on the screen (this is what is meant by the phrase "24-bit color"). However, many computers do not have this many bits per pixel—many, in fact, have only 8 bits per pixel, and support what is known as 8-bit color. In this case, a pixel can display at most 256 different colors, a far cry from the millions possible with 24 bits.

At the same time, a number shorter than 24 bits is too short to specify how much red, green, and blue to use, since you need 24 bits to fully specify the desired color. Thus, a system that has fewer than 24 bits per pixel needs a way of relating the number stored in a given pixel to the desired RGB color. The mechanism for doing so is called a *colormap* or *colormap table*.

Using an 8-bit system as an example, a colormap works as follows. Each pixel on such a system can contain an integer value ranging from 0 to 255. To determine the color corresponding to each of these integers, the system creates a colormap table that relates each integer to a full RGB color code. An example table is:

Integer	RGB Colors (decimal)			RGB Hex Code
0	00	00	00	000000
1	00	00	51	000033
2	00	00	102	000066
. . .	..	..	..	. . .
216	255	255	255	FFFFFF
. . .	..	..	..	. . .

Each 8-bit number now corresponds to one of the colors in the table. Thus, if a pixel is set to the number 2, the graphics system will look to the color table, pull out the RGB hex code 000033, and paint the pixel with this color.

Default System Colormaps

Microsoft Windows systems with 8-bit color use a default colormap, usually called the *Windows colormap*, which specifies a predefined relationship between pixel codes and RGB colors. This colormap defines 216 entries out of the total possible 256 colors. Each of the 216 different colors is defined using the six individual primary color codes 0, 51, 102, 153, 204, 255—the 216 comes from having six different shades of red, six different shades of green, and six different shades of blue, for a total of 6 x 6 x 6 = 216. Obviously, this scheme omits a lot of colors! But, it does evenly cover the range of possible colors, and provides a reasonable set of default values.

Color Substitution and Dithering

Problems then arise if the computer wishes to display a color that is not available in the system colormap. For example, a Web page might contain an image that employs the color 00192F, but a user's 8-bit color system can only display the colors 000000 and 000033. How, then, will the system display this color?

There are two possible approaches. First, the computer can look in the system colormap for the color "nearest" the color in the image, and substitute this color in its place. The computer might then take all pixels of color 00192F and paint them with color 000033. Unfortunately, the concept of "nearest" can lead to odd color replacements (light pink replacing light blue, for example), so this is often not an ideal approach.

The second way to approximate colors is via *color dithering*. With dithering, the program displaying the color tries to find a set colors in the local colormap that are close to the desired color, and then replaces blocks of the original color by a mixture of the colors that can actually be displayed.

This procedure is easily illustrated using a black-and-white example. Suppose a 1-bit display system (i.e., that can display only black and white), and an image that contains a block of gray. With dithering, the gray region would be displayed as a grid of alternating black and white pixels, which to the human eye will appear gray (provided you don't look too closely).

You can often detect dithering by looking at a region of an image that "should" appear as a solid color. If the area appears mottled, with lots of dots of slightly different colors, then the color has been dithered.

Dithering can be avoided by restricting oneself to colors present in the Windows colormap. Most Web design tools support this, by providing color palettes that let the user select Windows colormap colors for text and background colors.

Standardized Color—Standardized RGB

Unfortunately, just specifying an RGB code is not sufficient, since this code does not uniquely specify a color. Given the same RGB code, different computers will display slightly different shades of the specified color, due to system-to-system variations in how a given code is transformed into the displayed result.

These system-to-system variations can largely be parametrized via a quantity called the monitor *gamma*. Gamma is a number that describes how a given RGB code is converted, by the display, into a color. All monitors have slightly different gamma values, and as a result display the same RGB-specified color in slightly different ways.

In practice, this means that a *true color* is actually specified by two quantities: the RGB code and a standard specification for the monitor (and gamma) displaying that code. Such a standard does exist for RGB codes, and is called sRGB, for *standardized* RGB. In CSS, every RGB code is interpreted as specifying a color in this sRGB framework.

To display an sRGB-specified color correctly, the computer displaying the color must understand the sRGB system, and must know enough about its own monitor and display system that it can translate the sRGB-specified color into the correct RGB code to send to the display. At present, there are no browsers that do this transformation correctly.

Additional information about graphics issues on the Web, and on the sRGB system is particular, are available over the Web. The following URL is particularly useful for technical information about sRGB:

`http://www.w3.org/pub/WWW/Graphics/Color/sRGB.html`

B

CSS Length Units

CSS supports several different length measurement units. These can be divided into two categories: *absolute units*, which define lengths on an absolute scale independent of the display device, and *relative units*, which define lengths relative to other units known to the browser.

Absolute length measurements are available in five units: inches, centimeters, millimeters, points, and picas. Points and picas are commonly used typographic units, where 1 pica = 12 points. CSS defines a pica as being 1/72 of an inch—that is, 72 picas = 1 inch, which is the same definition used by the Adobe PostScript language commonly used by high-quality printers.

CSS also supports "absolute" lengths measured in pixels—a pixel, of course, being a single dot on a computer display. However, the absolute size of a pixel can vary significantly from display to display, owing to differences in pixel density, and the user's choice of screen resolution (the same display may support a resolution of 640 by 480 pixels as well as 1024 by 768 pixels). Thus, a pixel really is a *display*-dependent length. The advantage of using pixels as the unit for a computer display is that the pixel is well defined—a length of 10 pixels will always span 10 pixels of the display. Thus, if you have an image 90 pixels wide, you can be sure that a 91-pixel margin will position text just beyond this image. However, pixel units present problems when *printing* Web documents, as discussed later.

Absolute length units such as inches or centimeters are very useful for print typesetting, as they provide the absolute positioning required to lay out a document on a fixed size of paper. For this same reason, absolute lengths are not as useful for electronically displayed documents, since displays can vary from a 6" by 4" PDA display to a 21" diagonal monitor, and since there is no guarantee on a given display that the browser will display a document using a fixed window area (the user can choose to resize the window). To account for such variations, it is best to use lengths that automatically scale relative to the size of the display area or relative to the font size of the text. Fortunately, there are three CSS length units that allow precisely this behavior.

Relative length measurements are available in three forms: *em* units, *ex* units, and *percentages*. Em and ex units define lengths relative to the *size* of the font. As discussed in Chapter 3, em units define sizes relative to the actual font point size: Thus, if the current font is a 12pt font, then 1 em = 12 points. Ex units, in turn, define lengths relative to the font's *x-height*: essentially, the height of the letter "x" in the current font. Thus, the size of an ex-length unit can depend on both the font size and on the font family, since the actual x-height varies from family to family given the same point size.

At present, em units are more reliably implemented than ex units: For best compatibility across multiple browsers, it is best to use ems. Note, however, that both em and ex units lead to printing problems, as discussed later in this appendix.

Percentage units are the third relative length unit. This unit defines lengths as a percentage of a related length. According to the CSS specifications, this related length can be either the size of the parent element's font, or else the *width* of the parent formatting element—the particular case depends on the property in question. The CSS properties summary in Chapter 8 explains how percentage lengths are calculated for the different CSS properties that support this unit.

NOTE   Percentage Widths Not Calculated Relative to Parent Element Width

With current browsers (Navigator 4, MSIE 3 and 4), percentage lengths are *not* calculated relative to the width of the parent element, in contradiction with the CSS specifications. Instead, percentage lengths are calculated relative to the full width of the browser window. The ramifications of this behavior are discussed in the section of this appendix entitled "Problems with Percentage Length Values."

Problems with Percentage Length Values

An extremely important caveat is that current browsers *do not properly implement* percentage lengths calculated relative to element width. Instead, all current browsers (Navigator 4.0, MSIE 3 and 4) calculate non-font-related percentage lengths as a percentage of the *full width* of the browser window, and *not* as a percentage of the parent element width. As an example, consider a **DIV** inside the **BODY** of a document, with the **DIV** having the declarations `margin-left: 20%` and `margin-right: 0`: Thus, the **DIV** spans 80% of the width of the browser window. Now suppose that, inside the **DIV**, there is a paragraph with the CSS declaration `text-indent: -20%`. According to the CSS specifications, this hanging indent should have a size that is 20% of the width of the parent **DIV** element, and thus should be -20% x 80% = -16% of the full width of the browser window. Thus the negative indent should still leave the first line of the paragraph with a small, 4% indent relative to the left margin of the browser window. However, the browser actually calculates this hanging indent as a percentage of the full width of the window. Thus the negative indent is actually a full 20% of the browser window width, such that the hanging indent aligns precisely with the left margin of the browser window.

Problems with Table WIDTHs

This may seem convenient in this context, but presents particular problems with table layout and positioning. For example, suppose we wish to place a table within the **DIV** defined in the previous discussion, such that the left and right edges of the table span the full width of the **DIV**. According to the CSS specifications, one would anticipate the TABLE element start tag:

```
<TABLE WIDTH="100%">
```

since this should specify a table that is 100% the width of the **DIV**. However, this instead produces a table that is 100% of the width of the full browser window, but with a 20% left margin due to the parent **DIV**: Thus the table extends well out beyond the right edge of the browser window (it would be accessible via a scroll bar). In fact, one needs the attribute assignment **WIDTH="80%"** to generate a table the same width as the parent **DIV**.

Illustration of Percentage and Em Units

The following two examples illustrate the differences between percentage and relative lengths. In the first example, all lengths are calculated as percentages—the comments strings (in italics) describe what actually happens:

```
P {
    font-size:    200%;  /* The font inside P is twice as large as
                            the font in the surrounding element     */
    margin-left: 20%;   /* The left margin is indented 20% of the
                            full width of the parent element        */
    text-indent: 5%;    /* The paragraph start is indented 5% of the
                            width of the current paragraph element  */
}
```

On the other hand, the following example uses em units to request similar formatting. In this case, the interpretation of the units is quite different—again, the comment strings (in italics) describe the processing of each length:

```
P {
    font-size: 2em;     /* The font inside P is twice as large as
                            the font in the surrounding element     */
    margin-left: 10em;  /* The left margin is indented by an amount
```

```
                            equal to 10 times the font size in the
                            parent element                              */
   text-indent: 5em;    /* The paragraph text is indented 5em units
                            relative to the font size within the P    */
   }
```

Defining Length Units

In CSS, lengths are denoted by a string containing a number indicating the length, followed by a percent symbol, or by a two-letter suffix indicating the units of measure. Some examples are shown in Table B.1. Note that there can be no space between the number and the units code. Decimal lengths are allowed (e.g., 25.4mm), but you cannot use commas to denote groups of thousands, nor can you use exponential notation (i.e., 2e4 for 20000). Thus expressions such as 1232.2pt and 0.12in are allowed, but 1,323.2pt and 1.2e-1in are not.

Lengths can be either positive or negative, with negative values taking a leading negative sign (e.g., -30mm). If there is no negative sign, the value is assumed positive (as you probably suspected). Note, however, that some CSS properties, such as padding widths, border widths, and font sizes, do not support negative lengths. If an author tries to set these quantities to a negative value, the browser will ignore the declaration and will assume a standard default value (usually zero), or a value inherited from the parent element.

Finally, a length of zero can be indicated by the number 0, without any units. Obviously, zero is zero, regardless of units!

Table B.1 summarizes the different length units supported by CSS, and gives examples of how these lengths are expressed using CSS notation.

Length Units and Printing Support

One major issue with CSS-enabled pages is printing support: Many CSS-enabled pages, when printed, produce totally illegible output. This is largely due to the length units used in the document to define font sizes and element positioning. The problem can be illustrated by considering pixel units for font sizes: If a size is specified in pixels, it is unclear how this size should be translated into a physical length on a printer. The result today is that font sizes specified in pixels lead to printed output that uses tiny, totally illegible fonts.

Current browsers all have problems printing legible documents when the font size is specified using pixel units. In addition, most browsers also print illegible text when font sizes are specified in em, ex, or percentage units. This is most unfortunate, as these units are the most useful for Web-based design: Pixels are best for absolute positioning on the display, while em, ex, and percentage units are best for layouts that are designed to scale well on different displays or with different font sizes.

If printing is an important feature for your pages, then you must be very careful in your designs. First, you must specify *all* your font sizes using absolute units (points, inches, etc.). Then, it is a

Table B.1 Absolute and Relative Length Units Available with CSS
In CSS, 1 inch = 72 points.

Absolute Length Units	Example
Inches	1.0in
Centimeters	2.54cm
Millimeters	25.4mm
Points	12pt
Picas	1pc
Pixels (platform-dependent)	-8px
Relative Length Units	
Em units	1em
Ex units	-3.25ex
Percentage units	35%
Special Case—Zero Length	
(*no units required*)	0

matter of defining the remaining page layout using whatever units seem appropriate, and then testing the design for printability—what may seem like a simple design may simply not print, for seemingly unfathomable reasons. If it does not print, you will need to try modifications to the design (changing the structure or the length unit px, em, etc.)—in an attempt to get printable output. Finally, you will need to test the design with different browsers—just because it works on one browser is no guarantee that it will work on another!

In general, this can be so frustrating that it is often best to avoid CSS in documents that must be easily printed!

Endnote

1. Note that MSIE 3 does not support CSS properties attached to TABLE, TD, TH or TR elements, and that Netscape 4 does not support CSS properties attached to TABLE or TR elements, but does support CSS properties that apply to TD or TH. There are, however, many bugs in Netscape's TABLE formatting, as discussed at the end of Chapter 5.

Glossary

This glossary provides a list of terms relevant to typography, Cascading Stylesheets, and HTML: Items cross-referenced in the glossary are shown in italics. In many cases, more detailed descriptions are found in the body of the book, and you are advised to look there for more information about the more complicated terms.

If there are terms that you would like to see included in this glossary, please let me know, and I will include them in the next edition. Please send any suggestions to:

stylesheet-book@wiley.com

anchor The location of a hypertext link in a document, as marked by the **A** element. An *anchor* can be either the start of a hypertext link or the destination of a hypertext link.

antialiasing Characters are traditionally displayed on a computer screen as an array of black (or other color) pixels. *Antialiasing* instead represents the font as a collection of pixels in various shades of gray.

applet A program or mini-application that can be *downloaded* over a network and run on the user's computer. In HTML, the **APPLET** and **OBJECT** element support the embedding of applets within a document.

ASCII American Standard Code for Information Interchange. This is a 7-bit character code capable of representing 128 (2^7) characters. The printable characters in this set consist of the letters A–Z and a–z, the numbers 0–9, plus several common punctuation symbols. There are also several physical formatting characters (e.g., carriage return, line feed, tab, form feed). The remaining characters are special control characters, and are not printable.

attribute A quantity that defines a special property of an HTML element. Attributes are specified within an element *start tag*. For example, <IMG SRC="image.gif"> means that the element **IMG** has an attribute **SRC**, which is assigned the indicated value.

bitmapped font A font defined as a fixed pattern of dots. Bitmapped fonts are defined for only a fixed set of font sizes. See also *scalable font*.

block-level element Any HTML element that defines a block of text—that is, a section that is preceded and followed by a line break. **H1, P,** and **DIV** are examples of block-level elements. See also *inline element*.

browser Any program used to access and view material prepared for the World Wide Web. Mosaic, Netscape Navigator, Microsoft Internet Explorer, and lynx are some examples. A browser is also often called a *user-agent* or a Web client.

canvas The portion of the browser into which the document is rendered for display. This is also called the display *window*.

child element An element that is directly contained within another element. For example, in the markup sequence <P> some text <EM> emphasized <EM> more text </P>, the **EM** element is a *child* of the **P** element. For those who care about such things, this is equivalent, in SGML terminology, to a subelement.

contextual selector A *selector* that references an element dependent on the position of that element within the document. For example, the contextual selector P EM references only those **EM** elements that lie inside **P** elements, and so does not reference **EM** elements inside a heading. See also *selector*.

character reference A way, within an SGML language such as HTML, of referencing a character in terms of the character's position in the current character set. For example, if a document uses the ISO Latin-1 character set, then the character reference $#233; refers to the letter e with an acute accent (é). Note that character references may produce different characters if a different character set is used (e.g., using another character set, the character at position 233 net not be é). For a character representation that is independent of the character set being used, see *entity reference*.

class, or CLASS The CSS specification introduces a new **CLASS** attribute, allowed with almost all HTML elements. **CLASS** allows the author to specify subclass for an element. For example, the markup `<DIV CLASS="abstract"> ... </DIV>` indicates a **DIV** element belonging to the "abstract" class. CSS rules can define different formatting instructions for **DIV** elements of different classes. The value for **CLASS** must be a *name token*.

CRLF The combination of carriage-return (**CR**) and linefeed (**LF**) characters. This combination is used by several Internet protocols to denote the end of a line.

CSS Cascading Stylesheets—stylesheet language described in this book. The current definitive version of CSS is known as CSS1, or CSS Level 1. CSS1 specifies both **core features**—those features that must be supported by a browser that supports CSS1—and **advanced features** that are less widely supported.

CSS1 see *CSS*.

declaration A stylesheet *property* along with the value to be associated with that property. For example, the declaration `font-face: Arial, Helvetica` assigns the value `Arial, Helvetica` to the property `font-face`.

DSSSL Document Style Semantics and Specification Language. An ISO specification (ISO 10179) for defining stylesheets for SGML documents. DSSSL is an extremely sophisticated language, and is far more expensive (and complicated!) that CSS. A simplified version of DSSSL, known as DSSSL-Online, has been proposed as an alternative stylesheet language for HTML documents. However, there are currently no browsers that support this approach.

DTD Document Type Definition. An SGML document type definition is a specific description of a markup language. This description is written as a plain text file, often with the filename extension *.dtd*. The HyperText Markup Language, or HTML, is an SGML-based language, and thus has its own document type definition. CSS stylesheets will work properly only if the document obeys the HTML syntax rules specified by the DTD.

element type The name of the element. In most cases, the name is strongly related to the type or functional role of the element (e.g., **P** for paragraphs, **H1** for level-1 headings).

element The basic unit of an HTML document. HTML documents use start and stop *tags* to define structural elements in the document—an element generally consists of a *start tag*, a *stop tag*, and the content lying between them (e.g., `<EM> text </EM>` is an **EM** element). Elements are arranged hierarchically, to define the overall document structure. The *element type* is given by the name inside the tag, and indicates the meaning associated with the block. Elements that do not affect a block of text (e.g., **BR**) are called empty elements, and generally do not have end tags. Elements that have content are also often called *containers*.

em unit A length unit that defines a length relative to the size of the font being used. In CSS, one (1) em unit is equal to the defined height of the current font. For example, for a 12-point font, 1 em is equal to 12 points.

en unit A relative length unit, related to *em units*. In general, an en unit is one half of an em unit (1 en = 1/2 em). Note that en units are not supported by CSS.

end tag A markup that denotes the end of an *element*. An end tag has the general form `</NAME>`, where **NAME** is the name or *element type* of the element.

entity reference A way, within an SGML language such as HTML, of referencing a character using a symbolic string of ASCII characters. For example, the entity reference `&eacute;` is the reference for e with an acute accent (é). See also *character reference*.

ex unit An ex is a length unit that defines a length relative to the size of the font. One (1) ex is equivalent to the height of the letter "x" in the current font.

FAQ Frequently Asked Questions. On the Internet, a FAQ is a document that answers the most frequently asked questions on a particular topic. Most Internet newsgroups have FAQs that are frequently posted to the newsgroup.

floating element An HTML element that is allowed to float towards the left or right inner edge of the element that contains it. The remaining content of the parent element will flow around a floated element.

font A collection of symbols, sharing common size and design features, that represent a groups of characters. For example, Times-Roman and Arial are common fonts of the Latin character set. See also *glyph* and *serif*.

font size The size of a font; typically the distance from the bottom of the lowest letter with a descender (e.g., for an English language font, one of g, j, p, q, or y) to the top of the tallest letter with an ascender (e.g., one of b, d, f, h, k, l, or t), and perhaps a diacritical mark (i.e., an "accent"). Font sizes are often measured in *points* or *picas*.

GIF Graphics Interchange Format, a format for storing image files. It is the most common format for inline images in HTML documents. The other common formats are *JPEG* and *PNG*.

glyph The actual shape representation for a particular character or language symbol. For example, "e" is a glyph for the indicated letter. See also *font*.

header The leading part of a data message. HTTP messages are sent with an HTTP *header* that precedes the actual communicated data.

hinting Parameters used, with *scalable fonts*, to define special formatting characteristics that should only be applied at certain font sizes. Developing a good set of hinting parameters can be the most complicated (and expensive) aspect of developing a new scalable font.

HTML HyperText Markup Language. A markup language defined by an SGML document type definition (DTD). To a document writer, HTML is simply a collection of tags used to mark blocks of text and assign them special meanings.

hyperlink See *hypertext link*.

hypertext Any document that contains *hypertext links* to other documents. HTML documents are almost always hypertext documents.

hypertext link A hypertext relationship between two anchors, leading from the head anchor to the tail anchor. On the Web, this is usually a link from one hypertext document to another. Lining points are associated with *anchors*.

ID A new HTML attribute, introduced with CSS, used to uniquely label a particular element. For example, `<P ID="z23"> ... </P>` labels the paragraph with the given **ID**. An **ID** value must be a *name token*. IDs must be unique within a given document—that is, no two elements can have the same **ID** value. Using CSS, the author can give formatting instructions specific to an element labeled by a given **ID** value.

inline element An element that does not have a preceding and following line break. Examples include **EM**, **TT**, and **SUP**. **IMG** is also an inline element, unless it is transformed into a *floating* element.

Internet You mean you don't know? The Internet is a worldwide network of computers communicating via the Internet protocols.

intrinsic dimensions The width and height of an element as specified by the element itself. In CSS, the only elements with intrinsic dimensions are those that are replaced by special objects—namely **IMG, APPLET, EMBED, OBJECT,** and the form **INPUT, SELECT,** and **TEXTAREA** elements, which are replaced by the related form objects (text input fields, buttons, etc.)

ISO 10646 a multi-byte character set proposed by the ISO as a universal character set for the characters and symbols used by all the world's languages. The most important 2-byte subset of this language, known as the basic multilingual plane, is equivalent to the *Unicode* character set.

ISO Latin-1 An 8-bit character code developed by the International Standards Organization. An 8-bit code contains 256 different characters. In the ISO Latin-1 code, the first 128 characters are equivalent to the 128 characters of the US-*ASCII* character set (also called the ISO 646 character set). The remaining 128 characters consist of control characters and a large collection of accented and other characters commonly used in Western European languages.

JavaScript A scripting language developed by Netscape Inc. JavaScript script can be included within an HTML document, and are executed by the Web browser when the document is loaded. A similar scripting language, known as *VBScript*, has been developed by Microsoft.

JPEG Joint Photographic Experts Group, an image format. In general JPEG allows for higher quality photographic image reproduction than does GIF.

kerning The adjustment of spacing between two particular letters appearing in a particular order. Kerning is used to make text more readable, and is commonly used to reduce spacing between letters that might otherwise have too much *whitespace* between them. For example, a capital "T" followed by a lowercase "o" could be kerned to reduce the whitespace lying between them. CSS does not provide any control over kerning. See also *tracking.*

leading Pronounced as "ledding," this refers to the vertical space left above and below a line of text. In CSS, this is equivalent to line spacing. When pronounced as "leading," this refers to the first line of a block of text, as in "leading line indent" for the indent applied to the first line.

link See *hypertext link.*

lynx A popular character-mode (text-only) World Wide Web browser; lynx is commonly used by visually impaired users.

MIME Multipurpose Internet Mail Extensions, a scheme that lets electronic mail messages contain mixed media (sound, video, images, programs, arbitrary data, and text). The World Wide Web uses MIME content-types to specify the type of data contained in a file or being sent from an HTTP server to a client.

MSIE Microsoft Internet Explorer, a popular Web browser.

name token In SGML, a name token is a character string composed of a combination of the ASCII letters a–z or A–Z, the numerals, 0–9, a dash (-), or period (.), and beginning with a letter. In the case of HTML, name tokens are usually case-insensitive. Many *attribute* values are defined as name tokens.

OpenType A proposed scalable font format, designed to integrate, under the same format, *TrueType* and *PostScript* fonts. This format is still under development.

parent element The element that directly contains the current element. For example, if an **EM** element is inside a particular **P** element, then this **P** is the *parent element* of the given **EM** element.

pica A unit of length commonly used in typography. In general, 1 pica = 12 *points*.

point A unit of length commonly used in typography to define font sizes. For Web application using CSS, the definition is 1 point = 1/72 inch = 1 inch). Note also that 12 points = 1 *pica*. The actual length of a point varies slightly depending on the typographical system being used (printers traditionally use the definition 72.27 points = 1 inch).

pseudo-element Pseudo-elements define, within CSS *selectors*, typographical properties that do not apply to the entire HTML element. For example, pseudo-element can specify special formatting for the first line of a paragraph: first-line or special formatting for the first letter of the first word in the sentence: first-letter. In fact, these are the only two pseudo-elements supported in the CSS1 specification.

pseudo-class Pseudo-classes reference, within CSS *selectors*, class-like information about an element but that is obtained from *outside* the HTML document (that is, from the browser). Consequently, such information cannot be expressed using a fixed **CLASS** attribute. At present, the only element to support pseudo-classes is the **A** (anchor) element, where the three allowed pseudo-class values are related to the status of the hypertext link—that is, whether the hypertext link has or has not been visited, or whether the link is active (selected by the user).

partial URL A location scheme containing only partial information about the resource location. To access the resource, the client must construct a full URL, based on the partial URL. It does so by assuming that all the information not given in the partial URL is the same as that used when the client accessed the document containing the partial URL reference. A partial URL is often called a relative URL, since the location of the linked resource is determined relative to the location of the document containing the partial URL.

PNG Portable Network Graphics, a graphic file format developed for use on the Web. PNG is similar to *GIF* (images are stored in an uncompressed but non-degraded format) but has a number of important improvements upon *GIF*, such as improved support for transparency, and the ability to support greater than 8-bit color.

PostScript fonts A scalable font format developed by Adobe. There are two types: PostScript Type 1 and PostScript Type 3. PostScript fonts are the fonts most commonly used fonts in professional electronic typesetting work.

property A stylistic or layout feature that can be affected using CSS, and that can take an assigned value. In CSS, a *declaration* consists of a *property* plus the associated value. For example, font-style is a property.

replaced element An HTML element that is replaced by non-text content, such as an **IMG, APPLET,** or form **INPUT** element.

RGB Red-Green-Blue, a coding scheme used on most computers to represent colors. Each color is represented as a mixture of the primary colors red, green, and blue.

rule A collection of CSS *declarations* along with the *selector* to which the *declarations* should be applied. For example, P.booby: {font-family: helvetica; color: purple} combines the *selector* P.booby with two *declarations*.

scalable font A font that is defined by a computer algorithm, and that can be scaled to any desired size. Some examples are *TrueType* and *PostScript* fonts. See also *bitmapped fonts*.

sans-serif A font that uses no serifs—that is, that has no straight line segments extending from the ends of the strokes of a letter. The Arial font (e.g., **Arial**) is an example of a sans-serif font. See also *fonts* and *serif*.

selector A strong that identifies a set of elements. A *simple selector* references a single element or single class of elements (e.g., EM, or DIV.abstract). A *contextual selector* references elements depending on their position within other elements (e.g., DIV.abstract EM references only those **EM** elements lying within a **DIV** with **CLASS**="abstract").

serif Any of the short, straight line segments extending from the ends of the strokes of a letter. Most common fonts (for example, Times-Roman) are serified fonts. Serifs actually make a font easier to read. See also *fonts* and *sans-serif*.

server A program, running on a networked computer, that responds to requests from client programs, running on other networked computers. The server and client communicate using a client-server protocol

Glossary

SGML Standard Generalized Markup Language. An ISO standard (ISO 8879, to be precise) for describing and defining markup languages. HTML is defined as an instance of SGML. The SGML rules for defining a specific markup language are defined in the language's *DTD*.

simple selector See *selector*.

space band The physical spacing between words when text is typeset. When HTML text content is formatted, multiple adjacent *whitespace* characters are usually collapsed to leave a single such space. Also called the word space.

start tag A markup tag that denotes the start of an *element*. See also *tag*.

stylesheet Any collection of *rules* for specifying the formatting layout for a document.

tag HTML marks documents using *tags*. A simple tag consists of typed text surrounded by the less-than and greater-than signs, for example: <TAG>, where the name inside the tag defines the *element type*. An *end tag* has a slash in front of the tag name—for example </TAG>.

tracking Refers to the increase or reduction of the generic space left between characters. Tracking is adjusted to either tighten up or loosen the appearance of the text, and is used in typesetting to improve readability, or simply to make a section of text auto-fill a desired region of the page. CSS does not provide control over text tracking. See also *kerning*.

TrueDoc A portable, scalable font format developed by Bitstream. Netscape has integrated this technology into the Navigator 4 browser to support dynamically downloadable fonts.

TrueType A scalable font format developed by Microsoft and Apple. This is the most common format used on Windows and Macintosh computers.

Unicode A 2-byte character set, developed as a universal character set for international use. The current version of Unicode is equivalent to the basic multilingual plane subset of the *ISO 10646* character set. Internationalized HTML uses Unicode as its base character set.

UNIX An operating system, commonly used by the backbone mechanism on the Internet. Most Web servers are run under the UNIX operating system.

URL Uniform Resource Locator, the scheme used to address Internet resources on the World Wide Web. *Partial URLs* are an associated scheme that specify a location relative to the location of a document or resource containing the URL reference.

user-agent Any program used, by a user, to access Web resources—a user-agent acts as an "agent" on the user's behalf. Web browsers are thus user-agents.

VBScript A document scripting language developed by Microsoft, also known as Visual Basic Script. See *JavaScript* for a description of document scripting languages.

W3C World Wide Web Consortium, an academic and industrial consortium devoted to the development of Web standards and technologies.

weight In CSS, the priority assigned to a particular rule—rules are applied to order of decreasing weight. Natural weights are set by an element's position within the HTML element hierarchy (e.g., an **EM** element's formatting properties override those of the surrounding paragraph). Weights can also be artificially set by the stylesheet author.

whitespace Any combination of space or tab characters that separate two characters or two character strings.

Index

!important, 234-235, 236, 306, 307
    overview, 306
    support, 235
    use to eliminate rules, 241-242
@import, 231-233, 305-306
    support, 231
@media, 386
@page, 385-386
:active, 76, 77, 85
:first-letter, 118-120, 147
:first-line, 118-120, 147
:link, 76, 85
:visited, 76, 85-86

A

A, 29-30, 37
    pseudo-class selectors, 76
absolute values, 17
ACSS (Aural Cascading Stylesheets),
    383-385
active. See :active
ADDRESS, 37
advanced features, 351-352
    aural cascading stylesheets, 383-385
    CSS-aware software, 388-389
    font downloading and dynamic
        fonts, 378-283
    positioning and z-ordering, 352-374
    printing and other alternate media,
        385-388
    scripted stylesheets and document
        object model, 374-378
ALIGN attribute, 114
    float elements, 40-41
    ignored by browser, 32
alignment. See also text-align
    aligning and indenting text, 115-116
    vertical, 114, 131, 133-138
    and word/letter spacing, 129
Amaya, 45, 389
Andressen, Marc, 3
antialiasing, 65, 66
Arena browser, 45
APPLET, 37, 38, 40
    to float, 40, 41
AREA, 38, 40
    CLASS attribute, 75
    ID attribute, 77

ascender, 69, 71, 104
ASCII characters, 28
attributes, 29-30
    case sensitivity, 31
    literal strings, 32
    name tokens, 32
    notation, 35
Aural Cascading Stylesheets, 383-385
author control, 83
author declarations, 307

B

B, 37, 44
background, 228, 313
background-attachment, 227, 248,
    347
    overview, 313
background-color, 113-114, 168,
    214-215, 248
    background/foreground
        contrast, 215
    description, 127, 128, 314
    problems, 168
background-image, 215,
    217-219, 248
    overview, 314
background-position,
    222-226
    overview, 315-316
background-repeat,
    220-222, 248
    overview, 316
backgrounds, 313-316
    images, 215, 217-219
        controlling tiling pattern,
            220-222
        initial location, 222-226
        scrolling or fixed, 227-228, 313
BASE, 34
BASEFONT, 38, 40
baseline, 69, 71, 104, 134
BDO, 37, 44
Berners-Lee, Tim, 1, 2, 3
BGCOLOR, 214
BGSOUND, 38, 40
BIG, 37, 44
bitmapped formats, 65
Bitstream, 97-98

BLINK, 37, 44
    non-Netscape browsers, 4, 32
block elements, 34, 35, 37
    sample document, 38
    summary of, 37
block-level formatting, 154-155, 156-
    157. See also examples
    horizontal layout, 167-176
    vertical layout, 176-183
BLOCKQUOTE, 37
BODY, 33, 34-41, 58
    summary of elements, 37-38
    types of elements, 34-41
books
    Cascading Style Sheets: Designing
        for the Web, 22
    HTML: The Definitive Guide, 60
    The HTML Sourcebook, Third
        Edition, 60
    The SGML Handbook, 59
    SGML on the Web; Small Steps
        Beyond HTML, 59
    10 Minute Guide to HTML Style
        Sheets, 22
border, 162
    description, 163, 317
border-bottom, 317-318
border-bottom-width,
    162, 176
    description, 163, 318
border-color, 162-163
    color assignments, 319-320
    overview, 318-319
border-left, 319
border-left-width, 162, 167
    description, 163, 320
border-right, 320-321
border-right-width, 162, 167,
    189
    description, 163, 321
border-style, 163, 321-323
    property values, 164
border-top, 323
border-top-width, 162, 176, 323-
    324
    description, 163
border-width, 163, 324-325
borders, 156-157, 158, 210

413

border-related properties, 163
    problems with, 163-164
    description, 162-165
Bos, Bert, 11
BR, 29, 37
browsers. *See also* MSIE 3; MSIE 4;
    Navigator 4
    Amaya, 45
    Arena, 45
    comments, 28
    CSS stylesheet errors, 20, 21
    CSS support in, 347-350
    default CSS properties, 21
    and DSSSL, 21
    end tags, 29
    hiding stylesheets, 45-46, 230,
        304-305
    and HTML errors, 32
    inline formatting, 187
    pseudo-class-based simple
        selectors, 76
    readability without stylesheets, 56
    stylesheet abuse, 182-183

C

call-out, 199
canvas, 18
CAPTION, 37
cascading principle, 82-83
    example, 84-85
cascading rules, 306-307
Cascading Stylesheets. *See* CSS
    stylesheets
case control. *See* text-transform
case sensitivity, 31-32, 298
    and class values, 48
CENTER, 37
    avoid using, 37
    and CLASS attribute, 75
    and ID attribute, 77
centering block-level elements,
    173-175
CERN (European Centre for Nuclear
    Research), 1
characters
    allowed in HTML documents, 27-28
    character highlighting elements, 44
    fonts and character sets, 382-383
    non-ASCII, 28
    Unicode character set, 383
CITE, 37, 44
CLASS attribute, 41
class-based selectors, 74-75, 299,
    300-301

description, 47-48
example, 78-79
multiple values, 75
priority, 84
and pseudo-class, 76-77
and rule selection, 307
SPAN, 46
supported by, 75
clear, 198, 325
clip, 353, 355
    description, 369-370
    overflow, 358-359
clipping box. *See* clip
CODE, 37, 44
COL, 38, 40
COLGROUP, 38, 40
color, 127, 326
colors, 113-114, 128, 148, 308, 391
    background, 113-114, 128, 214-215
    background/foreground contrast, 215
    borders, 162-163
    colormap, 397-399
    dithering, 326, 399
    named colors, 308, 392-394
        extended, 394-396
        RGB color codes, 308, 391-396
            explicit, 396-397
        standardized, 399
        substitution, 398-399
comments
    in CSS stylesheets, 121-122,
        147, 298
    in HTML documents, 28
containers, 29
contextual selectors, 74, 122-125,
    147, 300, 303
    examples, 123
copyrights, and fonts, 63-64, 65
Corel WordPerfect
    font names, 96-97
CSS stylesheets, 10-11, 21. *See also*
    CSS formatting model;
    examples; rules; stylesheets
    advanced features, 16-17, 21
    author stylesheet, 236, 239-240
    backward compatibility, 290
    browser handling of errors, 20, 21
    cascading principle, 82-83
        example, 84-85
    comments, 121-122, 147, 298
    core features, 16-17, 21
    create full document stylesheet,
        236-240
    default properties, 18-20, 21, 79,
        81-82

default stylesheet, 81-82
    and author control, 83
design and management, 246-248
font specifications, 77-78
hiding stylesheets, 45-46, 230,
    304-305
importing stylesheets, 231, 305-306
limitations, 11
multiple stylesheets and cascade,
    235-236
    evaluating the cascade, 236-246
placing within an HTML
    document, 21
property inheritance, 17, 21, 82
reader stylesheet, 235, 239
reducing size, 121, 147
reuse, 290-293
stylesheet example, 12-20
support in current browsers,
    347-350
syntax, 71-77, 105, 117-125,
    297-310
and text formatting, 125, 127-128
CSS formatting model, 152-154
    block-level, 154-155, 156-157
    borders, 162-165
    floating, 155, 158
    the formatting box, 159-166
    height and width, 159-160
    inline, 155, 156, 157-158
    list-item type, 155, 156
    margins, 165-166
        inline elements, 158
    padding space, 160-161, 210
    replaced elements, 155-156
    setting formatting type, 155
CSS1, 21
cursive fonts, 68, 93, 94, 95, 96

D

dashed, 164
DD, 37, 38
declarations, 13, 21, 71-72, 105, 297-
    298. *See also* cascading rules
    author declarations, 307
    CSS advanced features, 17
    CSS core features, 17
    increase importance of, 234-235,
        236, 306, 307
    reader declarations, 306-307
default
    BASEFONT, 40
    properties, 18-20, 21, 79, 81-82

stylesheet, 18, 21, 81-82, 235
   author control, 83
stylesheet language, 50
depth, 354-355
descender, 69, 71, 104
design. *See also* stylesheets
   HTML standard, 4-5
   splintering of HTML, 3-4
DFN, 37, 44
DIR, 37
   modify properties of an element, 35
display, 155, 156, 326-327
   display: none, 353
display resolution, 5, 70-71
dithering, 326, 399
DIV, 37
   and CLASS, 75
   error handling, 51-55
   and margins, 179
DL, 37
Document Object Model (DOM),
   377-378
Document Style Semantics and
   Specification Language. *See*
   DSSSL
document template, 7
document type definition. *See* DTD
DOM (Document Object Model),
   377-378
dotted, 164
double, 164
dpi (dots per inch), 70
drop-cap lettering, 116
   problems with, 120
DSSSL (Document Style Semantics
   and Specification Language)
   stylesheets, 11-12, 21
   references, 22-23
DT, 37, 38
DTD (document type definition), 33,
   57, 60

E

element formatting, 166
   block-level, 166
      horizontal layout, 167-176
      list item elements, 183-186
      vertical layout, 176-183
   floating elements, 188-201
   inline elements, 186-187
   replaced elements, 202-204
elements, 28-29. *See also* positioning
   attributes, 29-30, 35
   BODY content, 34-41
   case sensitivity, 31-32

character highlighting, 44
containers, 29
element name, 28
element specifications key, 41-43
empty elements, 29, 33, 34
HEAD content, 33
hierarchy of HTML elements, 29
nesting, 29
structural rules, 33-41
and tags, 27, 28
unique identifier, 48-49
EM, 37, 44
   contextual selectors, 122-125
em unit, 70, 71
EMBED, 37, 38, 40
   floated, 41
end tags, 28, 29
entity reference, 28
error handling, 20, 21, 32, 306
   HTML errors, 50-55
European Centre for Nuclear
   Research (CERN), 1
examples
   clearing below floating images, 198
   floating next to block-level
      elements, 195-197
   floating non-img elements, 199-201
   font family and style specification,
      87-98
   formatting of inline elements, 186-
      187
   horizontal layout of block-level
      elements, 167-176
   line height in block elements,
      139-141
   multiple floating elements, 191-195
   simple CSS selectors and rules,
      78-83
   a single floated element, 188-191
   some more CSS selectors and rules,
      83-86
   special formatting of list item
      elements, 183-184
   special handling of replaced
      elements, 202-204
   specifying font sizes, 101-104
   specifying font weights, 98-101
   stylesheet designs, 251
      additional designs, 293-295
      chapter cover page, 267-275
      decorative page, 264-266
      newspaper Web page, 275-293
      stylized heading, 258-264
      title page, 254-258
   text formatting, 128-131

text indent, alignment, and
   whitespace, 141-145
text preceding floating elements, 191
vertical alignment, 131-138
vertical layout of block-level
   elements, 176-183
ex unit, 70, 71

F

family. *See* font-family
fantasy fonts, 68, 93, 94, 95, 96-97
first letter formatting, 116. *See also*
   :first-line
first-letter. *See* :first-
   letter
first line formatting, 116. *See also*
   :first-line
first-line. *See* :first-line
float, 41, ,188 ,327. *See also*
   examples
   modify properties of an
      element, 35
floating elements, 35, 41, 188. *See
   also* examples
   and clear, 325
   formatting, 155, 158
   and replaced elements, 40-41
FONT, in el 4, 37, 44
   and CLASS attribute, 75
   and ID attribute, 77
   and SPAN element, 46
font, 78, 104, 128, 140-141,
   327-328
font-family, 91-93, 105,
   328-329
   alternatives, 71, 78,
      92, 105
   available fonts, 93-97
   description, 78
   inheritance, 82
   purpose of, 64-65, 67
   rules for selecting, 92-93
   support, 93
font-size, 101-104, 329-330
   description, 78
font-style, 78, 330
   example, 87-89
   italic, 88-89, 105
   normal, 88-89, 105
   oblique, 88-89, 105
font-variant, 67, 105
   description, 78, 330-331
   example, 89-91
   normal, 89
   not supported by, 91, 105

small caps, 89, 330-331
  and text-transform, 131
font-weight, 67, 105
  absolute weights, 98
    avoiding, 105
  common terms, 101
  description, 78, 331-332
  example, 72, 73, 98-101
  fewer than nine weights, 99-
    100
  named weights, 98
    bold, 98
    normal, 98
  nine weights support,
    98-99
  relative weights, 100-101
fonts, 61-63
  ascender, 69, 71, 104
  baseline, 69, 71, 104
  bitmapped formats, 65
  character sets, 382-383
  cost, 67
  descender, 69, 71, 104
  downloading, 97, 105, 378-379
  em units, 70, 71
  ex units, 70, 71
  font foundries, 63
  formats, 65
  generic font families, 67-68, 105
  height, 69
  improve readability, 65
  matching fonts, 97-98, 105,
    381-382
  names, 63-65, 67-68, 105
    font-family, 64-65
    generic, 67-68, 105
    platform-dependent variations,
      64-65
    and trademarks, 63-64
    typeface family name, 63
  PANOSE number, 97, 105, 379,
    381-382
  point, 69, 104
  resolution, 70-71
  scalable fonts, 65, 66
    hinting parameters, 65, 70
  selecting fonts, 70-71
  size, 69-70
  standard fonts, 93-97
  style, 66, 67
  typeface, 64
  variations, 66-67
  where fonts come from, 63
FORM, 37

formatting. *See also* element
    formatting; stylesheets; text
    formatting
  procedural, 11-12
  rules-based, 10-11
  setting formatting type, 155
  TABLE formatting, 204-209
  types, 154-155
foundry, 63

G

German, Daniel M., 12
groove, 164
grouped, 74, 120-121, 147, 300,
    303-304

H

H1, 37
  and P elements, 33
H2, 37
H3, 37
H4, 37
H5, 37
H6, 37
HEAD, 33-34, 58
headings, 254-258
  individual headings, 256-258
  stylized heading, 258-264
height, 114-115, 159-160, 176,
    202-204, 210, 353. *See also*
    ascender
  block-level element height,
    176
  description, 332, 370
  and TABLE, 206
hiding
  stylesheets, 45-46, 230, 304-305
  visibility: hidden, 365, 367
hierarchy of HTML elements, 29
  example, 36
hinting parameters, 65, 70
HiP (HoTMetaL Intranet
    Publisher), 388
Homesite Version 2.5, 388-389
horizontal layout of block-level
    elements, 167-176
horizontal text spacing, 112-113, 146
HotDog, 388
HoTaMaLe, 389
HoTMetal, 27
HotMetal Intranet Publisher
    (HiP), 388
HR, 29, 37
HREF attribute, 30

HTML (HyperText Markup
    Language), 25-26. *See also*
    elements
  allowed characters, 27-28
  BODY content, 34-41
  comments, 28
  current version, 5, 27
  defining HTML, 27
  document example, 30
  error handling, 50-55
  HEAD content, 33-34
  history of, 2-4
  including stylesheets in documents,
    229-235, 304-305
  lack of universality, 4
  model, 28-32
  review, 26-28
  structural rules, 33-41
  and stylesheets, 8-9, 41-50
  summary, 57-58
HTML 3.2, 5, 27, 214. *See also*
    HTML
  floating an element, 41
HTTP (HyperText Transfer
    Protocol), 2-3
  and META, 50
HyperText Markup Language. *See*
    HTML
HyperText Transfer Protocol. *See*
    HTTP

I

I, 37, 44
ID attribute, 41
  description, 48-49
  ID-based selectors, 74, 77, 84
  and LINK element, 44
  and SPAN element, 46
  supported by, 77
ID-based selectors, 74, 77, 299, 303
  example, 83-85
  priority, 84-85
  and rule selection, 307
IFRAME, 37, 38, 40
  floated, 41
IMG, 29, 37, 38, 40
  ALIGN attribute, 114
  floated, 41, 43
importing stylesheets, 231, 305-306
InContext's Spider, 27
indenting. *See* text-indent
inheritance. *See* property inheritance
inline elements, 34, 39
  formatting, 186-187
  sample document, 38

inline formatting, 154, 155, 157-158
    summary of, 37
INPUT, 37, 38, 40
inset, 164
International Standards Organization
    (ISO), 27
Internet Engineering Task Forces, 3
Internet Explorer 3. *See* MSIE 3
Internet Explorer 4. *See* MSIE 4
ISINDEX, 33, 34
ISO (International Standards
    Organization), 27
italics, 67. *See also* font-style
italic value
    font-style, 88-89, 105

J

JASS (JavaScript Accessible
    Stylesheets). *See* JavaScript
JavaScript
    and SCRIPT, 40
    and SERVER, 40
    stylesheets, 375-377
JoyHTML, 389
JSSS (JavaScript Accessible
    Stylesheets). *See* JavaScript

K

KBD, 37, 44
kerning, 112, 113, 146

L

leading, 114-115, 147. *See also*
    line-height
left, 370-371
length units, 307-308, 401-404. *See*
    also font-size
    absolute units, 101, 307, 401-402,
        404-405
    defining, 404-405
    and font-size, 101-103
    percentage length values, 402-404
    pixel units, 102
    and printing support, 405
    relative units, 101-103, 307, 401,
        402, 405
    supported length units, 308
letter-spacing, 112,
    146, 148
    description, 127, 128-129, 332-
        333
    and text alignment, 129
LI, 37, 38, 184-185
    and contextual selectors, 123-125

Lie, Hakon, 11
Lilley, Chris, 384
line-height, 115, 128, 139-
    141, 333
line spacing, 114-115, 140-141
line-through, 129
link. *See* :link
LINK, 33, 34, 41, 229-230, 304
    alternate media, 386-387
    alternate stylesheets, 387-388
    description, 44-45
list-item, 35, 38
    browser support, 184-186
    special formatting, 183-184
    summary of, 37
list-item-type property values, 185
list-style, 185, 334
list-style-image, 185, 334
list-style-position, 184,
    334-335
    description, 185
list-style-type, 184,
    185, 335
literal strings, 32

M

Macintosh, standard fonts, 93-94
MAP, 38, 40
    and ID attribute, 77
margin, 165, 166, 335-336
margin-bottom, 165, 176,
    178-179
    description, 166, 336
    effects of, 186
margin-left, 165, 167, 173
    description, 166, 337
margin-right, 165, 167,
    173, 189
    description, 166, 337-338
margin-top, 165, 176, 178-179
    description, 166, 338
    effects of, 186
margins, 156-157, 158, 211
    auto/fixed margin/width, 172-173
    description, 165-166
    horizontal layout of block-level
        elements, 167-176
    negative margins and overlapping,
        169-171
    restrictions, 167-168
    TABLE, 206
    vertical margins, 176, 178-181
markup tags. *See* tags
MARQUEE, 4, 37, 44

MENU, 37
META, 34, 50, 234
meta-information elements, 34, 39-40
    summary of, 38, 40
Microsoft
    font embedding, 381
    scripted stylesheets, 377-378
    standard fonts, 95-96
    Word, 7-8
Microsoft Internet Explorer 3. *See*
    MSIE 3
Microsoft Internet Explorer 4. *See*
    MSIE 4
middle, vertical alignment, 134
MIME type, 44-45, 381
monospace fonts, 68, 93, 94, 96, 97
MSIE 3 (Microsoft Internet
    Explorer 3)
    @import, 231
    !important, 235
    background-color, 168, 169, 215
    background-image, 217
    background properties not
        implemented, 226
    and BODY elements, 37-38
    border properties, 163-164
    and CLASS values, 48
    CSS implementation problems, 152
    CSS support, 347-350
    display property, 155
    element positioning and
        formatting, 152
    font-family support, 93
    font-style support, 89, 105
    font-variant support, 91, 105
    generic font families, 93
    horizontal formatting
        characteristics, 175
    inline formatting, 187
    letter-spacing, 127, 129
    line-height, 128
    list item properties, 184
    margins, 167-168, 169
        vertical margins, 179
    pseudo-class support, 76, 86
    pseudo-elements support, 119
    relative font size units, 103
    replaced element resizing, 203
    summary of CSS support, 347-350
    TABLE formatting, 206-207
    text-align, 128
    text-decoration, 127
    text-transform, 127
    vertical-align, 127, 134
    weights in cascades, 246

white-space, 128
word-spacing, 127, 129
MSIE 4
!important, 235
background properties not
    implemented, 226
font-family support, 93
font size, 103
font-variant support, 91
generic font families, 93
inline formatting, 187
TABLE formatting, 205-207
MULTICOL, 37

N

NAME attribute
    and ID, 49
named colors, 308, 392-394
    extended, 394-396
name tokens, 32
navigation icons, 264-265
Navigator 3+, 37-38
Navigator 4.0
    @import, 231
    !important, 235
    background-color, 168, 169, 215
    background-image, 219, 226
    background properties not
        implemented, 226
    border properties, 163-164
    border support, 322
    and CLASS values, 48
    contextual selectors and LI, 125
    CSS implementation problems, 152
    CSS support, 347-350
    element formatting and
        positioning, 152
    font-family support, 93
    font-variant support, 91, 105
    horizontal formatting
        characteristics, 175-176
    inline formatting, 187, 188
    letter-spacing, 127, 129
    line-height, 128, 140
    list-item properties, 184-185
    margins, 167-168, 169, 180-181
        vertical margins, 179
    pseudo-class support, 76
    pseudo-elements support, 119
    relative font size units, 103
    replaced element resizing, 203
    summary of CSS support, 347-350
    TABLE formatting, 204-209
    text-decoration, 127
    and TrueDoc, 97-98

vertical-align, 127, 134
white-space, 128
word-spacing, 127, 129
nesting, 29
NetManage WebSurfer browser, 39
Netscape. *See* JavaScript; Navigator
    4.0; TrueDoc
Newspaper Web page, 275-293
    assembling the documents, 285-290
    backward compatibility, 290
    main news article page, 283-285
    major news column, 279-281
    navigation bar, 282-283
    page title or banner, 278-279
NOBR, 37, 44
NOEMBED, 37
none, 164
normal value
    font-style, 88-89, 105
    font-variant, 89
normal.dot, 7

O

OBJECT, 37, 38, 40
    floated, 41
oblique value
    font-style, 88-89, 105
OL, 37
OpenType, 99
outset, 164
overflow, 357-359, 371
overlapping elements, 169-171

P

P, 37
padding, 161, 338-339
    and TABLE, 206
padding-bottom, 176, 180
    description, 161, 339-340
    effects of, 186
padding-left, 161, 167, 340
padding-right, 167, 189
    description, 161 , 340-341
padding-top, 161, 176, 341
    effects of, 186
padding space, 156-157, 158
    description, 160-161
pair kerning, 112, 113
PANOSE number, 97, 105, 379,
    381-382
PARAM, 38, 40
    and CLASS attribute, 75
    and ID attribute, 77
parent-child relationship, 124
periods

and CLASS values, 48
and ID attribute, 49
pixel units (px), 102
placeholders, 155-156
platform independent, 2
point, 69, 104
position, 353, 372. *See also*
    positioning
    absolute, 354
    relative, 359
positioning, 151-152, 352
    absolute positioning, 354-359
    limits on, 171-172
    within another element, 361-365
    relative positioning, 359-361
    review, 368-374
    visibility, 365, 367
PRE, 37
printing, 385-386
    and length units, 405
problem diagnosis checklist, 347-350
procedural formatting, 11-12
property inheritance, 17, 21, 82,
    298-299
    and TABLEs, 204-207
property specifications, 310-347
pseudo-class-based selectors, 74, 76-
    77, 299, 301
    active, 76, 85
    combining with regular class, 76-77
    example, 84, 85-86
    link, 76, 85
    visited, 76, 85-86
pseudo-element-based, 74, 118-120,
    147, 299, 301-302
    not supported, 119
pt (point), 69, 104
pull-quote, 199-200
px (pixel units), 102

Q

Q, 37, 44
QuickSite 2.0, 389

R

Raman, T.V., 384
readability without stylesheets, 56
reader declarations, 306-307
references. *See also* books
    CSS
        designs, 293
        general information, 22
        references, drafts, and notes, 389
    DSSSL information, 22-23
    fonts

dynamic fonts, 389-390
general issues, 108
matching and substitution, 109, 389-390
Microsoft recommendations, 109
HTML
DTDs, 60
dynamic HTML, 390
element content rules, 60
Microsoft/Netscape HTML extensions, 60
specifications and notes, 59
syntax validation tools/sites, 60
Javascript Accessible Stylesheets, 390
SGML, Web-based resources, 59
stylesheet, general information, 22
REL attribute, 41, 44
relative length units, 101-103, 307, 401, 402, 405
relative values, 17
replaced elements, 35, 40-41, 155-156, 202-204
summary of, 38, 40
resolution, 5, 70-71
REV attribute, 41, 44
RGB color codes, 308, 391-396
background-color, 128, 214
explicit, 396-397
standardized, 399
ridge, 164
rules. *See also* cascading rules; declarations; examples; selectors
structural rules of markup, 33-41
stylesheet rules, 13-14, 21, 71, 297
illustration, 73
rules-based language, 10-11

S

S, 37, 44
SAMP, 37, 44
sans-serif fonts, 68, 93, 94, 95, 97
illustration, 69
scalable fonts, 65, 66
hinting parameters, 65, 70
SCRIPT, 33, 34, 38, 40
and CLASS attribute, 75
and ID attribute, 77
scripted stylesheets, 374-378
scrolling, 227-228, 313
SELECT, 37, 38, 40
selectors, 13-14, 21, 71, 105, 117, 299. *See also* examples
class-based, 74-75, 299, 300-301

contextual, 74, 122-125, 147, 300, 303
examples, 123
grouped, 74, 120-121, 147, 300, 303-304
ID-based, 74, 77, 299, 303
pseudo-class-based, 74, 76-77, 299, 301
pseudo-element-based, 74, 118-120, 147, 299, 301-302
not supported, 119
role of, 73
simple (name based), 74, 299, 300
types of, 73-77, 117
serif fonts, 68, 93, 94, 95-96, 97
illustration, 69
SERVER, 38, 40
SGML (Standard Generalized Markup Language), 6
defining HTML, 27, 57
and DSSSL, 11
references, 59
simple selectors (name based), 74
example, 79
simplicity and CSS, 11
size. *See* font-size
slant. *See* font-style
SMALL, 37, 44
small caps, 89, 131, 330-331
font-variant, 89
SoftQuad's HoTMetal, 27
software and CSS support, 388-389
solid, 164
space band, 112-113, 143, 146
SPACER, 37
spacing. *See also* letter-spacing; word-spacing
between words and letters, 128-129
horizontal text spacing, 112-113, 146
line spacing, 114-115, 140-141
space band, 112-113, 143, 146
tracking, 146
SPAN, 37, 41, 44
description, 46-47
mimic :first-letter, 119
STYLE attribute examples, 49-50
Spider, 27
stacking, 354-355
Standard Generalized Markup Language. *See* SGML
standards, HTML, 3-5
start tag, 27, 28
and STYLE attribute, 305
stop tag, 27, 28

STRIKE, 37, 44
strikethrough, 129
STRONG, 37, 44
error handling, 51-55
STYLE, element 33, 34, 41, 230-231, 304-305
alternate media, 387
description, 45
hiding stylesheets, 45-46, 230
STYLE attribute, 41, 234, 305
description, 49-50
and SPAN element, 46
stylesheet designs, 251-254
additional designs, 293-295
chapter cover page, 267-275
decorative page, 264-267
newspaper Web page, 275-293
stylized heading, 258-264
title page, 254-258
stylesheets, 6, 21. *See also* CSS stylesheets; DSSSL
advantages of, 9
approaches to stylesheets, 9-12
procedural (DSSSL), 11-12
rules-based (CSS), 10-11
default stylesheet language, 50
external, 44-45, 228-230, 285-290, 304
and font specifications, 77-78
and HTML, 8-9, 41-50
including in HTML documents, 229-235, 304-305
introduction to, 6-12
language in use on Web, 11
META specification, 50
references, 22-23
scripted stylesheets, 374-378
and word processors, 6-8
SUB, 37, 44
sub, vertical alignment, 134
subclassing
and CLASS attribute, 47
SUP, 37, 44
super, vertical alignment, 134

T

TABLE, 37
and COL, COLGROUP, 40
formatting, 204-209
bugs, 207-209
property inheritance, 204-207
table cells, 37
tags, 27, 28, 29
and STYLE, 305

TD, 37, 205, 207-209
text-align, 115-116, 148
  description, 128, 141-143,
    341-342
text-bottom, 134, 135
text-decoration, 113, 148
  description, 127, 129, 342-343
text-indent, 102-103,
    115-116, 148
  description, 128, 141
  example, 102-103, 343
text-top, 134, 135
text-transform, 114, 127, 129,
    131, 343-344
TEXTAREA, 37, 38, 40
text formatting, 112. *See* examples;
    text-decoration; text-transform
  aligning and indenting, 115-116,
    141-143
  color, 113-114
    background colors, 128
  first letter, 116, 118-120, 147
  first line, 116, 118-120, 147
  horizontal text spacing,
    112-113, 146
  line height, 139-141
  line spacing, 114-115
    shorthand font property,
      140-141
  spacing between words and letters,
    128-129
  strikethrough, 129
  stylesheets, examples, 125, 127-146
  summary, 146-148
  text variation, 113-114
  underlines, 113, 129
  vertical alignment, 114, 131,
    133-138
  within text blocks, 114-116
TH, 37, 205, 207, 209
thickness. *See* font-weight
tiling, 215, 217, 219-222. *See also*
    background-repeat
TITLE, 34
TITLE attribute, 387-388
  and LINK element, 44
  and STYLE element, 45
title page design, 254-258

top, 135, 136-139, 372-373
  and absolute
      positioning, 354
TR, 205, 206-207
tracking, 112, 113, 146
trademarks, and font names, 63-64
TrueDoc, 97-98, 379
TrueType, 381
TT, 37, 44
TYPE attribute
  and LINK element, 44
  and STYLE element, 45
typeface, 64. *See also* fonts

U

U, 37, 44
UL, 37
underlines, 113, 129
Unicode character set, 383
Uniform Resource Locators. *See* URLs
universality, 4
UNIX X-Windows, standard
      fonts, 94
URLs (Uniform Resource Locators),
    309-310
  history of, 2-3
  partial, 231-233, 309-310

V

VAR, 37, 44
vertical-align, 114, 133-134
  baseline, 134, 135
  bottom, 135, 136-138
  description, 127, 148, 344-345
  and line-height, 140
  middle, 134, 135
  sub, 134, 135
  super, 134, 135
  support for, 134
  text-top, 134, 135
  text-bottom, 134, 135
  top, 135, 136-138
  uses, 148
  values, 134-136
vertical alignment, 114, 131,
    133-138
vertical layout of block-level
    elements, 176-183

vertical spacing. *See* leading
visibility, 353, 365, 367
  description, 373
visited. *See* :visited

W

WBR, 37
Web. *See also* W3C
  Cascading Style Sheets: Designing
      for the Web, 22
  the early days, 3
  font naming, 64-65
  NetManage WebSurfer browser, 39
  newspaper Web page, 275-293
  SGML on the Web; Small Steps
      Beyond HTML, 59
  stylesheet language in use, 11
  WebMaker, 388
WebMaker, 388
weights, 66. *See also* font-weight
white-space, 128, 143-145, 148,
    345-346
  example, 146-147
width, 159-160, 167, 172-173, 202-
    204, 210, 353
  and absolute
      positioning, 354
  description, 346, 373-374
  and TABLE, 206
Windows 3.1/95/NT
  standard fonts, 93
word processors, 6-8
word-spacing, 148
  description, 127, 128-129, 347
  and space band, 113, 146
  and text alignment, 129
World Wide Web. *See* Web
World Wide Web Consortium. *See*
    W3C
W3C (World Wide Web
    Consortium), 5, 11
  CSS extensions, 352-353

Z

z-index, 352-353, 354-355
  description, 374
z-ordering, 352